THE
Expositor's
Bible
Commentary
with The New International Version

REVELATION

THE
Expositor's Bible Commentary

with The New International Version

REVELATION

Alan F. Johnson

ZondervanPublishingHouse

Grand Rapids, Michigan

A Division of HarperCollinsPublishers

General Editor:

FRANK E. GAEBELEIN

Former Headmaster, Stony Brook School

Former Coeditor, *Christianity Today*

Associate Editors:

J. D. DOUGLAS

Editor, *The New International Dictionary of the Christian Church*

RICHARD P. POLCYN

Revelation
Copyright © 1996 by Alan F. Johnson

Requests for information should be addressed to:
Zondervan Publishing House
Grand Rapids, Michigan 49530

Library of Congress Cataloging-in-Publication Data

The expositor's Bible commentary : with the New International Version of the Holy Bible /
Frank E. Gaebelein, general editor of series.
    p.   cm.
   Includes bibliographical references and index.
    Contents: v. 1–2. Matthew / D. A. Carson — Mark / Walter W. Wessel — Luke / Walter
L. Liefeld — John / Merrill C. Tenney — Acts / Richard N. Longenecker — Romans /
Everett F. Harrison — 1 and 2 Corinthians / W. Harold Mare and Murray J. Harris —
Galatians and Ephesians / James Montgomery Boice and A. Skevington Wood—Philippians,
Colossians, Philemon / Homer A. Kent Jr., Gurtis Vaughan, and Arthur A. Rupprecht—
1, 2 Thessalonians; 1, 2 Timothy; Titus / Robert L. Thomas, Ralph Earle, and D. Edmond
Hiebert—Hebrews, James / Leon Morris and Donald W. Burdick—1, 2 Peter;
1, 2, 3 John; Jude / Edwin A. Blum and Glenn W. Barker—Revelation / Alan F. Johnson
   ISBN: 0-310-20389-9 (softcover)
   1. Bible N.T.—Commentaries. I. Gaebelein, Frank Ely, 1899–1983.
BS2341.2.E96 1995
220.7-dc 00   94-47450
                                                CIP

Printed in the United States of America

   98 99 00 01 / ❖ DH / 10 9 8 7 6 5 4 3 2

CONTENTS

PREFACE

The title of this work defines its purpose. Written primarily by expositors for expositors, it aims to provide preachers, teachers, and students of the Bible with a new and comprehensive commentary on the books of the Old and New Testaments. Its stance is that of a scholarly evangelicalism committed to the divine inspiration, complete trustworthiness, and full authority of the Bible. Its seventy-eight contributors come from the United States, Canada, England, Scotland, Australia, New Zealand, and Switzerland, and from various religious groups, including Anglican, Baptist, Brethren, Free, Independent, Methodist, Nazarene, Presbyterian, and Reformed churches. Most of them teach at colleges, universities, or theological seminaries.

No book has been more closely studied over a longer period of time than the Bible. From the Midrashic commentaries going back to the period of Ezra, through parts of the Dead Sea Scrolls and the Patristic literature, and on to the present, the Scriptures have been expounded. Indeed, there have been times when, as in the Reformation and on occasions since then, exposition has been at the cutting edge of Christian advance. Luther was a powerful exegete, and Calvin is still called "the prince of expositors."

Their successors have been many. And now, when the outburst of new translations and their unparalleled circulation have expanded the readership of the Bible, the need for exposition takes on fresh urgency.

Not that God's Word can ever become captive to its expositors. Among all other books, it stands first in its combination of perspicuity and profundity. Though a child can be made "wise for salvation" by believing its witness to Christ, the greatest mind cannot plumb the depths of its truth (2 Tim. 3:15; Rom. 11:33). As Gregory the Great said, "Holy Scripture is a stream of running water, where alike the elephant may swim, and the lamb walk." So, because of the inexhaustible nature of Scripture, the task of opening up its meaning is still a perennial obligation of biblical scholarship.

How that task is done inevitably reflects the outlook of those engaged in it. Every biblical scholar has presuppositions. To this neither the editors of these volumes nor the contributors to them are exceptions. They share a common commitment to the supernatural Christianity set forth in the inspired Word. Their purpose is not to supplant the many valuable commentaries that have preceded this work and from which both the editors and contributors have learned. It is rather to draw on the resources of contemporary evangelical scholarship in producing a new reference work for understanding the Scriptures.

A commentary that will continue to be useful through the years should handle contemporary trends in biblical studies in such a way as to avoid becoming outdated when critical fashions change. Biblical criticism is not in itself inadmissible, as some have mistakenly thought. When scholars investigate the authorship, date, literary characteristics, and purpose of a biblical document, they are practicing biblical criticism. So also when, in order to ascertain as nearly as possible the original form of the text, they deal with variant readings, scribal errors, emendations, and other phenomena in the manuscripts. To do these things is essential to responsible exegesis and exposition. And always there is the need to distinguish hypothesis from fact, conjecture from truth.

The chief principle of interpretation followed in this commentary is the grammatico-historical one—namely, that the primary aim of the exegete is to make clear the meaning of the text at the time and in the circumstances of its writing. This endeavor to understand what in the first instance the inspired writers actually said must not be confused with an inflexible literalism. Scripture makes lavish use of symbols and figures of speech; great portions of it are poetical. Yet when it speaks in this way, it speaks no less truly than it does in its historical and doctrinal portions. To understand its message requires attention to matters of grammar and syntax, word meanings, idioms, and literary forms—all in relation to the historical and cultural setting of the text.

The contributors to this work necessarily reflect varying convictions. In certain controversial matters the policy is that of clear statement of the contributors' own views followed by fair presentation of other ones. The treatment of eschatology, though it reflects differences of interpretation, is consistent with a general premillennial position. (Not all contributors, however, are premillennial.) But prophecy is more than prediction, and so this commentary gives due recognition to the major lode of godly social concern in the prophetic writings.

THE EXPOSITOR'S BIBLE COMMENTARY is presented as a scholarly work, though not primarily one of technical criticism. In its main portion, the Exposition, and in Volume 1 (General and Special Articles), all Semitic and Greek words are transliterated and the English equivalents given. As for the Notes, here Semitic and Greek characters are used but always with transliterations and English meanings, so that this portion of the commentary will be as accessible as possible to readers unacquainted with the original languages.

It is the conviction of the general editor, shared by his colleagues in the Zondervan editorial department, that in writing about the Bible, lucidity is not incompatible with scholarship. They are therefore endeavoring to make this a clear and understandable work.

The translation used in it is the New International Version (North American Edition). To the International Bible Society thanks are due for permission to use this most recent of the major Bible translations. The editors and publisher have chosen it because of the clarity and beauty of its style and its faithfulness to the original texts.

To the associate editor, Dr. J. D. Douglas, and to the contributing editors—Dr. Walter C. Kaiser, Jr. and Dr. Bruce K. Waltke for the Old Testament, and Dr. James Montgomery Boice and Dr. Merrill C. Tenney for the New Testament—the general editor expresses his gratitude for their unfailing cooperation and their generosity in advising him out of their expert scholarship. And to the many other contributors he is indebted for their invaluable part in this work. Finally, he owes a special debt of gratitude to Dr. Robert K. DeVries, executive vice-president of the Zondervan Publishing House; Rev. Gerard Terpstra, manuscript editor; and Miss Elizabeth Brown, secretary to Dr. DeVries, for their continual assistance and encouragement.

Whatever else it is—the greatest and most beautiful of books, the primary source of law and morality, the fountain of wisdom, and the infallible guide to life—the Bible is above all the inspired witness to Jesus Christ. May this work fulfill its function of expounding the Scriptures with grace and clarity, so that its users may find that both Old and New Testaments do indeed lead to our Lord Jesus Christ, who alone could say, "I have come that they may have life, and have it to the full" (John 10:10).

FRANK E. GAEBELEIN

ABBREVIATIONS

A. General Abbreviations

A	Codex Alexandrinus	MT	Masoretic text
Akkad.	Akkadian	n.	note
ℵ	Codex Sinaiticus	n.d.	no date
Ap. Lit.	Apocalyptic Literature	Nestle	Nestle (ed.) *Novum*
Apoc.	Apocrypha		*Testamentum Graece*
Aq.	Aquila's Greek Translation	no.	number
	of the Old Testament	NT	New Testament
Arab.	Arabic	obs.	obsolete
Aram.	Aramaic	OL	Old Latin
b	Babylonian Gemara	OS	Old Syriac
B	Codex Vaticanus	OT	Old Testament
C	Codex Ephraemi Syri	p., pp.	page, pages
c.	*circa*, about	par.	paragraph
cf.	*confer*, compare	‖	parallel passage(s)
ch., chs.	chapter, chapters	Pers.	Persian
cod., codd.	codex, codices	Pesh.	Peshitta
contra	in contrast to	Phoen.	Phoenician
D	Codex Bezae	pl.	plural
DSS	Dead Sea Scrolls (see E.)	Pseudep.	Pseudepigrapha
ed., edd.	edited, edition, editor; editions	Q	Quelle ("Sayings" source
e.g.	*exempli gratia*, for example		in the Gospels)
Egyp.	Egyptian	qt.	quoted by
et al.	*et alii*, and others	q.v.	*quod vide*, which see
EV	English Versions of the Bible	R	Rabbah
fem.	feminine	rev.	revised, reviser, revision
ff.	following (verses, pages, etc.)	Rom.	Roman
fl.	flourished	RVm	Revised Version margin
ft.	foot, feet	Samar.	Samaritan recension
gen.	genitive	SCM	Student Christian Movement Press
Gr.	Greek	Sem.	Semitic
Heb.	Hebrew	sing.	singular
Hitt.	Hittite	SPCK	Society for the Promotion
ibid.	*ibidem*, in the same place		of Christian Knowledge
id.	*idem*, the same	Sumer.	Sumerian
i.e.	*id est*, that is	s.v.	*sub verbo*, under the word
impf.	imperfect	Syr.	Syriac
infra.	below	Symm.	Symmachus
in loc.	*in loco*, in the place cited	T	Talmud
j	Jerusalem or	Targ.	Targum
	Palestinian Gemara	Theod.	Theodotion
Lat.	Latin	TR	Textus Receptus
LL.	Late Latin	tr.	translation, translator,
LXX	Septuagint		translated
M	Mishnah	UBS	The United Bible Societies'
masc.	masculine		Greek Text
mg.	margin	Ugar.	Ugaritic
Mid	Midrash	u.s.	*ut supra*, as above
MS(S)	Manuscript(s)	viz.	*videlicet*, namely

vol.	volume		Vul.	Vulgate
v., vv.	verse, verses		WH	Westcott and Hort, *The*
vs.	versus			*New Testament in Greek*

B. Abbreviations for Modern Translations and Paraphrases

AmT	Smith and Goodspeed,	LB	The Living Bible
	The Complete Bible,	Mof	J. Moffatt, *A New Trans-*
	An American Translation		*lation of the Bible*
ASV	American Standard Version,	NAB	The New American Bible
	American Revised Version	NASB	New American Standard Bible
	(1901)	NEB	The New English Bible
Beck	Beck, *The New Testament in*	NIV	The New International Version
	the Language of Today	Ph	J. B. Phillips *The New Testa-*
BV	Berkeley Version (The		*ment in Modern English*
	Modern Language Bible)	RSV	Revised Standard Version
JB	The Jerusalem Bible	RV	Revised Version — 1881–1885
JPS	*Jewish Publication Society*	TCNT	Twentieth Century
	Version of the Old Testament		New Testament
KJV	King James Version	TEV	Today's English Version
Knox	R.G. Knox, *The Holy Bible:*	Wey	*Weymouth's New Testament*
	A Translation from the Latin		*in Modern Speech*
	Vulgate in the Light of the	Wms	C. B. Williams, *The New*
	Hebrew and Greek Original		*Testament: A Translation in*
			the Language of the People

C. Abbreviations for Periodicals and Reference Works

AASOR	*Annual of the American Schools*	BAG	Bauer, Arndt, and Gingrich:
	of Oriental Research		*Greek-English Lexicon*
AB	*Anchor Bible*		*of the New Testament*
AIs	de Vaux: *Ancient Israel*	BC	Foakes-Jackson and Lake: *The*
AJA	*American Journal of*		*Beginnings of Christianity*
	Archaeology	BDB	Brown, Driver, and Briggs:
AJSL	*American Journal of Semitic*		*Hebrew-English Lexicon*
	Languages and Literatures		*of the Old Testament*
AJT	*American Journal of*	BDF	Blass, Debrunner, and Funk:
	Theology		*A Greek Grammar of the*
Alf	Alford: *Greek Testament*		*New Testament and Other*
	Commentary		*Early Christian Literature*
ANEA	*Ancient Near Eastern*	BDT	Harrison: *Baker's Dictionary*
	Archaeology		*of Theology*
ANET	Pritchard: *Ancient Near*	Beng.	Bengel's *Gnomon*
	Eastern Texts	BETS	*Bulletin of the Evangelical*
ANF	Roberts and Donaldson:		*Theological Society*
	The Ante-Nicene Fathers	BJRL	*Bulletin of the John*
ANT	M. R. James: *The Apocryphal*		*Rylands Library*
	New Testament	BS	*Bibliotheca Sacra*
A-S	Abbot-Smith: *Manual Greek*	BT	*Babylonian Talmud*
	Lexicon of the New Testament	BTh	*Biblical Theology*
AThR	*Anglican Theological Review*	BW	*Biblical World*
BA	*Biblical Archaeologist*	CAH	*Cambridge Ancient History*
BASOR	*Bulletin of the American*	CanJTh	*Canadian Journal of Theology*
	Schools of Oriental Research	CBQ	*Catholic Biblical Quarterly*

CBSC — Cambridge Bible for Schools and Colleges
CE — Catholic Encyclopedia
CGT — Cambridge Greek Testament
CHS — Lange: Commentary on the Holy Scriptures
ChT — Christianity Today
Crem — Cremer: Biblico-Theological Lexicon of the New Testament Greek
DDB — Davis' Dictionary of the Bible
Deiss BS — Deissmann: Bible Studies
Deiss LAE — Deissmann: Light From the Ancient East
DNTT — Dictionary of New Testament Theology
EBC — The Expositor's Bible Commentary
EBi — Encyclopaedia Biblica
EBr — Encyclopaedia Britannica
EDB — Encyclopedic Dictionary of the Bible
EGT — Nicoll: Expositor's Greek Testament
EQ — Evangelical Quarterly
ET — Evangelische Theologie
ExB — The Expositor's Bible
Exp — The Expositor
ExpT — The Expository Times
FLAP — Finegan: Light From the Ancient Past
GR — Gordon Review
HBD — Harper's Bible Dictionary
HDAC — Hastings: Dictionary of the Apostolic Church
HDB — Hastings: Dictionary of the Bible
HDBrev. — Hastings: Dictionary of the Bible, one-vol. rev. by Grant and Rowley
HDCG — Hastings: Dictionary of Christ and the Gospels
HERE — Hastings: Encyclopedia of Religion and Ethics
HGEOTP — Heidel: The Gilgamesh Epic and Old Testament Parallels
HJP — Schurer: A History of the Jewish People in the Time of Christ
HR — Hatch and Redpath: Concordance to the Septuagint
HTR — Harvard Theological Review

HUCA — Hebrew Union College Annual
IB — The Interpreter's Bible
ICC — International Critical Commentary
IDB — The Interpreter's Dictionary of the Bible
IEJ — Israel Exploration Journal
Int — Interpretation
INT — E. Harrison: Introduction to the New Testament
IOT — R. K. Harrison: Introduction to the Old Testament
ISBE — The International Standard Bible Encyclopedia
ITQ — Irish Theological Quarterly
JAAR — Journal of American Academy of Religion
JAOS — Journal of American Oriental Society
JBL — Journal of Biblical Literature
JE — Jewish Encyclopedia
JETS — Journal of Evangelical Theological Society
JFB — Jamieson, Fausset, and Brown: Commentary on the Old and New Testament
JNES — Journal of Near Eastern Studies
Jos. Antiq. — Josephus: The Antiquities of the Jews
Jos. War — Josephus: The Jewish War
JQR — Jewish Quarterly Review
JR — Journal of Religion
JSJ — Journal for the Study of Judaism in the Persian, Hellenistic and Roman Periods
JSOR — Journal of the Society of Oriental Research
JSS — Journal of Semitic Studies
JT — Jerusalem Talmud
JTS — Journal of Theological Studies
KAHL — Kenyon: Archaeology in the Holy Land
KB — Koehler-Baumgartner: Lexicon in Veteris Testamenti Libros
KD — Keil and Delitzsch: Commentary on the Old Testament
LSJ — Liddell, Scott, Jones: Greek-English Lexicon
LTJM — Edersheim: The Life and Times of Jesus the Messiah

MM	Moulton and Milligan: *The Vocabulary of the Greek Testament*		*Testament aus Talmud und Midrash*
MNT	Moffatt: *New Testament Commentary*	SHERK	*The New Schaff-Herzog Encyclopedia of Religious Knowledge*
MST	McClintock and Strong: *Cyclopedia of Biblical, Theological, and Ecclesiastical Literature*	SJT	*Scottish Journal of Theology*
		SOT	Girdlestone: *Synonyms of Old Testament*
NBC	Davidson, Kevan, and Stibbs: *The New Bible Commentary*, 1st ed.	SOTI	Archer: *A Survey of Old Testament Introduction*
NBCrev.	Guthrie and Motyer: *The New Bible Commentary*, rev. ed.	ST	*Studia Theologica*
		TCERK	Loetscher: *The Twentieth Century Encyclopedia of Religious Knowledge*
NBD	J. D. Douglas: *The New Bible Dictionary*	TDNT	Kittel: *Theological Dictionary of the New Testament*
NCB	*New Century Bible*		
NCE	*New Catholic Encyclopedia*	TDOT	*Theological Dictionary of the Old Testament*
NIC	*New International Commentary*	Theol	*Theology*
NIDCC	Douglas: *The New International Dictionary of the Christian Church*	ThT	*Theology Today*
		TNTC	*Tyndale New Testament Commentaries*
NovTest	*Novum Testamentum*	Trench	Trench: *Synonyms of the New Testament*
NSI	Cooke: *Handbook of North Semitic Inscriptions*		
NTS	*New Testament Studies*	UBD	*Unger's Bible Dictionary*
ODCC	*The Oxford Dictionary of the Christian Church*, rev. ed.	UT	Gordon: *Ugaritic Textbook*
		VB	Allmen: *Vocabulary of the Bible*
Peake	Black and Rowley: *Peake's Commentary on the Bible*	VetTest	*Vetus Testamentum*
PEQ	*Palestine Exploration Quarterly*	Vincent	Vincent: *Word-Pictures in the New Testament*
PNFl	P. Schaff: *The Nicene and Post-Nicene Fathers* (1st series)	WBC	*Wycliffe Bible Commentary*
		WBE	*Wycliffe Bible Encyclopedia*
PNF2	P. Schaff and H. Wace: *The Nicene and Post-Nicene Fathers* (2nd series)	WC	*Westminster Commentaries*
		WesBC	*Wesleyan Bible Commentaries*
		WTJ	*Westminster Theological Journal*
PTR	*Princeton Theological Review*	ZAW	*Zeitschrift für die alttestamentliche Wissenschaft*
RB	*Revue Biblique*		
RHG	Robertson's *Grammar of the Greek New Testament in the Light of Historical Research*	ZNW	*Zeitschrift für die neutestamentliche Wissenschaft*
		ZPBD	*The Zondervan Pictorial Bible Dictionary*
RTWB	Richardson: *A Theological Wordbook of the Bible*	ZPEB	*The Zondervan Pictorial Encyclopedia of the Bible*
SBK	Strack and Billerbeck: *Kommentar zum Neuen*	ZWT	*Zeitschrift für wissenschaftliche Theologie*

D. Abbreviations for Books of the Bible, the Apocrypha, and the Pseudepigrapha

OLD TESTAMENT

Gen	2 Chron	Dan
Exod	Ezra	Hos
Lev	Neh	Joel
Num	Esth	Amos
Deut	Job	Obad
Josh	Ps(Pss)	Jonah
Judg	Prov	Mic
Ruth	Eccl	Nah
1 Sam	S of Songs	Hab
2 Sam	Isa	Zeph
1 Kings	Jer	Hag
2 Kings	Lam	Zech
1 Chron	Ezek	Mal

NEW TESTAMENT

Matt	1 Tim
Mark	2 Tim
Luke	Titus
John	Philem
Acts	Heb
Rom	James
1 Cor	1 Peter
2 Cor	2 Peter
Gal	1 John
Eph	2 John
Phil	3 John
Col	Jude
1 Thess	Rev
2 Thess	

APOCRYPHA

1 Esd	1 Esdras
2 Esd	2 Esdras
Tobit	Tobit
Jud	Judith
Add Esth	Additions to Esther
Wisd Sol	Wisdom of Solomon
Ecclus	Ecclesiasticus (Wisdom of Jesus the Son of Sirach)
Baruch	Baruch

Ep Jer	Epistle of Jeremy
S Th Ch	Song of the Three Children (or Young Men)
Sus	Susanna
Bel	Bel and the Dragon
Pr Man	Prayer of Manasseh
1 Macc	1 Maccabees
2 Macc	2 Maccabees

PSEUDEPIGRAPHA

As Moses	Assumption of Moses
2 Baruch	Syriac Apocalypse of Baruch
3 Baruch	Greek Apocalypse of Baruch
1 Enoch	Ethiopic Book of Enoch
2 Enoch	Slavonic Book of Enoch
3 Enoch	Hebrew Book of Enoch
4 Ezra	4 Ezra
JA	Joseph and Asenath
Jub	Book of Jubilees
L Aristeas	Letter of Aristeas
Life AE	Life of Adam and Eve
Liv Proph	Lives of the Prophets
MA Isa	Martyrdom and Ascension of Isaiah
3 Macc	3 Maccabees
4 Macc	4 Maccabees
Odes Sol	Odes of Solomon
P Jer	Paralipomena of Jeremiah

Pirke Aboth	Pirke Aboth
Ps 151	Psalm 151
Pss Sol	Psalms of Solomon
Sib Oracles	Sibylline Oracles
Story Ah	Story of Ahikar
T Abram	Testament of Abraham
T Adam	Testament of Adam
T Benjamin	Testament of Benjamin
T Dan	Testament of Dan
T Gad	Testament of Gad
T Job	Testament of Job
T Jos	Testament of Joseph
T Levi	Testament of Levi
T Naph	Testament of Naphtali
T 12 Pat	Testaments of the Twelve Patriarchs
Zad Frag	Zadokite Fragments

E. Abbreviations of Names of Dead Sea Scrolls and Related Texts

CD	Cairo (Genizah text of the) Damascus (Document)	1QSa	Appendix A (Rule of the Congregation) to 1QS
DSS	Dead Sea Scrolls	1QSb	Appendix B (Blessings) to 1QS
Hev	Nahal Hever texts	3Q15	Copper Scroll from Qumran Cave 3
Mas	Masada Texts		
Mird	Khirbet mird texts	4QFlor	Florilegium (or Eschatological Midrashim) from Qumran Cave 4
Mur	Wadi Murabba'at texts		
P	Pesher (commentary)		
Q	Qumran	4Qmess ar	Aramaic "Messianic" text from Qumran Cave 4
1Q,2Q,etc.	Numbered caves of Qumran, yielding written material; followed by abbreviation of biblical or apocryphal book.	4QPrNab	Prayer of Nabonidus from Qumran Cave 4
QL	Qumran Literature	4QTest	Testimonia text from Qumran Cave 4
1QapGen	Genesis Apocryphon of Qumran Cave 1	4QTLevi	Testament of Levi from Qumran Cave 4
1QH	*Hodayot* (Thanksgiving Hymns) from Qumran Cave 1	4QPhyl	Phylacteries from Qumran Cave 4
1QIsa[a, b]	First or second copy of Isaiah from Qumran Cave 1	11QMelch	Melchizedek text from Qumran Cave 11
1QpHab	Pesher on Habakkuk from Qumran Cave 1	11QtgJob	Targum of Job from Qumran Cave 11
1QM	*Milhamah* (War Scroll)		
1QS	*Serek Hayyahad* (Rule of the Community, Manual of Discipline)		

TRANSLITERATIONS

Hebrew

א = ʾ		ד = $\underline{d}$		י = y		ס = s		ר = r
ב = b		ה = h		כ = k		ע = ʿ		שׂ = ś
ב = $\underline{b}$		ו = w		ך = $\underline{k}$		פ = p		שׁ = š
ג = g		ז = z		ל = l		ף = $\underline{p}$		ת = t
ג = $\underline{g}$		ח = ḥ		מ = m		צ = ṣ		ת = $\underline{t}$
ד = d		ט = ṭ		נ = n		ק = q		

(ה)ָ = â (h)		ָ = ā		ַ = a		ֶ = ᵃ
ֵה = ê		ֵ = ē		ֶ = e		ֱ = ᵉ
ִ = î				ִ = i		ֲ = ᵉ (if vocal)
וֹ = ô		ֹ = ō		ָ = o		ֳ = ᵒ
וּ = û				ֻ = u		

Aramaic

ʾ b g d h w z ḥ ṭ y k l m n s ʿ p ṣ q r ś š t

Arabic

ʾ b t ṯ ǧ ḥ ḫ d ḏ r z s š ṣ ḍ ṭ ẓ ʿ ġ f q k l m n h w y

Ugaritic

ʾ b g d ḏ h w z ḥ ḫ ṭ ẓ y k l m n s ś ʿ ġ p ṣ q r š t ṯ

Greek

α	—	a	π	—	p	αι	— ai
β	—	b	ρ	—	r	αύ	— au
γ	—	g	σ,ς	—	s	ει	— ei
δ	—	d	τ	—	t	εύ	— eu
ε	—	e	υ	—	y	ηύ	— ēu
ζ	—	z	φ	—	ph	οι	— oi
η	—	ē	χ	—	ch	ού	— ou
θ	—	th	ψ	—	ps	υι	— hui
ι	—	i	ω	—	ō		
κ	—	k				ῥ	— rh
λ	—	l	γγ	—	ng	‘	— h
μ	—	m	γκ	—	nk		
ν	—	n	γξ	—	nx	ᾳ	— ā
ξ	—	x	γχ	—	nch	ῃ	— ē
ο	—	o				ῳ	— ō

REVELATION

Alan Johnson

REVELATION

Introduction

1. General Nature and Historical Background

The Book of Revelation fascinates and also perplexes the modern reader. For the present generation, it is the most obscure and controversial book in the Bible. Yet those who study it with care agree that it is a unique source of Christian teaching and one of timeless relevance. Accordingly, Swete says, "The Apocalypse offers to the pastors of the church an unrivaled store of materials for Christian teaching, if only the book is approached with an assurance of its prophetic character, chastened by a frank acceptance of the light which the growth of knowledge has cast and will continue to cast upon it" (p. viii). Indeed, it may well be that with the exception of the Gospels, the Apocalypse is the most profound and moving teaching on Christian doctrine and discipleship found anywhere in Holy Scripture.

Neither the fanaticism of some who have fixed their attention on prophecy but not on Christ, nor the diversity of interpretative viewpoints should discourage us from pursuing Christian truth in the marvelous book.

The title of the last book of the NT sheds light on its character. Revelation differs in kind from the other NT writings. The difference is not in doctrine but in literary genre and subject matter. It is a book of prophecy (1:3; 22:7, 18–19) that involves both warning and consolation—announcements of future judgment and blessing. For communicating its message, the Lord uses symbol and vision.

Why did the Lord use a method that seemingly makes his message so obscure? The answer is twofold. First, the language and imagery were not so strange to first-century readers as they are to many today. Faced with the apocalyptic style of the book, the modern reader who knows little about biblical literature and its parallels is like a person who, though unfamiliar with stocks and bonds, tries to understand the Dow-Jones reports. Therefore, familiarity with the prophetic books of the OT (especially Dan and Ezek), apocalyptic literature current during the first century, the

3

DSS, and the Targums (paraphrases of the OT into Aram. and Gr.) will help the reader grasp the message of the Apocalypse. (See the commentary for references to these cognate materials.)

Second, the subject matter, with its glimpses into the future and even into heaven itself, required the kind of language John used. Only through symbolism and imagery can we gain some understanding of the things the Lord was unveiling through the writer John. Moreover, while the symbolic and visionary mode of presentation creates ambiguity and frustration for many of us, it actually conduces to evocative description of unseen realities with a poignancy and clarity unattainable by any other method. For example, "evil" is an abstract term, but a woman "drunk with the blood of the saints" graphically sets forth the concrete and more terrible aspect of this reality. Such language can trigger all sorts of ideas, associations, existential involvement, and mystical responses that the straight prose found in much of the NT cannot attain.

The letters to the seven churches in the Roman province of Asia, modern Turkey, specifically locate the recipients of the book and give some broad indication of the historical situation. Some of the churches were experiencing persecution (2:10, 13). From this it has been customary to assume that persecution was quite intense and widespread. Revelation is then viewed as a "tract for the times" document, warning Christians against emperor worship and encouraging them to be faithful to Christ even to death. Recent studies, however, question how intense, widespread, or sustained the persecution was, even under Domitian.[1] Thus the primary occasion for the writing of the book must be sought elsewhere than in the persecution of that time.

The letters to the churches imply that five of the seven had serious problems. The major problem seemed to be disloyalty to Christ. This may indicate that the major thrust of Revelation is not sociopolitical but theological. John is more concerned with countering the heresy that was creeping into the churches toward the close of the first century than in addressing the political situation. Newman suggests that this heresy could well have been Gnosticism, an idea he derives from a critical study of Irenaeus's statements in the second century about the Book of Revelation.[2]

Revelation is also commonly viewed as belonging to the body of nonbiblical Jewish writings known as apocalyptic literature. The name for this type of literature (some nineteen books) is derived from the word "revelation" (*apocalypsis*) in Revelation 1:1 (q.v.). The extrabiblical apocalyptic books were written in the period from 200 B.C. to A.D. 200. Usually scholars stress the similarities of the Apocalypse of John to these noncanonical books—similarities such as the use of symbolism and vision, the mention of angelic mediators of the revelation, the bizarre images, the expectation of divine judgment, the emphasis on the kingdom of God, the new heavens and earth, and the dualism of this age and the age to come. Although numerous similarities exist, John's writing also has some clear differences from these writings, and these differences must not be overlooked.[3]

---

[1] F.F. Bruce, *New Testament History* (New York: Doubleday, 1972), pp. 412–13; Barclay Newman, "The Fallacy of the Domitian Hypothesis," NTS, 10 (1963), 133–39; G. Edmundson, *The Church in Rome in the First Century* (London: Longmans, Green, 1913).

[2] Newman, "Domitian Hypothesis," pp. 133–39; also his "A Consideration of the Apocalypse as an Anti-Gnostic Document" (Th.D. diss., Southern Baptist Theological Seminary, 1959) and *Rediscovering the Book of Revelation* (Valley Forge: Judson, 1968); also W. Foerster, TDNT, 3:135, n.11; Minear, *I Saw a New Earth*, pp. 250–56; cf. discussion at ch. 13 introduction.

[3] The literature on recent apocalyptic discussion is extensive. See esp. D.S. Russell, *The Method and Message of Jewish Apocalyptic* (Philadelphia: Westminster, 1964); idem, *Apocalyptic Ancient and Modern*

Unlike the Jewish and Jewish-Christian apocalyptic books, the Apocalypse of John clearly claims to be a book of prophecy (1:3; 22:7, 10, 18–19), the effect of which is to identify the message, as in the OT prophetic tradition, with the Word of God (1:2; 19:9). The Jewish apocalyptists used the literary form of prophecy to trace the course of history from ancient times down to their own day. John does not follow this method. He clearly places himself in the contemporary world of the first century and speaks of the future eschatological consummation in much the same way as Ezekiel and Jeremiah did. While extrabiblical apocalypses are clearly pseudonymous (e.g., Enoch, Abraham, Ezra, Baruch, et al.), the last book of the NT is plainly attributed to John. It does not, however, explicitly identify him as being well known or an apostle. Many of the noncanonical apocalyptic works are ethically passive; they blame the immediate plight of God's people, not on their unfaithfulness, but on the pervasive presence of evil in the world. While Revelation is not lacking in words of encouragement to the faithful, it also strongly urges the churches to repent.

Finally, and importantly, these apocalypses are pessimistic concerning the outcome of God's present activity in the world; and for hope they look wholly to the eschatological end, when God will once again intervene and defeat the evil in the world. Though Revelation is often read in this manner, there are great differences between it and the noncanonical apocalypses. In the latter, the turning point of history is the future event of the Messiah's coming as a conquering warrior-king. In Revelation the climactic event has already occurred in the victory of the slain Lamb (ch. 5). Now, however, the Lamb's victory is being worked out in history in the obedient suffering of his followers (12:11; 15:2). Their deaths are seen in Revelation as a part of the victory over evil that God is already effecting in the world. This partial victory through the suffering of the saints is combined with the hope of the final unambiguous victory of God at the end of history.

By viewing history in this way, the book makes clear that the source of Christian hope is not imminent in history itself but relates to a transcendent future. For John, there is no evolutionary progress of righteousness in history. Therefore, any identification of the Apocalypse with the writings of the extrabiblical apocalyptists must be

---

(Philadelphia: Fortress, 1978); Klaus Koch, *The Rediscovery of Apocalyptic*, Second Series, no. 22 (Naperville, Ill.: Allenson, 1972); Paul D. Hanson, *The Dawn of Apocalyptic* (Philadelphia: Fortress, 1975); idem, "Apocalypse," "Apocalyptic," IDB, 5:27–34; John J. Collins, who takes the position that the difference between Revelation and the Jewish apocalyptic writings are superficial except in the former's reference to the earthly Jesus, "Pseudonymity, Historical Reviews and the Genre of the Revelation of John," CBQ, 39 (March 1977), 329–43; idem, ed., *Apocalypse: The Morphology of a Genre*, Semeia 14 (Missoula, Mont.: Scholar's, 1979; J.H. Charlesworth, *The Pseudepigrapha in Modern Research* (Missoula, Mont.: Scholar's, 1976). For the primary documents, see R.H. Charles, *The Apocrypha and Pseudepigrapha of the Old Testament*, 2 vols. (Oxford: Clarendon, 1913) and J.H. Charlesworth, ed., *The Pseudepigrapha of the Old Testament* (Garden City, N.Y.: Doubleday, 1980). Those who point out the difference between the Apocalypse of John and other apocalyptic literature are G.E. Ladd, "The Revelation and Jewish Apocalyptic," EQ, 29 (1957), 95–100; idem, "Why Not Prophetic-Apocalyptic?" JBL, 76 (1957), 192–200; idem, "Apocalyptic and NT Theology," in *Reconciliation and Hope*, ed. Robert Banks (Grand Rapids: Eerdmans, 1974), pp. 285–96; James Kallas, "The Apocalypse—An Apocalyptic Book?" JBL, 86, (1967), 69–80; Leon Morris, *Apocalyptic* (Grand Rapids: Eerdmans, 1972), pp. 78–81; idem, *Revelation of St. John*, TNTC (Grand Rapids: Eerdmans, 1969), pp. 23–25. See esp. Elisabeth S. Fiorenza, *The Apocalypse* (Chicago: Franciscan Herald, 1976), who emphasizes that the book is a "Christian Prophetic-Apocalyptic Circular letter" (pp. 14–26). See also idem, "Composition and Structure of the Book of Revelation," CBQ, 39 (March 1977), 344–66. For a good survey of recent Roman Catholic views on Revelation, see John J. Pilch, *What Are They Saying About the Book of Revelation?* (New York: Paulist, 1978).

severely qualified. Indeed, the reader would do well to reexamine every method of interpreting Revelation that rests on this assumed similarity. For example, is it truly a "tract for the times" as other apocalyptic books, or should this supposed connection be questioned and the book freed to speak its own message about realities that are far more determinative of world events than immediate political powers?

John was no doubt quite familiar with the Jewish apocalyptists of the intertestamental period, and in some instances there seems to be a direct allusion to them (cf. comments at 2:7). But the relation is in general superficial. Only twice is an interpreting angel involved in the explanation of a vision (chs. 7 and 17), a feature constantly present in the other kind of apocalyptic writing. In no case can it be demonstrated that John depends on the assumed knowledge among his readers of the Jewish apocalyptists for clarity of meaning.[4] On the other hand, he is everywhere dependent on the OT canonical books, especially those where symbol and vision play a dominant role, such as portions of Isaiah, Ezekiel, Daniel, and Zechariah.

Although throughout the following pages frequent references to noncanonical apocalyptic literature appear, they are given as aids in understanding the background of John's writing and should not be taken as sources of his thought or method in the same way that the inspired canonical Scriptures influenced him.

Ladd's suggestion that we create a new category called "Prophetic-Apocalyptic" to distinguish canonical materials from the late Jewish apocalyptics, if not so much in form, certainly in world view, has much merit. Thus, in Ladd's view, the beast of chapters 13 and 17 is historical Rome, but it is far larger than the ancient city and is also the future Antichrist. The references to the persecution of Christians likewise go far beyond the known historical situation of John's day. Evil at the hands of Rome is realized eschatology. Recently this view has been held also by others.[5] The commentary on chapters 13 and 17 will reveal sympathy for Ladd's break with the dominant preterist interpretation while at the same time arguing that the preterist-futurist viewpoint, like that of the preterist, rests on the questionable assumption that John's Apocalypse is describing historical-political entities rather than theological archetypes (see Introduction: Interpretative Schemes; cf. also the introductions to chs. 13 and 17).

Much more important than the late Jewish apocalyptic sources is the debt John owes to the eschatological teaching of Jesus, such as the Olivet Discourse (Matt 24–25; Mark 13; Luke 21). The parallelism is striking and certainly not accidental. In the commentary, these connections are dealt with in more detail (cf. introduction to 6:1ff.). In short, we believe that the ultimate source of John's understanding of the future as well as his interpretation of the OT lies not in his own inventive imagination but definitely in Jesus of Nazareth.[6]

---

[4]J. Julius Scott, Jr., likewise arrives at the same conclusion for the connection between Paul and the apocalyptists: "Paul and Late-Jewish Eschatology—A Case Study, 1 Thess 4:13–18 and 2 Thess 2:1–12," JETS, 15 (1972), 3:133–43. See also Mounce, *Revelation*, pp. 18–25.

[5]See n.4; see also Ladd, *Commentary on Revelation*, pp. 8–10; idem, BDT, p. 53; Morris, *Revelation of St. John*, p. 24; Beasley-Murray, "The Revelation," pp. 1279ff.

[6]The development of this parallelism with the Olivet Discourse has been noted by Austin Farrer, *The Revelation of St. John the Divine* (Oxford: Clarendon, 1964), pp. 31–32; Swete, pp. cli-clii; Beckwith, pp. 139–40 and most recently by Louis A. Vos, *The Synoptic Traditions in the Apocalypse* (Kampen: J.H. Kok, 1965).

2. Unity

The question of the unity of Revelation is a relative one. Even Charles, who consistently advances a fragmentary approach to the book, recognizes the pervading unity of thought in the majority of the material (*Commentary on Revelation,* 1:lxxxviif.). Likewise Ford, who views the book as originating from three different authors, nevertheless insists that it displays an amazing and masterly literary unity that she ascribes to the work of still another person, an editor (p. 46).

The evidence that allegedly argues against a single author revolves around a number of internal difficulties. These fall into four categories: (1) the presence of doublets—the same scene or vision described twice; (2) sequence problems—persons or things introduced seemingly for the first time when in fact they had already been mentioned; (3) seeming misplaced verses and larger sections; and (4) distinctive content within certain sections that does not fit the rest of the book. In each case, however, there are satisfying alternative explanations. In fact, the difficulties just named stem more from the reader's presuppositions than from the text itself. Dissection of the text has been notoriously unfruitful in yielding further light on the book itself. We are more likely to discover the author's original intent if we approach Revelation with the assumption of its literary integrity than if we attempt at every turn to judge it by our modern and Western mentality.[7]

There is also a certain artificiality about interpolation theories that claim unity for the book until a passage is encountered that does not fit in with preconceived views, by which, without the slightest evidence, "interpolation" is cited to alleviate the embarrassment. Some of the best interpreters have succumbed to this temptation.[8]

Yet without belaboring the argument, we may affirm that the book everywhere displays both the literary and conceptual unity to be expected from a single author. This does not eliminate certain difficult hermeneutical problems nor preclude the presence of omissions or interpolations encountered in the extant MSS of the book. Nor does the view of single authorship preclude that John in expressing in written form the revelation given to him by Christ used various sources, whether oral or written (cf. comments at 1:2). Yet, under the guidance of the Holy Spirit, who is of course the primary author, John has everywhere made these materials his own and involved them with a thoroughly Christian orientation and content.

---

[7]This is precisely the point of three recent studies that look critically but fairly at the general trends of form and redaction criticism of NT documents: Northrop Frye, *Anatomy of Criticism: Four Essays* (Princeton: Princeton University, 1957); Walter Wink, *The Bible in Human Transformation* (Philadelphia: Fortress, 1973); and Leland Ryken, "Literary Criticism of the Bible: Some Fallacies," ch. 2 in *Literary Interpretations of Biblical Narratives,* edd. Louis, Ackerman, and Warshaw (Nashville: Abingdon, 1974). G. Mussies's recent and detailed work on the language of the Apocalypse has reaffirmed the unity of the entire book (*The Morphology of Koine Greek as Used in the Apocalypse of St. John* [Leiden: E.J. Brill, 1971], p. 351); as has also Vos, *Synoptic Tradition.*

[8]Thus Eller (pp. 159, 165–66), following M. Rissi ("The Kerygma of the Revelation to John," Int, 22 [1968], 4), chooses to dismiss John's number 666 as an interpolation mainly because it is unlike John to be a "calenderizer," which is contrary to his overall view of the Apocalypse. The issue, however, is not whether interpolations have crept into the text but the method of approach to determining interpolations. If there is no evidence to support such a view, there is no way of distinguishing whether an actual interpolation has occurred anywhere except in the mind of the commentator.

3. Authorship and Canonicity

The question of the authorship of Revelation is the same as that of the authorship of the other Johannine writings (the Gospel and the Epistles). The earliest witnesses ascribe Revelation to John the apostle, the son of Zebedee (Justin Martyr [d. 165]; Clement of Alexandria [d.c. 220]; Hippolytus [d.c. 236]; Origen [d.c. 254]) (Swete, pp. clxxif.). Not until Dionysius, the distinguished bishop of Alexandria and student of Origen (d.c. 264), was any voice raised within the church against its apostolic authorship.[9] Dionysius questioned the apostolic origin of Revelation because the advocates of an earthly eschatological hope ("Chiliasts"), whom he opposed, appealed to Revelation 20. He based his arguments on four main comparisons between the First Epistle of John and the Gospels at points where these differ from Revelation: (1) the Gospel and First Epistle do not name their author but Revelation does; (2) the Gospel and First Epistle contain parallels to each other but not to Revelation; (3) no reference to Revelation appears in the Gospel or First Epistle and no reference to the Gospel or First Epistle is found in Revelation; and (4) the Greek in which Revelation is written is faulty and entirely different from that of the Gospel and First Epistle (ANF, 6:82–84).

From the time of Dionysius, the apostolic origin of the book was disputed in the East until Athanasius of Alexandria (d.373) turned the tide toward its acceptance. In the West the story was different. From at least the middle of the second century, the book held its own, being widely accepted and listed in all the principal canon enumerations. The Reformation period witnessed a renewal of the earlier questions concerning its apostolic authorship and canonical status. Thus Luther, offended by the contents of Revelation, declared that he regarded it as "neither apostolic nor prophetic."[10]

Typical of current views is that of Moule, who claims that "few can now believe that the John of the Apocalypse is the same as the author (or authors) of what are commonly called the Johannine writings—the Gospel and the three epistles."[11] The chief

---

[9]Kümmel mentions certain heretical parties ("Alogoi") who opposed the Montanists as tracing the authorship of the book to the Gnostic Cerinthus. Gaius, the Roman anti-Montanist, likewise held such a view (Feine, Paul, and Behm, Johannes, *Introduction to the New Testament,* ed. W. Kümmel [Nashville: Abingdon, 1966], p. 330). Dionysius refers to these earlier views in his treatise against the apostolic authorship of the Apocalypse (ANF, 6:82). For the most extensive treatment of the canon evidence, see Ned. B. Stonehouse, *The Apocalypse in the Ancient Church* (Goes, Holland: Oosterboon and LeCointre, 1929).

[10]Feine-Behm, *Introduction to NT,* p. 330.

[11]C.F.D. Moule, *An Idiom Book of New Testament Greek,* 2d ed. (Cambridge: Cambridge University, 1960), p. 3; also Mussies, *Morphology,* p. 352: "The linguistic and stylistic divergence of the Apc. on the one hand and the Gospel and Letters of St. John on the other, proves beyond any reasonable doubt that all these works as we have them before us were not phrased by one and the same man." While Mounce (*Revelation,* pp. 28–30) probably underestimates the negative linguistic evidence against a common authorship of Gospel and Apocalypse, he does cite an early Gnostic text, the *Apocryphon of John,* which credits the passage in Revelation 1:19 to "John, the brother of James, these who are the two sons of Zebedee" (see also the review of Mounce by Alan F. Johnson, "A New Standard on the Apocalypse," CT [January 5, 1979], pp. 36–37). Elisabeth S. Fiorenza argues for a Johannine school as the explanation of the origin of both Gospel and Revelation: "The Quest for the Johannine School: The Apocalypse and the Fourth Gospel," NTS, 23 (April 1977), 402–27. Thus, recent NT scholarship is tending more toward the view that the writing of NT books was more located in "schools" or "communities" of disciples in various locations. Thus, a school of Matthew, or a school of John, Paul, or Peter, may account for the diversity

obstacle is the barbarous Greek style of Revelation as compared to that of the other Johannine writings. Of course, there is no good reason why the John of the Apocalypse could not have been the apostle John, while another John wrote the Gospel and the epistles.

However, despite the linguistic problem, a number of scholars have been convinced of the similarities between Revelation and the other Johannine books. So a group of dissenting scholars attribute the Apocalypse to the apostle, the son of Zebedee, or lean in that direction (e.g., most of the Roman Catholic scholars, Alford, Feine-Behm, Guthrie, Mounce, Stauffer, Swete, Zahn). Others leave the question open but do not deny apostolic authorship (Beasley-Murray, Beckwith, Bruce, Morris). Ford's view, that the book was not written by the apostle but was a composite writing by John the Baptist (chs. 4–11), a disciple of John the Baptist (chs. 12–22), and a later unknown Christian author (chs. 1–3), rests on conjectural evidence and has little to commend it to serious scholarly acceptance (pp. 28–40). Her arguments, instead, could be used to support the traditional view that the apostle, the son of Zebedee, who was a disciple of John the Baptist, was the author.

From the internal evidence, the following things can be said about the author with some confidence.

1. He calls himself John (1:4, 9; 22:8). This is not likely a pseudonym but instead the name of a well-known person among the Asian churches. Other than the apostle, John the Baptist, and John Mark, the only John we know about is the disputed "John, the presbyter" Papias spoke of (Eusebius *Ecclesiastical History* 3.39.1–7). (The John mentioned in Acts 4:6 would obviously not be a serious candidate.)

2. This John of the Apocalypse identifies himself as a prophet (1:3; 22:6–10, 18–19) who was in exile because of his prophetic witness (1:9). As such, he speaks to the churches with great authority.

3. His use of the OT and Targums make it virtually certain that he was a Palestinian Jew, steeped in the temple and synagogue ritual.[12] He may also have been a priest.[13]

To sum up, it must be admitted that the question of authorship of Revelation is problematic. On the one hand, the language and grammatical style are incompatible with the Gospel and the epistles; yet, on the other hand, in imagery, literary forms, liturgical framework, and symbolism, there are notable similarities to the Gospel and the epistles. Early and widespread testimony attributes the book to the apostle John, and no convincing argument has been advanced against this view. Perhaps we must be satisfied at present with a similar judgment for this book that Origen suggested for the authorship of Hebrews: "Who wrote the letter, God really knows."[14] Regardless of the problem of authorship, the church universal has come to acknowledge the Apocalypse as divinely authoritative, inspired Scripture.

---

in style and emphasis among the writings in the NT attributed to the same author. See E. Earl Ellis's "Further Reflections on John A.T. Robinson and the Dating of the New Testament," NTS, 26, no. 4 (1980): 487–502; also K. Stendahl, *The School of St. Matthew* (*Uppsala: Gleerup, 1954*) and Raymond E. Brown, *The Community of the Beloved Disciple* (New York: Paulus, 1979).

[12]L. Paul Trudinger, "Some Observations Concerning the Text of the Old Testament in the Book of Revelation," JTS, 17 (1966), 1:82–88.

[13]Ethelbert Stauffer, *New Testament Theology* (London: SCM, 1965), pp. 40–41.

[14]Daniel J. Theron, *Evidence of Tradition* (Grand Rapids: Baker, 1958), pp. 40–41.

4. Date

Only two suggested dates for Revelation have received serious support. An early date, shortly after the reign of Nero (A.D. 54–68), is supported by references in the book to the persecution of Christians, the "Nero redivivus" myth (a revived Nero would be the reincarnation of the evil genius of the whole Roman Empire), the imperial cult (ch. 13), and the temple (ch. 11), which was destroyed in A.D. 70 (so Westcott, Hort, Lightfoot, Ford). Some external evidence for the early date exists in the Muratorian Fragment (170–190) and the Monarchian Prologues (250–350). These documents claim that Paul wrote to seven churches following the pattern of John's example in Revelation.[15] But this would date the book before the Pauline Epistles!

The alternate and more generally accepted date rests primarily on the early witness of Irenaeus (185), who stated that the apostle John "saw the revelation . . . at the close of Domitian's reign" (A.D. 81–96) (*Contra Haereses* 5.30.3; ANF, 1:559–60). Both views appeal to the book's witness to persecution because of refusal to comply with emperor worship. On the other hand, if most of the persecution referred to in the book is anticipatory, and if the exegesis that sees in the book references to the succession of the emperors (ch. 17) and enforced emperor worship (ch. 13) is questionable, then no substantial argument can be advanced for either date. Therefore, though the slender historical evidence on the whole favors the later date (81–96), in the light of the present studies, the question as to when Revelation was written must be left open.[16]

---

[15]Ibid., pp. 59, 111; cf. Krister Stendahl, "The Apocalypse of John and the Epistles of Paul in the Muratorian Fragment," *Current Issues in New Testament Interpretation*, ed. W. Klassen and G.F. Snyder (New York: Harper, 1962), pp. 239–45. Stendahl argues that in addition to apostolic inspiration, a canonical book also needed to be universal in nature, i.e., written for the whole church. Apparently the Apocalypse served as a standard for including other books into the canon of the NT. Thus, the canon of Mommsen (c. early fourth century) states: "But as it is said in the Apocalypse of John, 'I saw twenty-four elders presenting their crowns before the throne,' so our fathers approved that these books are canonical and that the men of old have said this" (Theron, *Evidence of Tradition*, p. 121).

[16]See chs. 13 and 17, where the dating schemes are discussed in more detail and questioned. Kümmel suggests that since the congregation of Smyrna had been tried for a long time (2:8–11) and according to Polycarp (*Philippians* 11) the church did not exist in Paul's day, and since 3:17 describes the church at Laodicea as rich, though this city was almost completely destroyed by an earthquake in A.D. 60/61, the later date for the book is to be preferred (Feine-Behm, *Introduction to NT*, p. 329). However, John A.T. Robinson (*Redating the New Testament* [Philadelphia: Westminster, 1976], pp. 229–30) has recently challenged the above objection to the early date and favors a date prior to A.D. 70. He has effectively shown that this evidence is misinterpreted by Kümmel and others. Robinson's early date for the Apocalypse is conceded by D. Moody Smith ("A Review of John A.T. Robinson's *Redating the New Testament*," *Duke Divinity School Review*, 42 [1977], 193–205). Robinson claims that in addition to J.M. Ford and R.M. Grant, F.F. Bruce now inclines in the same direction (*Redating the New Testament*, p. 225, n.27). Morris correctly concludes that "the date of John is far from certain and there are some grounds for holding that it is to be dated before the destruction of Jerusalem in A.D. 70" (*Revelation of St. John*, p. 39). Albert A. Bell, Jr., has argued that the Domitian dating is not credible since the only direct evidence comes from Irenaeus ("The Date of John's Apocalypse. The Evidence of Some Roman Historians Reconsidered," NTS, 25 [1978], 93–102). Bell says, "Second-century traditions about the apostles are demonstrably unreliable, and Irenaeus' testimony is not without difficulties." Bell argues against the persecution theory as a backdrop to Revelation by refuting the evidence of Cassius Dio. He places the date of Revelation between June 68 and January 69!

5. Purpose

Swete captured the basic thrust of the book when he remarked, "In form it is an epistle, containing an apocalyptic prophecy; in spirit and inner purpose, it is a pastoral" (p. xc). As a prophet, John is called to separate true belief from false—to expose the failures of the congregations in Asia. He desires to encourage authentic Christian discipleship by explaining Christian suffering and martyrdom in the light of how Jesus' death brought victory over evil. John is concerned to show that the martyrs (e.g., Antipas [2:13]) would be vindicated. He also discloses the end both of evil and of those who follow the beast (19:20–21; 20:10, 15); he also describes the ultimate issue of the Lamb's victory and of those who follow him. John himself is centrally concerned with God's saving purpose and its implementation by Jesus. John writes to the church universal in every age so that they too might join him in confirming this witness of Jesus (1:9; 22:16).[17] Sadly, because of the sometime overemphasis on either the symbolic or the literal, and because of the theological problems (see below), the church has often been deprived of the valuable practical thrust of this book as through it God seeks to lead us into authentic Christian discipleship.

6. Theological Problems

From earliest times, certain theological emphases in Revelation are cited as objections to the whole book or to certain parts that are considered unworthy and sub-Christian. Among these are (1) its eschatological view of history, which includes an earthly Millennium (ch. 20); (2) the cry for vengeance in 6:10; (3) its "weakly Christianized Judaism";[18] and (4) its overuse of visions and symbols, according to Luther, who said that Christ is neither taught nor accepted in this book, and who considered it neither apostolic nor prophetic.

To sum up, Revelation is alleged to be sub-Christian in its Christology, eschatology, and doctrine of God, all three of which are thought to obscure or to contradict outright the central message of the NT.[19] While none of the above problems should be glossed over, it is becoming apparent that prior commitment to a certain viewpoint on these three areas, rather than the intrinsic incompatibility of John's ideas with the central NT message, often determines the negative judgments that some scholars pass on Revelation. A recent study by Beasley-Murray points out the basic difference in John's views from standard Jewish apocalyptic thought and wisely argues for the necessity to read Revelation in conjunction with the NT books that preceded it, not as contradictory, but as complementary to them.[20]

---

[17]Cf. Minear, *I Saw a New Earth*, pp. 213–17, for an excellent discussion of the prophet's motives in writing the book.

[18]Rudolph Bultmann, *Theology of the New Testament*, 2 vols. (New York: Scribner, 1951), 2:175.

[19]Cf. Kümmel (Feine-Behm, *Introduction to NT*), pp. 331–32. Even the conservative Morris complains that apocalyptic is not a good medium for expressing the "cruciality of the cross," and he believes that it does not express it: "Apocalyptic fails us at the heart of the faith" (*Apocalyptic*, p. 86). Yet the Book of Revelation seems to capture splendidly this cruciality of the Cross in its own unique way (cf. chs. 5 and 12) and provides a needed complement to the other NT descriptions of the Cross (see Beasley-Murray, n.20, below).

[20]G.R. Beasley-Murray, "How Christian Is the Book of Revelation?" in *Reconciliation and Hope, New Testament Essays on Atonement and Eschatology*, ed. Robert Banks (Grand Rapids: Eerdmans, 1974), pp.

7. Text

The MSS of Revelation are few compared to those of other NT literature. Thus, of the important early witnesses, only three papyri and scarcely half a dozen uncials of the Apocalypse are extant. While there are over a thousand minuscule MSS for each of most of the other books, Revelation has a total of only about 250.[21] Thus we have P[18] (third-fourth century), P[24] (fourth century), P[47] (late third century), ℵ (fourth century), A (fifth century), C (fifth century), P (ninth century), and a few minuscules cited in Metzger's apparatus and commentary.[22] In the Notes throughout this commentary, only those textual variants are discussed where, in my opinion, the sense of the passage is affected. I have also followed the practice of not citing all the textual evidence, since those who understand such technicalities have ready access to the standard critical editions of the Greek NT and works such as Metzger's (*Textual Commentary*) and Hoskier's collations (*Text of the Apocalypse*). In general, MSS A, ℵ, C, P[47] weigh heavily in the external evidence, especially where they agree. A alone is sometimes the preferred reading. Most of the cases must be settled on intrinsic probability and context. I have given Metzger's conclusions throughout but have occasionally dissented when the internal evidence seems to warrant it.

8. Interpretative Schemes

Four traditional ways of understanding Revelation 4–22 have emerged in the history of the church. In our day, additional mixed views have been developed by combining elements from these four traditions.

a. Futurist

This view is that, with the exception of chapters 1 to 3, all the visions in Revelation relate to a period immediately preceding and following the second advent of Christ at the end of the age. Therefore, the seals, trumpets, and bowls refer to events still in the future; the beasts of chapters 13 and 17 are identified with the future Antichrist, who will appear at the last moment in world history and will be defeated by Christ in his second coming to judge the world and to establish his earthly millennial kingdom.

Variations of this view were held by the earliest expositors, such as Justin Martyr (d.165), Irenaeus (d.c.195), Hippolytus (d.236), and Victorinus (d.c.303). After nearly a ten-century eclipse, during which time the allegorical method prevailed, the futurist view was revived in the late sixteenth century by Franciscus Ribera, a Spanish Jesuit. He held that the beast was the Antichrist of the end time and that Babylon was not Rome under papal rule but a degenerate Rome of a future age. Unlike many modern futurists, Ribeira founded his views on a thorough appreciation of the historical

---

275–84. See also Carl E. Braaten, *Apocalyptic Themes in Theology and Culture: Christ and Counter-Christ* (Philadelphia: Fortress, 1972), esp. ch. 1, "Apocalyptic Interpretation of History"; also G.E. Ladd, "The Theology of the Apocalypse," GR, 7 (1963–64), 73–86.

[21]H.C. Hoskier's monumental work has collated afresh all the uncial and minuscule witnesses to the book and is the best source for variants (*Concerning the Text of the Apocalypse*, 2 vols. [London: Bernard Quaritch, 1929]).

[22]Bruce M. Metzger, *A Textual Commentary on the Greek New Testament* (New York: UBS, 1971).

backgrounds of Revelation and its language. Thus he understood the first five seals to depict various elements of early Christianity. The white horse was the apostolic age; the red, the early persecutors; the black, heresies; the pale, the violent persecutions by Trajan. But when Ribera came to the sixth seal, he took this to indicate the signs that would precede the return of Christ; he also understood the seven trumpets and seven bowls to follow the three and a half years. This futurist approach to the book has enjoyed a revival of no small proportion since the nineteenth century and is widely held among evangelicals today. The chief problem with it is that it seems to make all but the first three chapters of Revelation irrelevant to the contemporary church. This objection is pressed more strongly when adherents to the futurist view affirm, as many do today, that the church will be removed from the earth before the events described in 6:1ff. occur.[23]

b. Historicist

As the word implies, this view centers on history and its continuity as seen in Revelation. It started with Joachim of Floris (d.1202), a monastic who claimed to have received on Easter night a special vision that revealed to him God's plan for the ages. He assigned a day-year value to the 1,260 days of the Apocalypse. In his scheme, the book was a prophecy of the events of Western history from the times of the apostles (in some varieties, from the Creation) until Joachim's own time. A short time after his death, the Franciscans considered themselves the true Christians of his vision. They interpreted Babylon not only as pagan Rome but also as papal Rome. In the various schemes that developed as this method was applied to history, one element became common: the Antichrist and Babylon were connected with Rome and the papacy. Later, Luther, Calvin, and other Reformers came to adopt this view. That this approach does not enjoy much favor today is largely because of the lack of consensus as to the historical identification it entails. The distinguished exegete Henry Alford (1810–71) held a guarded version of this view.

c. Preterist

According to this view, Revelation is to be seen as related to what happened in the time of the author; as to the time of its writing, it is a contemporary and imminent historical document. So the main contents of chapters 4–22 are viewed as describing events wholly limited to John's own time. This approach identifies the book with the Jewish apocalyptic method of producing "tracts for the times" to encourage faithfulness during intense persecution. The beasts of chapter 13 are identified respectively as imperial Rome and the imperial priesthood. This is the view held by a majority of contemporary scholars, not a few of whom are identified with the liberal interpretation of Christianity. As a system, it did not appear till 1614, when a Spanish Jesuit named Alcasar developed its main lines. Today some commentators argue that the events were imminent but not yet realized when John wrote; hence, they suggest an imminent historical view (so Caird). While they do not ignore the importance of the historical setting, those who accept Revelation as a book of genuine prophecy concerning events extending beyond the first six centuries are little attracted by this view.

---

[23]Some good sources for the history of interpretation are the works by Beckwith, Elliott, and Swete cited in the Bibliography.

d. *Idealist*

This method of interpreting Revelation sees it as being basically poetical, symbolic, and spiritual in nature. Indeed, it is sometimes called the spiritualist view—not, of course, in reference to the cult of spiritualism, but because it "spiritualizes" everything in the book. Thus Revelation does not predict any specific historical events at all; on the contrary, it sets forth timeless truths concerning the battle between good and evil that continues throughout the church age. As a system of interpretation, it is more recent than the three other schools and somewhat more difficult to distinguish from the earlier allegorizing approaches of the Alexandrians (Clement and Origen). In general, the idealist view is marked by its refusal to identify any of the images with specific future events, whether in the history of the church or with regard to the end of all things.[24] Undoubtedly, the book does reflect the great timeless realities of the battle between God and Satan and of divine judgment; undoubtedly, it sees history as being ultimately in the hand of the Creator. But certainly it also depicts the consummation of this battle and the triumph of Christ in history through his coming in glory.

Which view is the right one? Since there have been evangelicals who have held to each of the four views, the issue is not that of orthodoxy but of interpretation. In recent years many expositors have combined the stronger elements of the different views. The history of the interpretation of Revelation should teach us to be open to fresh approaches to it, even when this attitude goes contrary to the prevailing interpretations. Nothing short of the careful exegesis of the text uninhibited by prior dogmatic conclusions is required for the fullest understanding of the Apocalypse.

This commentary will pay close attention to the historical situation of first-century Christianity in its Judeo-Greco-Roman world setting. I do not, however, take the position that this emphasis necessarily leads to the conclusion that John's language and visions describe the political entities of imperial Rome or the imperial priesthood. Thus we feel that the preterist and to a lesser extent the preterist-futurist's views are misled.[25] On the other hand, we believe that John is describing the final judgment and the physical, bodily return of Christ to the world. This means that in every age Revelation continues to encourage the church in persecution as well as to warn the church of the beast's satanically energized, multifaceted deception. Its language describes the deeper realities of the conflict of Christ's sovereignty with satanic power rather than the mere temporary historical-political entities, whether past (such as Rome) or future.

Revelation may then be viewed, on the one hand, as an extended commentary on Paul's statement in Ephesians 6:12: "For our struggle is not against flesh and blood, but against the rulers, against the authorities, against the powers of the dark world and against the spiritual forces of evil in the heavenly realms." On the other hand,

---

[24]Recent interpreters who favor this view are Calkins, Hendriksen, and Milligan; see Bibliography, also.

[25]Beasley-Murray, Bruce, Ladd, Morris, Mounce, among others, are recent evangelical interpreters who have endeavored to combine the preterist and futurist schools. The key issue seems to be this: To what extent does the Apocalypse fit the literary genre of apocalyptic at the point of its view of history? The Jewish apocalyptists related their messages to the immediate historical-political entities. But does John in fact do this? Our answer is no. His language about the beast and Babylon describes more a theological than a political entity (see at chs. 13, 17). While the preterist-futurist view is a big step in the right direction away from the purely preterist or nonhistorical futurist views, in our opinion it falls short of the actual sense of the language throughout the book.

it also reveals the final judgment upon evil and the consummation of God's kingdom in time and eternity.

9. Use of the Old Testament

While Revelation does not have a single direct quotation, there are hundreds of places where John alludes in one way or another to the OT Scriptures. Swete mentions that of the 404 verses of the Apocalypse, 278 contain references to the Jewish Scriptures (p. cxxxv). UBS's Greek NT (2d ed.) cites over five hundred OT passages in connection with the book (pp. 897–920). In any case, the author's use of the OT is unique (e.g., Paul's epistles contain ninety-five direct quotations and possibly an additional one hundred allusions to the OT).

The OT used by John is primarily Semitic rather than Greek, agreeing often with the Aramaic Targums and occasionally reflecting Midrashic background materials to the OT passages; and it can be shown that he used a text other than the Masoretic that has a close affinity with the Hebrew text of the Qumran MSS.[26] From the Prophets, John refers quite frequently to Isaiah, Jeremiah, Ezekiel, and Daniel. John also refers repeatedly to the Psalms, Exodus, and Deuteronomy. Especially important are John's christological reinterpretations of OT passages he alludes to. He does not simply use the OT in its pre-Christian sense but often recasts the images and visions of the OT. While there is an unmistakable continuity in Revelation with the older revelation, the new emerges from the old as a distinct entity.[27]

10. Structure

The main contents of Revelation are given in terms of a series of sevens, some explicit, some implied: seven churches (chs. 2–3); seven seals (chs. 6–7); seven trumpets (chs. 8–11); seven signs (chs. 12–15); seven bowls (chs. 16–18); seven last things (chs. 19–22). It is also possible to divide the contents around four key visions: (1) the vision of the Son of man among the seven churches (chs. 1–3); (2) the vision of the seven-sealed scroll, the seven trumpets, the seven signs, and the seven bowls (4:1–19:10); (3) the vision of the return of Christ and the consummation of this age (19:11–20:15); and (4) the vision of the new heaven and new earth (21–22). Commendable attempts have also been made to show that the literary structure of the Apocalypse is patterned after the Easter liturgy of the early church.[28] All such schemes must, however, be subordinate to the exegesis of the book.

---

[26]DSS have shown that there were many text types in the first century, including a Masoretic-like text. John's use of the OT reflects some of the Qumran text types rather than the MT. See Trudinger, "Text of OT in Relevation," pp. 83–88; cf. D. Moody Smith, Jr., "The Use of the Old Testament in the New" in *The Use of the Old Testament in the New and Other Essays*, ed. James M. Efird (Durham: Duke University, 1972), pp. 58–63. See also Vos's excellent chapter "The Apocalyptist's Manner of Using Pre-Existent Material As Illustrated from His Employment of the Old Testament" (*Synoptic Traditions*, pp. 16–53).

[27]Austin Farrer (*A Rebirth of Images: the Making of St. John's Apocalypse* [London: Darce, 1949]) has opened my eyes to this dimension of the Apocalypse. The chief difficulty with Farrer is that his own book is more difficult to understand than Rev itself.

[28]Massey H. Shepherd, Jr., *The Paschal Liturgy and the Apocalypse* (Richmond: John Knox, 1960).

11. Bibliography

Space allows the mention of only representative books. Some defy exact categories and it may be unfair to classify them. We have used the interpretation of the beast (ch. 13) and Babylon (ch. 17) as the chief indicators of the nature of the books listed.

A. Futurist

1. Dispensational

Smith, J.B. *A Revelation of Jesus Christ*. Scottdale, Pa.: Herald, 1961.
Tenney, Merrill C. *Interpreting Revelation*. Grand Rapids: Eerdmans, 1957.
Walvoord, John F. *The Revelation of Jesus Christ*. Chicago: Moody, 1966.

2. Purely Eschatological

Eller, Vernard. *The Most Revealing Book of the Bible: Making Sense Out of Revelation*. Grand Rapids: Eerdmans, 1974.
Lilje, Hanns. *The Last Book of the Bible: The Meaning of the Revelation of St. John*. Philadelphia: Muhlenberg, 1955.

3. Preterist-Futurist

Beasley-Murray, G.R. "The Revelation." NBC rev. Edited by D. Guthrie, et al. Grand Rapids: Eerdmans, 1970.
Beckwith, Isbon T. *The Apocalypse of John*. New York: Macmillan, 1922.
Bruce, F.F. "The Revelation to John." In *A New Testament Commentary*. Edited by G.C.D. Howley, F.F. Bruce, and H.L. Ellison. Grand Rapids: Zondervan, 1969.
Ladd, George E. *A Commentary on the Revelation of John*. Grand Rapids: Eerdmans, 1972.
Morris, Leon. *The Revelation of St. John*. Grand Rapids: Eerdmans, 1969.
Mounce, Robert H. *The Book of Revelation*. NIC. Grand Rapids: Eerdmans, 1977.

B. Historicist

Alford, Henry. *The Revelation*. Alf. London: Cambridge, 1884.
Elliott, E.B. *Horae Apocalypticae*. 4 vols. Eng. tr. 3d ed. London: Seeley, Burnside, and Seeley, 1828.

C. Preterist

Barclay, William. *The Revelation of John*. 2 vols. The Daily Study Bible Series. Philadelphia: Westminster, 1959.
Caird, G.B. *The Revelation of St. John the Divine*. Harper's New Testament Commentaries. New York: Harper, 1966.
Charles, R.H. *A Critical and Exegetical Commentary on the Revelation of St. John*. 2 vols. ICC. Edinburgh: T. & T. Clark, 1920.
Ford, J. Massyngberde. *Revelation*. AB. New York: Doubleday, 1975.
Glasson, T.F. *The Revelation of John*. The Cambridge Bible Commentary on the New English Bible. New York: Cambridge at the University, 1965.
Harrington, Wilfred J. *The Apocalypse of St. John: A Commentary*. London: Geoffrey Chapman, 1969.
Heidt, William G. *The Book of the Apocalypse*. New Testament Reading Guide. Collegeville, Minn.: Liturgical, 1962.
Pieters, Albertus. *Studies in the Revelation of St. John*. Grand Rapids: Eerdmans, 1954.
Summers, Ray. *Worthy Is the Lamb*. Nashville: Broadman, 1951.

Sweet, J.P.M. *Revelation*. Philadelphia: Westminster, 1979.
Swete, Henry Barclay. *The Apocalypse of St. John*. New York: Macmillan, 1906.

D. *Idealist*

Calkins, Raymond. *The Social Message of the Book of Revelation*. New York: Woman's, 1920.
Carrington, Philip. *The Meaning of the Revelation*. New York: Macmillan, 1931.
Hendriksen, W. *More Than Conquerors*. Grand Rapids: Baker, 1940.
Kiddle, Martin. *The Revelation of St. John*. MNT. New York: Harper, 1940.
Milligan, William. *The Book of Revelation*. ExB. Hodder & Stoughton, 1909.
Minear, Paul S. *I Saw a New Earth: An Introduction to the Visions of the Apocalypse*. Cleveland: Corpus Books, 1968.
Rissi, Mathias. *Time and History*. Richmond: John Knox, 1966.

12. Outline and Map

I. Introduction (1:1–8)
   A. Prologue (1:1–3)
   B. Greetings and Doxology (1:4–8)

II. Vision of the Son of Man Among the Seven Churches of Asia (1:9–3:22)
   A. The Son of Man Among the Lampstands (1:9–20)
     1. Introduction and voice (1:9–11)
     2. The sight of the vision (1:12–20)
   B. The Letters to the Seven Churches (2:1–3:22)
     1. To Ephesus (2:1–7)
     2. To Smyrna (2:8–11)
     3. To Pergamum (2:12–17)
     4. To Thyratira (2:18–29)
     5. To Sardis (3:1–6)
     6. To Philadelphia (3:7–13)
     7. To Laodicea (3:14–22)

III. Vision of the Seven-Sealed Scroll, the Seven Trumpets, the Seven Signs, and the Seven Bowls (4:1–19:10)
   A. The Seven-Sealed Scroll (4:1–8:1)
     1. Preparatory: the throne, the scroll, and the Lamb (4:1–5:14)
       a. The throne (4:1–11)
       b. The scroll and the Lamb (5:1–14)
     2. Opening of the first six seals (6:1–17)
     3. First interlude (7:1–17)
       a. The 144,000 Israelites (7:1–8)
       b. The great white-robed multitude (7:9–17)
     4. Opening of the seventh seal (8:1)
   B. The Seven Trumpets (8:2–11:19)
     1. Preparatory: The angel and the golden censer (8:2–5)
     2. Sounding of the first six trumpets (8:6–9:21)
     3. Second interlude (10:1–11:14)
       a. The little book (10:1–11)
       b. The two witnesses (11:1–14)
     4. Sounding of the seventh trumpet (11:15–19)
   C. The Seven Signs (12:1–14:20)
     1. The woman and the dragon (12:1–17)
     2. The two beasts (13:1–18)
     3. The Lamb and the 144,000 (14:1–5)
     4. The harvest of the earth (14:6–20)
   D. The Seven Bowls (15:1–19:10)
     1. Preparatory: The seven angels with the seven last plagues (15:1–8)
     2. Pouring out of the seven bowls (16:1–21)
     3. The woman and the beast (17:1–18)
     4. The fall of Babylon the Great (18:1–24)

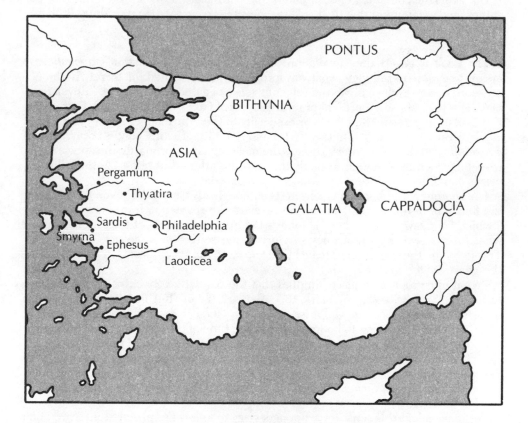

Text and Exposition

I. Introduction (1:1–8)

A. *Prologue*

1:1–3

¹The revelation of Jesus Christ, which God gave him to show his servants what must soon take place. He made it known by sending his angel to his servant John, ²who testifies to everything he saw—that is, the word of God and the testimony of Jesus Christ. ³Blessed is the one who reads the words of this prophecy, and blessed are those who hear it and take to heart what is written in it, because the time is near.

The Prologue contains a description of the nature of the book, a reference to the author, and a statement that the book was meant for congregational reading. Probably vv. 1–3 were written last.

1 The book is called the "revelation of Jesus Christ." "Revelation" (*apokalypsis*) means to expose in full view what was formerly hidden, veiled, or secret. In the NT the word occurs exclusively in the religious sense of a divine disclosure. "Revelation" may refer to either some present or future aspect of God's will (Luke 2:32; Rom 16:25; Eph 3:5) or to persons (Rom 8:19) or especially to the future unveiling of Jesus Christ at his return in glory (2 Thess 1:7; 1 Peter 1:7, 13). In this single occurrence of *apokalypsis* in the Johannine writings, the meaning is not primarily the appearing or revealing of Christ—though certainly the book does this—but rather, as the following words show, the disclosure of "what must soon take place."

The content of the book comes from its author, Jesus Christ. Yet even Christ is not the final author but a mediator, for he receives the revelation from God the Father ("which God gave him to show"). John is the human instrument for communicating what he has seen by the agency of Christ's messenger or angel (cf. 22:6, 8, 16). Through John the revelation is to be made known to the servants of God who comprise the churches (cf. 22:16).

"What must soon take place" implies that the revelation concerns events that are future (cf. Dan 2:28–29, 45; Mark 13:7; Rev 4:1; 22:6). But in what sense can we understand that the events will arise "soon" (*en tachei*)? From the preterist point of view (the events are seen to be imminent to the time of the author; cf. Introduction), the sense is plain: all will "soon" take place—i.e., in John's day. Others translate *en tachei* as "quickly" (grammatically this is acceptable) and understand the author to describe events that will rapidly run their course once they begin. However, it is better to translate *en tachei* as "soon" in the light of the words "the time is near" in v.3 (cf. 22:10).

Yet, if we adopt this sense, it is not necessary to follow the preterist interpretation of the book. In eschatology and apocalyptic, the future is always viewed as imminent without the necessity of intervening time (cf. Luke 18:8). That *en tachei* does not preclude delay or intervening events is evident from the Book of Revelation itself. In chapter 6 we hear the cry of the martyred saints: "How long, Sovereign Lord, holy and true, until you . . . avenge our blood?" They are told to "wait a little longer" (vv.10–11). Therefore, "soonness" means imminency in eschatological terms. The church in every age has always lived with the expectancy of the consummation of all things in its day. Imminency describes an event possible any day, impossible no day. If this sense is followed, we are neither forced to accept a "mistaken apocalyptic" view as Schweitzer advocated nor a preterist interpretation (Albert Schweitzer, *The Quest of the Historical Jesus* [New York: Macmillan, 1968]).

Two more focal points of the book are introduced by the words "by sending his angel to his servant John." First, they introduce us to the significance of angels in the worship of God, in the revelation of God's Word, and in the execution of his judgments in the earth. Angels are referred to sixty-seven times in Revelation.

The second focal point is the word "servant" (*doulos*). All of God's people are known in Revelation as his servants. No less than eleven times in the book are they so described (e.g., 2:20; 7:3; 22:3). John is one servant selected to receive this revelation and communicate it to other servants of God. "Servant," used throughout the NT to describe those who are so designated as the special representatives of the Lord Christ himself, becomes a beautiful title of honor for God's people. Here, then, in the Prologue are five links in the chain of authorship: God, Christ, his angel, his servant John, and those servants to whom John addressed his book.

2 Two elements in the book are of chief importance: "The word of God and the testimony of Jesus Christ." In referring to his visions as the "word of God," John emphasizes his continuity with the prophets in the OT as well as the apostles in the NT. The following passages show us John's concept of the Word of God: 1:9; 3:8, 10; 6:9; 12:11; 17:17; 19:9; 20:4. In 19:13 Jesus is himself identified with the name "the Word of God." Here, in chapter 1, the reference is not directly to Christ but to the promises and acts of God revealed in this book that are realized through Jesus, the Word of God incarnate (cf. John 1:1–2; 1 John 1:1). The church needs to be reminded that the neglected Book of Revelation is the very Word of God to us. While John's literary activity is evident throughout, he claims that what he presents he actually "saw" in divinely disclosed visions. And in the book God himself bears witness to the readers that these things are not the product of John's own mind (1:1–2; 21:5; 22:6; cf. 2 Peter 1:21).

"Testimony" translates the Greek *martyria*, another important term for the author. It is variously rendered as "witness," "attestation," "validation," "verification." "The testimony of Jesus" grammatically could be the testimony "to" Jesus—i.e., John's own testimony about Jesus (objective genitive). However, the alternate grammatical sense —the testimony or validation "from" Jesus (subjective genitive)—is to be preferred. John testifies both to the Word of God received in the visions and also to the validation of his message from Jesus himself. The important range of possible implications of the term in the following references is worthy of study: 1:9; 6:9; 12:11, 17; 19:10; 20:4; 22:16–20.

3 "The one who reads" reflects the early form of worship where a reader read the Scriptures aloud on the Lord's Day. "Those who hear" are the people of the congregation who listen to the reading. "This prophecy" is John's way of describing his writing and refers to the entire Book of Revelation (10:11; 19:10; 22:7, 9–10, 18). Prophecy involves not only future events but also the ethical and spiritual exhortations and

21

warnings contained in the whole writing. Thus John immediately sets off his writing from the late Jewish apocalyptic literature (which did not issue from the prophets) and at the same time puts himself on a par with the OT prophets (cf. 10:8–11; David Hill, "Prophecy and Prophets in the Revelation of St. John," NTS, 18 [1971–72], 401–18).

The twofold benediction "blessed" (*makarios*) pronounced on the reader and the congregation emphasizes the importance of the message in that they will be hearing not only the word of John the prophet but actually the inspired word of Christ (Rev contains six more beatitudes: 14:13; 16:15; 19:9; 20:6; 22:7, 14). John wrote in anticipation of the full and immediate recognition of his message as worthy to be read in the churches as the Word of God coming from Christ himself. In the ancient Jewish synagogue tradition in which John was raised, no such blessing was promised on anyone who recited a mere human teaching, even if from a rabbi, while one who read a biblical text (Scripture) performed a *mitzvah* (commanded act) and was worthy to receive a divine blessing.

All must listen carefully and "take to heart what is written" (*tērountes*, "observe," "watch," "keep") because "the time is near," the time or season (*kairos*) for the fulfillment of the return of Christ (v.7; cf. Luke 11:28, 21:8) and for all that is written in this book (cf. 22:10). The season (*kairos*) for Christ's return is always imminent—now as it has been from the days of his ascension (John 21:22; Acts 1:11).

A comparison of the Prologue (1:1–3) with the Epilogue (22:7–21) shows that John has followed throughout Revelation a deliberate literary pattern. This should alert us to the possibility that the entire book was designed to be heard as a single unit in the public worship service. As Minear says, "The student should not be content with his interpretation of any passage unless and until it fits into the message of the book as a whole" (*I Saw a New Earth*, p. 5). This should not in any way detract from the fact that John claims to have seen real visions ("saw," v.2), which we may assume were arranged by John in their particular literary form for purposes of communication.

Notes

1 Ἀποκάλυψις Ἰησοῦ Χριστοῦ (*apocalypsis Iēsou Christou*, "the revelation of Jesus Christ") raises two questions: (1) What is the relation of this book to the late Jewish apocalyptic literature (Enoch, T 12 Pat, etc.)? "Apocalyptic," as applied to this body of literature comes from the Gr. title of the Revelation (*apocalypsis*) of John (see p. 402). (2) Is "Jesus Christ" an objective or subjective genitive? If the latter, as most commentators suggest, the sense is the "revelation from Jesus Christ"; if the former, the meaning would be the "revelation about Jesus Christ." Grammatically, either is possible.

2 Τὴν μαρτυρίαν Ἰησοῦ Χριστοῦ (*tēn martyrian Iēsou Christou*, "the testimony of Jesus Christ") involves the same problem as above—viz, whether "Jesus Christ" is in an objective or subjective genitive relation to "witness." If the former, the sense is "the witness to Jesus Christ"; if the latter, it is "the witness received from Jesus Christ," i.e., attested by him (so TDNT, 4:500–501).

3 This is the first place in the book where synoptic parallels to the Apocalypse can be noted (cf. Luke 11:28; 21:8). No less than twenty-five direct and indirect uses of the sayings of Jesus can be identified in the Apocalypse. See the excellent work on this subject by Louis A. Vos, *The Synoptic Traditions in the Apocalypse* (Kampen: J.H. Kok, 1965).

B. *Greetings and Doxology*

1:4–8

⁴John,

¹To the seven churches in the province of Asia:

Grace and peace to you from him who is, and who was, and who is to come, and from the seven spirits before his throne, ⁵and from Jesus Christ, who is the faithful witness, the firstborn from the dead, and the ruler of the kings of the earth.

To him who loves us and has freed us from our sins by his blood, ⁶and has made us to be a kingdom and priests to serve his God and Father—to him be glory and power for ever and ever! Amen.

⁷Look, he is coming with the clouds,
 and every eye will see him,
even those who pierced him;
 and all the peoples of the earth will mourn
 because of him.

So shall it be! Amen.

⁸"I am the Alpha and the Omega," says the Lord God, "who is, and who was, and who is to come, the Almighty."

John now addresses the recipients of his book: "To the seven churches in the province of Asia" (cf. v.11; 2:1–3:22). Almost immediately he introduces an expanded form of the Christian Trinitarian greeting that merges into a doxology to Christ (vv.5b–6) and is followed by a staccato exclamation calling attention to the return of Christ to the world (v.7). The Father concludes the greeting with assurances of his divine sovereignty.

4 The epistolary form of address immediately distinguishes this book from all other Jewish apocalyptic works (cf. Introduction). None of the pseudepigraphical works contain such epistolary addresses. John writes to actual, historical churches, addressing them in the same way the NT epistles are addressed. These churches he writes to actually existed in the Roman province of Asia (the western part of present-day Turkey), as the details in chapters 2 and 3 indicate. But the question is this: Why did John address these churches and only these seven churches? There were other churches in Asia at the close of the first century. The NT itself refers to congregations at Troas (Acts 20:5–12), Colosse (Col 1:2), and Hierapolis (Col 4:13). There might also have been churches at Magnesia and Tralles, since Ignatius wrote to them less than twenty years later.

At present it is difficult to say why the Lord selected these seven churches. Some have suggested that the churches selected were prophetic of the church ages throughout history (J.A. Seiss, *The Apocalypse* [Grand Rapids: Zondervan, 1957], p. 64; the Scofield Reference Bible adopts this view in its notes). For example, Ephesus would represent prophetically the apostolic period until the Decian persecution (A.D. 250), followed by Smyrna, which represents the church of martyrdom extending until the time of Constantine (A.D. 316). However, after this initial agreement identifications become more difficult except for the last church. All agree that Laodicea is the final period of lukewarm apostasy. Yet there is no reason from the text itself to hold this view. The churches are simply churches found in every age. If the churches were genuinely prophetic of the course of church history rather than representative in every age, those who hold to the imminent return of Christ would have been quickly disillusioned once they realized this.

The reason seven churches were chosen and were placed in this order seems to be that seven was simply the number of completeness, and here it rounds out the literary pattern of the other sevens in the book (cf. Introduction: Structure). These seven churches contained typical or representative qualities of both obedience and disobedience that are a constant reminder throughout every age to all churches (cf. 2:7, 11, 17, 29; 3:6, 13, 22; esp. 2:23). Mounce suggests that the seven were possibly chosen because of some special relationship to emperor worship (*Revelation,* p. 68). As for the order of their mention (1:11), it is the natural ancient travel circuit beginning at Ephesus and arriving finally at Laodicea (see a map of the area).

"Grace and peace" are the usual epistolary greetings that represent the bicultural background of the NT—Greek (*charis,* "grace") and Hebrew (*šālôm,* "peace"; here the Gr. *eirēnē*). The source of blessing is described by employing an elaborate triadic formula for the Trinity:

"From him who is, and who was, and who is to come," i.e., the Father;
"From the seven spirits before his throne," i.e., the Holy Spirit;
"From Jesus Christ," i.e., the Son (v.5).

Similarly there follows a threefold reference to the identity and function of Christ: "the faithful witness, the firstborn from the dead, and the ruler of the kings of the earth"; and three indications of his saving work: "who loves us and has freed us from our sins . . . and has made us to be a kingdom and priests."

The descriptive name of the Father is "him who is [*ho ōn*], and who was [*ho ēn*], and who is to come [*ho erchomenos*]." Each name of God in the Bible is replete with revelatory significance. This particular title occurs nowhere else except in Revelation (4:8; cf. 11:17; 16:5). It is generally understood as a paraphrase for the divine name represented throughout the OT by the Hebrew tetragrammaton *YHWH*. In Exodus 3:14 the LXX has *ho ōn* for the Hebrew tetragrammaton, and in the LXX of Isaiah 41:4 the Lord is described as the one "who is to come." The complete combination of the three tenses does not occur in our Bibles but can be found in a Palestinian Targum on Deuteronomy 32:39. A case can be made that John has made a literal translation here of that Aramaic Targum (L. Paul Trudinger, "Some Observations Concerning the Text of the Old Testament in the Book of Revelation," JTS, 17, [1966], 87). The force of the name has been widely discussed. In 1:8 and 4:8 it is parallel with the divine name "Lord God, the Almighty." The tenses indicate that the same God is eternally present to his covenant people to sustain and encourage them through all the experiences of their lives.

"And from the seven spirits before his throne" seems clearly to focus on the Holy Spirit, not on angels. But why "seven spirits"? Some understand John to mean the "sevenfold spirit" in his fullness (NIV mg. and Ladd, *Commentary on Revelation,* in loc.). Borrowing from the imagery of Zechariah 4, where the ancient prophet sees a lampstand with seven bowls supplied with oil from two nearby olive trees, John seems to connect the church ("lampstands" [v.20]) to the ministry of the Holy Spirit (3:1; 4:5; 5:6). The "seven spirits" represent the activity of the risen Christ through the Holy Spirit in and to the seven churches. This figure brings great encouragement to the churches, for it is " 'not by might nor by power, but by my Spirit,' says the LORD Almighty" (Zech 4:6), that the churches serve God. Yet the figure is also a sobering one because the history of each church (chs. 2–3) is an unfolding of that church's response to the Holy Spirit—"He who has an ear, let him hear what the Spirit says to the churches" (2:7, 11, et al.).

Mounce opts for the view that the seven spirits are perhaps "part of the heavenly entourage that has a special ministry in connection with the Lamb" (*Revelation*, p. 70). However, to identify the seven spirits with angels is highly unlikely because (1) such reference to angels would break the symmetry of the Trinitarian address in 1:4–5 by the intrusion of an angelic greeting and (2) "spirit(s)" in the Book of Revelation refers only to the Spirit of God or to demons, with the exception of 11:11 and 13:15, neither of which refers to angels (for further objections to Mounce's view, see F.F. Bruce, "The Spirit in the Apocalypse," in *Christ and the Spirit in the New Testament*, edd. B. Lindars and S. Smalley [Cambridge: Cambridge University, 1973], pp. 333–37).

5 Finally, greetings come from the *Son*—"from Jesus Christ." John immediately adds three descriptive epithets about Christ and a burst of doxology to him. He is first the "faithful witness." His credibility is proved by his earthly life of obedience in the past; it is proved in the present by his witness to the true condition of the churches; and it will be proved in the future by the consummation of all things in him. In the past he was loyal to the point of death (cf. John 7:7; 18:37; 1 Tim 6:13), as was his servant Antipas (2:13). That Christ was a reliable witness to God's kingdom and salvation—even to the point of suffering death at the hands of the religious-political establishment of his day—is an encouragement to his servants who also are expected to be loyal to him—even to their death (2:10).

The fact that he is "the firstborn from the dead" brings further encouragement. As Christ has given his life in faithfulness to the Father's calling, so the Father has raised Christ from the dead, pledging him as the first of a great company who will follow (cf. 7:13–14). John nowhere else refers to Christ as the "firstborn" (*prōtotokos*), though Paul uses it in Romans 8:29 and Colossians 1:15, 18; and it also occurs in Hebrews 1:6. The same expression is found in Colossians 1:18, where it is associated with words of supreme authority or origin such as "head," "beginning" (*archē*, cf. Rev 3:14), and "supremacy." In Colossians 1:15 Paul refers to Christ as the "firstborn over all creation." This cannot mean that Christ was the first-created being but rather that he is the source, ruler, or origin of all creation (cf. EBC, 11:183). So for Christ to be the "firstborn" of the dead signifies not merely that he was first in time to be raised from the dead but also that he was first in importance, having supreme authority over the dead (cf. 1:18). In the LXX of Psalm 89:27 the same word is used of the Davidic monarch: "I will also appoint him my firstborn, the most exalted of the kings of the earth." Rabbinic tradition believed this reference was messianic (LTJM, 2:719).

The further title for Jesus, "the ruler of the kings of the earth," virtually connects John's thought with the psalm just quoted. Christ's rulership of the world is a key theme of John (11:15; 17:15; 19:16). Jesus Christ is the supreme ruler of the kings of the earth. But who are the "kings of the earth" over whom Jesus Christ rules? John could mean the emperors such as Nero and Domitian, the territorial rulers such as Pilate and Herod, and their successors. In that case John was affirming that even though Jesus is not physically present and the earthly monarchs appear to rule, in reality it is he, not they, who rules over all (6:15; 17:2). Another approach holds that Jesus rules over the defeated foes of believers, e.g., Satan, the dragon, sin, and death (1:18). A third possibility sees believers as the kings of the earth (2:26–27; 3:21; cf.

11:6). Support for this view comes from the reference to Christ's redeeming activity in the immediate context as well as by the reference to believers in v.6 as a "kingdom." All three ideas are true; so it is difficult to decide which was uppermost in John's mind. We should be careful, however, not to read into the term "king" our own power concepts but to allow the biblical images to predominate.

The mention of the person and offices of Christ leads John to a burst of praise to his Savior: "To him who loves us . . . be glory and power." In the present, Christ is loving us. Through all the immediate distresses, persecutions, and even banishment, John is convinced that believers are experiencing Christ's continual care. Moreover, in the past Christ's love was unmistakably revealed in his atoning death, by which he purchased our release from the captivity of sin. Christ's kingly power is chiefly revealed in his ability to transform individual lives through his "blood" (i.e., his death; cf. 5:9; 7:14). Through his death on the cross, he defeated the devil; and those who follow Christ in the battle against the devil share this victory. "They overcame him [the devil] by the blood of the Lamb and by the word of their testimony" (12:11).

6 This transformation simultaneously involves the induction of blood-freed sinners into Christ's "kingdom" and priesthood. Of Israel it was said that they would be a "kingdom of priests and a holy nation" (Exod 19:6; cf. Isa 61:6). The OT references as well as John's probably refer to both a "kingdom" and "priests" rather than a "kingdom of priests" (RSV). As Israel of old was redeemed through the Red Sea and was called to be a kingdom under God and a nation of priests to serve him, so John sees the Christian community as the continuation of the OT people of God, redeemed by Christ's blood and made heirs of his future kingly rule on the earth (5:10; 20:6). Furthermore, all believers are called to be priests in the sense of offering spiritual sacrifices and praise to God (Heb 13:15; 1 Peter 2:5). While John sees the church as a kingdom, this does not mean that it is identical with the kingdom of God. Neither do the new people of God replace the ancient Jewish people in the purpose of God (cf. Rom 11:28–29).

7 What Christ will do in the future is summed up in the dramatic cry: "Look, he is coming." This is a clear reference to the return of Christ (22:7, 12, 20). The preceding affirmation of Christ's rulership over the earth's kings and the Christians' share in the messianic kingdom leads to tension between the believers' actual present condition of oppression and suffering and what seems to be implied in their royal and priestly status. So the divine promise of Christ's return is given by the Father, and the response of the prophet and congregation follows in the words "So shall it be! Amen." Or we might think of Christ as saying, "So shall it be!" and the prophet and the congregation responding, "Amen" (cf. 22:20). The promise combines Daniel 7:13 with Zechariah 12:10 (taken from the Heb. text rather than LXX, as in John 19:37; cf. Matt 24:30, which also refers to the coming of Christ). Daniel 7 provides a key focus for John throughout the whole book (there are no fewer than thirty-one allusions to it).

Christ's coming will be supernatural ("with the clouds") and in some manner open and known to all ("every eye"), even to those who "pierced" him, i.e., put him to death. "Those who pierced him" might be those historically responsible for his death—such as Pilate, Annas, and Caiaphas—and those Jewish leaders of the Sanhedrin who pronounced him guilty. And yet, when he comes, there will be mourning among "all the peoples of the earth." From the NT point of view, Pilate, Annas, Caiaphas, and the others were acting as representatives for all mankind in crucifying

Jesus. While it is possible to see this mourning as a lament of repentance and sorrow for putting the Son of God to death, more probably the mourning results from the judgment Christ brings upon the world. The expression "peoples of the earth" (*phylai*; lit., "tribes") is normally used throughout the LXX and NT of the tribes of Israel (7:4ff; 21:12; cf. Matt 19:28; 24:30). John, however, uses *phylai* in a number of places to refer more broadly to the peoples of all the nations (5:9; 7:9; 11:9; 13:7; 14:6)—a usage that seems natural here, also.

8 Such a stupendous promise requires more than the prophet's own signature or even Christ's "Amen." God himself speaks and, with his own signature, vouches for the truthfulness of the coming of Christ. Of the many names of God that reveal his character and memorialize his deeds, there are four strong ones in this verse: "Alpha and Omega," "Lord God," "who is, and who was, and who is to come," and "the Almighty" (cf. v.4 for comments on the second title). Alpha and omega are the first and last letters of the Greek alphabet. Their mention here is similar to the "First" and "Last" in v.17 and is further heightened by the "Beginning" and the "End" in 21:6 and 22:13. Only the Book of Revelation refers to God as the "Alpha and the Omega." God is the absolute source of all creation and history. Nothing lies outside of him. Therefore, he is the "Lord God" of all and is continually present to his people as the "Almighty" (*pantokratōr*, lit., "the one who has his hand on everything"; cf. 4:8; 11:17; 15:3; 16:7, 14; 19:6, 15; 21:22; 2 Cor 6:18).

Notes

4 Ἀπὸ (*apo*, "from") plus the nominative in the divine name presents a problem. G. Mussies (*The Morphology of Koine Greek as Used in the Apocalypse of St. John* [Leiden: E.J. Brill, 1971], p. 93) takes the nominative as an appositional nominative and not as an instance of *apo* with the nominative case.
5 Textual problems exist as to whether λύσαντι (*lysanti*, "freed") or λούσαντι (*lousanti*, "washed") is correct and whether ἀγαπῶντι (*agapōnti*, present tense, "loves") or ἀγαπή-σαντι (*agapēsanti*, aorist tense, "loved") is the correct reading. In both cases the evidence is divided, but more diverse witnesses favor the adoption of the readings "freed" and "loves."

II. Vision of the Son of Man Among the Seven Churches of Asia (1:9–3:22)

A. *The Son of Man Among the Lampstands* (1:9–20)

1. *Introduction and voice*

1:9–11

⁹I, John, your brother and companion in the suffering and kingdom and patient endurance that are ours in Jesus, was on the island of Patmos because of the word of God and the testimony of Jesus. ¹⁰On the Lord's Day I was in the Spirit, and I heard behind me a loud voice like a trumpet, ¹¹which said: "Write on a scroll what you see and send it to the seven churches: to Ephesus, Smyrna, Pergamum, Thyatira, Sardis, Philadelphia and Laodicea."

9 This verse begins a third introduction in which the author again identifies himself as John and adds further significant information about where and when the visions took place together with their divinely appointed destination. John stresses his intimate identification with the Asian Christians and the reason for his presence on Patmos.

One of the Sporades Islands, Patmos lies about thirty-seven miles west-southwest of Miletus, in the Icarian Sea. Consisting mainly of volcanic hills and rocky ground, Patmos is about ten miles long and six miles wide at the north end. It was an island used for Roman penal purposes. Tacitus refers to the use of such small islands for political banishment (*Annals* 3.68; 4.30; 15.71). Eusebius mentions that John was banished to the island by the emperor Domitian in A.D. 95 and released eighteen months later by Nerva (*Ecclesiastical History* 3.20. 8–9).

John indicates that it was "because of the word of God and the testimony of Jesus" that he was formerly on Patmos (cf. 1:2; 6:9; 20:4). He was not there to preach that Word but because of religious-political opposition to his faithfulness to it. John sees his plight as part of God's design and says he is a partner with Christians in three things: "suffering" ("ordeal," "tribulation," "distress," "agony"), "kingdom," and "patient endurance" (or "faithful endurance"). John and the Asian believers share with Christ and one another the suffering or agony that comes because of faithfulness to Christ as the only true Lord and God (John 16:33; Acts 14:22; Col 1:24; 2 Tim 3:12). Also, they share with Christ in his "kingdom" (power and rule). In one sense they already reign (1:6), though through suffering. Yet, in another sense, they will reign with Christ in the eschatological manifestation of his kingdom (20:4, 6; 22:5).

Finally, John sees the present hidden rule of Christ and his followers manifested through their "patient endurance." As they look beyond their immediate distresses and put their full confidence in Christ, they share now in his royal dignity and power. Whether those distresses were imprisonment, ostracism, slander, poverty, economic discrimination, hostility (both violent and nonviolent by synagogue, marketplace, and police), disruption of the churches by false prophets, and the constant threat of death from mob violence or judicial action, believers are to realize their present kingship with Christ in their faithful endurance.

Endurance is "the spiritual alchemy which transmutes suffering into royal dignity" (Charles, *Commentary on Revelation*, 1:21). It is the Christians' witness and their radical love in all spheres of life. It produces the conflict with the powers of the world, and it calls for long-suffering as the mark of Christ's kingship in their lives (2:2, 19; 3:10; 13:10; 14:12; cf., e.g., Luke 8:15; 21:19; Rom 2:7; 1 Cor 13:7; Col 1:11). Christ's royal power does not now crush opposition but uses suffering to test and purify the loyalty of his servants. His strength is revealed through their weakness (2 Cor 12:9). Christians are called, as was John, to reign now with Christ by willingly entering into suffering conflict with the powers of this age.

10 "I was in the Spirit" describes John's experience on Patmos. The words imply being transported into the world of prophetic visions by the Spirit of God (4:2; 17:3; 21:10; cf. Ezek 3:12, 14; 37:1; Acts 22:17). At least the first vision—if not the whole Book of Revelation—was revealed on "the Lord's Day" (*kyriakē hēmera*). Since this is the only place in the NT where this expression is used, its identification is difficult. Paul uses *kyriakē* as an adjective in 1 Corinthians 11:20 in reference to the "Lord's supper" (*kyriakon deipnon*). Some feel that John was transported into the future day of the Lord, the prophetic day of God's great judgment and the return of Christ (E.W.

Bullinger, *The Apocalypse,* 2d ed. [London: Eyre & Spottiswoode, 1909], p. 152). The major objection to this is that John does not use the common expression for the eschatological "day of the Lord" (*hēmera kyriou*). Others find a reference here to Easter Sunday and base it on the tradition reported in Jerome's commentary on Matthew 24, that Christ would return on Easter Eve (Friedrich Bleek, *Lectures on the Apocalypse,* ed. and trans. L.T. Hossbach and S. Davidson [London: Williams & Norgate, 1875], p. 156).

More recently a convincing attempt has been made to link the literary form of Revelation with the paschal (Easter) liturgy of the ancient church (Massey H. Shepherd, Jr., *The Paschal Liturgy and the Apocalypse* [Richmond: John Knox, 1960]). Most commentators, both ancient and modern, have, however, taken the expression to mean Sunday, the first day of the week (W. Stott, "A Note on *kyriakē* in Rev 1:10," NTS, 12 [1965], 70–75). This usage occurs early in the apostolic fathers (*Didache* 14; Ignatius *To the Magnesians* 9). Tendencies toward recognizing Sunday as a day designated by Christ to celebrate his redemption occur even in the earlier parts of the NT (Acts 20:7; 1 Cor 16:2). Such a reference would bind the exiled apostle to the worshiping churches in Asia through his longing to be with them on Sunday. It is not impossible, however, that the day referred to here was an Easter Sunday.

11 The "voice" John heard could be Christ's or, more likely, that of the angel who appears frequently to John (4:1; 5:2). What John sees (visions and words), he is to write down in a papyrus scroll and send to the seven Asian churches (v.4). This writing would include the substance of the whole book, not just the first vision. (For a map of the seven churches, see page 415.)

Notes

9 Newman, in defending his thesis that Revelation is an anti-Gnostic document, proposes that 1:9 should be repunctuated as follows: "I John, . . . was on the island called Patmos. On account of the Word of God and the testimony of Jesus, I was in the Spirit on the Lord's day." John's words would, then, "indicate that the revelation which he received was given to him while he was *in the Spirit.* This revelation would be a direct rebuttal against his Gnostic opponents, who claimed to possess revelations which came to them while they were under the influence of the Spirit" (italics his) (Barclay Newman, *Rediscovering the Book of Revelation* [Valley Forge: Judson, 1968], p. 15).

2. *The sight of the vision*

1:12–20

> [12]I turned around to see the voice that was speaking to me. And when I turned I saw seven golden lampstands, [13]and among the lampstands was someone "like a son of man," dressed in a robe reaching down to his feet and with a golden sash around his chest. [14]His head and hair were white like wool, as white as snow, and his eyes were like blazing fire. [15]His feet were like bronze glowing in a furnace, and his voice was like the sound of rushing waters. [16]In his right hand he held seven stars, and out of his mouth came a sharp double-edged sword. His face was like the sun shining in all its brilliance.

¹⁷When I saw him, I fell at his feet as though dead. Then he placed his right hand on me and said: "Do not be afraid. I am the First and the Last. ¹⁸I am the Living One; I was dead, and behold I am alive for ever and ever! And I hold the keys of death and Hades.
¹⁹"Write, therefore, what you have seen, what is now and what will take place later. ²⁰The mystery of the seven stars that you saw in my right hand and of the seven golden lampstands is this: The seven stars are the angels of the seven churches, and the seven lampstands are the seven churches.

Certain important literary features of John's first vision are noted:

1. Beginning with v.12, the vision extends as a unit through chapter 3. The quotation that begins in v.17 is not closed till the end of chapter 3.

2. The introductory section (1:12–20) can be divided into two sections—the sevenfold features in the description of the glorified Christ (vv.12–16) and the address to John (vv.17–20).

3. In this symbolic picture the glorified Lord is seen in his inner reality that transcends his outward appearance. The sword coming out of his mouth (v.16) alerts us to this. In words drawn almost entirely from imagery used in Daniel, Ezekiel, and Isaiah of God's majesty and power, John uses hyperbole to describe the indescribable reality of the glorified Christ. These same poetic phrases reappear in the letters to the churches in chapters 2 and 3 as well as throughout the rest of the book (14:2; 19:6, 12, 15).

4. The words of Christ give his absolute authority to address the churches. And the vision (vv.12–16) leads to John's transformed understanding of Jesus as the Lord of all through his death and resurrection (vv.17–18).

12 For the OT tabernacle, Moses constructed a seven-branched lampstand (Exod 25:31ff.). Subsequently this lampstand symbolized Israel. Zechariah had a vision of a seven-branched golden lampstand fed by seven pipes—explained to him as the "eyes of the Lord, which range through the earth" (4:10). Thus the lampstand relates directly to the Lord himself. Since other allusions to Zechariah's vision of the lampstand appear in the Revelation—e.g., "seven eyes, which are the seven spirits of God" (5:6) and the "two witnesses" that are "the two olive trees" (11:3–4)—it is logical to assume here a connection with that vision as well.

But there are problems in any strict identification. In v.20 Christ tells John that the "seven lampstands are the seven churches" and in 2:5 that it is possible to lose one's place as a lampstand through a failure to repent. Therefore, the imagery represents the individual churches scattered among the nations—churches that bear the light of the divine revelation of the gospel of Christ to the world (Matt 5:14). If Zechariah's imagery was in John's mind, it might mean that the churches, which correspond to the people of God today, are light bearers only because of their intimate connection with Christ, the source of the light, through the power of the Holy Spirit (1:4b; 3:1; 4:5; 5:6).

13 Evidently the words "someone 'like a son of man'" are to be understood in connection with Daniel 7:13 as a reference to the heavenly Messiah who is also human. Jesus preferred the title Son of Man for himself throughout his earthly ministry, though he did not deny, on occasion, the appropriate use of "Son of God" as well (John 10:36; cf. Mark 14:61). Both titles are nearly identical terms for the

Messiah. The early church, however, refrained from using "Son of Man" for Jesus except rarely, such as when there was some special connection between the suffering of believers and Christ's suffering and glory (e.g., Acts 7:56; Rev 14:14; cf. Richard N. Longenecker, *The Christology of Early Jewish Christianity* [London: SCM, 1970], p. 92).

"Dressed in a robe" begins the sevenfold description of the Son of Man. The vision creates an impression of the whole rather than of particular abstract concepts. John saw Christ as the divine Son of God in the fullest sense of that term. He also saw him as fulfilling the OT descriptions of the coming Messiah by using terms drawn from the OT imagery of divine wisdom, power, steadfastness, and penetrating vision. The long robe and golden sash were worn by the priests in the OT (Exod 28:4) and may here signify Christ as the great High Priest to the churches in fulfillment of the OT Aaronic priesthood or, less specifically, may indicate his dignity and divine authority (Ezek 9:2, 11). In Ecclesiasticus 45:8, Aaron is mentioned as having the symbols of authority: "the linen breeches, the long robe, and the ephod."

14 In an apparent allusion to Daniel, Christ's head and hair are described as "white like wool, as white as snow" (Dan 7:9; cf. 10:5). For John, the same functions of ruler and judge ascribed to the "Ancient of Days" in Daniel's vision relate to Jesus. In Eastern countries, white hair commands respect and indicates the wisdom of years. This part of the vision may have shown John something of the deity and wisdom of Christ (cf. Col. 2:3). Christ's eyes were like a "blazing fire," a detail not found in Daniel's vision of the Son of man (Dan 7) but occurring in Daniel 10:6. This simile is repeated in the letter to Thyatira (2:18) and in the vision of Christ's triumphant return and defeat of his enemies (19:12). It may portray either his penetrating scrutiny or fierce judgment.

15 "His feet were like bronze glowing in a furnace" (cf. 2:18). The Greek is difficult (see Notes). His feet appeared like shining bronze, as if it were fired to white heat in a kiln. A similar figure of glowing metal is found in Ezekiel 1:13, 27; 8:2; Daniel 10:6. In both Ezekiel and Daniel the brightness of shining metal like fire is one of the symbols connected with the appearance of the glory of God. Revelation 2:18ff. might imply that the simile of feet "like burnished bronze" represents triumphant judgment (i.e., treading or trampling down) of those who are unbelieving and unfaithful to the truth of Christ.

"His voice was like the sound of rushing [lit., 'many'] waters" describes the glory and majesty of God in a way similar to that in Ezekiel (1:24; 43:2). Anyone who has heard the awe-inspiring sound of a Niagara or Victoria Falls cannot but appreciate this image of God's power and sovereignty (Ps 93:4). The same figure occurs in 14:2 and 19:6 (cf. also the Apocalypse of Ezra, a late Jewish book written about the same time or slightly earlier than Revelation; it similarly refers to the voice of God [4 Ezra 6:17]).

16 "In his right hand he held seven stars." The right hand is the place of power and safety, and the "seven stars" Christ held in it are identified with the seven angels of the seven churches in Asia (v.20). This is the only detail in the vision that is identified. Why the symbolism of stars? This probably relates to the use of "angels" as those to whom the letters to the seven churches are addressed (chs. 2–3). Stars are associated in the OT and in Revelation with angels (Job 38:7; Rev 9:1) or faithful witnesses to God (Dan 12:3). The first letter (that to Ephesus) includes in its introduction a reference to the seven stars (2:1), and in 3:1 they are associated closely with the "seven spirits of God."

John sees a "sharp double-edged sword" going forth from the mouth of Christ. Originally this was a large broad-bladed sword used by the Thracians (HDB, 4:634). The metaphor of a sword coming from the mouth is important for three reasons: (1) John refers to this characteristic of Christ several times (1:16; 2:12, 16; 19:15, 21); (2) he uses a rare word for sword (*rhomphaia*) that is found only once outside Revelation (Luke 2:35); and (3) there is no scriptural parallel to the expression except in Isaiah 11:4, where it is said that the Messiah will "strike the earth with the rod of his mouth" and "with the breath of his lips he will slay the wicked."

The sword is both a weapon and a symbol of war, oppression, anguish, and political authority. But John seems to intend a startling difference in the function of this sword, since it proceeds from the mouth of Christ rather than being wielded in his hand. Christ will overtake the Nicolaitans at Pergamos and make war with them by the sword of his mouth (2:12, 16). He strikes down the rebellious at his coming with such a sword (19:15, 21). The figure points definitely to divine judgment but not to the type of power wielded by the nations. Christ conquers the world through his death and resurrection, and the sword is his faithful witness to God's saving purposes. The weapons of his followers are loyalty, truthfulness, and righteousness (19:8, 14).

Finally, the face of Christ is likened to "the sun shining in all its brilliance." This is a simile of Christ's divine glory, preeminence, and victory (Matt 13:43; 17:2; cf. Rev 10:1; 1 Enoch 14:21).

17–18 These verses identify Christ to John and connect the vision of the glorified Christ (vv.13–16) with his existence in history. The vision is seen in the light of the Eternal One who identifies himself in these verses. "I fell at his feet as though dead" indicates that in the vision John actually saw a supernatural being and was stricken with trembling and fear, as had the prophets before him (Ezek 1:28; Dan 8:17; 10:9). Immediately Christ placed his hand on John and assured him that he would not die: "Do not be afraid" (cf. 2:10; 19:10; 22:8; Matt 17:6–7). The title "the First and the Last," which belongs to God in Isaiah 44:6 and 48:12 (where it means that he alone is God, the absolute Lord of history and the Creator), shows that in John's Christology Christ is identified with the Deity.

Christ is also "the Living One" in that he, like God, never changes. Probably this expression is a further elaboration of what it means to be "the First and the Last," i.e., he alone of all the gods can speak and act in the world (Josh 3:10; 1 Sam 17:26; Ps 42:2; Rev 7:2). These divine qualities of his person are now linked to his earthly existence in first-century Palestine—"I was dead, and behold I am alive for ever and ever!" This passage is sufficient to counter the claim that John's view of Christ does not revolve around atonement theology. On the contrary, his whole view of Jesus and his kingdom revolves around the Cross and resurrection—an interpretation that should serve to set the tone for all the visions that follow.

It was through Jesus' suffering, death, and resurrection that he won the right to have the "keys of death and Hades." Keys grant the holder access to interiors and their contents, and in ancient times the wearing of large keys was a mark of status in the community (cf. 3:7; 9:1; 20:1; 21:25). "Hades" translates the Hebrew term *šeʾôl* ("death," "grave") almost everywhere in the LXX. In the NT the word has a twofold usage: in some cases it denotes the place of all the departed dead (Acts 2:27, 31); in others, it refers to the place of the departed wicked (Luke 16:23; Rev 20:13–14). Since

Christ alone has conquered death and has himself come out of Hades, he alone can determine who will enter death and Hades and who will come out of these. He has the "keys." For the Christian, death can only be seen as the servant of Christ.

19 John is told to "write, therefore, what you have seen." This verse faces us with an important exegetical problem concerning the sense of the words and the relationship of the three clauses: "what you have seen, what is now and what will take place later." Does Christ give John a chronological outline as a key to the visions in the book? Many think he does. If so, are there three divisions: "seen," "now," and "later"? Or are there two: "seen," i.e., "now" and "later"? In the latter case, where does the chronological break take place in the book? For others, v.19 simply gives a general statement of the contents of all the visions throughout the book as containing a mixture of the "now" and the "later" (Moffatt, EGT, 5:347; Caird, p. 26).

While no general agreement prevails, the key to the problem may lie in the middle term "what is now." The Greek simply reads "which [things] are" (*ha eisin*). There are two possibilities. First, the verb can be taken temporally ("now") as NIV has done. This would refer to things that were present in John's day, e.g., matters discussed in the letters to the churches (2–3). Or second, the verb can be taken in the sense of "what they mean" (Alf, 4:559). This later explanation agrees with John's usage of the verb *eisin* throughout the book (cf. 1:20; 4:5; 5:6, 8; 7:14; 17:12, 15). "What they are [mean]" would immediately be given in the next verse, i.e., the explanation of the mystery of the lamps and stars. The change from the plural verb *eisin* in the second term to the singular *mellei* ("will") in the third tends to distinguish the last two expressions from both being time references.

Again, most commentators understand the phrase "what you have seen" as referring to the first vision (1:12–16); but it may refer to the whole book as the expression "what you see" in v.11 does (EGT, 5:347). In this case the translation could be either "what you saw, both the things that are and the things that will occur afterwards," or "what you saw, both what it means and what will occur afterwards." "What will take place later" clearly refers to the future, but to the future of what? Some have taken the similar but not identical phrase in 4:1 (q.v.) to mean the same as here and have rendered it "what shall take place after these present things," i.e., after the things relating to the seven churches (2–3). This results in either the historicist view of chapters 4–22 or in the futurist view of them. But if the future is simply the future visions given to John after this initial vision, then the statement has little significance in indicating chronological sequence in the book. While v.19 may provide a helpful key to the book's plan, on careful analysis it by no means gives us a clear key to it (see Notes).

John is told to write down a description of the vision of Christ he has just seen, what it means, and what he will see afterward, i.e., not the end-time things, but the things revealed later to him—whether they are wholly future, wholly present, or both future and present depends on the content of the vision. This leaves the question open concerning the structure of the book and its chronological progression, as John may have intended.

20 The first vision is called a "mystery" (*mystērion*). In the NT a "mystery" is something formerly secret but now revealed or identified. Thus John identifies the "mystery" of the harlot in chapter 17 by indicating that she is the "great city" that rules over the kings of the earth (vv.7, 18; cf. 10:7). The seven stars represent the "angels of the seven churches." Who are the angels? There is no totally satisfactory answer to this question. The Greek word for angels (*angeloi*) occurs sixty-seven times in Revelation and in every other instance refers to heavenly messengers, though occasionally in the NT it can mean a human messenger (Luke 7:24; 9:52; James 2:25 [Gr.]).

A strong objection to the human messenger sense here is the fact that the word is not used that way anywhere else in apocalyptic literature. Furthermore, in early noncanonical Christian literature no historical person connected with the church is ever called an *angelos*. Mounce and others (Beckwith, Morris) following Swete, who claims the idea comes from the Spanish Benedictine Beatus of Liebana (c. 785) (p. 22), identify the angels as a "way of personifying the prevailing spirit of the church" (Mounce, *Revelation*, p. 82). Though this is an attractive approach to our Western way of thinking, it too lacks any supporting evidence in the NT use of the word *angelos* and especially of its use in Revelation. Therefore, this rare and difficult reference should be understood to refer to the heavenly messengers who have been entrusted by Christ with responsibility over the churches and yet who are so closely identified with them that the letters are addressed at the same time to these "messengers" and to the congregation (cf. the plural form in 2:10, 13, 23–24).

As stated in v. 16, the stars are clearly linked in 3:1 with the seven spirits of God. Whatever may be the correct identification of the angels, the emphasis rests on Christ's immediate presence and communication through the Spirit to the churches. There is no warrant for connecting the seven stars with the seven planets or with images on Domitian's coins (Stauffer). In some sense, the reference to angels in the churches shows that the churches are more than a gathering of mere individuals or a social institution; they have a corporate and heavenly character (cf. 1 Cor 11:10; Eph 3:10; Heb 1:14). (See H. Berkhof, *Christ and the Powers* [Scottdale, Penn.: Herald, 1962] for further insight on the angelic ministries.) That the "seven lampstands are the seven churches" not only shows that the churches are the earthly counterpart of the stars but links the vision of Christ with his authority to rule and judge his churches.

Notes

11 The words "I am the Alpha and Omega, the first and the last" found in KJV have very little MS support, though the expression is represented in vv. 8, 11.

13 Rowland has recently argued that the elements in this vision are not only taken from the angelophany of Dan 10:5ff. and the "son of man" image in Dan 7:15ff. but that these texts also can be traced to a theological history within Judaism that stretches back to the call-vision of the prophet Ezekiel (1:4–28). Apparently a trend developed in Jewish angelology that separated the human figure from the throne chariot in Ezekiel 8:2. Rowland suggests that Revelation 1:13ff. reflects this history and attempts to develop a Christology based on the "angel of the Lord" figure in the Old Testament. (C. Rowland, "The vision of the Risen Christ in Rev. 1:13ff.: The Debt of an Early Christology to an Aspect of Jewish Angelology" JTS, N.S., 31/1 (1980), 1–11.)

15 While πεπυρωμένης (*pepyrōmenēs*, "glowing") is supported by only A C, Bruce M. Metzger favors the reading (*A Textual Commentary on the Greek New Testament* [New York: UBS, 1971], p. 732). This ending would modify καμίνω (*kaminō*, "furnace"), which is feminine, but Mussies says it could just as well go with χαλκολιβάνω (*chalkolibanō*, "brass") (*Morphology*, p. 98).

19 W.C. VanUnnik argues from early Christian and Gnostic literature, especially from the Apocryphon of John, that this threefold expression was a standing formula to identify the true Christian prophet (NTS, 9:86–94).

B. *The Letters to the Seven Churches* (2:1–3:22)

1. *To Ephesus*

2:1–7

¹"To the angel of the church in Ephesus write:
These are the words of him who holds the seven stars in his right hand and walks among the seven golden lampstands: ²I know your deeds, your hard work and your perseverance. I know that you cannot tolerate wicked men, that you have tested those who claim to be apostles but are not, and have found them false. ³You have persevered and have endured hardships for my name, and have not grown weary.
⁴Yet I hold this against you: You have forsaken your first love. ⁵Remember the height from which you have fallen! Repent and do the things you did at first. If you do not repent, I will come to you and remove your lampstand from its place. ⁶But you have this in your favor: You hate the practices of the Nicolaitans, which I also hate.
⁷He who has an ear, let him hear what the Spirit says to the churches. To him who overcomes, I will give the right to eat from the tree of life, which is in the paradise of God.

The letters are more in the nature of messages than letters. Each message to an individual church was apparently also intended for the other six churches (2:7, 11, 17, etc., esp. 2:23). By reading and comparing each similar component of all the letters, one may gain a fuller insight into the messages. Each message generally follows a common literary plan consisting of seven parts:

1. The addressee is first given. This pattern occurs in the same way at the beginning of each letter; viz., "To the angel of the church in Ephesus write," etc.

2. Then the speaker is mentioned. In each case, some part of the great vision of Christ and of his self-identification (1:12–20) is repeated as the speaker identifies himself; e.g., "him who holds the seven stars in his right hand and walks among the seven golden lampstands" (2:1; cf. 1:13, 16). This identification is preceded in each case with the significant declaration "These are the words of him"—a declaration strongly reminiscent of the OT formula for introducing the words of God to the congregation of Israel.

3. Next, the knowledge of the speaker is given. His is a divine knowledge. He knows intimately the works of the churches and the reality of their loyalty to him, despite outward appearances. Each congregation's total life is measured against the standard of Christ's life and the works they have embraced. In two cases that assessment proves totally negative (Sardis and Laodicea). In the message to Philadelphia, the speaker designates himself as "holy and true" (3:7); to the Laodiceans, he is "the faithful and true witness" (3:14). The enemy of Christ's churches is the deceiver, Satan, who seeks to undermine the churches' loyalty to Christ (2:10, 24).

4. Following his assessment of the churches' accomplishments, the speaker pronounces his verdict on their condition in such words as "You have forsaken your first love" (2:4) or "You are dead" (3:1). While two letters contain no unfavorable verdict

(Smyrna, Philadelphia) and two no word of commendation (Sardis, Laodicea), yet since all seven letters would be sent to each church together with the entire Book of Revelation (cf. 1:11), we may assume that Christ intended that all the churches hear words of both commendation and blame. In the letters all derelictions are viewed as forms of inner betrayals of a prior relation to Christ. Each congregation is responsible as a congregation for its individual members and for its leaders; each leader and each individual believer is at the same time fully responsible for himself and for the congregation. This responsibility especially involves the problem of self-deception concerning good and evil, the true and the false, in situations where they are easily confused. The evil appears under the cloak of good; the good appears as apparent evil. Christ's verdict sets before each church the true criteria for leading it out of self-deception into the truth.

5. To correct or alert each congregation, Jesus issues a penetrating command. These commands further expose the exact nature of the self-deception involved. We are mistaken if we believe that the churches readily identified the heretics and heresies involved in Christ's descriptions. Because they were deceptions, they would not easily be identified; thus there is the use of OT figures such as Balaam, Jezebel, etc., to alert the churches to the deceptiveness of the error. The greater the evil, the more deceptive the cloak. In the exposition of the letters, the commands must be carefully considered so as to determine precisely the particular nature of the various errors. The thrust of the commands is not in the direction of consolation for persecuted churches. It is rather the opposite—viz., that John, like Jesus, was concerned to bring not peace but a sword.

6. Each letter contains the general exhortation "he who has an ear, let him hear what the Spirit says to the churches" (2:7, et al.). Seven exactly identical exhortations occur with only the position in the letter as a variable. The words of the Spirit are the words of Christ (cf. 19:10). Actually, the commands of Christ in the letters are somewhat ambiguous. Therefore, they require the individual and the congregation to listen also to the Spirit's voice that accompanies the words of Jesus if they are truly to realize the victory he considers appropriate for them. The exhortations provide warnings about apathy as well as words of challenge and encouragement. Even though the words of Christ refer initially to the first-century churches located in particular places, by the Spirit's continual relevance they transcend that time limitation and speak to all the churches in every generation.

7. Finally, each letter contains a victor's promise of reward. These promises are often the most metaphorical and symbolic portions of the letters and thus in some cases present interpretive difficulties. Each is eschatological and is correlated with the last two chapters of the book (21–22). For example, "the right to eat from the tree of life, which is in the paradise of God" (2:7) is parallel to "the tree of life" in 22:2; protection from "the second death" (2:11) finds its counterpart in 21:4: "There will be no more death," etc. Furthermore, the promises are echoes of Genesis 2–3: what was lost originally by Adam in Eden is more than regained in Christ. The expression "I will give" or "I will make" identifies Christ as the absolute source and donor of every gift. Probably we are to understand the multiple promises as different facets that combine to make up one great promise to believers, that wherever Christ is, there will the overcomers be. Who are the "overcomers"? Certainly it is those who are fully loyal to Christ as his true disciples, those who are identified with him in his suffering and death (1 John 5:4–5). Compare those who do not overcome in 21:8 with those

referred to in the letters, e.g., the "cowardly" (2:10, 13), the "sexually immoral" (2:14, 20), the "idolaters" (2:14, 20), and the "liars" (2:2, 9, 20; 3:9).

The church at Ephesus is addressed in the first letter. Ephesus was a crossroads of civilization. Politically, it had become the de facto capital of the province, known as "Supreme Metropolis of Asia." The Roman governor resided there. It was a "free" city, i.e., self-governed. Located on the western coast of Asia Minor, at the convergence of three great highways, from the north, east, and south, Ephesus was the trade center of the area. It has been called "The Vanity Fair of the Ancient World" (William Barclay, *Letters to the Seven Churches* [New York: Abingdon, 1957], p. 12).

Religiously, Ephesus was the center for the worship of the fertility "bee" goddess known in Greek as "Artemis," or Romanized as "Diana" (Acts 19:23ff.). The temple with its statue of Artemis was one of the wonders of the ancient world. Thousands of priests and priestesses were involved in her service. Many of the priestesses were dedicated to cult prostitution. (This may be related to the "practices of the Nicolaitans" in v.6.) The temple also served as a great bank for kings and merchants, as well as an asylum for fleeing criminals. To what extent the temple phenomena contributed to the general moral deterioration of the population cannot be assessed, but one of Ephesus' own citizens, the weeping philosopher Heraclitus, said that the inhabitants of the city were "fit only to be drowned and that the reason why he could never laugh or smile was because he lived amidst such terrible uncleanness" (ibid., p. 17). The church at Ephesus was probably founded jointly by Aquila, Priscilla, and (later) Paul (Acts 18:18–19; 19:1–10). The Ephesians were cosmopolitan and transient, and their city had a history of cultural-political change; these factors may have influenced the apostasy of the congregation at Ephesus from its first love (cf. 2:4).

1 The speaker identifies himself by a reference to the vision of chapter 1: "Him who holds the seven stars in his right hand" (cf. 1:16). These words strike both a note of reassurance signaling Christ's strong protection and control of the church and his vital concern. On the other hand, there is a note of warning in the description of Christ as the one who "walks [travels] among the seven golden lampstands," since he may journey to Ephesus to remove their lampstand (2:5).

2–3 The speaker's knowledge includes awareness of their activity, their discernment of evil, and their patient suffering. Their "deeds," their "hard work" (*kopos*, "wearisome toil"), and their "perseverance" are underlined by the phrase "you have . . . endured hardships for my name, and have not grown weary" (v.3). The Ephesian Christians did not lack serious and sustained activity, even to the point of suffering for Christ's name. Paul attributes the same threefold activity to the Thessalonians and there adds to each quality its motivating source: "faith," "love," and "hope" (1 Thess 1:3).

Christ also knows that doctrinal discrimination accompanies the toil and patience of the Ephesians. They "cannot tolerate wicked men." These were not the pagans in Ephesus but false brethren who "claim to be apostles but are not." It is not easy, however, to determine precisely who these people were, what they taught, or how the church tested them. An "apostle" is one who is sent as a representative of another and bears the full authority of the sender (TDNT, 1:421). The word is applied first in the NT to the original circle of the Twelve (Mark 3:14; Acts 1:2, 26), who had a special place historically in the foundation of the church (Eph 2:20; Rev 21:14). But

37

the NT further broadens this original circle to include others such as Paul (Gal 1:1), Barnabas (Acts 14:14), James the brother of Jesus (Gal 1:19), and still others (cf. Rom 16:7). The name was applied to those who were authentically and specially called by Christ to be his authoritative spokesmen.

Miracles were the signs of apostolic authority (2 Cor 12:12; Heb 2:4), but miracles may also accompany false prophets (Mark 13:22; 2 Thess 2:9; 2 Tim 3:8; Rev 13:13–14). Thus it was necessary to "test the spirits to see whether they are from God, because many false prophets have gone out into the world" (1 John 4:1). Beyond their denial of Jesus as Lord, these self-proclaimed apostles also sought selfish advantage through their claims (2 Cor 11:5, 13; 12:11).

As to whether the authoritative function of apostles continued after the first century, the apostolic fathers are instructive. In no case do the many references to apostles in the writings of Clement of Rome, Ignatius, Barnabas, and the Shepherd of Hermas relate to any recognized apostles other than those associated with the NT. The Fathers apparently understood the special apostolic function to have ceased with the end of the apostolic era.

About fifteen years later than John's writing of Revelation, Ignatius wrote to the church of Ephesus and commended them for refusing to give a "home" to any heresy (*To the Ephesians* 6, 7, 9, 16). Thyatira had failed (2:20ff.), but the Ephesians had won the victory over false teachers. They had heeded Paul's earlier warning (Acts 20:28–30).

4 The speaker's verdict shows, on the other hand, that however much had been gained at Ephesus by resisting the false apostles, not all was well there. They had "forsaken," or "let go" (*aphiēmi*), their "first love." This was a serious defect. If uncorrected, it would result in their loss of light bearing (v.5). The majority of commentators take the first love to refer to the original Christian love the Ephesians had for one another. Paul's exhortation to the Ephesian elders to "help the weak" (Acts 20:35) and the warm commendation he gives them in their early years for their fervent love of one another (Eph 1:15) may lend support to this view.

Other commentators, however, see the "first love" as a reference to their inner devotion to Christ that characterized their earlier commitment, like the love of a newly wedded bride for her husband (John R.W. Stott, *What Christ Thinks of the Church* [Grand Rapids: Eerdmans, 1958], p. 27; Alf, 4:563). This interpretation is supported by the fact that the letters to the other churches reveal problems of inner betrayal to Christ as subjects of his complaint. Neither view necessarily eliminates the other. Loving devotion to Christ can be lost in the midst of active service, and certainly no amount of orthodoxy can make up for a failure to love one another. "First" (*prōtos*) love would suggest that they still loved, but with a quality and intensity unlike that of their initial love.

5 The speaker's command further exposes the problem and offers a way to correct the fault. The imperatives are instructive: "Remember. . . . Repent . . . do." The Ephesians are called on to reflect on their earlier works of fervent love (like the Sardians [3:3]), to look in comparison at the present situation, to ponder how far they have fallen from their former devotion and enthusiasm, to humbly "repent" (totally change) before God, and to do the former works motivated by love. These imperatives are all part of a single action designed to keep the Ephesians from the judgment of Christ, which would effectively remove them as his representatives in the world.

How many churches today stand at this same crossroads? Do we sense the importance to Christ of not only honoring his name by our true confession but also reflecting his life by our loving relationship to others? This threat of loss of light bearing (or witness) applies doubtless equally to the other four churches, to whom a similar exhortation to repent is given (Pergamos, Thyatira, Sardis, and Laodicea).

6 Christ adds a further commendation concerning the Ephesians' hatred of the practices of the Nicolaitans (cf. 2:15)—a hatred directed at the practices of the Nicolaitans, not the people themselves (cf. Ps 139:21). It is difficult to determine exactly who the Nicolaitans were and what they taught. Etymologically the name means "to conquer [or 'consume,' *nikao*] the people [*laos*]." Did they call themselves by this name or is it a derogatory title Christ applied to them? The close association of the name with the Balaamites in 2:14–15 may suggest either identity with this group or similarity to their teachings (see comments on 2:14–15).

Information about the Nicolaitans is limited, ambiguous, and based on John's references here in Revelation. Irenaeus claims that John wrote the Gospel to thwart the teaching of the Gnostic Cerinthus whose error was similar to the earlier offshoot of the same kind of teaching known as Nicolaitanism (*Contra Haereses* 3.11.7, cited by Daniel J. Theron, *Evidence of Tradition* [Grand Rapids: Baker, 1958], p. 73). Eusebius mentions that the Nicolaitans lasted only a short time (*Ecclesiastical History* 3.29.1). Seeing the sect as a heresy would agree with the reference in 2:14 and 2:20, which warns against mixing Christian faith with idolatry and cult prostitution. Fiorenza identifies the group as Gnostics and summarizes the problem well: "The Nicolaitans are according to Revelation a Christian group within the churches of Asia Minor and have their adherents even among the itinerant missionaries and the prophetic teachers of the community. They claim to have insight into the divine or, more probably, into the demonic. They express their freedom in libertine behavior, which allows them to become part of their syncretistic pagan society and to participate in the Roman civil religion" (Elisabeth S. Fiorenza, "Apocalyptic and Gnosis in the Book of Revelation," JBL, 92 [1973], 570; see also Barclay Newman, *Rediscovering the Book of Revelation* [Valley Forge: Judson, 1968], pp. 11–30, who sees the entire Book of Revelation as an anti-Gnostic polemic rather than a political-religious persecution document). Others understand the Nicolaitans as Christians who still showed devotion to the emperor by burning incense to his statue or image (William M. Ramsay, *The Letters to the Seven Churches of Asia* [London: Hodder & Stoughton, 1904], pp. 300–301). (See also the letters to Pergamum and Thyatira.)

7 On the general exhortation and the meaning of "overcomes," see the introduction to this section (2:1). The overcomer is promised access to the "tree of life, which is in the paradise of God." The "tree of life" is first mentioned in Genesis 2:9 as one of the many trees given to Adam and Eve for food and was off bounds after their fall into sin (Gen 3:22, 24). It is last mentioned in Revelation 22:19.

Rabbinic and Jewish apocalyptic works mention that the glorious age of the Messiah would be a restoration to Edenic conditions before the Fall (see also Isa 51:3; Ezek 36:35; cf. Ezek 28:13; 31:8–9). Jewish thought joined the concepts of the renewed city of God, the tree of life, and the paradise of God. In the apocalyptic book the Testament of Levi it is promised that God (or Messiah) "shall open the gates of Paradise, and shall remove the threatening sword against Adam, and he shall give the saints to eat from the tree of life, and the spirit of holiness shall be on them" (18:10–11).

"Paradise" (*paradeisos*) is a Persian loan word meaning "a park" or "a garden." The LXX uses it to translate the Hebrew expression the "garden" of Eden (Gen 2:8–10). John seems to reinterpret the Jewish idea of Paradise. First, Jesus Christ is the restorer of the lost Paradise (22:1–4, 14). He gives access to the tree of life. Paradise means to be with him in fellowship rather than the idea of a hidden paradise with its fantastic sensual delights (TDNT, 6:772). The tree of life conveys symbolically the truth of eternal life or the banishment of death and suffering (22:2). Those at Ephesus who truly follow Christ in deep devotion and thus experience the real victory of Christ will share the gift of eternal life that he alone gives.

Notes

1 In addition to Ramsay's and Barclay's work on the seven churches, see also Otto F.A. Meinardus, *St. John of Patmos and the Seven Churches of the Apocalypse* (Athens, Greece: Lycabettus, 1974); idem, "The Christian Remains of the Seven Churches of the Apocalypse," BA, 37 (March 1974), 69–82; Minear, *I Saw a New Earth;* Ramsay, *Seven Churches;* R.C. Trench, *Commentary on the Epistles to the Seven Churches in Asia: Revelation II and III* (New York: Scribner's, 1862); J.R.W. Stott, *What Christ Thinks of the Church.* Two very detailed and accurate treatments of the historical interpretation and archaeological research regarding the cities of the seven churches, with extensive bibliographies, are Edwin Yamauchi's *Archaeology of New Testament Cities in Western Asia Minor* (Grand Rapids: Baker, 1980) and Colin Hemer's four excellent articles on the seven churches in *Buried History,* 11 (1975), 4–27; 56–83; 110–35; 164–90. In 1969 Hemer wrote a dissertation at Manchester University entitled "A Study of the Letters to the Seven Churches of Asia with Special Reference to Their Local Background," which in revised form is to be published in the New Testament Monographs series by Cambridge University.

2. To Smyrna

2:8–11

8"To the angel of the church in Smyrna write:

These are the words of him who is the First and the Last, who died and came to life again. 9I know your afflictions and your poverty—yet you are rich! I know the slander of those who say they are Jews and are not, but are a synagogue of Satan. 10Do not be afraid of what you are about to suffer. I tell you, the devil will put some of you in prison to test you, and you will suffer persecution for ten days. Be faithful, even to the point of death, and I will give you the crown of life.

11He who has an ear, let him hear what the Spirit says to the churches. He who overcomes will not be hurt at all by the second death.

Smyrna (modern Izmir) lay almost due north of Ephesus, a distance of about forty miles. The city was exceptionally beautiful and large (c. 200,000 pop.) and ranked with Ephesus and Pergamum as "First of Asia." Known as the birthplace of Homer, it was also an important seaport that commanded the mouth of the Hermus River valley. Smyrna was a wealthy city where learning, especially in the sciences and medicine, flourished. An old city (third millennium B.C.), allegedly founded by a mythical Amazon who gave her name to it, Smyrna repeatedly sided with Rome in different periods of her history, and thus earned special privileges as a free city and assize (self-governed) town under Tiberius and successive emperors. Among the beautiful paved streets traversing it from east to west was the "Golden Street," with the temples to Cybele and Zeus at either end and along which were temples to Apollo, Asclepius, and Aphrodite.

Smyrna was also a center of the emperor worship, having won the privilege from the Roman Senate in A.D. 23 (over eleven other cities) of building the first temple in honor of Tiberius. Under Domitian (A.D. 81–96) emperor worship became compulsory for every Roman citizen on threat of death. Once a year a citizen had to burn incense on the altar to the godhead of Caesar, after which he was issued a certificate. Barclay (*Seven Churches*, p. 29) quotes a request for such a certificate, and the certificate itself.

> To those who have been appointed to preside over the sacrifices, from Inares Akeus, from the village of Theoxenis, together with his children Aias and Hera, who reside in the village of Theadelphia. We have always sacrificed to the gods, and now, in your presence, according to the regulations, we have sacrificed and offered libations, and tasted the sacred things, and we ask you to give us a certification that we have done so. May you fare well.

> We, the representatives of the Emperor, Serenos and Hermas, have seen you sacrificing. (*Seven Churches*, p. 29).

Such an act was probably considered more as an expression of political loyalty than religious worship, and all a citizen had to do was burn a pinch of incense and say, "Caesar is Lord [*kyrios*]." Yet most Christians refused to do this. Perhaps nowhere was life for a Christian more perilous than in this city of zealous emperor worship. About sixty years later (c. 156), Polycarp was burned alive at the age of eighty-six as the "twelfth martyr in Smyrna" (IDB, 4:393). His words have echoed through the ages: "Eighty-six years have I served Christ, and he has never done me wrong. How can I blaspheme my King who saved me?" (Eusebius *Ecclesiastical History* 4.15.25). There was a modern-day parallel to the predicament of Christians under Roman emperor worship when the Japanese occupied Korea in 1937–40 and ordered Christians to worship at their Shinto shrines. Many Christians refused and were imprisoned and tortured (Keun, Han Woo, *History of Korea*, ed. G.K. Muntz, tr. Lee Kyuen-Shik [Seoul: Eul-Woo, 1970], p. 496). A large and hostile Jewish community at Smyrna was prominent in Polycarp's death and no doubt troubled the church also in John's day (2:9) (Barclay, *Seven Churches*, p. 31). Concerning the founding of the Smyrna church, we have no information other than this letter to it.

8 The speaker identifies himself as "him who is the First and the Last, who died and came to life again" (cf. comments on 1:17–18). The "First and Last" might remind those suffering persecution and rejection from their countrymen (vv. 9–10) that the one they belong to is the Lord of history and the Creator. He is in control regardless of appearances of evil. Ramsay suggests that the term may allude by contrast to Smyrna's claim to be the "first" of Asia in beauty and emperor loyalty (*Seven Churches*, pp. 269–70). But Christians at Smyrna were concerned with him who was truly first in everything.

He who is "the First and the Last" is also the one "who died" (lit., "became a corpse") and "came to life again." To a congregation where imprisonment and death impend, the prisoner who died and came back to life again can offer the crown of life to other executed prisoners and protect them from the second death (vv. 8, 10–11).

41

There might also be an allusion here to the history of the city of Smyrna, which had been destroyed in the seventh century B.C. and rebuilt in the third century B.C. (ibid., p. 269).

9 The speaker's knowledge is threefold: (1) He knows their "afflictions" (*thlipsis*)—a word later translated "persecution" (v. 10). (2) He knows their "poverty." This can only mean material poverty because the speaker (Christ) immediately adds, "Yet you are rich" (toward God). Why was this church so poor in such a prosperous city? We do not know. Perhaps the high esteem of emperor worship in the city produced economic sanctions against Christians who refused to participate. In Smyrna, economic pressure may have been the first step toward persecution. Sometimes, even today, for Christians to be loyal to their Lord entails economic loss (cf. 3:17). (3) The risen Lord also knows "the slander of those who say they are Jews and are not, but are a synagogue of Satan." Trouble arose from the Jewish community (cf. commentary on v. 8). Certain Jews (not all of them) used malicious untruths ("slander") to incite persecution to the impoverished saints in Smyrna. They "say they are Jews but are not" shows that even though these men claimed descent from Abraham, they were not his true descendants because they did not have faith in Christ, the "Seed" of Abraham (Gal 3:16, 29). These unbelieving and hostile Jews probably viewed the Jewish Christians at Smyrna as heretics of the worst sort, deserving ridicule and rejection. Whether Christians in general were now the "true" Jews, or whether it is those Jews in Smyrna who became Christians who are the "true" Jews is debatable (cf. comments on 7:4).

"But are of the synagogue of Satan" reveals for the first time in Revelation the ultimate source of the persecution of Christians—Satan. Many further references to the archenemy of the followers of Christ are found throughout the book (2:13; 3:9; 9:11; 12:9–10, 12; 13:4; 20:2, 7, 10). In fact, he is one of the principal actors in the apocalyptic drama. While Satan is the author of persecution and wicked men are his instruments, God remains sovereign in that he will give "the crown of life" to those who are "faithful, even to the point of death" (v. 10). "Synagogue of Satan" refers, then, to certain Jews in ancient Smyrna who, motivated by Satan, slandered the church there. The term should never be indiscriminately applied to all Jewish synagogues.

10 The speaker's command immediately follows since no word of verdict or fault is spoken of. The prospect of further and imminent suffering may have made the believers at Smyrna fearful: "Do not be afraid of what you are about to suffer" (lit., "Stop being afraid . . ."). The risen Christ reveals that some of them will be imprisoned by the devil in order to test them, and they will have ten days of persecution. Who will do this—whether Jew or pagan—is not stated. The testing will show where their true loyalty lies. For a faithful and suffering church, Christ offers further trial and suffering, even "to the point of death." The "ten days" may be ten actual days. Or it may be a Semitism for an indeterminate but comparatively short period of time (cf. Neh 4:12; Dan 1:12). In the first-century Roman world, prison was usually not punitive but the prelude to trial and execution, hence the words "Be faithful, even to the point of death."

For those who would face martyrdom out of loyalty to Christ, there was to be a "crown of life" given by Christ himself. Those at Smyrna would be very familiar with the term "the crown of Smyrna," which no doubt alluded to the beautiful skyline formed around the city by the "hill Pagos, with the stately public buildings on its rounded sloping sides" (Ramsay, *Seven Churches*, p. 256). The "crown" usually referred to a garland of flowers worn chiefly in the worship of the pagan gods such as Cybele or Bacchus, who was pictured on coins with a crown of battlements. Faithful servants of the city appeared on coins with laurel wreaths on their heads (Barclay, *Seven Churches*, p. 39). As the patriots of Smyrna were faithful to Rome and to their crown city, so Christ's people are to be faithful unto death to him who will give them the imperishable crown of life (James 1:12; 1 Peter 5:4).

11 The general exhortation to all the churches is identical to the parallel passages in the other letters (cf. introduction to letters). For those who overcome, the promise is that they "will not be hurt at all by the second death." Death was a real possibility for these believers. But greater than the fear of physical death should be the fear of God's eternal judgment (Luke 12:4–5). The "second death" is a well-known Targumic expression, but it does not occur elsewhere in Jewish literature. Moses prays, "Let Reuben live in this world, and not die in the second death, in which death the wicked die in the world to come" (paraphrase of Deut 33:6 found in the Paris MS 110, cited by M. McNamara, *Targum and Testament: Aramaic Paraphrases of the Hebrew Bible; A Light on the New Testament*, [Grand Rapids: Eerdmans, 1962], p. 148). Even though death was the outcome of Adam's sin, in Christ there is a complete reversal for man (Gen 2:16–17; Rom 5:15ff.). Since the messianic believers at Smyrna were under attack by some in the Jewish community, it was reassuring indeed to hear the Lord himself say that his followers would not be harmed by the second death—viz., the lake of fire (20:14; 21:8).

Notes

8 Besides Ramsay's studies already cited, cf. C.J. Cadoux, *Ancient Smyrna* (Oxford: Blackwell, 1938), esp. pp. 228–366.

---

3. *To Pergamum*

2:12–17

12"To the angel of the church in Pergamum write:

These are the words of him who has the sharp, double-edged sword. 13I know where you live—where Satan has his throne. Yet you remain true to my name. You did not renounce your faith in me, even in the days of Antipas, my faithful witness, who was put to death in your city—where Satan lives.

14Nevertheless, I have a few things against you: You have people there who hold to the teaching of Balaam, who taught Balak to entice the Israelites to sin by eating food sacrificed to idols and by committing sexual immorality. 15Likewise you also have those who hold to the teaching of the Nicolaitans. 16Repent therefore! Otherwise, I will soon come to you and will fight against them with the sword of my mouth.

17He who has an ear, let him hear what the Spirit says to the churches. To him who overcomes, I will give some of the hidden manna. I will also give him a white stone with a new name written on it, known only to him who receives it.

The inland city of Pergamum lay about sixty-five miles north of Smyrna along the fertile valley of the Caicus River. Pergamum held the official honor of being the provincial capital of Roman Asia, though this honor was in fact also claimed by Ephesus and Smyrna. Among its notable features were its beauty and wealth; its library of nearly two hundred thousand volumes (second only to the library of Alexandria); its famous sculpture; its temples to Dionysus, Athena, Asclepius, and Demeter and the three temples to the emperor cult; its great altar to Soter Zeus; and its many palaces. The two main religions seem to have been the worship of Dionysus, the god of the royal kings, symbolized by the bull, and Asclepius, the savior god of healing, represented by the snake (Ramsay, *Seven Churches*, p. 284). This latter feature made Pergamum the "Lourdes of the ancient world" (Charles, *Commentary on Revelation*, 1:60). Tradition also records that in Pergamum, King Eumenes II (197–159 B.C.) planned to build a library to rival the one in Alexandria. Ptolemy Epiphanes of Egypt (205–182 B.C.) took action to stop this venture by cutting off the export of papyrus sections. It was this embargo that forced Eumenes to develop vellum or parchment (*pergamēnē*, "from Pergamum"), a writing material made from animal skins. Josephus mentions a Jewish community at Pergamum (Antiq. XIV, 247 [x. 22]).

12 The speaker identifies himself as "him who has the sharp, double-edged sword" (cf. comments on 1:16 and cf. Isa 49:2). In dealing with the Pergamum congregation, divided by deceptive teaching, the risen Lord will use this sword to fight against the Balaamites and the Nicolaitans (v.16). It is interesting that Pergamum was a city to which Rome had given the rare power of capital punishment (*ius gladii*), which was symbolized by the sword. The Christians in Pergamum were thus reminded that though they lived under the rule of an almost unlimited *imperium*, they were citizens of another kingdom—that of him who needs no other sword than that of his mouth (Caird, p. 38).

13 The speaker's knowledge is searching: he knows that they live in a hostile and difficult place—"where Satan has his throne." This certainly refers to the fact that Pergamum was a center for worship of the pagan gods, especially the emperor cult. The first temple in the empire was established in honor of Augustus in A.D. 29 at Pergamum because it was the administrative capital of Asia. In succeeding years the city boasted of being the official *neokoros* ("temple sweeper") of the "temple where Caesar was worshiped" (Barclay, *Seven Churches*, p. 45). Others see the reference to the altar of savior Zeus or the center of worship of Asclepius, the snake god of healing. Pergamum was an idolatrous center; and to declare oneself in that place a Christian who worships the one true God and Savior, Jesus Christ, would certainly provoke hostility.

Furthermore, the risen Lord knew their loyalty to him in all that he is revealed to be ("my name") even when "Antipas, my faithful witness, . . . was put to death in [their] city." Nothing further is known about Antipas than the meaning of his name— viz., "against all." The proximity of the name "Satan" before and after Antipas in v.13 makes it virtually certain that his death was instigated by the enmity of pagans in Pergamum. He may have been the first or most notable of martyrs. Christ pays this hero of the faith a noble tribute: "faithful witness"—words that John applies to Christ himself in 1:5. Satan tries to undermine loyalty to Christ by persecution; Christ strengthens that loyalty by commending those who are true to him and by exposing those who are deceitful.

14–15 The speaker's verdict reveals that the church in Pergamum was divided. Some had followed Antipas and did not deny Christ's name or his faith (v.13). Others held to the teaching and practice of the Balaamites and Nicolaitans that Christ hates (2:6). Since the name "Balaam" can mean to "conquer the people" (Heb. *ba'al 'am*), which means the same as "Nicolaitans," and since they are mentioned together in this letter, both groups may be closely related (see Notes, v.15). In fact, the error in the church at Thyatira through the teaching of the woman Jezebel may also be similar to this one. In that letter and this one, the more deadly effects of the error are described as "eating food sacrificed to idols and committing sexual immorality" (2:14, 20).

The OT names Balaam and Jezebel serve to alert the church community to the insidious nature of the teaching that was not until now recognized as overtly evil. Since Satan's chief method is deception, his devices are not known until they are clearly pointed out. Christ exposes error here by identifying the false teaching in Pergamum with clear-cut evil such as that of Balaam and Jezebel. Balak, king of Moab, could not succeed in getting the venial prophet Balaam to curse Israel directly. But Balaam devised a plan whereby the daughters of the Moabites would seduce the Israelite men and lead them to sacrifice to their god Baal-peor and worship him (Num 25:1ff.; 31:16; cf. 2 Peter 2:15; Jude 11). So God's judgment fell on Israel because of fornication and idolatry. What Balak was not able to accomplish directly, he got through Balaam's deception. While the Ephesians recognized the Nicolaitan error (v.6), apparently Pergamum and Thyatira were deceived by it; it was an unconscious subversion. What Satan could not accomplish at Smyrna or Pergamum through intimidation, suffering, and death from outside the church, he achieved from within.

The combination of "food sacrificed to idols" with "sexual immorality" may refer to the common practice of participating in the sacrificial meal of the pagan gods (cf. 1 Cor 10:19–22) and indulging in sexual intercourse with temple priestesses in cult prostitution. This is the more normal way to understand the term "sexual immorality" in the context of the pagan gods. Some feel, however, that the term refers to spiritual unfaithfulness and apostasy from Christ (cf. Isa 1:21; Ezek 23:37). But the prevalence of sexual immorality in first-century pagan society makes it entirely possible that some Christians at Pergamum were still participating in the holiday festivities and saw no wrong in indulging in the "harmless" table in the temples and the sexual excitement everyone else was enjoying (cf. 1 John 5:21). Will Durant made the following observation on the pagan festivities:

> At the center and summit of [each Greek] city was the shrine of the city god; participation in the worship of the god was the sign, the privilege, and the requisite of citizenship. In the spring, the Greek cities celebrated the Athesterion, or feast of flowers, a three-day festival to Dionysus [a chief deity at Pergamum!] in which wine flowed freely and everybody was more or less drunk. At the end of March came the great Dyonysia, a widely observed series of processional and plays accompanied by general revelry. At the beginning of April various cities in Greece celebrated [Aphrodite's] great festival, the Aphrodisia; and on that occasion, for those who cared to take part, sexual freedom was the order of the day (*The Story of Civilization* [New York: Simon and Schuster, 1939], vol. 2, *Life of Greece*, pp. 75, 185).

16 The speaker's command includes both a call to the whole congregation to repent and a special threat to the heretical members if they do not repent. Since those who

45

did not indulge in these things tolerated their practice by some of the church's members, they, along with the guilty, needed to repent. If those at Pergamum will not heed the word of Christ's warning, that word from his mouth will become a "sword" to fight against the disloyal. (Curiously, Balaam himself was slain by the "sword" [Num 31:8].) The words "I will soon come to you" should be understood as a coming "against" the congregation in judgment, as in v.5, and not as a reference to Christ's second coming.

17 The promise to the overcomer includes three difficult symbols: "hidden manna," "a white stone," and "a new name." The "hidden manna" is reminiscent of the manna hidden in the ark of the covenant by Moses (Exod 16:33–34; Heb 9:4). Since Moses' pot of manna was designed to remind the Israelites of God's grace and faithfulness in the wilderness (Ps 78:24), there may be a similar thought here. In apocalyptic Jewish teaching, however, the messianic era will see the restoration of the hidden wilderness manna: "And it shall come to pass at that self-same time (in the days when the Messiah comes) that the treasury of manna shall again descend from on high, and they will eat of it in those years" (2 Baruch 29:8; Sib Oracles 7:149). To those at Pergamum who refused the banquets of the pagan gods, Christ will give the manna of his great banquet of eternal life in the kingdom (John 6:47–58).

The "white stone" is a puzzle. It has been thought of in relation to voting pebbles, an inscribed invitation to a banquet, a victory symbol, an amulet, or a counting pebble. It seems best to link the stone to the thought of the manna and see it as an allusion to an invitation that entitled its bearer to attend one of the pagan banquets.

The "new name . . . known only to him who receives it" is either the name of Christ himself, now hidden from the world but to be revealed in the future as the most powerful of names (3:12; 14:1), or the believer's new name or changed character through redemption (Isa 62:2; 65:15). Pritchard cites an Egyptian text concerning the goddess Isis plotting to learn the secret name of the supreme god Re to gain his hidden power for herself. The one who knew the hidden name received the power and status of the god who revealed it (ANET, p. 12). Hence the name was jealously guarded by the god. This background would fit the context here in Revelation—viz., to Christians tempted to compromise their loyalty to Christ to gain the favor of the pagan gods, Christ generously offers himself and the power of his name so that those who have faith in him may overcome.

Notes

---

13 The reading καὶ ὅπου ὁ θρόνος τοῦ Σατανᾶ (kai hopou ho thronos tou Satana, "even the throne of Satan") in the TR and reflected by KJV seems warranted on good MS evidence (046 plus many late MSS). Καὶ (kai, "even") modifies the sense slightly by broadening the faithfulness of those in Pergamum beyond Antipas's time. Copyists probably omitted the word, not recognizing its ascensive use in the sentence (Bruce M. Metzger, A Textual Commentary on the Greek New Testament, [New York: UBS, 1971], p. 733).

Wood has argued that the reference to "Satan's throne" may be "topographical" rather than merely religious: "The actual shape of the city-hill towered, as it still does, like a giant throne above the plain" (Peter Wood, "Local Knowledge in the Letters of the Apocalypse," ET, 73 [1962], 264).

15 The TR has ὁ μισῶ (*ho misō,* "which I hate") instead of ὁμοίως (*homoiōs,* "likewise"). However, *homoiōs* agrees with οὕτως (*houtōs,* "also," "in this way") to call attention to the strong similarity of the two teachings—possibly to imply their identity. The sentence might then read, "In fact, you have people there who similarly hold the teaching of the Nicolaitans."

---

4. *To Thyatira*

2:18–29

18"To the angel of the church in Thyatira write:

These are the words of the Son of God, whose eyes are like blazing fire and whose feet are like burnished bronze. 19I know your deeds, your love and faith, your service and perseverance, and that you are now doing more than you did at first. 20Nevertheless, I have this against you: You tolerate that woman Jezebel, who calls herself a prophetess. By her teaching she misleads my servants into sexual immorality and the eating of food sacrificed to idols. 21I have given her time to repent of her immorality, but she is unwilling. 22So I will cast her on a bed of suffering, and I will make those who commit adultery with her suffer intensely, unless they repent of her ways. 23I will strike her children dead. Then all the churches will know that I am he who searches hearts and minds, and I will repay each of you according to your deeds. 24Now I say to the rest of you in Thyatira, to you who do not hold to her teaching and have not learned Satan's so-called deep secrets (I will not impose any other burden on you): 25Only hold on to what you have until I come. 26To him who overcomes and does my will to the end, I will give authority over the nations—

27'He will rule them with an iron scepter;
he will dash them to pieces like pottery'—

just as I have received authority from my Father. 28I will also give him the morning star. 29He who has an ear, let him hear what the Spirit says to the churches.

On the inland route about forty-five miles due east of Pergamum was the city of Thyatira. Although not a great city, it was nevertheless important through commerce in wool, linen, apparel, dyed stuffs, leatherwork, tanning, and excellent bronzework. Associated with its commerce was an extensive trade guild or labor union network, which must have played a prominent role in the social, political, economic, and religious life of the city. Each guild had its own patron deity, feasts, and seasonal festivities that included sexual revelries. Religiously, the city was unimportant, though worship of Apollo and Artemis (Diana) was prominent. Acts 16:14 mentions that Lydia, a proselyte of the gate, came from the Jewish settlement at Thyatira. She was a distributor of garments made of the purple dye substance known as "Turkey red" and no doubt a member of the dyers' guild. It has been suggested that some of Paul's converts at Ephesus went out and evangelized Thyatira (Acts 19:10).

18 The speaker of this fourth letter, the longest of the seven, identifies himself as "the Son of God, whose eyes are like blazing fire and whose feet are like burnished bronze" (cf. comments on 1:14–15). The expression "Son of God" appears only here in the book. It is a designation for the Messiah and is almost equivalent to the more frequently used title "Son of Man" and probably anticipates the quotation from the messianic second Psalm in v.27, which implies the term. But the name might also have captured the attention of those who were enticed by the emperor cult into calling Caesar the Son of God. That Christ's eyes are here described as blazing fire might be an allusion to the sun god, Apollo, worshipped at Thyatira. More likely, however, it refers to his penetrating discernment of the false prophetess Jezebel (v.23). The feet of Christ, which are like burnished bronze, would no doubt have special significance to the bronze-workers at Thyatira.

19 The speaker's knowledge of the Thyatirans' works is essentially twofold: he knows their love and faithfulness. Their love manifests itself in "service" and their faithfulness in "perseverance" during trial. Their present state reflects outstanding progress, but there is a perilous flaw in the church there.

20 The speaker's verdict reveals that the congregation had allowed a woman prophetess (a false one, according to Christ's assessment) to remain in the church and to continue to teach the saints to indulge in "sexual immorality" and to "eat food sacrificed to idols." The genuine gift of prophecy was highly respected in the early church. Along with apostles, teachers, and elders, prophets were often elevated to leadership (1 Cor 12:28; Eph 4:11). Women also received the genuine gift of prophecy (Luke 2:36; Acts 21:9; 1 Cor 11:5). Prophets generally brought direct revelation from God in the form of teaching as well as occasional predictions of the future (Acts 11:27). Tests for a true prophet, as for the true apostle (2:2), were available but often difficult to apply.

This supposedly Christian woman at Thyatira had claimed to be a "prophetess," gifted as such by the Holy Spirit. She must have been elevated to prominence in the church because of her unusual gifts. But only a small minority saw through her pious deception (v.24); the rest either followed her or ignored her views without objecting to her presence in the church. In order to expose her true character, she is labeled "Jezebel"—the name of the Canaanite wife of Israel's King Ahab. Jezebel had not only led Ahab to worship Baal but through Ahab had promulgated her teachings of idolatry throughout all Israel (1 Kings 16:31–33; 2 Kings 9:22).

We must not, however, press the similarity too far. As this wicked and deceptive woman in the OT led Israel astray and persecuted the true prophets of God, so this woman at Thyatira was enticing the servants of God to abandon their exclusive loyalty to Christ. Her teaching was no doubt similar to that of the Nicolaitans and Balaamites at Ephesus and Pergamum. While most commentators prefer to see the "sexual immorality" as spiritual adultery (i.e., idolatry), the possibility of cultic fornication should not be ruled out for reasons cited above (cf. 2:14). The distinction between the woman and those who follow her (v.22) may argue against the view that she is symbolic of a group in the church, unless the "woman" represents the false prophets and her "children" are those who follow the teaching. In 2 John the "chosen lady" is probably a reference to the faithful congregation, while "her children" refers to individuals in the congregation who represent her.

21–22 Christ's verdict continues with his strongest accusation directed against, not Jezebel's perversion, serious as that is, nor even against her successful deception of fellow Christians, but against her refusal to repent. Although Christ has dealt with her over a period of time, she will not change her ways or her thinking. The Lord, therefore, will judge Jezebel by two swift acts. She will be "hurled" (NIV, "cast") into a bed, and her children will be put to death. The "bed" or "couch" (*klinē*) can mean a bed used for resting, for guild-banqueting, or for sickness. Ramsay adopts the banqueting sense and relates it to the idol-feast couches (*Seven Churches,* p. 352). Others suggest a bed of sickness or suffering, seen as an act of God's visitation or judgment. On a bed she sinned, on a bed she will suffer; and those who committed adultery with her will also suffer intensely.

As in the case of Jezebel, Christ's strongest threat to the offenders is not in regard to their sin, serious as that is, but to their reluctance to repent. The Lord is walking among his churches. He judges evil; but he also offers deliverance to those who have fallen, if they repent and stop doing Jezebel's deeds.

23 For those who follow Jezebel ("her children") and refuse to repent, a fatal judgment will be meted out by the Lord Christ: "I will strike her children dead" (lit., "I will kill her children with death"—perhaps a Heb. idiom denoting "pestilence" [6:8]). Some understand "her children" to refer to her actual children, born of the sexual sins, rather than to her followers (Beckwith, p. 467). This cannot be decided with certainty. Whatever the exact nature of the judgment, it is announced beforehand by Christ so that when it occurs not just Thyatira but "all the churches will know that I am he who searches hearts and minds," since they too will read the same letter and will later hear of the historical outcome. OT references ascribe omniscience to God alone (Ps 7:9; Prov 24:12; Jer 17:10). "Heart" is literally "kidneys" (Heb., $k^e l\bar{a}y\hat{o}t$; Gr., *nephroi*), which in Semitic thought represented the moral center of the life, while "mind" is literally "heart" (Heb., $l\bar{e}\underline{b}$; Gr., *kardia*), which represents the totality of the feelings, thoughts, and desires traced back to one's deepest inner life. There is nothing in our thoughts or desires that is hidden from Christ's penetrating gaze (Heb 4:12–13). Our only safety from judgment is in repentance. The risen Lord does not stop with searching hearts and minds but brings recompense according to deeds: for faithfulness, reward; for unfaithfulness, judgment.

24–25 Christ's only command to the church at Thyatira was probably for the minority who had sufficient insight to penetrate Jezebel's deception. They are to simply "hold on to what you have" (i.e., their insight into Jezebel's teaching and evil deeds) till Christ returns (v.25). This small group may have been nearer his standard than any other group mentioned in Revelation because they could discriminate between authentic and spurious worship.

The reference to "Satan's so-called deep secrets" is ambiguous (cf. "the deep things of God" [1 Cor 2:10]). It may mean the "deep things," i.e., the secret knowledge of God reserved only for the initiates into the heretical teaching. This would suggest a form of Christian Gnosticism, an early heretical teaching. The words "so-called" would then be a mocking remark of John's—"the so-called deep things of God, which are in fact of Satan" (Bruce, "Revelation," p. 639).

However, this view rests on the doubtful thesis of a developed Christian Gnosticism in the first century (cf. Edwin Yamauchi, *Pre-Christian Gnosticism* [Grand Rapids: Eerdmans, 1973], pp. 55, 185) and strains the normal sense of the Greek. Therefore, another sense is preferable—viz., that the "deep secrets of Satan" is the actual phrase Jezebel used. But could she lure Christians by using such a term? The reasoning of some in the early church (the Nicolaitans) might have gone something like this: The only effective way to confront Satan was to enter into his strongholds; the real nature of sin could only be learned by experience, and therefore only those who had really experienced sin could truly appreciate grace. So by experiencing the depths of paganism ("the deep secrets of Satan"), one would better be equipped to serve Christ, or be an example of freedom to his brothers (cf. 1 Cor 8:9–11). Thus the sin of Jezebel was deadly serious because of the depths of its deception. Only a few perceived where the teaching was leading.

"Until I come" is the first of several references to the second coming of Christ in these letters (cf. 1:7).

26–27 The promise to the overcomers is twofold: "authority over nations" and the gift of "the morning star." It contains one important modification of the regular overcomer's formula. Added to the words "to him who overcomes" is "and does my will to the end" (lit., "who keeps my works until the end"). It reminds us of Jesus' statement in his great eschatological discourse, that "he who stands firm to the end will be saved (Matt 24:13), and of Paul's words to the Colossians about continuing in the faith "established and firm" (Col 1:23). The proof of authentic trust in Jesus is steadfastness of belief and continuance in the will of God till Christ returns or death comes.

The first promise is a fulfillment of Psalm 2, which is messianic and tells how the Father gave the Messiah the rule over the nations of the world. This psalm plays an important part in thinking about Christ (11:18; 12:5; 19:15). The coming reign of the Messiah over the world is to be shared with his disciples (1:6; 3:21; 20:6; 1 Cor 6:2). In the pre-Christian apocryphal Psalms of Solomon, the same psalm is used with reference to the Messiah and the Jews who will reign with him (17:23–24). Here in vv.26–27 its use seems to indicate that the overcomers will participate with Christ in fulfilling the promise of Psalm 2:9. There is a paradox in the combination of the mild word "rule" (*poimainō*, lit., "to shepherd") with the harsh words "with an iron scepter; he will dash them to pieces like pottery" (cf. comments on 19:11ff.). The prospect of such a reversal of their present experience of oppression and persecution would be a constant encouragement for suffering Christians.

28 Second, the overcomers in Thyatira are promised "the morning star" (*astera ton prōinon*). Some link this expression to Christ himself as in 22:16. Believers would then receive Christ as their very life. Or it may refer to the Resurrection in the sense that the morning star rises over the darkness of this world's persecution and offers victory over it. Perhaps a combination of the two thoughts may be intended. The promise of Christ's return is like the "morning star [*phōsphoros*]" (2 Peter 1:19). (See 22:16, where Jesus calls himself "the bright Morning Star" [*ho astēr ho lampros ho prōinos*], in apparent reference to his return.)

29 In this fourth letter and in the three that follow it, the general exhortation comes at the very end; in the first three letters, however, it precedes the promise (cf. comments at introduction to the seven letters).

Notes

20 Alexandrinas (A), generally a good witness in Rev, and a number of other witnesses include the word σου (*sou*, "your") after γυναῖκά (*gynaika*, "woman"), giving the sense "your wife." This implies taking "angel" in 1:18 and elsewhere in chs. 2–3 as the bishop or overseer of the church. This inferior reading probably arose through scribal confusion with other frequent references to *sou* in the letters.

The TR has ὀλίγα (*oliga*, "a few things") included in the verdict words, thus reading,

"I have a few things against you." NIV rightly follows the numerous and varied witnesses that omit *oliga*.

27 According to Trudinger's analysis (L. Paul Trudinger, "Some Observations Concerning the Text of the Old Testament in the Book of Revelation," JTS, 17 [1966], 84–85), the text that John follows in the OT quotation from Ps 2:9 is closer to a Semitic original than to the LXX, from which it is generally thought to be derived. He finds at least thirty-nine direct quotations and as many allusions in Rev that go against the LXX in favor of a Semitic text.

---

5. To Sardis

3:1–6

1"To the angel of the church in Sardis write:

These are the words of him who holds the seven spirits of God and the seven stars. I know your deeds; you have a reputation of being alive, but you are dead. 2Wake up! Strengthen what remains and is about to die, for I have not found your deeds complete in the sight of my God. 3Remember, therefore, what you have received and heard; obey it, and repent. But if you do not wake up, I will come like a thief, and you will not know at what time I will come to you.
4Yet you have a few people in Sardis who have not soiled their clothes. They will walk with me, dressed in white, for they are worthy. 5He who overcomes will, like them, be dressed in white. I will never erase his name from the book of life, but will acknowledge his name before my Father and his angels. 6He who has an ear, let him hear what the Spirit says to the churches.

Sardis was about thirty miles south of Thyatira. Its location commanded the trade of the Aegean Islands and the military road through the important Hermus River valley. Sardis enjoyed prominence as a commercially prosperous and militarily strategic city throughout its history. The city's topography was notable for the acropolis, the temple of Artemis, and the necropolis. The acropolis rose about eight hundred feet above the north section of Sardis and was virtually impregnable because of its rock walls, which were nearly vertical, except on the south side. Formerly the site of the original city, the acropolis became a refuge for the inhabitants in time of siege.

Only twice in the history of Sardis was its fortress ever captured, though attacks on it were frequent. When Cyrus attacked it in the sixth century B.C., a shrewd Persian soldier observed a Sardian descending the southern winding path to retrieve his fallen helmet. Unknown to the soldier, the Persians followed his path back up to the summit and captured the whole city, taking them quite by surprise. There was a similar occurrence when Antiochus attacked Sardis about two hundred years later.

The temple to Artemis (possibly Cybele) equaled in size the famous temple of Artemis in Ephesus. However, the temple at Sardis was never finished.

A third feature of Sardis was the impressive necropolis, or cemetery, of "a thousand hills" (modern Bin Tepe), so named because of the hundreds of burial mounds visible on the skyline some seven miles from Sardis.

Sardis retained its wealth into the first two centuries of the Christian Era. But its political brilliance as the capital city of Asia for Persia lay in the past. Ramsay aptly remarks, "No city of Asia at that time showed such a melancholy contrast between past splendor and present decay as Sardis" (William M. Ramsay, *The Letters to the Seven Churches of Asia* [London: Hodder & Stoughton, 1904], p. 375). In A.D. 26, Sardis begged the Roman Senate to grant it the coveted honor of building a temple to Caesar. The distinction, however, went to Smyrna. The luxurious living of the Sardians led to moral decadence. Herodotus (fifth century B.C.) wrote despairingly of Sardis and its people as "the tender-footed Lydians, who can only play on the cithara, strike the guitar, and sell by retail" (William Barclay, *Letters to the Seven Churches* [New York: Abingdon, 1957], p. 71). Sardis was a city of peace, not the peace won through battle, but "the peace of the man whose dreams are dead and whose mind is asleep, the peace of lethargy and evasion" (ibid., p. 72). A great wool industry flourished at Sardis, and this may account for Christ's reference to clothing (v.4).

1 The speaker identifies himself as "him who holds the seven spirits of God and the seven stars" (cf. comments on 1:4 and 1:16, 20; 2:1). To the Sardians, Christ reveals himself as the one who controls the seven spirits of God. If the Sardian church is strong, it is because Christ has sent his Spirit to encourage and quicken the Sardian believers; if they are dead like Sardis, it is because in judgment he has withdrawn his Spirit from them. Yet the faithful minority at Sardis (v.4) can count on that divine power of Christ to sustain, give life, and mobilize them to do his will even though the majority are dead. (On the "seven stars," cf. comments at 2:1.)

The speaker's knowledge of the church in Sardis reveals their true condition. He knows their "deeds." It is not clear whether this alludes to their past accomplishments, which gave them their reputation of being alive, or whether the reference is to their present deeds, which were not those Christ sought from them. This latter view is supported by v.2, where he mentions their deeds again and says they are incomplete. He also knows that though they claim to be a healthy Christian church, in reality they are "dead."

How does a church die? Why does Christ use this expression for Sardis even though the churches in Thyatira and Laodicea also had serious problems? Sardis had had significant fame as a royal city, but now it was nothing. The citizens were living off past fame. Apparently the same spirit had affected the church. Their loyalty and service to Christ was in the past. Now they were nothing. It may be that they had so made peace with the surrounding society that the offense of the Cross had ceased, and they were no longer in jeopardy of life or vulnerable to suffering. Further facts emerge when we consider the series of commands in vv.2–3. Death was a special preoccupation of the Sardians, as witnessed by the impressive necropolis seven miles from the city. What had been a part of the pagan rites had also crept into the church. But again this work of the enemy came through deception. The Sardian church was for the most part a duped church.

2 The command "Wake up!" or "Be watchful" (present tense, "Be constantly alert") is a call to reverse their attitudes radically. The congregation must be alerted to the seriousness of the situation. Their complacency led them to give up their identification with Christ and their mission for him. The situation was dire but not totally hopeless. Immediate steps were to be taken to "strengthen what remains." Some persons and things were salvageable if quick and decisive action were taken. Otherwise, death would follow.

The Sardians' deeds are in danger of judgment because Christ has not found them "complete [*peplērōmena*, 'full,' 'fulfilled,' 'filled up to measure'] in the sight of my God." Though this could refer to incompleteness in the number of their deeds, more likely it describes the quality of their deeds—they do not measure up to the standard

52

Christ sets. In the other letters, works acceptable to Christ are love, faithfulness, perseverance, keeping Christ's words, and not denying his name.

3 Like those in Ephesus, the Sardians must remember what they "have received and heard." What they "received" was the apostolic tradition of the gospel; what they "heard" probably were the teachings of the apostles and prophets who brought the gospel to them. Unlike the church at Philadelphia (v.8), the Sardians were not holding to the word of Christ. For them repentance was the only way out of certain and final death. So they were to repent by restoring the gospel and the apostolic doctrine to its authority over their lives. This would mean they would once more start obeying (*tēreō*, "keep," "watch") the truth of Christ's word. Today's church needs to hear this challenge to take the word of Christ seriously. Unless the church at Sardis repents, Christ says that he will come to them in judgment "as a thief"—i.e., by surprise—just as Sardis had been attacked and defeated by Cyrus long before. "As a thief" should probably not be taken as referring to the Second Coming but to Christ's coming against them (opposing them) in judgment (cf. his threat to the church in Ephesus in 2:5).

4 While the majority had departed from faithful obedience to Christ, a few at Sardis remained true. Here an allusion to the wool industry at Sardis intensifies the image of soiled and defiled garments. Those with soiled garments were removed from the public lists of citizens in Sardis. In the pagan religions it was forbidden to approach the gods in garments that were soiled or stained (Barclay, *Seven Churches,* p. 77). Soiling seems to be a symbol for mingling with pagan life and thus defiling the purity of one's relation to Christ (14:4; 1 Cor 8:7; 2 Cor 7:1; 11:2; Jude 23). To "walk with Christ" symbolizes salvation and fellowship with him—something the others at Sardis had forfeited through their sin (1 John 1:6–7). "White" garments are symbolic of the righteousness, victory, and glory of God (3:18; 6:11; 7:9, 13f.; 19:14). As Caird (p. 49) observes, this passage shows that not all faithful Christians were martyrs, nor can we make emperor worship the sole source of the problems of the early Christians. Ironically, the Sardians were occupied with their outward appearance, but they were not concerned with inner purity toward Christ and their outward moral life in a pagan society.

5 The overcomer's promise is threefold and grows out of the reference to white clothing.
    1. "Like" the faithful Sardian Christians who would receive white clothes from Christ, the others there who overcame the stains of pagan society would similarly be dressed in white.
    2. Furthermore, the pure relationship to Christ is permanently guaranteed: "I will never erase his name from the book of life." In ancient cities the names of citizens were recorded in a register till their death; then their names were erased or marked out of the book of the living. This same idea appears in the OT (Exod 32:32–33; Ps 69:28; Isa 4:3). From the idea of being recorded in God's book of the living (or the righteous) comes the sense of belonging to God's eternal kingdom or possessing eternal life (Dan 12:1; Luke 10:20; Phil 4:3; Heb 12:23; Rev 13:8; 17:8; 20:15; 21:27). For Christ to say that he will never blot out or erase the overcomer's name from the book of life is the strongest affirmation that death can never separate us from Christ and his life (Rom 8:38–39). A person enrolled in the book of life by faith remains in

it by faithfulness and can be erased only by disloyalty. There is some evidence that a person's name could be removed from the city register before death if he were convicted of a crime. In the first century, Christians who were loyal to Christ were under constant threat of being branded political and social rebels and then stripped of their citizenship. But Christ offers them an eternal, safe citizenship in his everlasting kingdom if they only remain loyal to him.

3. Finally, to the overcomer Christ promised to "acknowledge his name before [the] Father and his angels." "Acknowledge" (*homologeō*) is a strong word for confession before the courts. It is Christ's confession of our name before the Father and his angels (implying our fellowship with him) that assures our heavenly citizenship (Matt 10:32; Luke 12:8).

What ultimately counts, then, is not our acceptance by this world's societies but that our relationship to Christ is genuine and hence will merit his approbation in the coming kingdom.

6 Again, the general exhortation comes last, as in the previous letter (cf. comments in the introduction to the seven letters).

Notes

1 See also John G. Pedley, *Ancient Literary Sources on Sardis* (Cambridge, Mass.: Harvard University Press, 1972).

2 The imperfect tense in ἃ ἔμελλον ἀποθανεῖν (*ha emellon apothanein*, "what is about to die") probably looks back from the reader's point of view to the time when John saw the vision. At the same time, it expresses the conviction of the writer that the worst would soon be past (Swete, p. 48; Ernest Burton, *Syntax of the Moods and Tenses of New Testament Greek*, 3d ed. [Edinburgh: T. & T. Clark, 1898], par. 73).

4 S. David Garber argues that the white robes mentioned throughout the Book of Revelation refer to the divine gift of salvation that can be preserved only through continued discipleship. He also sees a possible allusion to the idea of a heavenly or spiritual body of glory that accompanies the resurrection—an idea that occurs frequently in the Jewish apocalyptic literature but which is different than the white-clothing imagery found among the Gnostic religions ("Symbolism of Heavenly Robes in the New Testament in Comparison with Gnostic Thought" [Ph.D. diss., Princeton Theological Seminary, 1974], pp. 307–14).

5 The reading οὕτως (*houtōs*, "like them") over οὗτος (*houtos*, "this one") is by no means certain. While Metzger et al. argues for the first reading on superior MS evidence (Bruce M. Metzger, *A Textual Commentary on the Greek New Testament* [New York: UBS, 1971], p. 736), Alford (Alf, in loc.) and Beckwith (in loc.) have a point in suggesting that the author would have used ὁμοίως (*homoiōs*, "likewise"), not *houtōs* to express similarity.

6. To Philadelphia

3:7–13

7"To the angel of the church in Philadelphia write:

These are the words of him who is holy and true, who holds the key of David. What he opens, no one can shut; and what he shuts, no one can open. 8I know your deeds. See, I have placed before you an open door that no one can shut. I know that you have little strength, yet you have kept my word and have not denied my name. ⁹I will make those who are of the synagogue of Satan, who claim to be Jews though they are not, but are liars—I will make them come and fall down at your feet and acknowledge that I have loved you. ¹⁰Since you have kept my command to endure patiently, I will also keep you from the hour of trial that is going to come upon the whole world to test those who live on the earth.

¹¹I am coming soon. Hold on to what you have, so that no one will take your crown. ¹²Him who overcomes I will make a pillar in the temple of my God. Never again will he leave it. I will write on him the name of my God and the name of the city of my God, the new Jerusalem, which is coming down out of heaven from my God; and I will also write on him my new name. ¹³He who has an ear, let him hear what the Spirit says to the churches.

About twenty-five miles southeast of Sardis, along the Hermus River valley, lay the important high plateau city of Philadelphia, modern Alasehir. A main highway that ran through the city connected Smyrna (about a hundred miles due west) to northwest Asia, Phrygia, and the east. Furthermore, the imperial post road of the first century A.D., which came from Rome via Troas, Adramyttium, Pergamum, and Sardis, passed through this valley and Philadelphia on the way to the east. So situated, Philadelphia became a strong fortress city. To the northeast was a great vine-growing district, which, along with textile and leather industries, contributed greatly to the city's prosperity.

Philadelphia was established by the Pergamenian king Attalus II (159–138 B.C.), who had been given the epithet "Philadelphus" ("brother lover") because of his love for his brother. The city was to be a mission city for disseminating Greco-Asiatic culture and language in the eastern part of Lydia and in Phrygia. Its success is attested by the fact that the Lydian language ceased to be spoken in Lydia by A.D. 19 and Greek took over (Ramsay, *Seven Churches*, p. 391). But beyond this language achievement, Philadelphia had not been successful in converting the Phrygians (Barclay, *Seven Churches*, p. 80).

According to Strabo, the whole region was earthquake prone (*Geography* 12.579; 13.628). In A.D. 17 an earthquake that destroyed Sardis and ten other cities also destroyed Philadelphia. Consequently, many people preferred to live in the rural area surrounding the city. The fear of earthquakes caused those who continued to live in the city to leave it at the slightest sign of a tremor.

After the devastating earthquake, Tiberius came to the peoples' aid and had the city rebuilt. In gratitude the citizens renamed it Neocaesarea ("New Caesar"). Later the name was changed to Flavia (A.D. 70–79), and this, along with Philadelphia, continued to be its name through the second and third centuries A.D. Later, the establishment of the emperor cult in the city earned it the title "Neokoros," or "Temple Warden" (c. 211–17). In the fifth century, it was nicknamed "Little Athens" because of its proliferation of festivals and pagan cults. Whether this indicates something of its early period is uncertain. Since wine was one of the city's important industries, some have assumed that the worship of Dionysus was a chief pagan cult in it (Swete, p. 52).

Although nothing is known about the origin of the Philadelphian church, in A.D. 100–160 the church prospered under the ministry of a prophetess named Ammia, who was universally recognized as ranking with Agabus and the four daughters of Philip in her possession of the gift of prophecy (Eusebius *Ecclesiastical History* 5.17.2). Long after all the surrounding country had succumbed to Muslim control under

Turkey, Philadelphia held out as a Christian populace till 1392. Even Gibbon admired its fortitude (Ramsay, *Seven Churches*, p. 400).

7 The letter to the church in Philadelphia begins with the speaker's identifying himself as "him who is holy and true, who holds the key of David. What he opens, no one can shut; and what he shuts, no one can open." Each of these identifications calls attention to Jesus as the true Messiah. "Holy and true" relate to God himself and describe aspects of his presence among us (cf. 6:10). Holiness is the attribute of God whereby we sense the presence of the "Wholly Other," the one who says, "I am God, and not man—the Holy One among you" (Hos 11:9). He is the "True One" in that he is wholly trustworthy and reliable in his words and actions. For this congregation for whom Christ has only commendation, these titles would bring encouragement, despite their "little strength" (v.8) to go on in their faithfulness, in contrast to those described in v.9.

The reference to the "key of David" alludes to Isaiah 22:20ff. and the incident of transferring the post of secretary of state in Judah from the unfaithful Shebna to the faithful Eliakim. The "key" signifies the power of the keys that were normally held by the king himself, unless delegated to another. The use of the name "David" points to Christ as the Messiah, who alone determines who will participate in his kingdom and who will be turned away: "He opens, no one can shut; . . . he shuts, no one can open." This may allude to the false claims of certain Jews at Philadelphia who argued that they, not the heretical Nazarenes, would inherit the kingdom of David (v.9) and thus excluded the followers of Jesus. But the true Messiah, Jesus, will exclude them!

8 Here the knowledge of the speaker and his verdict blend together in untarnished praise as in the letter to Smyrna. Between the declaration "I know your deeds" and the words "you have little strength, yet you have kept my word and have not denied my name" is the somewhat awkward interjection "See, I have placed before you an open door that no one can shut."

Since Christ has absolute authority from the Father, he has opened a door for the Philadelphians that even their enemies cannot close. But an open door to what? Swete (in loc.) sees an inference here to Philadelphia as a missionary city. As the easternmost of the seven cities and an outpost on the high tableland of upper Asia, it was effective in evangelizing the area with Hellenism. So the witness of the church in Philadelphia will be effective despite its small strength (1 Cor 16:9; Col 4:3). Others feel that v.8 refers to Christ's opening the door to his kingdom for those who love him and thus reinforces the statement in v.7 about opening and shutting.

Beckwith protests against the first view: "Such a reference to future missionary activity of the church is singularly out of place, thrust in as a parenthesis between the parts of a sentence concerned with commendation of the church for its steadfastness in the past" (p. 430). The context strongly favors the second view (so Ladd, *Commentary on Revelation*, in loc.). What became a serious problem at Sardis (v.3) was not the case with the Philadelphian congregation, to whom the risen Christ said, "You have kept my word." They had been faithful to the Gospel and the apostles' teaching even during the trial of their faith alluded to in the words "and have not denied my name" (cf. 2:13).

9 Here those opposing the witness of the congregation are characterized as "those who are of the synagogue of Satan, who claim to be Jews though they are not, but are liars." The words are like those spoken to the church in Smyrna (cf. comments on 2:9). A "synagogue of Satan" appears to describe a Jewish element that vehemently denied Jesus as the Messiah and that actively persecuted others who made this claim. A true Jew in the view of Jews like John and Paul is one who has found forgiveness and life in Jesus the Messiah, while a false Jew is one who rejects those who believe in Jesus and openly persecutes them; such a one is an antichrist (1 John 2:22).

In writing to the church in Philadelphia a few years later, Ignatius warned them not to listen to "any one propounding Judaism unto you" (*To the Philadelphians* 6.1)—a warning that might refer to certain Christians who tried to lead others into Judaism as did the Judaizers of Paul's day (Acts 15:1; Gal 3:4). Perhaps the words "have not denied my name" in v.8 relate to this. But Christ will make those who have persecuted the followers of Jesus as heretics acknowledge that God is indeed with the church in Philadelphia and that they are not heretics but are God's people.

We catch a glimpse here of the ever-widening gap between Judaism and Christianity toward the end of the first century. The church is the true people of God, loved by Christ, and in some real sense inheritors of the covenant promises in the OT made to the people of God (Isa 43:4; 45:14; 49:23; 60:14). In these OT passages it is the Gentiles, or heathen nations, who bow before Israel and acknowledge that God is with them. In this letter Christ reverses these roles: his followers are the people of God, and Jewish unbelievers are the pagans who come and acknowledge the love of the Messiah for the church! There is, however, no indication of when such acknowledgment will come or of what nature it will be. Ladd (*Commentary on Revelation*, p. 61) sees this as a fulfillment of Paul's expectation of the conversion of "all Israel" (i.e., of the majority of the Jewish people) at some time in the future (Rom 11:25–26; cf. esp. v.28). Most commentaries evade this issue.

Against Ladd's view, however, is the fact that the context seems to require retribution on Christ's enemies, not their conversion. Be that as it may, underlying v.9 is the same truth Paul expressed in Philippians 2:10–11: "At the name of Jesus every knee should bow, . . . and every tongue confess that Jesus Christ is Lord, to the glory of God the Father." Some will do this joyfully and some remorsefully—not penitently (cf. 6:12–17). Mounce (*Revelation*, p. 118) calls this the eschatological interpretation and refers to Isaiah 60:14 ("the sons of your oppressors will come bowing before you"), where Israel in the eschatological future will receive the acknowledgment from the pagan nations that their God is indeed the true Lord. What the Jews expected from the pagans, they themselves will be forced to render to the followers of Jesus.

10 This is another promise given the church in Philadelphia. Though not part of the promise to the overcomers in Philadelphia (v.12), like the special promises to Smyrna and Sardis (2:10; 3:4), it may be taken as a promise to all the churches. The words "since you have kept my command to endure patiently" (lit., "kept the word of my patience") refer to the condition under which the promise is valid. Some translate the phrase as in NIV, inferring that the "word of my patience" means the command of Christ to endure suffering, or to endure till he returns (Luke 21:19; cf. Heb 10:36). Others translate it as "the word enjoining Christ's patient endurance" (Ladd, *Commentary on Revelation*, p. 61). In that case it would refer to an apostolic teaching (such as Paul's) encouraging Christians to endure the contrariness of a sinful world after the pattern of Christ's own endurance (2 Thess 3:5; Heb 12:3). The Greek text slightly favors the latter translation, though the former is also possible.

Related to the promise "I will also keep you from the hour of trial that is going to come upon the whole world to test those who live on the earth" are two problems: the identification of the "hour of trial" and the precise sense of the phrase "keep you from the hour of trial." Both involve the ongoing debate among evangelical eschatologists over the Tribulation-Rapture question.

We can dismiss the view that the "hour of trial" refers to some general or personal distress that will come upon the Philadelphian community and from which the church will be delivered (so J. Barton Payne, *The Imminent Appearing of Christ* [Grand Rapids: Eerdmans, 1962], pp. 78–79). Though the universality of the expression "the whole world" is reason enough to refute Payne's view, the phrase "those who live on the earth" is repeated in Revelation a number of times and refers not to believers but to unbelievers who are the objects of God's wrath—i.e., the "beast-worshipers" (6:10; 8:13; 11:10; 12:12; 13:8, 12, 14; cf. Isa 24; Jer 13:12–14; IQH 8.19–36).

According to some interpreters (Ladd, Mounce, Walvoord), the "hour of trial" (*hōras tou peirasmou,* "time of temptation") is better understood as the time known to the Jews as the "messianic woes," a time of intense trouble to fall on the world before the coming of Christ and known as the eschatological "day of the Lord," or the "Great Tribulation" (Dan 12:1; Joel 2:31; Mark 13:14; 2 Thess 2:1–12; Rev 14:7). This "hour of trial," then, will be the one described in such detail in the following chapters of the book. In that case what, then, is the effect of the promise "I will also keep you from the hour of trial"? There are two possibilities. Some argue, with reference to the same Greek expression (*tēreō ek,* "keep from") in John 17:15, that the sense is preservation while in the trial, since to be kept from evil or the evil one does not mean to be removed from his presence but simply to be kept from his harmful power. Therefore, the church universal will experience preservation from harm in the trial of persecution and suffering and will not be raptured till the end of the period (Ladd; cf. 1 Thess 4:13ff.).

On the other hand, some writers offer these objections to this exegesis: (1) The "hour of trial" John describes is a judgment from God on the unbelieving inhabitants of the world, not a form of evil such as John 17:15 describes. (2) It is not true that the saints of the Tribulation period are exempt from harm during this period; a great group of them will be martyred (6:9–11; 7:9–14, etc.). (3) In the Gospel of John, preservation is from the devil; in Revelation, from a time period—the "hour" of trial (J.B. Smith, pp. 88–89).

Ladd offsets some of this criticism by advocating that the hour of trial has two aspects—the fierce persecution of believers by the beast and the outpouring of divine judgments on a rebellious world represented in the trumpet and bowl plagues. Believers are kept from the harm of the latter but not the former (*Commentary on Revelation,* p. 62). The difficulty in this view lies in Ladd's failure to identify clearly the hour of trial in this verse. It cannot refer to both the Great Tribulation (7:14) on believers and the wrath of God.

In our opinion, this confusion may be avoided by clearly identifying "the hour of trial" as the wrath of God, deliverance from which is promised to every one of Christ's overcomers. As a matter of fact, the expression *tēreō ek* ("keep out of") cannot be proved exegetically to be different from *tēreō apo* ("keep from"). In the LXX of Proverbs 7:5 the sense of this latter expression is to deliver the man from contact with or the presence of the harlot. In James 1:27 the same expression means to be kept from the pollution of the world. In both instances the sense is that of exemption from something. Can one, then, be exempt from the "hour of trial" that will try the whole world by famines, earthquakes, wars, floods, etc., and still be present on the earth? Yes, but removal is still a possible method of protection.

The above discussion shows that v. 10 does not settle the question of the time of the Rapture in relation to the Tribulation. Rather, it remains ambiguous. One might be on the earth and yet be exempt from the "hour of trial" if (1) the "hour of trial" is an equivalent derived from the briefer term "trial" and (2) if this "trial" is directed only at the unbelievers in the world while the believers are divinely immune, not from trial or persecution in general, but from a specific type of trial (God's wrath) that is aimed at the rebellious on the earth. To this writer, the most natural way to understand the expression to be "kept from the hour" of something that is universal in the world is not to be preserved through it but to be kept from being present when it happens. In any event, we have here a marvelous promise of Christ's protection (*tēreō*, "keep") for those who have protected (*tēreō*) his word by their loving obedience.

11 Here the words of Christ "I am coming soon" (cf. 22:7, 12, 20) are not a threat of judgment but a promise of Christ's second coming, such as the promise the faithful Christians in Thyatira received (2:25). The testing that faced the Philadelphians was not the same as that facing the unbelieving earth dwellers (v. 10). Loyal disciples must face one type of conflict, the world with its earth dwellers quite another (Minear, *I Saw a New Earth,* in loc.). Some such conflict is envisioned when Christ says, "Hold on to what you have, so that no one will take your crown." They had kept his word and had not denied his name in the face of persecution. Either Satan or men could rob them of their crown by diverting them from exclusive loyalty to Jesus (on crown, see comments on 2:10).

12 The promise to the overcomer is again twofold and related to the experience and memory of the inhabitants of the city. First, Christ will make the overcomer a "pillar in the temple of my God." As has already been noted, the city was constantly threatened with earthquakes. Often the only parts of a city left standing after a severe quake were the huge stone temple columns. Christ promises to set believers in his temple (the future kingdom?) in such a secure fashion that no disturbance can ever force them out.

Moreover, a faithful municipal servant or a distinguished priest was sometimes honored by having a special pillar added to one of the temples and inscribed with his name (Barclay, *Seven Churches,* p. 89). This may well be the sense of the second promise, "I will write on him the name of my God and the name of the city of my God, the new Jerusalem, . . . and . . . my new name." The inscribed name signifies identification and ownership. To those who have "little strength" (little influence) because of being ostracized, Christ promises recognition in his kingdom worthy of the most noble hero of any society.

Remembering how in days past the changes of name their city received (e.g., Neocaesarea; see comments on v. 7), the Philadelphians would be impressed that God himself (not the emperor) had chosen to identify himself with them and to insure their citizenship in the New Jerusalem (cf. 21:2ff.; Ezek 48:35). Christ's "new name" could be either the unknown name that he alone knows, signifying his absolute power over all other powers (19:12), or the new name of Christ given to the believer, i.e., his possession by Christ through redemption (Isa 62:2; 65:15).

13 The general exhortation follows the promise. (See comments in the introduction to the seven letters.)

Notes

10 A recent addition to the whole debate is Robert Gundry's *The Church and the Tribulation* (Grand Rapids: Zondervan, 1973), pp. 53–61. Gundry follows closely Ladd's views on this question, yet with much more elaborate weaponry.

Commenting on Rev 15:1, Victorinus (d.c.303) says, "For the wrath of God always strikes the obstinate people with seven plagues, that is, perfectly, as it is said in Leviticus; and these shall be in the last time, *when the Church shall have gone out of the midst*" (italics mine) (ANF, 7:357).

7. To Laodicea

3:14–22

14"To the angel of the church in Laodicea write:

These are the words of the Amen, the faithful and true witness, the ruler of God's creation. 15I know your deeds, that you are neither cold nor hot. I wish you were either one or the other! 16So, because you are lukewarm—neither hot nor cold—I am about to spit you out of my mouth. 17You say, 'I am rich; I have acquired wealth and do not need a thing.' But you do not realize that you are wretched, pitiful, poor, blind and naked. 18I counsel you to buy from me gold refined in the fire, so you can become rich; and white clothes to wear, so you can cover your shameful nakedness; and salve to put on your eyes, so you can see.

19Those whom I love I rebuke and discipline. So be earnest, and repent. 20Here I am! I stand at the door and knock. If anyone hears my voice and opens the door, I will go in and eat with him, and he with me.

21To him who overcomes, I will give the right to sit with me on my throne, just as I overcame and sat down with my Father on his throne.

22He who has an ear, let him hear what the Spirit says to the churches."

Laodicea was about forty-five miles southeast of Philadelphia and about one hundred miles due east of Ephesus. Along with Colosse and Hierapolis, it was one of the cities in the fertile Lycus valley. The great Roman road stretching to the inland of Asia from the coast at Ephesus ran straight through its center, making Laodicea an important center of trade and communication. In addition, its wealth came from the production of a fine quality of famous glossy black wool—whether dyed or natural in color is not known. That the city's banking assets were noteworthy is evidenced by the fact that Cicero cashed huge bank drafts in Laodicea. So wealthy was Laodicea that after the great earthquake of A.D. 17, which destroyed it, the people refused imperial help in rebuilding the city, choosing rather to do it entirely by themselves.

Laodicea had a famous school of medicine; and a special ointment known as "Phrygian powder," famous for its cure of eye defects, was either manufactured or distributed there, as were ear ointments also. Near the temple of the special god associated with healing, Men Karou (who later became identified with Asclepius), there was a market for trading all sorts of goods (Ramsay, *Seven Churches*, p. 417). Zeus, the supreme god, was also worshiped in the city.

Ramsay notes that Laodicea is difficult to describe because no one thing stands out. There were no excesses or notable achievements to distinguish it. It was a city with a people who had learned to compromise and accommodate themselves to the needs and wishes of others (ibid., p. 423). They did not zealously stand for anything. A six-mile-long aqueduct brought Laodicea its supply of water from the south. The water came either from hot springs and was cooled to lukewarm or came from a cooler source and warmed up in the aqueduct on the way. For all its wealth, the city had poor water. A large and influential Jewish population resided there. As for the church in Laodicea, it may have been founded by Epaphras (Col 4:12–13).

14 The speaker identifies himself by a threefold affirmation: "The Amen, the faithful and true witness, the ruler of God's creation." The normal Hebrew adverb that is rendered by the Greek *amēn* means the acknowledgment of that which is sure and valid. It is a word of human response to the divine verity or action. Jesus is the "Amen" in the sense that he is the perfect human, obedient response to the divine promises (cf. Isa 65:16; TDNT, 1: 337). Jesus' response to God's will was the perfect response of obedience and suffering: he is the "faithful and true witness" (cf. comments on 1:5, 9; 2:13). The same thought is expressed by Paul in 2 Corinthians 1:20: "For no matter how many promises God has made, they are 'Yes' in Christ. And so through him the 'Amen' is spoken by us to the glory of God." In one sense, all Christians are called to be "little amens" after the example of Christ.

The "ruler" (*archē*, "source," "origin") further amplifies the Amen statement. Paul used *archē* in Colossians 1:18 to describe Christ as the source or origin of all creation (not the first created; cf. Prov 8:22; John 1:3), no doubt to correct a heresy. Since Colosse was a neighboring city of Laodicea, it is not improbable that the same heresy was also affecting the sister church at Laodicea. But this is not explicit. What is plain is this: When Christ addresses a church that is failing in loyalty and obedience, he is to them the "Amen" of God in faithfulness and in true witness, the only one who has absolute power over the world because he is the source and origin of all creation (1:17; 2:8; 22:13).

15–16 Sadly, the speaker's knowledge reveals an unqualified condemnation of the Laodicean church. The verdict is the exact opposite of the church's own evaluation and expectations. Their deeds were "neither cold nor hot." The expression "cold nor hot" may refer to their lack of zeal (v.19) or their uselessness, for Christ says, "I wish you were either one or the other" (lit., "either cold or hot"). There is good reason why we should not try to take both of these words as if Christ meant I wish you were either spiritually cold (i.e., unsaved or hostile) or spiritually hot (i.e., alive and fervent). In the first place, it is inconceivable that Christ would wish that people were spiritually cold, or unsaved and hostile. Furthermore, the application of "hot" and "cold" to spiritual temperature, though familiar to us, would have been completely foreign to first-century Christians. The two adjectives in "neither hot nor cold" should be understood together as equivalent to "lukewarmness" (v.16). That is to say, they were useless to Christ because they were complacent, self-satisfied, and indifferent to the real issues of faith in him and of discipleship.

Since the city of Hierapolis, seven miles north of Laodicea, had famous "hot springs," it may be that similar springs were located south of Laodicea and affected the temperature of the water supply. "I am about to spit [*emesai*, 'vomit'] you out of my mouth" seems to allude to the lukewarm water. "Cold" could refer to the useful cool water located at Colosse, less than ten miles away. "Hot" would remind the Laodiceans of the beneficial "hot springs" to the north of Hierapolis. Yet Laodicea, for all its wealth, had an insipid water supply—one that induced vomiting! Christ detests a Laodicean attitude of compromise, one that seeks easy accommodation and peace at any cost. With such a condition, he must deal harshly. To be a Christian means to be useful to Christ.

17 The deeper problem in the Laodicean church was not simply their indifference. It was their ignorance of their real condition: "You say, 'I am rich; I have acquired wealth and do not need a thing.'" Observe the way this indictment is related to the general condition of the populace at large—rich in material possessions and self-sufficient. The spirit of the surrounding culture had crept into the congregation and had paralyzed their spiritual life. But did they actually claim to be materially rich or spiritually rich? Since it is difficult to see how a Christian community would boast of material wealth, many prefer the latter interpretation. Yet the Laodiceans may have interpreted their material wealth as a blessing from God and thus have been self-deceived as to their true spiritual state. In any case, they had misread their true condition.

Christ's revelation of the Laodiceans' actual situation shatters their illusions and calls them to repentance: "But you do not realize that you are wretched, pitiful, poor, blind and naked." Probably the first two characteristics—"wretched" and "pitiful"— are to be linked together, while the latter three explain this twofold condition in more detail (cf. v. 18). They are not, as they thought, rich and without need; they are pitifully wretched and in great need, being "poor, blind and naked." Conversely, Jesus said to the church at Smyrna, "I know . . . your poverty—yet you are rich!" (2:9).

To be "wretched" physically describes life when everything one owns has been destroyed or plundered by war (Ps 137:8 LXX). Here it refers to the Laodiceans' spiritual destitution and pitiableness before God. "Poor, blind and naked" refer to the three sources of their miserable condition. "Lukewarmness," then, does not refer to the laxity of Christians but the condition of not really knowing Christ as Savior and Lord and thus being useless to him. Origen likewise understood the passage to refer not to lapsed Christians but to the unregenerate (*Principiis* 3.4.3).

18 The commands of Christ correspond exactly to the self-deceptions of the Laodiceans. Gold, a source of the wealth of the city, was to be bought from Christ and to become the spiritually poverty-stricken's true wealth. Their shameful nakedness was to be clothed, not by purchasing the sleek, black wool of Laodicea, but by buying from Christ the white clothing that alone can cover shameful nakedness (16:15). For those who were blind to their true condition, the "Phrygian powder" was useless (cf. comments on v. 14). They needed to buy salve from Christ so that they could truly see. The reference to buying would recall the famous market near the temple of Men Karou, where the commodities manufactured at Laodicea could be bought, along with imports from other areas. But to what do gold, white clothes, and salve symbolically refer? Minear suggests the following:

> The only cure for poverty-stricken disciples was to purchase from Christ gold which is refined in the agonies of the shared passion. For their nakedness (did Hans Christian Andersen find here the theme of "The Emperor's New Clothes"?) the only recourse was to buy such clothes as the naked Christ had worn on the cross. The blindness of self-deception could be cured only by understanding the correlation between Christ's love and his discipline. These three purchases constitute a substantial definition of the kind of zeal and repentance which was the burden of all John's prophecies. The thrust of these commands moves in the direction of

rigorous warning. They are tantamount to saying "Open your eyes" and "Carry your cross." This letter argues against the widespread assertion of many interpreters to the effect that John's chief concern was to provide consolation to a persecuted church. Nearer the mark would be the opposite assertion; that John, like Jesus, was concerned to bring not peace but a sword (*I Saw a New Earth*, p. 57).

The three figures all point to the Laodiceans' need of authentic salvation through Christ.

19 Even though the state of a church, such as that in Laodicea verges on disaster, all is not lost if there are those in it who will receive Christ's loving rebuke and come back to him. "I love" is the Greek *phileō* ("to have affection for"). This verb does not necessarily connote a lower level of love than *agapaō*. Sometimes it has the force of *agapaō* (e.g., John 5:20; 16:27; 20:22; cf. BAG, s.v.). Christ's statement "I rebuke and discipline" speaks of his love (Prov 3:12; 1 Cor 11:32; Heb 12:6). He spits out those he does not love and "rebukes" (*elenchō*, "reproves," "convicts") and disciplines those who hear his voice. The difference between the expelled and the disciplined lies in their response: "So be earnest [*zeleuō*, 'zealous,' 'enthusiastic'] and repent." The Laodiceans' repentance would come from a rekindling of their loyalty to Christ.

20 To those who hear the words of rebuke, Christ extends an invitation to dine with him. Some older commentators find the reference to the "door" as parallel to the new age that will dawn at the advent of Christ (Swete, Beckwith; cf. Matt 24:33; James 5:9). So the challenge is to be ready to enter the banquet of Christ at his return. This view, however, does not seem to fit the immediate context, nor does it agree with other NT teaching on the Lord's return.

Others hold that the figure represents Christ standing at the door to the hearts of the members of the congregation at Laodicea. Christ will come and have fellowship with anyone who hears his voice of rebuke and thus proves himself Christ's friend by zeal and repentance. The "eating" (*deipneō*) refers to the main meal of the day, which in Oriental fashion was a significant occasion for having intimate fellowship with the closest of friends. It is through the Holy Spirit that Christ and the Father come to have fellowship with us (John 14:23).

While most commentators have taken this invitation as addressed to lapsed, halfhearted Christians, the terminology and context (v. 18) suggest that these Laodiceans were for the most part mere professing Christians who lacked authentic conversion to Christ, which is the essential prerequisite for true discipleship. Verse 20 is, therefore, more evangelistic than admonitory. Those who find in it an allusion to the Lord's Supper may be right. Cullman sees v. 20 as a response to the old eucharistic prayer: Maranatha (*marana tha*, "Our Lord, come!") (Oscar Cullmann, *Early Christian Worship* [London: SCM, 1953], in loc.).

21 The promise to the overcomers concerns the sharing in Christ's future reign in the eschatological kingdom: "I will give the right to sit with me on my throne." Such a joint reign with Christ has already been referred to earlier in the book (1:6, 9; 2:26–27) and appears later on (5:10; 20:4–6). The kingdom reign is also a theme in other NT writings (Luke 22:28–30; Rom 8:17; 2 Tim 2:12). As Christ overcame through his suffering and death (John 16:33) and entered into the highest honor God could bestow, that of being seated at his "right hand" of sovereignty (Mark 16:19; Acts

2:22ff.; Rev 22:1), so believers who suffer with Christ even to the point of death will share in the honor of Christ's exalted position. The distinction between the Father's throne and Christ's throne is no mere rhetoric. On the contrary, it differentiates aspects of God's program in history (1 Cor 15:24–28). Christ is reigning now, for there is a sense in which the eschatological or messianic kingdom of God was inaugurated in Christ's earthly ministry, death, and resurrection. But the promise here, as elsewhere in the NT, foresees a final earthly consummation of the kingdom that awaits the return of Christ.

22 The general exhortation closes the seventh letter (cf. comments in the introduction to the seven letters).

Notes

15–16 On the meaning of "hot" and "cold" and "lukewarm" as related to the city water supply and the consequent reinterpretation this suggests, see the helpful article by M.J.S. Rudwick and E.M.B. Green, "The Laodicean Lukewarmness," ET, 69 (1958), 176–78.

III. Vision of the Seven-Sealed Scroll, the Seven Trumpets, the Seven Signs, and the Seven Bowls (4:1–19:10)

A. *The Seven-Sealed Scroll* (4:1–8:1)

1. *Preparatory: the throne, the scroll, and the Lamb* (4:1–5:14)

a. *The throne*

4:1–11

¹After this I looked, and there before me was a door standing open in heaven. And the voice I had first heard speaking to me like a trumpet said, "Come up here, and I will show you what must take place after this." ²At once I was in the Spirit, and there before me was a throne in heaven with someone sitting on it. ³And the one who sat there had the appearance of jasper and carnelian. A rainbow, resembling an emerald, encircled the throne. ⁴Surrounding the throne were twenty-four other thrones, and seated on them were twenty-four elders. They were dressed in white and had crowns of gold on their heads. ⁵From the throne came flashes of lightning, rumblings and peals of thunder. Before the throne, seven lamps were blazing. These are the seven spirits of God. ⁶Also before the throne there was what looked like a sea of glass, clear as crystal.

In the center, around the throne, were four living creatures, and they were covered with eyes, in front and in back. ⁷The first living creature was like a lion, the second was like an ox, the third had a face like a man, the fourth was like a flying eagle. ⁸Each of the four living creatures had six wings and was covered with eyes all around, even under his wings. Day and night they never stop saying:

"Holy, holy, holy
is the Lord God Almighty,
who was, and is, and is to come."

9Whenever the living creatures give glory, honor and thanks to him who sits on the throne and who lives for ever and ever, 10the twenty-four elders fall down before him who sits on the throne, and worship him who lives for ever and ever. They lay their crowns before the throne and say:

> 11"You are worthy, our Lord and God,
>   to receive glory and honor and power,
>   for you created all things,
>   and by your will they were created
>   and have their being."

In view of the elaborate use of imagery and visions from 4:1 through the end of Revelation and the question of how this material relates to chapters 1–3, it is not surprising that commentators differ widely regarding them. One problem is that of interpretation: What do the imagery and visions mean? Another problem involves chronology: When do the things spoken of occur? Furthermore, how does John use his frequent OT images? Does he interpret them in exact accordance with their OT sources, or does he freely reinterpret these images and figures? What is symbolic and what is literal? Answers to such questions will determine the interpreter's approach. Since few of these questions are capable of dogmatic answers, there is a need for tolerance of divergent approaches in the hope that the Spirit may use open-minded discussion to bring us further into the meaning of the Apocalypse.

Chapters 4–5 form one vision of two parts—the throne (ch. 4) and the Lamb and the scroll (ch. 5). In actuality, the breaking of all seven seals (chs. 6–8:1) together with the throne vision (chs. 4–5) form a single, continuous vision and should not be separated. Indeed, the throne pictures (chs. 4–5) should be viewed as dominating the entire seven-seal vision (4:1–8:1).

1 Seeing a "door standing open in heaven," John is told to "come up here" (cf. Ezek 1:1, where the prophet says he saw the heavens opened). A new view of God's majesty and power (throne) is disclosed to John so that he can understand the events on earth that relate to the seven-seal vision (cf. 1 Kings 22:19). For the first time in Revelation, the reader is introduced to the frequent interchange between heaven and earth found in the remainder of the book. What happens on earth has its inseparable heavenly counterpart.

Chapter 4 focuses on the throne vision that provides the setting for the dramatic action of the slain Lamb in chapter 5. There is a connection between this throne vision and the vision of the glorified Christ in 1:10–16. Here we are told that John heard the same voice speaking to him that he "had first heard speaking . . . like a trumpet" (cf. 1:10). The words of the messenger relate to what has just transpired: "I will show you what must take place after this" (*meta tauta*, "after this," "next"; i.e., after the time of the historical churches in Asia [cf. 1:19]).

There is no good reason for seeing the invitation for John to come up into the opened heaven as a symbol of the rapture of the church. Some have so interpreted it and have inferred that the absence of the word "church" (*ekklēsia*) from Revelation till 22:16 and the continued references to the "saints" indicate that at this point the church departs from the earth. But the word "church" or "churches" always stands in Revelation for the historic seven churches in Asia and not just for the universal body of Christ. Since 4:1–22:15 concerns the believing community as a whole, it would be inappropriate at least for John's usage to find the narrower term "church" in this section (cf. 3 John 6, 9–10).

Finally, it is significant that in the visions that continue to the end of the book, there are references to the throne, the book, the crowns, the four living creatures, the twenty-four elders, and the victory of the Lamb. In all this, the center of focus appears to be the five hymns of praise that begin in 4:8 and continue through chapter 5.

2–3 Chapter 4 is above all a vision of the royal throne of God. The prophet ascends "in the Spirit" to see the source of all that will happen on earth (cf. 1:10). It will all be an expression of the throne's purpose; nothing happens, nothing exists in the past, present, or future apart from God's intention. Whatever authority is given to an angel or to a horseman is given by God. The throne symbolizes God's majesty and power. Yet his majestic transcendence is fully safeguarded—John does not attempt to describe the "someone sitting on" the throne (cf. 1 Kings 22:19; 2 Chron 18:18; Ps 47:8; Isa 6:1ff.; Ezek 1:26–28; Ecclus 1:8).

The minerals "jasper" and "carnelian" portray the supernatural splendor of God, while the "rainbow, resembling an emerald" conveys the impression of God's encircling brilliance (cf. Ezek 1:27–28). But we need not find symbolism in each element of the vision; it is enough to allow the archetypical imagery to create the impression of transcendant glory. Whether John intends God's judgment to be part of the symbolism of the throne vision (cf. Ps 9:4, 7) is not clear. What is unmistakably clear is that all—whether elders, angels, lamps, sea of glass, or living creatures—centers on the throne and the one who sits on it, "who lives for ever and ever" (v.9).

It is significant that the earliest Jewish mysticism is throne mysticism (Merkabah Mysticism). Its essence is not absorbed contemplation of God's true nature but perception of his appearance on the throne, as described by Ezekiel, and cognition of the mysteries of the celestial throne world (Gershorn G. Scholem, *Major Trends in Jewish Mysticism* [New York: Schocken Books, 1961], esp. ch. 2).

4 John also sees "twenty-four elders." It would be helpful if we could ask an interpreting angel, "Who are the elders?" There are at least thirteen different views of their identity, ranging from the twenty-four ruling stars (or judges) in the heavens to the simple figure of wholeness and fullness (cf. *I Saw a New Earth,* p. 83). Part of the discussion hinges on the correct text in 5:10 (cf. Notes). The following passages are pertinent to the elders' identification: 4:9–11; 5:5–14; 7:11–17; 11:16–18; 12:10–12; 14:3; 19:4.

The elders are always associated with the "four living creatures" (4:6ff.) and engage in acts of worship of God and the Lamb. While not entirely ruling out the elders' possible representative or symbolic significance (a view held by many good expositors), the arguments of Stonehouse, Mounce (*Revelation,* p. 135), and others who have argued that the elders are a class of heavenly spirit-beings belonging to the general class of angels and living creatures seem more compelling (Ned B. Stonehouse, *Paul Before the Areopagus* [Grand Rapids: Eerdmans, 1957], pp. 88–108). From this viewpoint, the "angels," the "twenty-four elders," and "the four living creatures" all designate actual supernatural beings involved with the purpose of God on earth and his worship in heaven. They are always distinguished from the "saints" (5:8; 11:17–18; 19:1–4), and the text of 5:10 is uncertain.

In the Bible twelve appears to be the number of divine government—twelve months in a lunar year, twelve tribes of Israel, twelve apostles, twelve gates in the

New Jerusalem, twelve angels at each gate, twelve foundations, twelve thousand sealed from each tribe, twelve thousand stadia (the length of the New Jerusalem), etc. Multiples of twelve—such as twenty-four, etc.—probably have a similar significance. Thrones are related to the heavenly powers in Colossians 1:16. In Revelation "white" clothing generally belongs to the saints but relates to angelic beings elsewhere in the NT (e.g., John 20:12). While the "crowns of gold" are likewise usually related to the redeemed, here they refer to the royal dignity of those so closely associated with the throne of God (cf. 1 Kings 22:19; Ps 89:7). Golden crowns are referred to in 4:4, 10; 9:7; 14:14.

5 "Flashes of lightning, rumblings and peals of thunder" coming from the throne are symbolic of God's awesome presence and the vindication of the saints and occur with slight variation four times in Revelation (4:5; 8:5; 11:19; 16:18; cf. Exod 19:16; Ezek 1:13; Ps 18:13–15). On the expression "seven blazing lamps," see comments on 1:4 (cf. Ezek 1:13).

6–8 "A sea of glass, clear as crystal" simply adds to the magnificence of the scene (15:2). Caird considers the "sea of glass" identical to the "sea" in Revelation 13:1 and 21:1 and identifies it as "a reservoir of evil" (p. 65). But a sea of "glass" may be an intentional reversal of this sea imagery (cf. Exod 24:10; Ezek 1:22, 26). The mirrorlike reflecting quality could symbolize the fact that before the sight of God all is revealed; i.e., "Everything is uncovered and laid bare before the eyes of him to whom we must give account" (Heb 4:13).

The "four living creatures" should be linked with Isaiah's seraphim and Ezekiel's cherubim (cf. Isa 6:3; Ezek 1:5–25; 10:1–22). They, like the elders and angels, are heavenly creatures of the highest order involved with the worship and government of God. "Covered with eyes" may give the impression of their exceeding knowledge of God, while the faces of a "lion," "ox," "man," and a "flying eagle" suggest qualities that belong to God, such as royal power, strength, spirituality, and swiftness of action. Each of the creatures mentioned is the chief of its species. Together they embody the reflection of God's nature as the fullness of life and power. Their six wings (cf. Isa 6:2) give the impression of unlimited mobility in fulfilling God's commands. Their position "in the center, around the throne" suggests that one might be before and one behind the throne with one on either side (Beckwith). The four living creatures appear throughout Revelation (cf. 5:6, 8, 14; 6:1ff.; 7:11; 14:3; 15:7; 19:4).

The four living creatures ceaselessly proclaim the holiness of God: "Holy, holy, holy" (v.8; Isa 6:3). In Hebrew, the double repetition of a word adds emphasis, while the rare threefold repetition designates the superlative and calls attention to the infinite holiness of God—the quality of God felt by creatures in his presence as awesomeness or fearfulness (Ps 111:9: "Holy and awesome is his name"). The living creatures celebrate God's holiness and power as manifested in his past, present, and future activity. Such holiness cannot tolerate the presence of evil (21:27). (On these titles of God, see comments on 1:4, 8.) The trisagion ("Holy, holy, holy") is a liturgical expression used in both ancient Jewish and Christian worship. Its use does not, however, reach back to the first century.

This hymn is the first not only of the five sung by the heavenly choirs in chapters 4–5 but also of a number of others in Revelation (4:8, 11; 5:9–10, 12, 13; 7:12, 15–17; 11:15, 17–18; 12:10–12; 15:3–4; 16:5–7; 18:2–8; 19:2–6). These hymns relate to the interpretation of the visions and provide a clue to the literary structure of Revelation.

In these two chapters, the sequence of hymns shows that the first two are addressed to God, the next two to the Lamb, and the last one to both. There is also a gradual enlargement in the size of the choirs. The internal movement also builds as the last hymn is sung by "every creature in heaven and on earth and under the earth" to "him who sits on the throne and to the Lamb" (5:13).

9–11 The second hymn is sung by the twenty-four elders. When the living creatures confess the truth of God's holy deeds, the response of the highest order of God's heavenly creatures is to relinquish their crowns of honor before the feet of him who alone is "worthy" of "glory and honor and power" because he alone (no man, not even the emperor) is the source and stay of every created thing (Ps 33:6–9; 102:25; 136:5ff.).

The expression "by your will they were created and have their being" (v.11) presents a translation difficulty because the Greek text has two different tenses (*ēsan*, "they were" [NIV, "have their being"], imperfect; *ektisthēsan*, "they were created," aorist). Although a number of possible explanations have been advanced, Alford's remains the best: the imperfect tense describes the *fact* of their existence while the aorist captures the sense of the *beginning* of their existence (Alf, 4:602–3). Consequently, the phrase might be translated thus: "Because of [not 'by'] your will they continually exist and have come into being."

Notes

1 The expression ἃ δεῖ γενέσθαι μετὰ ταῦτα (*ha dei genesthai meta tauta* "what must take place after this") is found in the LXX of Dan 2:29, 45, where it has the sense of "next" in historical sequence from the time of the writer. "After this" does not mean "at some future time" but refers to what is after that which is at present (KD, *Daniel* p. 111).

8 John's Gr. text of this verse agrees with 1QIsa at Isa 6:2 against both the MT and the LXX (L. Paul Trudinger, "Some Observations Concerning the Text of the Old Testament in the Book of Revelation," JTS, 17 [1966], 88).

---

b. *The Scroll and the Lamb*

5:1–14

¹Then I saw in the right hand of him who sat on the throne a scroll with writing on both sides and sealed with seven seals. ²And I saw a mighty angel proclaiming in a loud voice, "Who is worthy to break the seals and open the scroll?" ³But no one in heaven or on earth or under the earth could open the scroll or even look inside it. ⁴I wept and wept because no one was found who was worthy to open the scroll or look inside. ⁵Then one of the elders said to me, "Do not weep! See, the Lion of the tribe of Judah, the Root of David, has triumphed. He is able to open the scroll and its seven seals."

⁶Then I saw a Lamb, looking as if it had been slain, standing in the center of the throne, encircled by the four living creatures and the elders. He had seven horns and seven eyes, which are the seven spirits of God sent out into all the earth. ⁷He came and took the scroll from the right hand of him who sat on the throne. ⁸And when he had taken it, the four living creatures and the twenty-four elders fell down before the Lamb. Each one had a harp and they were holding golden bowls full of incense, which are the prayers of the saints. ⁹And they sang a new song:

"You are worthy to take the scroll
and to open its seals,
because you were slain,
and with your blood you purchased men for God
from every tribe and language and people and nation.
¹⁰You have made them to be a kingdom and priests to
serve our God,
and they will reign on the earth."

¹¹Then I looked and heard the voice of many angels, numbering thousands upon thousands, and ten thousand times ten thousand. They encircled the throne and the living creatures and the elders. ¹²In a loud voice they sang:

"Worthy is the Lamb, who was slain,
to receive power and wealth and wisdom and strength
and honor and glory and praise!"

¹³Then I heard every creature in heaven and on earth and under the earth and on the sea, and all that is in them, singing:

"To him who sits on the throne and to the Lamb
be praise and honor and glory and power,
for ever and ever!"

¹⁴The four living creatures said, "Amen," and the elders fell down and worshiped.

1 This chapter is part of the vision that begins at chapter 4 and continues through the opening of the seven seals (6:1–8:1; cf. comments in introduction to ch.4). Its center of gravity lies in the three hymns (vv.9, 12, 13). These are addressed to the Lamb. They beautifully combine the worship of the Lamb (hymns one and two) with the worship of the one who sits on the throne (hymn three, which is addressed to both God and the Lamb). The movement of the whole scene focuses on the slain Lamb as he takes the scroll from the hand of the one on the throne. The actions of all other participants are described in terms of worship directed to the Lamb and the one on the throne. The culminating emphasis is on the worthiness of the Lamb to receive worship because of his death.

John sees "in the right hand of him who sat on the throne a scroll with writing on both sides and sealed with seven seals." This raises a problem involving the phrase "with writing on both sides." Papyrus codices (which were like books as we know them) did not originate until the second century A.D., or perhaps the late first century (Bruce M. Metzger, *The Text of the New Testament* 2d ed. [Oxford: Clarendon, 1964], p. 6). In ancient times, papyrus rolls were used for public and private documents. Usually the writing was on one side only—the inside part, arranged in successive vertical columns. Occasionally a scroll was written on both sides; in that case it was called an "opisthograph." Such double-sided writing was for private, nonsalable use in contrast to the usual scrolls written on only one side, which were sold (Edward Maunde Thompson, *An Introduction to Greek and Latin Paleography* [Oxford: Clarendon, 1912], pp. 49–50). In the context of chapter 5, an opisthograph would signify a scroll full of words. The importance of establishing the scroll rather than codex character of the document lies in the interpretation of the opening of the seals. If the book was a codex, the seals could have been opened one at a time and portions of the book disclosed; a scroll, however, could be opened only after *all* the seals were broken.

Scrolls, or folded sheets, were sealed with wax blobs impressed with a signet ring to protect the contents or guarantee the integrity of the writing. Only the owner could open the seals and disclose the contents. Original documents were usually sealed; copies were not. Sealed documents were kept hidden while unsealed copies were made public (Rev 22:10) (TDNT, 7:941ff.).

The phrase "with writing on both sides" (*gegrammenon esōthen kai opisthen*) is literally "written inside and on the back side," where "on the back side" (*opisthen*) is generally understood as going with "written" (*gegrammenon*). Zahn, however, argues that "back side" (*opisthen*) should go with the verb "sealed" (*katesphragisme-non*) and not with "written" (Theodore Zahn, *Introduction to the New Testament*, 3 vols. [Grand Rapids: Kregel, 1953], 3.405–6). While tempting and grammatically possible, Zahn's view has not found acceptance among exegetes; and the adverbial use of *opisthen* in the rest of Revelation and the NT favors taking it always with a preceding rather than a following verb.

As to the identity and significance of the scroll, there are a number of different views.

1. Ancient Roman wills or "testaments" were sealed with six seals, each of which bore a different name of the sealer and could only be opened by him (TDNT, 7:941). This has led some to identify the scroll as the testament of God concerning the promise of the inheritance of his future kingdom (Zahn, *NT Introduction*, 3:395–96). A slight variation of this view refers the scene to the Roman law of *mancipatio*. Under this law an heir received either an inheritance at the death of the testator or the use of *mancipatio* in connection with transference of the inheritance to an executor, known as the *familiae emptor*. The executor could use the property till the death of the testator, at which time he was obligated to distribute the possessions in accordance with the instructions of the testator (Emmet Russell, "A Roman Law Parallel to Revelation Five," BS, 115 [1958], 258–64).

2. Others find the scroll containing, like Ezekiel's scroll, "words of lament and mourning and woe" (Ezek 2:9–10) and depicting the future judgment of the world (Walvoord, p. 113).

3. Still others find the significance to be the progressive unfolding of the history of the world. As each successive seal is opened, the further contents of the book are revealed. J.A. Seiss (*The Apocalypse* [Grand Rapids: Zondervan, 1957], p. 112) connects the scroll with a "title-deed" (Jer 32:10–14). It is the "title-deed" to creation that was forfeited by sin in Genesis. By his redeeming death Christ has won the authority to reclaim the earth.

4. A more recent study finds the scroll to be the OT Torah (Law) (Lucetta Mowry, "Revelation 4–5 and Early Christian Liturgical Usage," JBL, 71 [1952], 75–84).

Each of these views has merit and may provide elements of truth for the background of the striking imagery in these chapters. Yet each view is vulnerable to criticism. Only from Revelation itself can the content and nature of the scroll be determined. Since the seals hinder the opening of the scroll till they are all broken, we may assume that the seals are preparatory to the opening of the scroll and the disclosure of its contents. This means that the seals have the effect of hiding the contents of the scroll till they are broken (Isa 29:11).

The following internal evidence relating to the contents of the scroll may be noted:

1. Just prior to the opening of the seventh seal, in connection with the events under the sixth seal, we read, "For the great day of their [i.e., of the One sitting on the throne and the Lamb] wrath has come, and who can stand?" (6:17).

2. When the seventh seal is opened (8:1–5), no immediate events as such follow on earth—except for the earthquake—as in the first six seals, unless the opening of the seventh seal includes among its events the blowing of the seven trumpets of judgment (8:6–11:15). This appears to be precisely the case.

3. The seventh trumpet likewise is not immediately followed by any specific events on earth (11:15ff.), except for an earthquake and a hailstorm (11:19). However, just before the seventh trumpet is sounded, we read, "The second woe has passed; the third woe is coming soon" (11:14). When the seven angels prepare to pour out "the seven last plagues," symbolized by the bowls, we read that with these bowls "God's wrath is completed" (15:1, 7). Thus it seems reasonable to identify the content of the seventh trumpet with the seven bowls of judgment (chs. 16–19).

Furthermore, frequent references to the events of the seals, trumpets, and bowls appear throughout the remaining visions in Revelation (cf. 19:19ff.; 20:4; 21:9), indicating that the content of the seven-sealed scroll ultimately includes the unfolding of the consummation of the mystery of all things, the goal or end of all history, for both the conquerors and the worshipers of the beast. In 10:7 we are told that in the days of the sounding of the seventh trumpet "the mystery of God will be accomplished, just as he announced to his servants the prophets." From this it may be concluded that the scroll contains the unveiling of "the mystery of God" that OT prophets foretold (cf. comments at 10:7). Thus the "seals" conceal the mystery, which only Christ can disclose (Dan 12:9; Rev 10:4), of how God's judgment and his kingdom will come. In 11:15, when the final trumpet sounds, heavenly voices say, "The kingdom of the world has become the kingdom of our Lord and of his Christ," indicating that the scroll also contains the announcement of the inheritance of Christ and the saints who will reign with him (5:10).

The scroll, then, is not only about judgment or about the inheritance of the kingdom. Rather, it contains the announcement of the consummation of all history— how things will ultimately end for all people: judgment for the world and the final reward of the saints (11:18). Christ alone, as the Messiah, is the executor of the purposes of God and the heir of the inheritance of the world. He obtained this by his substitutionary and propitiatory death on the cross (5:9).

2–4 A mighty angel shouts out a challenge for anyone to come forth who is "worthy" to open the great scroll and its seals. All creation in heaven and earth and under the earth stood motionless and speechless. No one was worthy to open the scroll; i.e., no one had the authority and virtue for such a task. If the scroll contains both the revelation and the carrying out of the final drama of history, then John's despair can be appreciated. In this vision, the execution of events on earth is ascribed to the Lamb. As the seals are broken and the roll opened, salvation history unfolds till history culminates in the kingdom reign of the Messiah over the whole earth. History, then, has its center in Jesus Christ and its goal in his triumphant reign over all the powers of the world.

5 John's sorrow is assuaged. One of the elders announces that there is one who has "triumphed" (*nikaō*, "overcome," "conquer," "win a victory"—same word as 2:7; 3:21; et al.). He has triumphed because of his death (v.9). Two figurative titles are used of the one who is worthy—"the Lion of the tribe of Judah" and "the Root of David." Both are familiar OT messianic titles (Gen 49:9–10; cf. Isa 11:1, 10; Jer 23:5; 33:5; Rev 22:16). But they are linked together only here and in the Qumran literature

71

(cf. 4Q Patriarchal Blessings; L. Paul Trudinger, "Some Observations Concerning the Text of the Old Testament in the Book of Revelation," JTS, 17 [1966], 88). In Jewish apocalyptic literature contemporary with John, the figure of a lion was used to designate the conquering Messiah who would destroy Rome (4 Ezra 11:58). Close attention should be paid to John's understanding of the role and function of the Messiah, observing where it is similar to the Jewish understanding of the Messiah and where it differs from it.

6 As John looked to see the mighty Lion (the conquering warrior-Messiah from the Root of David), he saw instead the striking figure of a "Lamb" (*arnion*, "a young sheep") as if it had been slaughtered, standing in the center of the throne court. This new figure portrays sacrificial death and links the Messiah to the OT passover lamb (Exod 12:5f.; Isa 53:7; John 1:29, 36; Acts 8:32; 1 Peter 1:19). Here John joins the OT royal Davidic Messiah with the Suffering Servant of Isaiah (Isa 42–53). Both prophetic themes come together in Jesus of Nazareth, the true Messiah. "As if it had been slain" (*esphagmenon*, "with its throat cut") could refer to the "marks of death" the living Lamb still bore or to his appearance "as if being led to the slaughter," i.e., "marked out for death" (Minear, *I Saw a New Earth*, in loc.). The "lamb" metaphor dominates John's thought in the rest of the book (e.g., 6:1ff.; 7:9ff.; 12:11; 13:8; 21:9).

John notices that the Lamb who bears the marks of death is also the ruler who bears the signs of the fullness of divine omnipotence, dominion, and omniscience ("seven horns and seven eyes"). Following Charles, Mounce (*Revelation*, p. 145) suggests that the figure of a lamb with seven horns is undoubtedly drawn from the apocalyptic tradition, citing 1 Enoch 90.9 (the Maccabees are symbolized by "horned lambs") and the Testament of Joseph 19.8–9 (a *lamb* destroys the enemies of Israel). However, the Enoch passage bears little relationship to the messianic Lamb as portrayed in Revelation, and the Testament of Joseph is notorious for Christian interpolations. Since the lamb image is used by the fourth Gospel to depict the Suffering Messiah in passages where apocalyptic connections would be quite remote, it may still be better to connect the lamb vocabulary to the OT Passover motif and Isaiah's Suffering Servant (Isa 53:7), especially in light of the author's interest in the Passover theme elsewhere in the book (e.g., 19:1ff.).

The "eyes" are more explicitly identified as the "seven spirits of God sent out into all the earth," probably a symbolic reference to the divine Holy Spirit who is sent forth by Christ into the world (1:4; 4:5). The teaching of the fourth Gospel is similar, where the Spirit is sent forth to exalt Christ and convict the world of sin (John 14:26; 15:26; 16:7–15).

7 Next the Lamb acts: "He came and took the scroll." The Greek conveys a dramatic action in the tense of the verb "took" (perhaps a dramatic perfect?): "He went up and took it, and now he has it." Symbolically, the one on the throne thus authorizes the slain messianic King to execute his plan for the redemption of the world because in and through the Lamb, God is at work in history for the salvation of humanity. Observe that this dramatic act of seizing the scroll is not itself the act of victory referred to in v.6 and later in v.9. Christ's victorious death on the cross is the basis of his authority to redeem the world by taking and opening the seven-sealed scroll.

8 The Lamb's act calls forth three hymns of praise (vv.9, 12, 13) from the living creatures and elders. John sees them fall down in worship before the Lamb as they had earlier done before the one on the throne (4:10), thus acknowledging the deity of the Lamb. They have "harps", which are the "lyres" used for the older psalmody (cf., e.g., Pss 33:2; 98:5) but will now be used for the "new song" of praise to the Lamb (v.9; 15:2–3).

The "bowls full of incense" represent the "prayers of the saints" (8:3–4). Prayer (*proseuchē*) in this scene is not praise but petition. Why would John mention the saints on earth as petitioning God? In 6:10 the martyrs are seen as calling to God for his judgment on those who killed them, and in 8:3–4 the prayers of the saints are immediately connected with the trumpets of God's judgment. These prayers, then, are evidently for God's vindication of the martyred saints. And since v.10 refers to the coming kingdom, it may be that the prayers are petitions for God to judge the world and to extend his kingdom throughout the earth (Luke 18:7–8). "Saints" here, as elsewhere in the NT and the rest of Revelation, is simply the normal term for the rank and file of Christians, i.e., those set apart for God's purposes (2 Cor 1:1; Phil 1:1; Rev 11:18; 13:7, 19; 19:8; 22:21).

9 The three hymns interpret the symbolism of the scroll and the Lamb. The number of singers increases from twenty-eight in v.8 to every creature in all creation in v.13. The first two hymns are songs of praise to the Lamb, whereas the last is praise to both the one on the throne and the Lamb (v.13). The first hymn (vv.9–10) is called a "new" song because there was never any like it before in heaven (cf. comments on 14:3).

"You are worthy" (*axios*, "comparable," "equal to," "deserving") refers to the qualifications of this person who alone has won the right to take the scroll and open its seals. His worthiness for this task was won by his loving sacrifice on the cross— "because you were slain." This must be understood as a direct reference to the earthly death of the human Jesus of Nazareth (the Gr. aorist tense supports this). It is no mythological death or salvation. Like other NT writers, John views the death of Jesus as a redeeming death—"and with your blood [or 'by the price of your blood'] you purchased [or 'redeemed,' *agorazo*] men for God."

The death of Jesus broke the stranglehold of the "powers and authorities" over the creation and produced a great victory of liberation for mankind (Col 2:15). It is this victory, obtained through suffering and death, that entitles Christ to execute the unfolding of the mystery of God's consummation of history. The centrality of the Cross and its meaning as a redemptive act comes repeatedly to the fore and should dominate our understanding throughout Revelation. (1:5; 5:12; 7:14; 12:11; 13:8; 14:4; 15:3; 19:7; 21:9, 23; 22:3, et al.). Jesus' death secured a salvation universally applied to all classes and peoples of the earth—"every tribe and language and people and nation" (cf. 7:9).

10 The Lamb's right to open the scroll rests also on the fact that he has made the ransomed into a "kingdom" and made them "priests" (to serve God in praise; cf. Heb 13:15–16). Christians "will reign on the earth" with Christ because they have been given "kingly authority" through his death (1:6; 20:4–6). While not excluding the present reign of believers, the reference to "the earth" is best taken to refer to the future eschatological kingdom reign of Christ (see Notes for various problems in this verse).

11–12 Now John sees a new feature in the vision: "thousands upon thousands, and ten thousand times ten thousand" angels surrounding the throne. The vision is similar to Daniel's vision of the countless multitude before the Ancient of Days (Dan 7:10). The imagery suggests the infinite honor and power of the one who is at the center of it all. The angels shout out their song of praise to the Lamb who was slain (cf. Heb 1:6). Their sevenfold shout rings out like the sound from a huge bell—"power . . . wealth . . . wisdom . . . strength . . . honor . . . glory . . . praise." All these are intrinsic qualities of Christ except the last, which is the expression of the creatures' worship: "praise" (lit., "blessing"). Elsewhere the same qualities are ascribed to God himself (5:13; 7:12). The sevenfold multiplication of these attributes by angel choirs is a Qumran liturgical method for creating the feeling of God's majesty and glory (7:12; 4QSL).

13–14 Finally, far beyond the precincts of the throne, there arises an expression of praise and worth from the whole created universe to the one on the throne and to the Lamb. John beautifully blends the worship of the Father (ch. 4) and the worship of the Son (5:8–12) together. In appropriate response, the living beings utter their "Amen" (cf. comments on 3:14), and the elders fall down in worship.

Notes

---

1 The difficult expression ὄπισθεν (opisthen, "behind," "back of ") has textual variants here. A strongly supported tradition in the versions and Fathers has the reading ἔξωθεν (exōthen, "outside"), which probably arose when codices replaced scrolls in the Christian community, making the expression "back side" sound strange (Bruce M. Metzger, A Textual Commentary on the Greek New Testament, [New York: UBS, 1971], p. 737).

5 While evidence supporting a pre-Christian Jewish understanding of a suffering Messiah is meager, there do exist some traces of it. Edersheim points out that Isaiah 53 was applied to the Messiah in the Targum and in the Midrash on Samuel, "where it is said that all sufferings are divided into three parts, one of which the Messiah bore" (LTJM, 2:727).

6 The word for "lamb" or young sheep used in Rev some twenty-eight times is ἀρνίον (arnion), which occurs only once outside in John 21:15 (pl.). The alternate word elsewhere is ἀμνός (amnos), which occurs only four times and is used of Christ (John 1:29, 36; Acts 8:32; 1 Peter 1:19). Both words occur in the LXX and are used in Exod 12 to refer to the Passover sacrificial lamb. No distinction between arnion and amnos should be pressed; their use merely reflects the author's preference. The diminutive ending ιον (ion) has lost its diminutive force (G. Mussies, The Morphology of Koine Greek as Used in the Apocalypse of St. John [Leiden: E.J. Brill, 1971], p. 109).

9–10 Here the chief problem is whether the text should read "redeemed us [ἡμᾶς (hēmas, 'us')] to God" or simply "redeemed to God," omitting hēmas (NIV, "purchased men"). The reading is crucial to the identification of the elders. If hēmas is original, it would be difficult to argue that the elders are angelic beings. The evidence for the shorter reading consists of one Gr. MS (A) and one version (Ethiopic), while all other versional and Gr. evidence has the word hēmas. Unless unusual weight is given to A (it is considered the best witness), the most reasonable conclusion is to charge A at this point with an omission. On the other hand, Metzger argues that the reading of A best accounts for the origin of the longer variations since scribes were unsatisfied with a less-direct object for ἠγόρασας (ēgorasas, "redeemed"; NIV, "purchased") and supplied the awkward hēmas, which does not fit the αὐτούς (autous, "them") of v.10 (Textual Commentary, p. 738). It is a difficult question to settle with certainty, but this commentary follows the shorter reading (like NIV) and views the elders as angels.

More difficult are the readings βασιλεύουσιν (basileuousin, "they reign" [present tense]) or βασιλεύσουσιν (basileusousin, "they will reign" [future tense]). Both have nearly equal MS support. Although NIV has the future tense here, it would seem better to adopt—with reservations—the present-tense reading and understand it as a "future present," in keeping with John's other references to the future reign of the saints (20:4). Mounce concurs (*Revelation*, p. 149, n.27). For a helpful inductive discussion of the whole chapter, see also Robert H. Mounce, "Worthy is the Lamb," ch. 5 in *Scripture, Tradition, and Interpretation*, edd. W. Ward Gasque and William Sanford LaSor, (Grand Rapids: Eerdmans, 1978).

John's expression "a kingdom and priests" is a combination of the LXX rendering of Exod 19:6 and that of the Targum's (M. McNamara, *Targum and Testament: Aramaic Paraphrase of the Hebrew Bible; A Light on the New Testament* [Grand Rapids: Eerdmans, 1962], p. 156). The source of this idea of the saints' reign could well be Dan 7:10ff., though no direct verbal allusion appears in Rev (R.T. France, *Jesus and the Old Testament* [Downers Grove, Ill.: InterVarsity, 1971], p. 204).

---

2. Opening of the first six seals

6:1–17

[1] I watched as the Lamb opened the first of the seven seals. Then I heard one of the four living creatures say in a voice like thunder, "Come!" [2] I looked, and there before me was a white horse! Its rider held a bow, and he was given a crown, and he rode out as a conqueror bent on conquest.

[3] When the Lamb opened the second seal, I heard the second living creature say, "Come!" [4] Then another horse came out, a fiery red one. Its rider was given power to take peace from the earth and to make men slay each other. To him was given a large sword.

[5] When the Lamb opened the third seal, I heard the third living creature say, "Come!" I looked, and there before me was a black horse! Its rider was holding a pair of scales in his hand. [6] Then I heard what sounded like a voice among the four living creatures, saying, "A quart of wheat for a day's wages, and three quarts of barley for a day's wages, and do not damage the oil and the wine!"

[7] When the Lamb opened the fourth seal, I heard the voice of the fourth living creature say, "Come!" [8] I looked, and there before me was a pale horse! Its rider was named Death, and Hades was following close behind him. They were given power over a fourth of the earth to kill by sword, famine and plague, and by the wild beasts of the earth.

[9] When he opened the fifth seal, I saw under the altar the souls of those who had been slain because of the word of God and the testimony they had maintained. [10] They called out in a loud voice, "How long, Sovereign Lord, holy and true, until you judge the inhabitants of the earth and avenge our blood?" [11] Then each of them was given a white robe, and they were told to wait a little longer, until the number of their fellow servants and brothers who were to be killed as they had been was completed.

[12] I watched as he opened the sixth seal. There was a great earthquake. The sun turned black like sackcloth made of goat hair, the whole moon turned blood red, [13] and the stars in the sky fell to earth, as late figs drop from a fig tree when shaken by a strong wind. [14] The sky receded like a scroll, rolling up, and every mountain and island was removed from its place.

[15] Then the kings of the earth, the princes, the generals, the rich, the mighty, and every slave and every free man hid in caves and among the rocks of the mountains. [16] They called to the mountains and the rocks, "Fall on us and hide us from the face of him who sits on the throne and from the wrath of the Lamb! [17] For the great day of their wrath has come, and who can stand?"

1 The opening of the seals continues the vision begun in chapters 4 and 5. Now the scene shifts to events on earth. Before the exposition of each of the seals, it will be helpful to consider their overall meaning. As we have already seen (cf. comments on 5:1), the scroll itself involves the rest of Revelation and has to do with the consummation of the mystery of all things, the goal or end of history for both the overcomers and the beast worshipers. But what relationship do the seals have to this mystery? Are the events of the seals representative and simultaneous world happenings that occur throughout the church age (Minear)? Do they occur sequentially? Are they part of the final drama (Bruce) or merely preparatory to it (Ladd)? One thing is certain: the Lamb has the scroll and he himself opens the seals (6:1, 3, 5, et al.).

With the opening of the fifth seal, the martyrs cry out, "How long, . . . until you judge the inhabitants of the earth?" and are told to wait "a little longer" (vv.10–11). And when the sixth seal is opened, the judgment appears to be imminent (v.17), and this seems to indicate that there is a time progression in the seals. The writer of this commentary tentatively suggests that the seals represent events preparatory to the final consummation. Whether these events come immediately before the end or whether they represent general conditions that will prevail throughout the period preceding the end is a more difficult question.

The seals closely parallel the signs of the approaching end times spoken of in Jesus' Olivet Discourse (Matt 24:1–35; Mark 13:1–37; Luke 21:5–33). In these passages the events of the last days fall into three periods: (1) the period of false Christs, wars, famines, pestilences, earthquakes, and death, called "the beginning of birth pains" (Matt 24:8); (2) the period of the Great Tribulation (Matt 24:21; NIV, "great distress") and, (3) finally, the period "immediately after the distress of those days," when the sun, moon, and stars will be affected and Christ will return (Matt 24:29–30). This parallel to major parts of Revelation is too striking to be ignored. Thus the seals would correspond to the "beginning of birth pains" found in the Olivet Discourse. The events are similar to those occurring under the trumpets (8:2–11:19) and bowls (15:1–16:21) but they should not be confused with those later and more severe judgments. In Jewish apocalyptic literature (cf. 2 Baruch 25–30), the Great Tribulation precedes the age to come and is divided into twelve parts of various trials lasting possibly a week of seven weeks, or forty-nine years (C.K. Barrett, *The New Testament Background: Selected Documents* [New York: Harper and Row, 1961], pp. 245–48). Moreover, in the eschatological reckoning of time (cf. comments on 1:1), the events immediately preceding the end can stretch out over the whole age of the church, from John's time until now, and can still be viewed as "next" (4:1) in the sense that the "last days" began in the first century and are still continuing (cf. 1 John 2:18).

The first four seals are distinct from the last two in that they describe four horses of different colors with four riders who are given different powers over the earth. Background for the imagery of these four seals reflect Zechariah 1:8ff. and 6:1–8. In Zechariah's visions the horsemen and chariots are divine instruments of judgment on the enemies of God's people, while the colors represent geographical points of the compass. This may also be the best interpretation of the horses and their riders in Revelation 6, where each is sent by Christ through the instrumentality of the living creatures. The emphatic call "Come!" (vv.1, 3, 5, 7) should not be viewed as addressed either to John (some ancient Gr. MSS and many commentators, cf. Notes, v.1) or to Christ (Alford, Swete) but, rather, to the horsemen in each case. An analogy may be a first-century amphitheater or circus with various charioteers being summoned forth into the arena of the world by the call "Come!" or "Go forth!"

2 The identification of the first rider seated on a white horse has given interpreters great difficulty. Essentially, the difficulty is whether the rider on the white horse represents Christ and the victory of the gospel (Alford, Ladd) or whether he represents the Antichrist and the forces of evil (Beckwith, Bruce, Caird, Mounce, Swete, Walvoord). In favor of the first identification is the striking similarity of this rider to the portrayal of Christ in 19:11–16, the symbolism of white throughout Revelation always being associated with righteousness and Christ (e.g., 1:14; 2:17; 3:4–5, 18; 4:4; 7:9, 13–14; 20:11), and the references in the Olivet Discourse to the preaching of the gospel throughout the world before the end.

Support for the identification of the white horse with the Antichrist and his forces is the parallelism with the other three horses, which are instruments of judgment. The references in 19:11–16 to the rider on the white horse as "Faithful and True" and of whom it is said that "with justice he judges and makes war" may stand in contrast to the rider in 6:2 who is not faithful or true and who wages war for unjust conquest. As for the Lamb, he opens the seals and would not be one of the riders. Moreover, it would be inappropriate to have an angelic being call forth Christ or his servants. Again, the "bow" would most naturally be connected with the enemy of God's people (Ezek 39:3; cf. Rev. 20:7–8). Finally, the parallelism to the Olivet Discourse shows that the first events mentioned are the rise of "false Christs and false prophets" (Matt 24:24).

It must be admitted that the problem of the identity of the rider on the white horse may be solved either way, depending on the presuppositions one brings to the passage. The evidence, however, seems to favor slightly the second solution, which identifies the white horse with the Antichrist and his forces that seek to conquer the followers of Christ. John sensed that these persecutions were already present in his day and that they would culminate in a final, more severe form (1 John 2:18; Rev 13:7).

Each of the first four seals, then, represents conflict directed at Christians to test them and to sift out false disciples (6:10). This interpretation need not necessarily eliminate the fact that the seals may also refer to judgments on mankind in general. Yet since the fifth seal stresses the cry of the martyred Christians, probably the thought of Christian persecution belongs also in the first four seals (Minear, *I Saw a New Earth*, pp. 78, 266–69). Each of them unleashes events that separate false belief from true. The destruction of Jerusalem is a case in point (Luke 21:20ff.). The white horse is released to conquer. As he goes forth, judgment falls on the unbelief of Israel (Luke 21:22–23), while at the same time there is a testing of believers to separate the chaff from the wheat (cf. Luke 21:12–19).

Although the bow could be a symbol of either the Parthian or Cretan invaders bent on the conquest of Rome, in this context it suggests forces opposed to Christians (cf. Matt 24:5). A "crown" refers to victorious conquest in 19:12, where Christ wears "many crowns." "He was given" is the formula for the sovereign permission to carry out acts that, from a human viewpoint, seem contrary to God's character but nevertheless accomplish his will (cf. 13:5, 7, 15). Thus the rider on the white horse may also point to the attacks of the false Jews (2:9; 3:9) and to the affront to Christians from pagan religionists and the persecutions from Rome as well as all future, limited victories over the church by Satan (cf. 2:13; 12:17).

While v.2 would be sobering for first-century believers, at the same time it would encourage them, provided they understood that the Lamb had, for his own beneficent ends, permitted their testing and suffering. So they could trust that in the midst of seeming defeat from their enemies, he would ultimately be the victor (17:14).

3–4 The second horseman is war and bloodshed. He rides on a "fiery red steed," whose color symbolizes slaughter (2 Kings 3:22–23). Therefore, he is given the "large sword" because the number of those he kills is so great (cf. 13:10, 14). John might have thought of Nero's slaughter of Christians, the martyrdom of Antipas (2:13), or perhaps those slain under Domitian's persecutions (cf. Matt 10:34; 24:9).

5–6 The third horseman is poverty and famine. He rides on a "black horse" and symbolizes the effects of war and bloodshed: sorrow, mourning, and desolation (Isa 50:3; Jer 4:28; Lam 5:10 KJV). In the rider's hand there is a "pair of scales." A voice is heard interpreting its significance in economic terms: "a quart of wheat . . . and three quarts of barley for a day's wage" (lit., "for a denarius," a Gr. coin). This amount suggests food prices about twelve times higher than normal (Beckwith, p. 520) and implies inflation and famine conditions (Matt 24:7). A quart of wheat would supply an average person one day's sustenance. Barley was used by the poor to mix with the wheat. The expression "Do not damage the oil and wine" is less clear. Some view oil and wine as luxuries not necessary for bare survival, and the rich would have them while the poor were starving (cf. Prov 21:17). Others take oil and wine as showing the extent of the famine, since a drought affecting the grain may not be severe enough to hurt the vines and olive trees (ibid., p. 521). Moreover, oil and wine are staple foods in the East, both in dearth and in prosperity (e.g., Deut 7:13; Hos 2:8, 22). So in this view the third seal brings poverty and partial, though not severe, famine. As Mounce notes, "This interpretation is in harmony with the increasing intensity of the three cycles of judgment. The fourth seal affects 'the fourth part of the earth' (6:8), the trumpets destroy a third (8:7, 8, 10, 12), and the destruction by the bowls is complete and final (16:1ff.)" (*Revelation,* p. 155).

7–8 The fourth seal reveals a rider on a "pale horse." "Pale" (*chlōros*) denotes a yellowish green, the light green of a plant, or the paleness of a sick person in contrast to a healthy appearance (cf. BAG, p. 890). This cadaverous color blends well with the name of the rider—"Death" (*thanatos*). This probably refers to the death brought by pestilence, or plague, which often follows famine (cf. Jer 14:12; Ezek 5:17; 14:21; Luke 21:11). "Hades was following close behind him [Death]." But how? On foot? On the back of the same horse? On a separate horse? Scripture does not say. (On "Hades," cf. comments on 1:18.) There seems to be a growth of intensity in the judgments as they are carried out by various agencies—the sword (human violence), famine, plague, and now the wild beasts of the earth.

9–11 The fifth seal changes the metaphor of horsemen and discloses a scene of martyred saints under the altar crying out for justice upon those who killed them. They are told to wait a little longer till their fellow servants are also killed. Who are these martyrs? They are referred to again in 18:24 as "all who have been killed on the earth" and in 20:4 as "those who had been beheaded." In 13:15 they are referred to as those who refused to worship the image of the beast and were "killed." Others also take the group seen in 7:9ff. as martyred saints in heaven. At any rate, the question arises as to why the martyrs alone receive so much attention rather than all suffering or persecuted Christians. One solution understands John to be referring to all those who so faithfully follow Christ as to form a group that may be characterized as the slain of the Lord. They may or may not actually suffer physical death for Christ, but they have (like John) so identified themselves with the slain Lamb that they have in effect already offered up their lives ("because of the word of God and the testimony they had maintained" [cf. 1:2, 9]); and they are seen as a group (cf. Rom 8:36).

John says that he saw the "souls" (*psychas*) of those slain (v.9). This is generally understood to mean the disembodied souls of these saints. However, the Greek word *psychē* has various meanings and probably stands here for the actual "lives" or "persons" who were killed rather than for their "souls." They are seen by John as persons who are very much alive though they have been killed by the beast. "Under the altar" sets the scene as occurring in the temple of heaven. Depending on which altar is meant, one of two different ideas is connoted. In 8:3, 5 and 9:13 the altar is the golden altar of incense that stood in the tabernacle either in or before the Most Holy Place (Exod 30:1ff.; Heb 9:4). Likewise, the other references in Revelation to "altar" also can be understood as referring to this altar of incense (11:1; 14:18; 16:7). In accord with this sense, the prayers of the saints would be for God's vindication of the martyrs of Christ (cf. Luke 18:7–8). On the other hand, some understand this as the brazen altar of sacrifice and see in the imagery the blood of the martyrs at the base or "under the altar" (Ladd, *Commentary on Revelation*, in loc.). But if the symbolism was sacrificial, it would be more natural to read "on" the altar, not "under" it.

The martyred address God as "Sovereign Lord" (*despotēs*) (v.10). This term implies "ownership" (TDNT, 2:44) and is used elsewhere in the NT to denote slave masters (1 Tim 6:1; Peter 2:18), God (Luke 2:29; Acts 4:24), or Jesus Christ (2 Peter 2:1; Jude 4). (On the phrase "holy and true," cf. comments on 3:7.) The martyrs cry for God's vengeance on the evildoers. The word "avenge" (*ekdikeō*) relates everywhere in the OT (LXX) and in the NT to the idea of punishment or retribution (TDNT, 2:442ff.). These saints are following the teaching of Paul in Romans 12:19: "Do not take revenge, my friends, but leave room for God's wrath, for it is written: 'It is mine to avenge, I will repay,' says the Lord." Though believers are forbidden to take revenge, God will vindicate his elect by punishing those who killed them (Luke 18:7f.; 2 Thess 1:8).

The martyrs were each given a "white robe" as an evidence of their righteousness and victory before the Judge of all the earth, who will speedily avenge their deaths. The wait of a "little longer" is in God's estimate but a fleeting moment, though for us it may stretch out for ages (cf. 12:12; 20:3). The DSS refer to the final reward of the righteous as "the garment of honour in everlasting light" (1QS 4.8). The expression "until the number of their fellow servants . . . was completed" presents a slight exegetical difficulty (cf. Notes). It is usually taken to mean that the number of either the martyred or their companions on earth who will be killed will be completed (so NIV). However, another sense may be possible. The verb "completed" (*plēroō*) may mean "until their fellow servants complete their course," or "fulfill their Christian calling," which will involve also martyrdom. In any event, what constitutes the essence of Christian discipleship in John's eyes should not be overlooked. As Lilje says, "Every believer in Christ ought to be prepared for martyrdom; for Christians . . . cannot express their priestly communion with their Lord more perfectly than when they accept the suffering and the glory of martyrdom" (p. 130).

12–14 The sixth seal is broken by the Lamb, and John witnesses certain eschatological signs heralding the imminent, final day of the Lord so often described in Scripture (e.g., Isa 2:10, 19, 21; 13:10; 34:4; Jer 4:29; Ezek 32:7–8; Joel 2:31; 3:15; Zeph 1:14–18; Matt 24:29; Luke 21:11, 25–26). The signs are threefold: (1) the great earthquake and its storm affecting the sun and moon, (2) the stars falling, and (3) the terror on earth (vv.15–17). It is difficult to know how literally the whole description should be taken. Some of the events are described from the standpoint of ancient cosmology—e.g., the falling of the stars to earth like figs from a shaken tree, or the sky rolling up like a scroll. The firmament suspended like a roof over the earth is shaken by the great earthquake.

The scene, whether taken literally or figuratively, is one of catastrophe and distress for the inhabitants of the earth. As later biblical authors seized on the earlier imagery of the theophany on Sinai to describe appearances of God to man (e.g., Hab 3:3ff.), so John utilizes the archetypal imagery of the OT to describe this terrible visitation of God's final judgment to the earth. In much the same manner as we would describe a chaotic situation by saying "all hell broke loose" (though not intending to be taken in a strictly literal sense), so the biblical writers use the language of cosmic turmoil to describe the condition of the world when God comes to judge the earth (v.17). "Earthquakes" are mentioned in Revelation 8:5; 11:13, 19; 16:18 and sun, moon, and/or stellar disturbances in 8:12; 9:2; 16:8. Of course, actual physical phenomena may also accompany the final judgment.

15–17 These verses record the terror of all classes of people at these events and at the wrath of God and the Lamb. "The kings of the earth, the princes [dignitaries], the generals" describe the powerful; "the rich, the mighty" describe the affluent and the heroes. Finally, political distinctions of the widest kind—"every slave and every free man"—are referred to. Since all kinds of people are included, we cannot say that God's wrath is directed only at the powerful, at the rich, or at false Christians. His judgment will fall on all who refuse to repent and instead worship demons and idols and persecute Christ's followers (9:20–21; 16:6, 9).

The plea of people for the rocks and mountains to fall on them (v.16) occurs in OT contexts of God's judgment (Isa 2:19, 21; Hos 10:8). It expresses the desire to be buried under the falling mountains and hills so as to escape the pains and terrors of the judgment (K D, *Minor Prophets*, 1:131). Jesus said that in this way the inhabitants of Jerusalem would cry out when God's judgment fell on the city, in A.D. 70 (Luke 23:30).

The "wrath" (*orgē*, "anger") of the Lamb is not only a new metaphor but a paradoxical one. Lambs are usually gentle. But this Lamb shows "wrath" against those who have refused his grace (cf. John 5:27). Henceforth in Revelation the wrath of God and of the Lamb is a continuing theme and is described under the figures of the trumpets and bowls (11:18; 14:7, 10, 19; 15:1, 7; 16:1, 19; 19:15). Moreover, God's wrath is a present historical reality as well as an eschatological judgment (cf. Rom 1:18ff.; 2:5). So great is the day of destruction that "who can stand?" (cf. Joel 2:11; Nah 1:6; Mal 3:2).

Notes

1 Ἔρχου (*erchou*) can mean "go forth" rather than "come," thus clearly showing that the horseman rather than John is being addressed. In 16:1, however, John uses a different word, Ὑπάγετε (*hypagete*), for "go forth." ℵ understands *erchou* as addressed to John and adds καὶ ἴδε (*kai ide*, "and see") here and also in vv.3, 5, 7 (as does the TR). "Come and see" could be understood as a rabbinic invitation to enlightenment (cf. John 1:46). There is,

however, stronger MS support for the abbreviated readings that also agree with the sense given in the exposition. When John himself is addressed, another word is used, Δεῦρο (*deuro*, "come"; 17:1; 21:9).

On the problem of the identification of the white horse and its rider, see Mathias Rissi, "The Rider on the White Horse," Int, 18 (1964), 407–18, who argues for antichristic forces; Zane Hodges, "The First Horseman of the Apocalypse," BS, 119 (October 1962), 324–34, who argues for the Christ identification following the early father Irenaeus.

11 Πληρωθῶσιν (*plērōthōsin*, "was completed"), an aorist passive subjunctive, is supported by A C et al. and is followed by NIV. An alternative reading, πληρώσωσιν (*plērōsōsin*, "was complete"), the plain aorist subjunctive, is supported ℵ P et al. The passive would mean that the "number" was complete, while the plain aorist subjunctive reading favors either the sense that the fellow servants will be complete (rare intransitive sense for the verb, cf. BAG, pp. 677–78, pars. 5 and 6) or that they will complete their course.

---

3. First Interlude (7:1–17)

Indications that chapter 7 is a true interlude are the change in tone from the subject matter referred to in the sixth seal as well as the delay until 8:1 in opening the seventh seal. Two main subjects may be distinguished in the chapter. John first sees the angels who will unleash destruction on the earth restrained until the 144,000 servants of God from every tribe of Israel are sealed (vv. 1–8). Then he sees an innumerable multitude clothed in white standing before the throne of God, who are identified as those who have come out of the "great tribulation" (vv. 9–17). As Charles remarks, this chapter is in many respects one of the most difficult and yet most important in the book (*Commentary on Revelation*, 1:189). Lilje calls the whole picture one of the most glorious in the entire Apocalypse. It probably functions both prospectively and retrospectively.

The principal exegetical difficulty in chapter 7 centers around the identification of the 144,000 (vv. 1–8) and the identification of the innumerable multitude (vv. 9–17). Is the reference to the tribes of Israel symbolic, representative, or literal? What is the "great tribulation" (v. 14)? Are those described in 7:9ff. martyrs? There is considerable divergence of opinion about these questions. The dialogue can be traced only briefly.

a. The 144,000 Israelites

7:1–8

> [1]After this I saw four angels standing at the four corners of the earth, holding back the four winds of the earth to prevent any wind from blowing on the land or on the sea or on any tree. [2]Then I saw another angel coming up from the east, having the seal of the living God. He called out in a loud voice to the four angels who had been given power to harm the land and the sea: [3]"Do not harm the land or the sea or the trees until we put a seal on the foreheads of the servants of our God." [4]Then I heard the number of those who were sealed: 144,000 from all the tribes of Israel.
>
> > [5]From the tribe of Judah 12,000 were sealed,
> > from the tribe of Reuben 12,000,
> > from the tribe of Gad 12,000,
> > [6]from the tribe of Asher 12,000,
> > from the tribe of Naphtali 12,000,
> > from the tribe of Manasseh 12,000,

81

> [7] from the tribe of Simeon, 12,000,
> from the tribe of Levi 12,000,
> from the tribe of Issachar 12,000,
> [8] from the tribe of Zebulun 12,000,
> from the tribe of Joseph 12,000,
> from the tribe of Benjamin 12,000.

1–3 The "four angels" at "the four corners of the earth" hold "the four winds of the earth" from blowing on the earth until the servants of God are sealed on their foreheads. The expression "the four corners of the earth" was used in antiquity among the Near-Eastern nations much as we use "the four points of the compass." Since nowhere in Revelation do we read of the four winds actually blowing, they may be taken as representing the earthly catastrophes that occur under the trumpets and bowls.

Another angel comes from the "east" (possibly from Jerusalem or Zion, to emphasize its mission of salvation?) and calls to the four others not to release their destruction until the servants of God have a "seal" on their foreheads. Such a seal surely indicates ownership by God and the Lamb (14:1). Furthermore, a seal may offer protection or security for the bearers. Such seems to be the emphasis in 9:4, where the demonic forces are told to harm "only those people who did not have the seal [sphragis] of God on their foreheads." Charles believes that only protection from demonic forces is involved in the sealing rather than escape from physical harm from the plagues, from the Antichrist, or protection from spiritual apostasy (R.H. Charles, *Studies in the Apocalypse* [Edinburgh: T. & T. Clark, 1913], p. 124f.).

By examining references to events that happened to those who, by contrast, have the "mark" (*charagma*) of the beast (13:16–17), Charles's view may be evaluated. In 13:16–17, those who do not have the mark of the beast face severe socio-economic sanctions. Those who have the mark of the beast are not only identified as beast worshipers but become the objects of the irreversible wrath of God (14:9, 11). This implies, by contrast, that those who have "the seal [sphragis] of God" are God worshipers and will be the objects of his abiding grace. In 16:2, the bowl of God's wrath appears to be directed exclusively toward those who have the mark of the beast, thus excluding those with the seal of God (cf. 16:6). Those having the mark of the beast are deluded by the beast (19:20), this statement implying that the sealed of God are not thus deceived. Finally, a martyred group is seen just prior to their resurrection and thousand-year reign with Christ and are described as not having the mark of the beast or worshiping him (20:4).

In the light of these passages, we may say that the "sealed" are the people of God and that their sealing must be related to their salvation as in the comparable figure used by Paul (2 Cor 1:22; Eph 1:13; 4:30; cf. 4 Ezra 6:5). This is also evident in 14:3–4, where the sealed are described as those who were redeemed from the earth as firstfruits to God (cf. Rom 8:23; James 1:18). In fact, "baptism" was considered a "seal" of salvation in the early church (cf. BAG, p. 804, s.v. *sphragis*).

Furthermore, while the seal may not protect the sealed against harm inflicted by human agency (13:7; 20:4), they are protected from the divine plagues (16:2). It is clear that the protection from famine, pestilence, and sword afforded the sealed in the apocryphal Psalms of Solomon (15:6, 9) cannot also apply to John's sealed, since they are beheaded (20:4). As for OT background for the problem, Ezekiel 9:4–7 may well be primary. In this passage a divine messenger with stylus in hand was to go through the apostate Jerusalem of Ezekiel's day and put a mark upon the foreheads of those who deplored the faithless idolatry of the Israelites. Those so marked were the faithful and true servants of God in contrast to the professed but false servants who had abandoned him. The sealed would be spared the divine slaughtering of the rebellious inhabitants of the city. Interestingly, the "mark" (*taw*) in the Phoenician script looked like a cross (✝) and was later adopted by early Jewish Christians as a symbol of their faith in Jesus ("The Chi-Rho-Sign-Christogram and/or Staurogram," Matthew Black, *Apostolic History and the Gospel*, ed. W. Gasque and R.P. Martin [Grand Rapids: Eerdmans, 1970], pp. 319–27).

The sealing language would have the effect of assuring the people of God of his special concern and plan for them. Even when facing persecution and martyrdom at the hand of the beast, they can be certain that no plague from God will touch them but that they will be in his presence forever because they are his very own possession. Therefore, the seal on the forehead is equivalent to the divine mark of ownership on them that elsewhere in the NT is referred to the presence of the Holy Spirit (2 Cor 1:22; Eph 1:13; 4:30). This act of God will fulfill the promise to the Philadelphian church: "Since you have kept my command to endure patiently, I will also keep you from the hour of trial that is going to come upon the whole world to test those who live on the earth" (3:10). Consequently, those thus sealed must be Christians and not unconverted Jews or Gentiles (contra Robert Gundry, *The Church and the Tribulation* [Grand Rapids: Zondervan, 1973], p. 83).

4 John next gives the number of those sealed—144,000—and their identification: "From all the tribes of Israel." There are two principal views regarding the identification of this group: (1) The number and the tribal identifications are taken literally and refer to 144,000 Jewish Christians who are sealed (to protect them from destruction) during the time of the Great Tribulation (J.A. Seiss, *The Apocalypse* [Grand Rapids: Zondervan, 1957], pp. 160f.; Walvoord, pp. 140f.). (2) According to another viewpoint, John is understood to use the language of the new Israel and thus refers to the completed church composed of Jew and Gentile (Alf, p. 624; Beckwith, p. 535; Caird, p. 95; Swete, pp. 96–97).

In support of the first view is the normal usage of "Israel" in the NT as referring to the physical descendants of Jacob. Galatians 6:16 is no exception, as Peter Richardson observes: "Strong confirmation of this position [i.e., that 'Israel' refers to the Jews in the NT] comes from the total absence of an identification of the church with Israel until A.D. 160; and also from the total absence, even then, of the term 'Israel of God' to characterize the church" (*Israel in the Apostolic Church* [Cambridge: Cambridge University, 1969], pp. 74–84). Reference to the Twelve Tribes (vv.5–8) would most naturally be understood to refer to the ancient historic Israel and not to the church. The view that the Ten Tribes were "lost" in the first-century, though it is popular, hardly needs refuting (cf. IDB, 4:699f.; F.F. Bruce, *The Book of Acts*, NIC [Grand Rapids: Eerdmans, 1954], p. 489, n.13). Thus, in this first view, John would symbolically be describing the beginning of what Paul foretold in Romans 11:25–29 as the salvation of "all Israel."

In support of the second view, which identifies Israel with the church, is the fact that the NT identifies the followers of Christ as "Abraham's seed" (Gal 3:29), as "the true circumcision" (Phil 3:3) and as the "Israel of God" (Gal 6:16; though disputed, cf. above). Furthermore, John himself earlier in Revelation makes a distinction between the true Jew and the false (cf. 2:9; 3:9) and that could imply that here in chapter 7 he intends also to designate the true Israel or the church (Ladd, *Commentary on Revelation*, p. 116). Additional support for this view is found if there is a unity between the first and second groups in chapter 7, groups that otherwise must be treated as different and unconnected.

Without discussing at length the disputed issue of the Jew as Israel versus the church as Israel (though it obviously bears on the interpretation of this passage), we may agree with Walvoord, who says, "The decision as to who are included in the term 'Israel' should be reached on the basis of exegesis and usage" (p. 143). Those who argue that the term "Israel" in other NT books refers exclusively to Jews are in our opinion correct (so Richardson). Strict exegesis, however, must also ask whether the author of Revelation wishes the term to have this same more restricted usage or whether he uses it differently. It is possible that the usage of the term "Jew" among Christians had undergone a historic change from the earlier days when Paul wrote Romans (A.D. 56) until Revelation was written toward the close of the century.

By the middle of the first century, Paul made a distinction between the true, spiritual Jew and the physical descendants of Abraham (Rom 2:28–29; 9:8). Only those Jews who recognized Jesus as Messiah could rightly be called "Israel" in the strictest sense (Rom 9:6), though the term might be used with qualifications to refer to the historic descendants of Jacob ("Israel after the flesh" [1 Cor 10:18 Gr.]). Peter likewise described the church (Jew and Gentile) in terms drawn from the OT that historically describe the true people of God among the Jewish descendants ("holy priesthood . . . chosen people . . . royal priesthood . . . holy nation" [1 Peter 2:4, 9]). Moreover, even Gentiles who received Jesus as the Messiah and Lord were considered "Abraham's seed" (Gal 3:29) and the true "circumcision" (Phil 3:3).

Already in Revelation there has been the distinction between Jews who were Jews in name only and not true Jews because they did not acknowledge Jesus as Lord (2:9; 3:9). Also, the OT image of the people of Israel as a kingdom and priests to God is used by John of the followers of Jesus (1:6). Similarly, many of the promises to the victors in the churches of Asia (chs. 2–3) are fulfillments of OT promises given to the true people of Israel. In Christ's rebuke to the churches, we have the OT imagery of "Balaam" and "Jezebel" describing error that had influenced not the OT Israel but the NT church. In chapter 12, it is again difficult to distinguish whether the "woman" represents the ancient Jewish covenant people or the NT followers of Jesus. In Revelation 21:9–12, the church is called the "bride, the wife of the Lamb"; she is identified with the New Jerusalem, and on its twelve gates are inscribed the "names of the twelve tribes of Israel." Even in the Gospel of John (assuming the apostle wrote it as well as Revelation), Jesus is the "true vine," which many commentators understand to be an allusion to the vine that decorated the temple entrance and stood as a symbol for Israel (cf. Isa 5:1ff. with John 15:1ff.). Jesus is claiming to be the true Israel and his followers, then, the branches, would be related to the true Israel (cf. Rom 11:17–24).

The usage seems evident in the NT itself; the only question is whether John takes the final step in Revelation and, in the context of a largely Gentile church, uses the OT terminology to speak of the church. Richardson's summary is provocative:

> As long as the church was viewed as a community gathered from Gentiles and Jews, it could not readily call itself "Israel." But when it was sharply separated from both, and when it had a theory that Judaism no longer stood in continuity with Israel *ante Christum,* and when Gentiles not only could take over other titles but in some

cases could claim exclusive rights to them, then the church as an organizational entity could appropriate "Israel" (*Apostolic Church,* p. 204).

All this simply suggests the possibility that in John's mind the followers of Jesus (14:4) are the true servants of God, the Israel of God (cf. John 11:51–52). Richardson also observes that in Qumranic and late Jewish apocalyptic literature the term "Israel" was jealously and exclusively restricted to members of certain Jewish groups who even denied its use to other Jews and claimed that only they were the true Israel of God (ibid., pp. 217ff.).

The identification of the 144,000 with the whole elect people of God, including both Jews and Gentiles, does not negate Paul's teaching to the effect that the majority of the Jews themselves will one day be brought back into a relationship of salvation before God. John simply is not dealing with Paul's emphasis at this point in Revelation (but cf. at 11:2f.).

Mounce has a further suggestion on the identity of the two groups in the chapter. He states:

> The position taken in the following pages is that in both visions it is the church which is in view, but from two vantage points. Prior to the trumpet judgments the last generation of believers is sealed so as to be saved from the destruction coming upon the earth and to be brought safely into the heavenly kingdom. The second vision is anticipatory of the eternal blessedness of all believers when in the presence of God they realize the rewards of faithful endurance (*Revelation,* p. 164).

But Mounce later identifies the "great tribulation" (7:14) through which the second group passes as "that final series of woes which will immediately precede the end" (ibid., p. 173). This seems to contradict the earlier statement that the second group represents "all believers." Confessedly this is a difficult chapter. Perhaps the confusion revolves around our inability to understand John's precise perspective on "the great tribulation."

The number 144,000 is obviously obtained by combining 12,000 for each of the twelve tribes of Israel (vv.5–8). Earlier in Revelation (cf. 4:4), twenty-four (a multiple of twelve) serves as a symbolic number. The "thousand" multiple appears again—this time in relation to the size of the Holy City: "He measured the city with the rod and found it to be 12,000 stadia in length, and as wide and high as it is long" (21:16). Thus, 12,000 is symbolic of completeness and perfection. Even the wall is "144 cubits" (twelves times twelve) (v.17). The tree of life bearing "twelve crops of fruit, yielding its fruit every month" (i.e., twelve months) (22:2) further supports the view that John intends the number twelve to be taken symbolically and not literally. By 144,000, he signifies the sealing of *all* or the *total* number of God's servants who will face the Great Tribulation.

Those who are sealed come from "all the tribes of Israel," and this emphasizes even more the universality and comprehensiveness of the Christian gospel. Whereas in first-century Judaism there were many sects with exclusive tribal claims to being the true Israel, for the followers of Jesus all such sectarianism is broken down and all groups, regardless of race, culture, religious background, or geographical location, are accepted before God (7:9; 14:4). There is an exclusivism in Revelation, but it is based on loyalty to Christ, not on historical or liturgical continuity.

5-8 John goes even further. He enumerates each of the twelve tribes and their number: "From the tribe of Judah 12,000 were sealed," etc. Why was it necessary to provide this detailed enumeration? And why the particular tribal selection? In answering these difficult questions, some facts about the list should be noted. John places Judah first, evidently to emphasize the priority of the messianic King who came from the tribe of Judah (Rev 5:5; Heb 7:13–14). Nowhere in the tribal listings of the OT except in the space arrangement of the wilderness camp (Num 2:3ff.) does Judah come first. This exception may itself be linked with the messianic expectation through Judah (Gen 49:10; 1 Chron 5:2). John's priority of Judah is comparable to the emphasis placed in late Judaism on the tribe of Levi (the priestly tribe). It is significant that John includes Levi among the other tribes, and thus gives no special place to the Levitical order, and that he also places Levi in the comparatively unimportant eighth place.

The particular order and names of the tribes as given here by John is unique. The OT has no fewer than twenty variant lists of the tribes, and these lists include anywhere from ten to thirteen tribes, though the number twelve is predominant (cf. Gen 49; Deut 33; Ezek 48). The grouping of twelve may be a way of expressing the corporate identity of the elect people of God as a whole and may be maintained—even artificially at times—to preserve this identity (cf. the need to make up the "twelfth" apostle when Judas fell [Act 1:25–26]). John omits Dan (which elsewhere is always included) and Ephraim. In order to maintain the ideal number twelve with these omissions, he must list both Joseph and Manasseh as tribes. This is peculiar because the tribe of Joseph is always mentioned in the other lists by either including Joseph and excluding his two sons, Ephraim and Manasseh (Gen 49), or by omitting Joseph and counting the two sons as one tribe each (Ezek 48). It is not until the Levitical priesthood gains more prominence that the tribe of Levi is omitted from the lists and is replaced by the two sons of Joseph.

Various efforts have been made to solve the enigma of John's list and especially to explain the absence of the tribe of Dan. As yet, we have no completely satisfactory solution. Ladd's proposal is interesting: "John intends to say [by the irregular list] that the twelve tribes of Israel are not really literal Israel, but the true, spiritual Israel—the church" (*Commentary on Revelation,* p. 115). While this may be true, whether the mere irregularity of the list is intended to convey it is questionable. It might be more helpful to seek some satisfactory reason why John specifically omitted Dan and Ephraim.

The early church held that the Antichrist would arise from the tribe of Dan. Charles has argued that this belief is in fact pre-Christian Jewish tradition, first mentioned in Christian sources in Irenaeus (d. second century A.D.) (R.H. Charles, *The Apocrypha and Pseudepigrapha of the Old Testament,* 2 vols. [Oxford: Clarendon, 1913], 2:334). Furthermore, Dan was associated in the OT with idolatry (Judg 18:18–19; 1 Kings 12:29–30). This may be the clue. If John sought to expose Christian idolatry and beast worship in his day by excluding Dan from the list of those sealed, it may also be possible to explain, on the same basis, why Manasseh and Joseph were chosen to fill up the sacred number rather than Manasseh and Ephraim. In the OT Ephraim was also explicitly identified with idolatry (Hos 4:17). Qumran literature is of little help because in it both Ephraim and Manasseh are apostate tribes (4Qp Nah 7; 4Qp Ps 37:3—cited by Richardson, *Apostolic Church,* p. 227 and A. Dupont-Sommer, *The Essene Writings from Qumran,* tr. G. Vermes [Cleveland: World, 1962], p. 269, n.2; p. 273, n.2).

If idolatry, then, seems to be the reason for omitting both Dan and Ephraim, the readjustment of the list to include Joseph and Manasseh to complete the twelve can be understood. Since Dan will be reckoned first in the tribal listing of the restored eschatological Jewish community (Ezek 48) and John's list puts Judah first, it may be that John's listing describes the church rather than ethnic Israel.

It is important to note that John does not equate the 144,000 with all in the tribes. Rather, his repeated use of the preposition *ek* ("from") in vv. 4–8 implies that the sealed were an elect group chosen out of the tribes: "144,000 from all the tribes of Israel. . . . From the tribe of Judah 12,000 were sealed," etc. If John had the actual Jewish Israel in view, this use of "from" would indicate an election from the whole nation. On the other hand, if he intended to imply something about the church, his language might indicate God's selecting the true church out "from" the professing church. This thought has been mentioned earlier (cf. 2:14ff., 20ff.; 3:16ff.) and is supported by Ezekiel 9:4–7, where the seal identified the true servants of God from the false ones among the professing people of God (see above under vv. 2–3). Paul stated the same thought when he wrote, "Nevertheless, God's solid foundation stands firm, sealed with this inscription: 'The Lord knows those who are his,' and 'Everyone who confesses the name of the Lord must turn away from wickedness'" (2 Tim 2:19).

The description of the judgments under the sixth seal (6:12ff.) ends with the question "The great day of their wrath has come, and who can stand?" (6:17). Chapter 7 answers this question by implying that only the true servants of God, who are divinely sealed, can be protected from the wrath of God and the Lamb.

Notes

4–8 For a more thorough discussion of the various views on the identification of the 144,000, see Gundry, *Church and the Tribulation*, pp. 81ff.; Charles *Studies in the Apocalypse*, pp. 114–15; Elliott, 1:226ff.

b. *The great white-robed multitude*

7:9–17

9After this I looked and there before me was a great multitude that no one could count, from every nation, tribe, people and language, standing before the throne and in front of the Lamb. They were wearing white robes and were holding palm branches in their hands. 10And they cried out in a loud voice:

"Salvation belongs to our God,
who sits on the throne,
and to the Lamb."

11All the angels were standing around the throne and around the elders and the four living creatures. They fell down on their faces before the throne and worshiped God, 12saying:

"Amen!
Praise and glory
and wisdom and thanks and honor
and power and strength
be to our God for ever and ever.
Amen!"

¹³Then one of the elders asked me, "These in white robes—who are they, and where did they come from?"

¹⁴I answered, "Sir, you know."

And he said, "These are they who have come out of the great tribulation; they have washed their robes and made them white in the blood of the Lamb. ¹⁵Therefore,

"they are before the throne of God
and serve him day and night in his temple;
and he who sits on the throne will spread his tent
over them.
¹⁶Never again will they hunger;
never again will they thirst.
The sun will not beat upon them,
nor any scorching heat.
¹⁷For the Lamb at the center of the throne will be
their shepherd;
he will lead them to springs of living water.
And God will wipe away every tear from their eyes."

John now sees a great multitude from every nation and cultural background, standing before the throne of God and clothed in white robes. They are identified by the angel as those "who have come out of the great tribulation" (v.14). Again, the question is that of identity. Are they the Gentiles who are saved in the Tribulation in contrast to the Jews in vv.1–8? Beckwith answers no because they are described as coming from every nation and tribe and language, and this would mean both Jews and Gentiles (p. 539). Are they, then, martyrs who have given their lives in the Great Tribulation and have been slain by the beast? If martyrs, are they the remainder of those to be killed referred to when the fifth seal is opened (6:11)? Are they the complete group of martyrs? Or do they represent the whole company of the redeemed in Christ as seen in glory?

Although there is no direct evidence that the great multitude are martyrs, there are some indications of this: (1) they are seen in heaven "before the throne" (v.9) and "in his temple" (v.15); (2) they are described as those "who have come out of the great tribulation" (v.14). Thus it is assumed that, since they have died in the Great Tribulation, they have most likely been martyred because the Tribulation will be a time of great killing of the saints (17:6; 18:24; 19:2; 20:4, etc.).

The multitude would not be the whole company of the martyred throughout history but only those who were victims of the beast persecution during the Great Tribulation. The group is probably those future martyrs referred to under the fifth seal as those "who were to be killed as they had been" (6:11). Neither, then, would they be the whole redeemed church as Beckwith and Eller suggest, unless all Christians are to be identified with the martyrs.

The identification of this second group is related to the identification of the first one (vv.1–8). Some argue that the two groups must be different because the first is numbered, the second innumerable; the first is limited to Jews, the second refers to every nation (Gundry, *Church and the Tribulation*, p. 81). These objections are not serious if we recall the exposition of vv.1–8, where it was noted that (1) the number of the sealed was symbolic and not literal and that (2) the delineation of the Twelve Tribes was seen as John's deliberate attempt to universalize the election of God. Thus, what some have seen as contrasts may actually be designed to complement each other and show the continuity of the first group with the second. Furthermore, we should bear in mind that John does not see any group at all in vv.1–8 but merely hears the number of the sealed, whereas in vv.9–17 he actually sees a group and describes what he sees and hears. Therefore, the unity of both groups can be maintained and vv.9–17 understood as the interpretative key to the 144,000. John's vision then leaps ahead to a scene in heaven after the Great Tribulation has run its course and views the glorified Tribulation saints as being in God's presence, at rest from their trial, and serving him continually.

Two slightly different variations of the more literal Jewish identity of those in vv.1–8 and the relationship of this first group to the second (vv.9ff.) are quite popular today. Some see the 144,000 as a select group of Jews who will be converted to Jesus shortly after the rapture of the church to heaven. These Jewish evangelists will preach the gospel to the world during the Tribulation. As a result of their preaching, a great multitude of Gentiles will be converted to Christ (A.C. Gaebelein, *The Revelation*, [New York: Our Hope, 1915], pp. 58–59).

Others, accepting a posttribulational view of the church's rapture, understand the 144,000 as a literal Jewish remnant preserved physically through the Tribulation and converted immediately after the Rapture. They will be the people who will constitute the beginning of the restored Jewish Davidic Kingdom at the inception of the millennial reign of Christ on the earth (Gundry, *Church and the Tribulation*, pp. 82–83).

The Bible speaks of three different types of tribulation or distress, and it is important to distinguish between them:

1. There is tribulation that is inseparable from Christian life in the world (John 16:33; Acts 14:22; Rom 5:3; 2 Tim 2:11–12; 1 Peter 4:12; Rev 1:9; 2:10, etc.). All Christians during all ages participate in tribulation. Thus they share in the continuing sufferings of Christ (Col 1:24).

2. The Bible also speaks of an intense tribulation that will come on the final generation of Christians and climax all previous persecutions. Daniel 12:1 refers to such a time: "There will be a time of distress [*thlipseōs*, LXX] such as has not happened from the beginning of nations until then." Likewise, Jesus predicts such an unprecedented persecution: "For then there will be great distress [*thlipsis*], unequaled from the beginning of the world until now—and never to be equaled again" (Matt 24:21). Paul's mention of "the rebellion" (*apostasia*) and "the man of lawlessness" surely refers to this same period (2 Thess 2:3ff.). In Revelation this more intense persecution is mentioned in 7:14; 11:7–10; 13:7; 16:6, and possibly the events under the fifth seal should be included here (6:9–11; so J. Barton Payne, *The Imminent Appearing of Christ* [Grand Rapids: Eerdmans, 1962], p. 115). This future tribulation is distinguished from previous persecutions of the church in its intensity, in its immediate connection with Christ's second coming, and in the presence of Antichrist during it.

3. Scripture also speaks of a future time of God's intense wrath on unbelievers. Revelation refers to this as "the great day of their wrath" (6:17) and "the hour of trial that is going to come upon the whole world to test those who live on the earth" (3:10). Such wrath from God comes especially under the trumpets and bowls (8:2ff.; 16:1ff.). Probably drawing on the teaching of Jesus in the Olivet Discourse (Matt 24), Paul refers to this punitive action of God in 2 Thessalonians 1:6–10 and even uses the word *thlipsis* ("trouble"). While for Christians the Great Tribulation may be concurrent with a portion of the period of God's wrath on the rebellious, the final and more intense judgment of God seems to *follow* the Great Tribulation itself and is directly connected with the coming of Christ (Matt 24:29; Rev 6:12ff.; 19:11ff.).

9 "A great multitude . . . from every nation, tribe, people and language" pictures what Swete calls a "polyglot cosmopolitan crowd" (p. 97). The words might well describe the crowds common to the agora or the quay of a seaport in first-century Asia. (Similar fourfold descriptions of the members of the Christian community or of the inhabitants of the world also occur in Rev 5:9; 11:9; 13:7; 14:6; 17:15.) "Standing before the throne and in front of the Lamb" signifies their position of acceptance and honor as God's true servants (cf. v.15) and reminds us of the continuity of this vision with the earlier vision of the throne and the Lamb (chs.4–5). This group seems to complete the full circle of participants before the throne begun in chapter 4.

Their "white robes" impress John and are an important feature of the vision (vv.9, 13–14). We cannot fail to connect them with the white robes given the martyrs under the fifth seal (6:11). The white robes symbolize salvation and victory (v.10), and their possessors obtained them by "[washing] their robes and [making] them white in the blood of the Lamb" (v.14). This implies that they were true recipients of Christ's redemption in contrast to others who, though professing belief in Christ, were not genuine overcomers (cf. 3:5–6, 18).

"The blood of the Lamb" connotes here more even than the profound reference to the sacrificial death of Jesus (5:9); it also suggests faithful witness in following Jesus in his death (2:13; 12:11).

"Palm branches" are referred to only one other time in the NT (John 12:13), where they are connected to the Passover celebration. Moses provided that palms should be used at the Feast of Tabernacles (Lev 23:40). Later they were used on other festal occasions (1 Macc 13:51; 2 Macc 10:7). Jewish coins of the period 140 B.C. to A.D. 70 frequently contain palms and some have the inscription "the redemption of Zion" (IDB, 3:646). Palms were emblems of victory. In John 12 they denote the triumph of Christ, while here in Revelation the reference is to the victory of the servants of Christ (Deiss BS, pp. 368–70).

10 In accord with the literary symmetry of chapters 4–7, this group also expresses their worship of the King and the Lamb. Their praise to God is for his "salvation" (*sōtēria*), not their own accomplishments. Since the same word is associated with the final manifestation of God's power and kingdom (12:10; 19:1), here it may also denote God's final victory over sin and the principalities of this world that crucified Christ and that kill his true disciples (cf. Isa 49:8; 2 Cor 6:2).

11–12 Finally, the angelic hosts respond to the cry of the redeemed (v.10) with "Amen" and voice their praise and worship of God for the salvation given to men (cf. Luke 15:10). Compare this doxology with 5:12–13.

13–14 After the manner of the OT apocalyptic passages, the interpreting angel asks concerning the white-robed throng, "Who are they, and where did they come from?" (cf. Dan 7:15–16; Zech 1:9, 19; 4:1–6). Here and in 5:5 are the only references in Revelation to an elder speaking individually, a fact that supports the view that the elders in Revelation are angels and not a symbolic group representing the church.

The reference to the washed robes should be viewed in relation to 3:4, where soiled clothes represent defection from Christ through unbelief and worship of false gods (cf. 21:8). On the "great tribulation," see the introduction to this section.

15 This and the following verses describe the activity and condition of the true servants of God in their future and eternal relation to the Lamb. The scene is one of the most beautiful in the Bible. In it those who have washed their robes in the blood of the Lamb are described as being before the throne of God without fear or tremor, fully accepted by the divine Majesty. What are they doing? Theirs is no state of passivity but of continual service of God in praise and worship.

The reference to the "temple" of God raises the question whether the scene describes the final state of the saints or an intermediate state, as 21:22 tells us that the New Jerusalem has no temple. However, the language used in vv. 15–17 (esp. v. 17) seems to depict the same condition as that of the saints in chapters 21 and 22 (cf. 21:3–4, 6; 22:1). Since 7:15 relates to worship, it would be appropriate to refer to the presence of God and the Lamb as "in" the temple. In 21:22, however, the future existence of the people of God is described as a city; and in that glorious city, unlike the pagan cities of the present world, there will be no special temple in which to worship God because God himself and the Lamb will be present everywhere.

To "spread his tent [*skēnoō*] over them," or to "reside permanently" (TDNT, 7:385), calls to mind the shekinah presence in the OT tabernacle or temple (Exod 40:34–38; 1 Kings 8:10–11; cf. Ezek 10:4, 18–19) and later in Jesus (John 1:14) and also the idea of a permanent residence (Rev 21:3). Never again will these people endure torment. They have the supreme protection of the living God himself.

16 The condition described here contrasts to the earthly experience of those who suffered much for their faith (cf. Heb. 11:37–38). For them, starvation, thirst, and the burning desert are forever past. There may be allusion here to Isaiah 49:10, which places the time of relief from such distresses in the days of Messiah's kingdom. There may also be an allusion to what the four horsemen bring (6:1–8; cf. Matt 24:7).

17 We now have a beautiful pastoral figure—that of the Lamb shepherding his people (cf. John 10:1–8; Heb 13:20; 1 Peter 2:25). It is not through some perfect environment but through the presence and continual ministry of the Lamb that their sufferings are forever assuaged. Whereas on earth their enemies may have tormented them, now the Lamb guides them: "He will lead [*hodēgēsei*, the same verb is used of the Holy Spirit in John 16:13] them to springs of living water." In contrast to the burning thirst experienced in their tribulation, now they will enjoy the refreshing waters of life. Thus in the future life the saints will not know stagnation, boredom, or satiation (Ps 23:1f.; Jer 2:13; Ezek 47:1–12; Zech 14:8).

Finally, even the sorrowful memory of the pain and suffering of the former days will be mercifully removed by the Father: "God will wipe away every tear from their eyes" (cf. 21:4). Tribulation produces tears. Like a tenderhearted, devoted mother, God will wipe each tear from their eyes with the eternal consolations of glory itself. Never again will they cry out because of pain or suffering. Only through the Resurrection can all this become real (Isa 25:8; 1 Cor 15:54).

Notes

---

14 The correct translation of the nominative participle οἱ ἐρχόμενοι (*hoi erchomenoi*, "they who have come out of") is a problem. Grammatically, present participles depend on the main verb for their time of action and are generally coincident in time with it. But is the time of action here the time of John's writing or, for John, some future time? If it is present time for John, the translation would be "they who are coming out of the great tribulation." If future, two possibilities arise: (1) The time is in the future when the vision is to be fulfilled. In this case, the description looks back to the earthly scene that preceded the heavenly bliss: "They who have come [or 'were coming'] out of the great tribulation" (NIV). (2) The time is in the present of John's writing. In this case, the words predict what will happen: "They who will come out of the great tribulation" (cf. 1 Thess 1:10). Charles understands the construction as a Semitism and favors the idea of an imperfect participle—"were coming" (*Commentary on Revelation*, 1:213). One's theology and general exegesis of Rev will determine which rendering is preferred.

---

4. *Opening of the seventh seal*

8:1

> When he opened the seventh seal, there was silence in heaven for about half an hour.

1 After the long interlude of chapter 7, the sequence of the opening of the seals is resumed by the opening of the final or seventh seal. This action provides both a conclusion to the seals and a preparation for the seven trumpets. The praises ordinarily heard uninterruptedly in heaven (4:8) now cease in order to allow the prayers of the suffering saints on earth to be heard: "There was silence in heaven for about half an hour." Even heaven's choirs are subdued to show God's concern for his persecuted people in the Great Tribulation (8:4; cf. Luke 18:2–8). A Jewish teacher states, "In the fifth heaven are companies of angels of service who sing praises by night, but are silent by day because of the glory of Israel," i.e., that the praises of Israel may be heard in heaven (Charles, *Commentary on Revelation*, 1:223). But in John's view heaven is quieted, not to hear praises, but to hear the cries for deliverance and justice of God's persecuted servants (6:10). Most interpreters, however, understand the silence to refer to the awesome silence before the great storm of God's wrath on the earth. A kind of Sabbath pause might be thought of here. (The relation between the seals, trumpets, and bowls is discussed at 8:6.)

B. *The Seven Trumpets* (8:2–11:19)

1. *Preparatory: the angel and the golden censer*

8:2–5

> ²And I saw the seven angels who stand before God, and to them were given seven trumpets.
> ³Another angel, who had a golden censer, came and stood at the altar. He was given much incense to offer, with the prayers of all the saints, on the golden altar before the throne. ⁴The smoke of the incense, together with the prayers of the saints, went up before God from the angel's hand. ⁵Then the angel took the censer, filled it with fire from the altar, and hurled it on the earth; and there came peals of thunder, rumblings, flashes of lightning and an earthquake.

2 While the seven seals are opened by the Lamb himself, the judgments of the seven trumpets and the seven bowls (15:1) are executed by seven angels. In 1 Enoch 20:2–8, reference is made to seven angels who stand before God and are named Uriel,

Raphael, Raguel, Michael, Saraqael, Gabriel (cf. Luke 1:19), and Remiel. John may not have these in mind, but the offering up of the prayers of the saints was in Jewish thought connected with archangels (Tobit 12:15; Levi 3:7).

3–4 Before the trumpet judgments are executed, another angel enacts a symbolic scene in heaven. He takes a golden censer filled with incense and offers the incense on the altar in behalf of the prayers of all God's people. Earlier, in connection with the martyred saints (6:9), John mentioned the altar that was near God's presence. Likewise, a strong assurance is here given to the suffering followers of Christ that their prayers for vindication are not forgotten because God will speedily vindicate them from their enemies' assaults. So close is the altar to God that the incense cloud of the saints' prayers rises into his presence and cannot escape his notice (cf. Ps 141:2).

5 The censer or firepan is now used to take some of the burning coals from the altar and cast them to the earth. Symbolically, this represents the answer to the prayers of the saints through the visitation on earth of God's righteous judgments. God next appears on earth in a theophany. The language, reminiscent of Sinai with its thunder, lightning, and earthquake, indicates that God has come to vindicate his saints (Exod 19:16–19; Rev 4:5; 11:19; 16:18).

2. *Sounding of the first six trumpets*

8:6–9:21

⁶Then the seven angels who had the seven trumpets prepared to sound them.

⁷The first angel sounded his trumpet, and there came hail and fire mixed with blood, and it was hurled down upon the earth. A third of the earth was burned up, a third of the trees were burned up, and all the green grass was burned up.

⁸The second angel sounded his trumpet, and something like a huge mountain, all ablaze, was thrown into the sea. A third of the sea turned into blood, ⁹a third of the living creatures in the sea died, and a third of the ships were destroyed.

¹⁰The third angel sounded his trumpet, and a great star, blazing like a torch, fell from the sky on a third of the rivers and on the springs of water—¹¹the name of the star is Wormwood. A third of the waters turned bitter, and many people died from the waters that had become bitter.

¹²The fourth angel sounded his trumpet, and a third of the sun was struck, a third of the moon, and a third of the stars, so that a third of them turned dark. A third of the day was without light, and also a third of the night.

¹³As I watched, I heard an eagle that was flying in midair call out in a loud voice, "Woe! Woe! Woe to the inhabitants of the earth, because of the trumpet blasts about to be sounded by the other three angels!"

⁹:¹The fifth angel sounded his trumpet, and I saw a star that had fallen from the sky to the earth. The star was given the key to the shaft of the Abyss. ²When he opened the Abyss, smoke rose from it like the smoke from a gigantic furnace. The sun and sky were darkened by the smoke from the Abyss. ³And out of the smoke locusts came down upon the earth and were given power like that of scorpions of the earth. ⁴They were told not to harm the grass of the earth or any plant or tree, but only those people who did not have the seal of God on their foreheads. ⁵They were not given power to kill them, but only to torture them for five months. And the agony they suffered was like that of the sting of a scorpion when it strikes a man. ⁶During those days men will seek death, but will not find it; they will long to die, but death will elude them.

⁷The locusts looked like horses prepared for battle. On their heads they wore something like crowns of gold, and their faces resembled human faces. ⁸Their hair

was like women's hair, and their teeth were like lions' teeth. [9]They had breastplates like breastplates of iron, and the sound of their wings was like the thundering of many horses and chariots rushing into battle. [10]They had tails and stings like scorpions, and in their tails they had power to torment people for five months. [11]They had as king over them the angel of the Abyss, whose name in Hebrew is Abaddon, and in Greek, Apollyon.

[12]The first woe is past; two other woes are yet to come.

[13]The sixth angel blew his trumpet, and I heard a voice coming from the horns of the golden altar that is before God. [14]It said to the sixth angel who had the trumpet, "Release the four angels who are bound at the great river Euphrates." [15]And the four angels who had been kept ready for this very hour and day and month and year were released to kill a third of mankind. [16]The number of the mounted troops was two hundred million. I heard their number.

[17]The horses and riders I saw in my vision looked like this: Their breastplates were fiery red, dark blue, and yellow as sulfur. The heads of the horses resembled the heads of lions, and out of their mouths came fire, smoke and sulfur. [18]A third of mankind was killed by the three plagues of fire, smoke and sulfur that came out of their mouths. [19]The power of the horses was in their mouths and in their tails; for their tails were like snakes, having heads with which they inflict injury.

[20]The rest of mankind that were not killed by these plagues still did not repent of the work of their hands; they did not stop worshiping demons, and idols of gold, silver, bronze, stone and wood—idols that cannot see or hear or walk. [21]Nor did they repent of their murders, their magic arts, their sexual immorality or their thefts.

6 Two questions confront the interpreter at this point: What is the relationship of the trumpets to the preceding seals and the following bowls? Are the events described symbolic or more literal? In answer to the first question, there are two basic options: either the series are parallel and simultaneous or they are sequential or successive. It is not possible to decide with certainty for either of these views. Each contains elements of truth. Both sequential factors and parallel ingredients are evident. This commentary has already argued for the chronological priority of the first five seals to the events of the trumpets and bowls (see comments at 6:1). But the sixth seal seems to take us into the period of the outpouring of God's wrath that is enacted in the trumpet and bowl judgments (6:12–17).

The sequential factors are as follows: (1) There is a rise in the intensity of the judgments (only a part of earth and men are affected in the trumpets, but all are affected under the bowls). (2) There is a difference in sequence and content of the events described in each series. (3) The reference to those not sealed in 9:4 (fifth trumpet) presupposes the sealing of 7:1–8. (4) The explicit statement in 8:1–2 implies a sequence between seals and trumpets—"When he opened the seventh seal, . . . And I saw the seven angels . . . to them were given seven trumpets"—on which Tenney remarks, "The vision of the angels with the trumpets follows the seals directly, and conveys the impression that the seals and the trumpets are successive" (Merrill C. Tenney, *Interpreting Revelation* [Grand Rapids: Eerdmans, 1957], p. 71). (5) The bowl judgments are directly called the "last plagues" because with them God's wrath is "completed" (15:1), indicating the prior trumpet judgments. When the seventh bowl is poured out, the words "It is done" are spoken (16:17).

On the other hand, there are parallelisms. The sixth-seventh seal, the seventh trumpet (11:15ff.), and the seventh bowl (16:17ff.) all seem to depict events associated with the second coming of Christ. This last event parallelism may indicate that all these series (seals, trumpets, bowls) are parallel in their entirety or that there is a partial recapitulation or overlap in the three series. This is especially evident in connection with the sixth-seventh seal (6:12ff.), the seventh trumpet (11:15ff.), and the seventh bowl (16:17ff.). The text seems to demand some type of sequential understanding and hence rules out a complete parallelism.

The main question is whether the parallelism indicates that the events described under the sixth-seventh seal, seventh trumpet, and seventh bowl are identical or merely similar and hence really sequential and not exactly parallel. Here the following points are relevant: (1) The sixth seal brings us into the period of God's wrath on the beast worshipers but does not actually advance beyond that event to refer to the coming of Christ (6:12–17). (2) The seventh seal introduces the trumpet judgments, which run their course, and the seventh trumpet seems to bring us into the kingdom of Christ (11:15–18). (3) The seventh bowl likewise brings us to the consummation and return of Christ, that is, if we keep in mind that the incident of Babylon's destruction is an elaboration of events under the seventh bowl (16:17ff.; 19:11ff.).

But are all three series parallel in their last events (for the affirmative, see Dale Ralph Davis, "The Relationship Between the Seals, Trumpets, and Bowls in the Book of Revelation," JETS, 16 [Summer 1973], 149–58) or only parallel in the last trumpet and last bowl (so Ladd and Mounce)? Ladd and Mounce, following Beckwith, have correctly noted that the "third woe" (9:12, 11:14) is never fulfilled by the seventh trumpet, unless, that is, the content of the seventh trumpet is the seven bowls, which is also the "third woe." This is another way of saying that there is some limited recapitulation or overlap with the seventh seal and the first trumpets and in the seventh trumpet with the first bowls. This might be called a telescopic view of the seals, bowls, and trumpets. Further support for this view is also found in observing that interludes come between the sixth and seventh seals and between the sixth and seventh trumpets but not between the sixth and seventh bowls, which would be expected if the trumpets were strictly parallel to the bowls.

The second problem concerns the literalness of the events described under each trumpet. The important but hard question is not literal versus nonliteral but what did John intend? Some things may need to be understood more literally and others quite symbolically. For example, the reference to the army of 200 million (9:16–19) can hardly be literal (cf. comments on 9:16). Either the number is figurative or the army refers to demonic powers rather than human soldiers. It is also difficult to handle literally the reference to the eagle that speaks human words (8:13). While there is no way to settle this problem finally, the exposition will attempt to steer between a literal approach and a totally symbolic one.

As in the seals, there is a discernible literary pattern in the unfolding of the trumpets. The first four trumpets are separated from the last three, which are called "woes" (8:13; 9:12; 11:14), and are generally reminiscent of the plagues in Exodus. While John refers in 15:3 to the Song of Moses (Exod 15:1–18), he does not follow out the plague parallelism precisely, and the connections should not always be pressed.

Shofar trumpets (usually made of a ram's horn) were used in Jewish life as signaling instruments. They sounded alarms for war or danger as well as for peace and announced the new moon, the beginning of the Sabbath, or the death of a notable. Trumpets were also used to throw enemies into panic (Judg 7:19–20). Their use as eschatological signals of the day of the Lord or the return of Christ is well established in the OT and NT (Isa 27:13; Joel 2:1; Zeph 1:16; Matt 24:31; 1 Cor 15:52; 1 Thess 4:16). The Dead Sea community had an elaborate trumpet signal system patterned after Joshua 6 (cf. 1QM).

7 The first trumpet. Hail and fire are reminiscent of the fourth Egyptian plague of the Exodus (Exod 9:23–26), with added intensity suggested by the reference to hail and fire mixed with blood (cf. Ezek 38:22). A "third" refers to a relative fraction of the total and should not be construed as a specific amount (cf. Ezek 5:2; Zech 13:8–9).

8–9 The second trumpet. A huge blazing mass like a mountain is thrown into the sea and turns part of the sea into blood. This suggests the first plague, when the Nile was turned blood red and the fish destroyed (Exod 7:20–21; cf. Zeph 1:3). Reference to the destruction of ships shows the intense turbulence of the sea.

10–11 The third trumpet. John next sees a huge fiery star fall on the rivers and springs of water and turn a part of these fresh-water supplies into very bitter water. The star's name is "Wormwood," which refers to the quite bitter herb *Artemesia absinthium* found in the Near East and mentioned elsewhere in the Bible (Jer 9:15; 23:15; Lam 3:15, 19; Amos 5:7). It is not clear whether John intended the star to be understood as an angel as in 9:1 and in 1:20. Here is the first reference in the plagues to the loss of human life (cf. 9:15, 20). This plague, aimed at the fresh water, is a counterpart of the preceding one, which was aimed at the sea.

12 The fourth trumpet. The heavens are struck with partial darkness, reminiscent of the ninth plague (Exod 10:21–23). The references to "a third of . . ." refer to a partial impairment of the ordinary light from these bodies. In the OT the darkening of the heavens appears in connection with the theophany of God in judgment (cf. Isa 13:10; Ezek 32:7–8; Joel 2:10; 3:15; cf. Matt 24:29). An unusual darkness also attended the crucifixion of Christ (Matt 27:45).

13 Before the last three trumpets sound, John hears a flying eagle call out "woe" three times. His cry announces the especially grievous nature of the last three plagues, which kill a third part of the population of the earth (9:18). Two of the woes are identified with the fifth and sixth trumpets (9:12; 11:14). (See the comments at 8:6, which argue that the third woe should be seen as the seven bowl judgments (in 16:1ff.) The "inhabitants of the earth" distinguishes the Christ rejectors of the world from the true, faithful followers of the Lamb (cf. comments at 3:10). A flying "eagle" announces these words. This must be taken symbolically. In Revelation there are two other references to eagles (4:7; 12:14). Since 4:7 relates to the description of one of the four living beings, it may be that John intends the eagle mentioned here to have the same significance.

9:1–11 The fifth trumpet. John now focuses attention on the fifth and sixth trumpets (first and second woes) by giving more than twice the space to their description that he gives the previous four trumpets together. The fifth trumpet releases locusts from the Abyss. For five months these locusts torment the inhabitants of the earth who do not have the seal of God. John sees a "star" that has fallen to the earth. Since this star is given a key to open the Abyss, it is reasonable to understand it as being a symbolic reference to an angel. This is supported by v.11, where "the angel of the Abyss" is mentioned and named "Abaddon," as well as 20:1, where reference is also made to "an angel coming down" (i.e., stars "fall") and having the key to the Abyss, where Satan is thrown.

The Abyss is also referred to in 11:7 and 17:8 as the place from which the beast arises. The word *abyssos* ("Abyss") refers to the underworld as (1) a prison for certain demons (Luke 8:31; cf. 2 Peter 2:4; Jude 6) and (2) the realm of the dead (Rom 10:7; TDNT, 1:9). When the Abyss is opened, huge billows of smoke pour out, darken the sky, and release horselike locusts on the earth.

Locust plagues are one of the severest plagues of mankind. The imagery of locusts, appearing like armies, advancing like a cloud, darkening the heavens, and sounding like the rattle of chariots, goes back to Joel's vision of the locust army that came on Israel as a judgment from God (Joel 1:6; 2:4–10). But the locusts of the Apocalypse inflict agony like scorpion stings (vv.3, 5, 10). This, together with the fact that they do not eat grass (v.4), shows that these locusts are something other than ordinary earthly insects. Indeed, they have the special task of inflicting a nonfatal injury only on the beast worshipers, who do not have the seal of God on their foreheads (v.4); (cf. comments on 7:3). This may imply that these locustlike creatures are not simply instruments of a physical plague such as that in Moses' or Joel's day or under the first four trumpets but are demonic forces out of the Abyss from whom the true people of God are protected (cf. John's use of frogs to represent demonic powers in 16:13). The five months of agony (vv.5, 10) may refer to the life span of the locust (i.e., through spring and summer [Charles, *Commentary on Revelation*, 1:243]). So severe is the torment they inflict that their victim will seek death (v.6; cf. Job 3:21; Jer 8:3; Hos 10:8).

John describes the locusts as an army of mounted troops ready for the attack (v.7). The heads of the locusts resemble horses' heads. John does not say that the locusts had crowns of gold on their heads but that they wore "something like crowns of gold" on their heads. Charles suggests that this might refer to the yellow green of their breasts (ibid., 1:244). This, combined with their resemblance to human faces, suggests something unnatural, hence demonic. The comparison of their "hair" with that of women may refer (as in other ancient texts) to the locusts' long antennae, while their lionlike teeth suggest the terrible devastation they can bring (cf. Joel 1:6–7). The "breastplates of iron" refer to their scales, which appeared as a cuirass of metal plates across the chest and long flexible bonds of steel over the shoulders. Their sound was like the rushing of war chariots into battle (v.9; cf. Joel 2:5).

This description creates an image of the fearful onslaught of demonic powers in the last days. Therefore, their leader is called "Abaddon" in Hebrew and "Apollyon" in Greek. The Hebrew term *'aḇaddôn* means "destruction" or "ruin" (Job 26:6 mg.; Prov 27:20 mg.), and more often "the place of ruin" in Sheol (Job 26:6 mg.; Prov 15:11 mg.; 27:20 mg.), or "death" (Job 28:22 mg.), or "the grave" (Ps 88:11 mg.). In late Jewish apocalyptic texts and Qumran literature, it refers to the personification of death (IQH 3.16, 19, 32; IQ ap Gen 12:17 [TDOT, 1:23]).

The Greek term *apollyōn* means "exterminator" or "destroyer" and does not occur elsewhere in the Bible, though it can be readily understood as John's way of personifying in Greek what is personified in the Hebrew word *'aḇaddôn* (LXX *apōleia*). Some understand Apollyon as a separate angel entrusted with authority over the Abyss. Attempts to identify Apollyon with the Greek god Apollo, who in some Greek texts of Revelation is connected with the locusts, or another Greco-Roman deity have not met with much success. The creature, his name, and his responsibility seem to be original with the author of the Apocalypse.

Why John names the king of the Abyss in both Hebrew and Greek is open to question. Perhaps his readers' background in Hebrew, on which John's names and thoughts seem to turn (cf. 16:16), was so slender that an additional help here and there was necessary. This stylistic trait of giving information in bilingual terms is peculiar to Revelation and the fourth Gospel (John 6:1; 19:13, 17, 20; 20:16). It may also reveal a mind steeped in the Targum tradition of the ancient synagogue, where it was customary to render Scripture in Hebrew and then in either Aramaic or Greek for those who did not understand Hebrew.

12 This seems to be a transitional verse, indicating that the "first woe" (fifth trumpet) is finished and two woes are yet to come (presumably the sixth and seventh trumpets; cf. 8:13 with 11:14). There may be in this verse a resumption of the eagle's words (cf. 8:13).

13–19 The sixth trumpet: The second woe. Here we find a description of disasters that reach to the death of a third of mankind (vv.15, 18; cf. 8:7). "Four angels," the instruments of God's judgment, are held at the river Euphrates, whence traditionally the enemies of God's ancient people often advanced on the land of Israel (Jer 2:18 mg.; 13:4f. mg; 51:63; Rev 16:12) and which was recognized as its eastern extremity (Gen 15:18). John here makes use of the ancient geographical terms to depict the fearful character of the coming judgment of God on a rebellious world. While the language is drawn from historical-political events of the OT, it describes realities that far transcend a local geographical event. God's dealings are not accidental but planned and precise in time as to a definite hour of a definite day of a definite month of a definite year. By a reference to the "golden altar" of incense, the release of these angels is again connected with the prayers of God's saints for vindication (6:9; 8:3).

At v.16 a mounted army of some 200 million horses and riders is rather abruptly introduced. While some (e.g., Walvoord) argue for a literal human army here, several factors point to their identity as demonic forces. First, the horsemen are not in themselves important but wear brightly colored breastplates of fiery red, dark blue, and sulfurous yellow, more suggestive of supernatural than natural riders. More important are the horses, which not only have heads resembling lions but are, rather than their riders, the instruments of death by the three plagues of fire, smoke, and sulfur that come from their mouths. Furthermore, these horses have tails like snakes that are able to kill (vv.17–19), unlike the locusts' scorpionlike tails that do not inflict death but only injury (v.5). Finally, according to General William K. Harrison (an expert in military logistics), an army of 200 million could not be conscripted, supported, and moved to the Middle East without totally disrupting all societal needs and capabilities ("The War of Armageddon," xerographic copy of unpublished, undated article). As General Harrison brings out on this aspect of Revelation, God has made men with certain limitations; and the actual raising and transporting of an army of the size spoken of in v.16 completely transcends human capability. All the Allied and Axis forces at their peak in World War II were only about 70 million (*The World Almanac, 1971,* ed. L.H. Long [New York: Newspaper Enterprise Association, 1970], p. 355).

Thus it seems better to understand the vast numbers and description of the horses as indicating demonic hordes. Such large numbers do occasionally indicate angelic hosts elsewhere in Scripture (Ps 68:17; Rev 5:11; cf. 2 Kings 2:11–12; 6:17). This would not eliminate the possibility of human armies of manageable size also being involved. But the emphasis here (vv.16–19) is on their fully demonic character, utterly cruel and determined, showing no mercy to man, woman, or child. These demons might also be manifest in pestilences, epidemic diseases, or misfortunes as well as in armies. Such would explain the use of "plagues" to describe these hordes (vv.18, 20; cf. 11:6; 16:9, 21).

20–21 God's purpose for the plagues is first of all a judgment on man for his willful choice of idolatry and the corrupt practices that go with it (v.21). John had earlier called the churches to "repent" of their faithless tendencies lest they too should share in God's judgment (2:5, 16, 21–22; 3:19). In these verses we see the end result of refusing to turn to God. This stubbornness leads to worship of demons as well as worship of cultic objects made by human hands (gold, silver, bronze, stone, and wood; cf. Pss 115:4–7; 135:17; Jer 10:1–16; Dan 5:23). "Demons" may mean either pagan deities (Deut 32:17; Ps 106:37) or malign spirits (1 Cor 10:20–21; 1 Tim 4:1). But since the Greek here in Revelation distinguishes the cultic objects from the demons, John no doubt shared Paul's concept of demons as evil spirits (Rev 16:14; 18:2). Hence, there is a twofold evil in idol worship: it robs the true God of his glory (Rom 1:23) and it leads to consorting with evil spirits that corrupt man.

This demonic corruption is manifest in the inhuman acts of those who have given up God for idols—acts of murder, sexual immorality, and thefts (cf. Rom 1:24; 28–31). In general, these are violations of the ten commandments. "Magic arts" (*pharmakōn*) means "a practice of sorceries" or "witchcraft" (LXX Exod 7:11; 9:11; Gal 5:20; Rev 21:8; 22:15). Usually drugs were involved in these arts. Sometimes the word *pharmakōn* means "to poison," as in a Jewish prayer from the first century B.C.: "I call upon and pray the Most High, the Lord of the spirits and of all flesh, against those who with guile murdered or poisoned [*pharmakōn*] the wretched, untimely lost Heraclea, shedding her innocent blood wickedly" (MM, p. 664).

The second purpose of God revealed in the agonizing plagues described in chapters 8 and 9 is to bring societies to repentance (cf. 16:9, 11). God is not willing that any person should suffer his judgment but that all should repent and turn to him (Luke 13:3, 5; 2 Peter 3:9). But when God's works and words are persistently rejected, only judgment remains (Eph 5:6; Heb 10:26–31).

Notes

8:13 In place of ἀετός (*aetos*, "eagle") read by ℵ A B and most MSS and versions, other texts read ἄγγελος (*angelos*, "angel") (P and some minuscules). Metzger suggests *aetos* was corrupted to *angelos* by scribal concerns "to harmonize what is done by the eagle into line with what is ascribed to angels elsewhere" (Bruce M. Metzger, *A Textual Commentary on the Greek New Testament* [New York: UBS, 1971], p. 743).

9:1 Ἄβυσσος (*abyssos*, "Abyss") (from Heb. תהום [*tᵉhôm*, "the deep"]) is referred to in 1 Enoch in the sense of both an intermediate and a final abode for fallen angels, Satan, demons, and fallen men (1 Enoch 18:12–16; 21:7–10; 108:3–6; Charles, *Commentary on Revelation*, 1:240–41).

11 Ἑβραϊστί (*Hebraisti*) has generally been understood here and elsewhere in the NT to mean "Aramaic," but recent studies are questioning this identification and arguing for the sense "in Hebrew" rather than "in Aramaic" (Philip Edgcumbe Hughes, "The Language Spoken by Jesus," *New Dimensions in New Testament Study*, ed. R.N. Longenecker and M.C. Tenney [Grand Rapids: Zondervan, 1974], pp. 127–28).

16 The words δισμυριάδες μυριάδων (*dismyriades myriadōn*, "200 million") are Heb. and not Aram. in background (G. Mussies, *The Morphology of Koine Greek as Used in the Apocalypse of St. John* [Leiden: E.J. Brill, 1971], p. 353).

3. *Second interlude* (10:1–11:14)

a. *The little book*

10:1–11

> ¹Then I saw another mighty angel coming down from heaven. He was robed in a cloud, with a rainbow above his head; his face was like the sun, and his legs were like fiery pillars. ²He was holding a little scroll, which lay open in his hand. He planted his right foot on the sea and his left foot on the land, ³and he gave a loud shout like the roar of a lion. When he shouted, the voices of the seven thunders spoke. ⁴And when the seven thunders spoke, I was about to write; but I heard a voice from heaven say, "Seal up what the seven thunders have said and do not write it down."
>
> ⁵Then the angel I had seen standing on the sea and on the land raised his right hand to heaven. ⁶And he swore by him who lives for ever and ever, who created the heavens and all that is in them, the earth and all that is in it, and the sea and all that is in it, and said, "There will be no more delay! ⁷But in the days when the seventh angel is about to sound his trumpet, the mystery of God will be accomplished, just as he announced to his servants the prophets."
>
> ⁸Then the voice that I had heard from heaven spoke to me once more: "Go, take the scroll that lies open in the hand of the angel who is standing on the sea and on the land."
>
> ⁹So I went to the angel and asked him to give me the little scroll. He said to me, "Take it and eat it. It will turn your stomach sour, but in your mouth it will be as sweet as honey." ¹⁰I took the little scroll from the angel's hand and ate it. It tasted as sweet as honey in my mouth, but when I had eaten it, my stomach turned sour. ¹¹Then I was told, "You must prophesy again about many peoples, nations, languages and kings."

1–4 As in the seals, the sequences of the sixth and seventh trumpets is interrupted to provide additional information bearing on the previous events and to prepare the reader for further developments. The author sees a mighty angel (possibly Michael, "the great prince" [Dan 12:1]) whom he describes in such dazzling terms (cloud, rainbow, sun, fiery pillars) that some have identified him with Christ. But angels are always angels in the Apocalypse, as well as in the rest of the NT, and should not be identified with Christ. The voice that speaks in vv. 4, 8 could, however, be that of Jesus.

The angel has in his hand a small scroll (v.2). This scroll should not be confused with the Lamb's scroll of chapters 5–7. It should be connected with the symbolic scroll of Ezekiel (Ezek 2:9–3:3; cf. Jer 15:15–17). This prophet was told to "eat" the scroll just as John was told to eat the scroll given him (vv.9–10). Such an action symbolized the reception of the Word of God into the innermost being as a necessary prerequisite to proclaim it with confidence. John could see the words on the scroll because it "lay open" in the angel's hand. The angel standing on both land and sea symbolizes that the prophetic message is for the whole world.

When the angel shouted (v.3), seven thunders spoke, and John proceeded to write down their words. But he is interrupted and is commanded, "Seal up what the seven thunders have said and do not write it down" (v.4). Conceivably, this might have been another series of sevens. Either the seven thunders were intended for John's own illumination and were not essential to the main vision of the seven trumpets or the reference is designed to strike a note of mystery with reference to God's revelatory activities (cf. 2 Cor 12:4). As the visible portion of an iceberg is only a small part of the iceberg, most of which is hidden from man's sight, so God's disclosures reveal only part of his total being and purposes.

5-7 The angel's action of raising his right hand to heaven doubtless alludes to the Jewish oath-swearing procedure (Deut 32:40; Dan 12:7). He swears that "there will be no more delay" (v.6). Clearly there is some type of progression in the seals, trumpets, and bowls that nears its conclusion as the seventh trumpet is about to sound (v.7). When the seventh trumpet is finally sounded, there is an announcement that "the kingdom of the world has become the kingdom of our Lord and of his Christ" and that the time has come to judge the dead, to reward the saints, and to destroy the earth destroyers (11:15, 18). These events are recorded in the remaining chapters of the book, which include the seven bowl judgments and the new heavens and the new earth. Thus here in 10:7 it is announced that "the mystery of God" is accomplished. "The mystery of God" is his purposes for man and the world as revealed to both OT and NT prophets.

The way NIV translates v.7 suggests that the consummation comes before the blowing of the seventh trumpet: "when the seventh angel is about to sound his trumpet. . . ." While this is grammatically possible, it is also possible to render the expression "about to sound" as "when he shall sound." Thus understood, the meaning is that "in the days of " (i.e., during the period of) the sound of the seventh trumpet, when the angel sounds, the final purposes of God will be completed. This rendering clarifies the statement in 11:14, "The second woe has passed: the third woe is coming soon," a statement made just before the seventh trumpet sounds. Hence, the seventh trumpet will reveal the final judgments of the bowls and the final establishment of God's rule on the earth (cf. Notes).

8-11 John, like Ezekiel, is now commanded to take the prophetic scroll and eat it. The scroll tasted "as sweet as honey" but was bitter to the stomach. Receiving the Word of God is a great joy; but since the Word is an oracle of judgment, it results in the unpleasant experience of proclaiming a message of wrath and woe (cf. Jer 15:16, 19). The symbolic act of eating the scroll might also mean that the prophetic message was mixed with joy and comfort as well as gloom. Mounce, following Bruce, argues that the content of the scroll is

> a message for the believing church and is to be found in the following verses (11:1-13). . . . It is *after* the eating of the book that John is told he must prophesy again, this time concerning many peoples, nations, tongues, and kings (Rev. 10:11). This begins with chapter 12. The sweet scroll which turns the stomach bitter is a message for the church. Before the final triumph believers are going to pass through a formidable ordeal. . . . So the little scroll unveils the lot of the faithful in those last days of Satanic opposition (*Revelation*, p. 216).

In any case, the sweetness should not be taken to refer to the joy of proclaiming a message of wrath, for to all God's prophets this was a sorrowful, bitter task (Jer 9:1).

101

The chief import of chapter 10 seems to be a confirmation of John's prophetic call as v.11 indicates: "You must prophesy again about many peoples, nations, languages and kings." This prophesying should not be understood as merely a recapitulation in greater detail of the previous visions but a further progression of the events connected with the end. Notice the use of the word "kings" instead of "tribes" (as in 5:9; 7:9; 13:7; 14:6). This may anticipate the emphasis on the kings of the earth found in 17:9–12 and elsewhere.

Notes

6 The Gr. word χρόνος (*chronos;* "delay," NIV) can refer to time in a number of aspects. Other verses where *chronos* means "delay" are Matt 25:5 and Heb 10:37.
7 There are two possibilities for rendering μέλλω (*mellō*) plus the infinitive: (1) imminence ("about to," NIV) or (2) strong future certainty ("shall"). I have opted for the second sense to throw the action into the time of the blowing of the seventh trumpet and not to the time *before* its sound.
11 The preposition ἐπί (*epi*) translated correctly "about" in NIV may, with the dative, also mean "upon," "over," "against," "near," "to," "with." The KJV rendering "before" would not be accurate unless the genitive were used (BAG, p. 287).

b. *The two witnesses*

11:1–14

[1]I was given a reed like a measuring rod and was told, "Go and measure the temple of God and the altar, and count the worshipers there. [2]But exclude the outer court; do not measure it, because it has been given to the Gentiles. They will trample on the holy city for 42 months. [3]And I will give power to my two witnesses, and they will prophesy for 1,260 days, clothed in sackcloth." [4]These are the two olive trees and the two lampstands that stand before the Lord of the earth. [5]If anyone tries to harm them, fire comes from their mouths and devours their enemies. This is how anyone who wants to harm them must die. [6]These men have power to shut up the sky so that it will not rain during the time they are prophesying; and they have power to turn the waters into blood and to strike the earth with every kind of plague as often as they want.

[7]Now when they have finished their testimony, the beast that comes up from the Abyss will attack them, and overpower and kill them. [8]Their bodies will lie in the street of the great city, which is figuratively called Sodom and Egypt, where also their Lord was crucified. [9]For three and a half days men from every people, tribe, language and nation will gaze on their bodies and refuse them burial. [10]The inhabitants of the earth will gloat over them and will celebrate by sending each other gifts, because these two prophets had tormented those who live on the earth.

[11]But after the three and a half days a breath of life from God entered them, and they stood on their feet, and terror struck those who saw them. [12]Then they heard a loud voice from heaven saying to them, "Come up here." And they went up to heaven in a cloud, while their enemies looked on.

[13]At that very hour there was a severe earthquake and a tenth of the city collapsed. Seven thousand people were killed in the earthquake, and the survivors were terrified and gave glory to the God of heaven.

[14]The second woe has passed; the third woe is coming soon.

Some have considered this chapter one of the most difficult to interpret in the Book of Revelation (Lilje, p. 159). Alford agrees: "This passage may well be called . . . the *crux interpretum;* as it is undoubtedly one of the most difficult in the whole Apocalypse" (Alf, 4: 655). In it John refers to the temple, the Holy City, and the two prophets who are killed by the beast and after three and one-half days are resurrected and ascend to heaven. Does John intend all this to be understood simply as it is given—viz., the literal temple in Jerusalem; two people prophesying for 1,260 days, who are killed by the Antichrist, raised from the dead, and ascend to heaven; a great earthquake that kills seven thousand people and the survivors of which glorify God? Or does he intend all or part of these as symbols representing something? Most commentators take at least part of these things as symbolic. Furthermore, how does this section (11:1–13) relate to the total context (10:1–11:19)?

While details of interpretation vary, there are but two main approaches to the chapter: (1) the temple, altar, worshipers, and Holy City have something to do with the Jewish people and their place in the plan of God; or (2) John is here referring to the Christian church. As in chapter 7, John's references to particular Jewish entities create the chief source of the problem. Does he use these references in a plain, one-to-one sense, or does he use them representatively or symbolically?

At the outset, it may be helpful to state why the Jewish view is less preferable. Actually, this approach has two slightly different aspects. One school of commentators, generally dispensational, understands the "temple" and the "city" to refer to a rebuilt Jewish temple in Jerusalem. While in this view elements in the description may be symbolic, the main import of the passage is seen as depicting a future protection of the nation of Israel prior to her spiritual regeneration. The Antichrist (beast) will permit the rebuilding of the temple in Jerusalem as well as the restoration of Jewish worship for three and a half years; but then he will break his covenant and trample down a part of the temple and the Holy City until Christ returns to deliver the Jewish people (cf. Dan 9:27; so J.B. Smith, Seiss, Walvoord).

More recently Ladd, following Beckwith, Zahn, and perhaps Swete, has argued for a modified Jewish view. He contends that John is prophetically predicting the "preservation and ultimate salvation of the Jewish people" much in the manner of Paul in Romans 11:26 ("And so all Israel will be saved") (*Commentary on Revelation,* pp. 150ff.). Unlike those who hold the strict dispensational view, Ladd believes that the temple and the city of Jerusalem are not the literal Jewish restored temple or the city located in Palestine. Rather, they represent, on the one hand, the believing Jewish remnant (temple, altar, and worshipers) and, on the other hand, the Jewish people or nation as a whole who are now under Gentile oppression (outer court and city) (ibid.). Both Jewish views suffer from their inability to relate this chapter to the context of chapter 10, to the parallelism in the seal interlude (ch. 7), to the ministry and significance of the two witnesses, or to the further chapters in Revelation (esp. chs. 12–13). Therefore, it is better to understand John as referring in chapter 11 to the whole Christian community.

1 John is given a "reed" (*kalamos*), or "cane," long and straight like a "rod," and thus suitable for measuring a large building or area. (The measuring rod referred to in Ezek 40:5 was about ten feet long.) The purpose of the reed is to "measure the temple of God and the altar." Most agree that the principal OT passage in John's mind was Ezekiel's lengthy description of the measuring of the future kingdom temple (Ezek

40:3–48:35). Since interpreters are confused about what Ezekiel's vision means, the ambiguity extends also to John's description. In the ancient world, measuring was accomplished for shorter lengths by the reed cane (Ezek 40:2ff.) or, for longer distances, with a rope line (1 Kings 7:23; Isa 44:13). Measuring with a line may have various metaphorical meanings. It may refer to the promise of restoration and rebuilding, with emphasis on extension or enlargement (Jer 31:39; Zech 1:16). Measuring may also be done to mark out something for destruction (2 Sam 8:2; 2 Kings 21:13; Isa 28:17; Lam 2:8; Amos 7:7–9). In Ezekiel 40:2ff., this latter sense would be inappropriate. But what does John's measuring mean?

Since John is told in v.2 not to measure the outer court but to leave it for the nations to overrun, it may be that here in chapter 11 the measuring means that the temple of God, the altar, and the worshipers (who are to be counted) are to be secured for blessing and preserved from spiritual harm or defilement. So in 21:15–17, John similarly depicts the angel's measuring of the heavenly city (with a golden rod), apparently to mark off the city and its inhabitants from harm and defilement (21:24, 27). As a parallel to the sealing of 7:1–8, the measuring does not symbolize preservation from physical harm but the prophetic guarantee that none of the faithful worshipers of Jesus as the Messiah will perish even though they suffer physical destruction at the hand of the beast (13:7). Such seems also to be the sense of the measuring passage in 1 Enoch 62:1–5 (Charles, *Commentary on Revelation*, 1:276).

In Ezekiel 43:10, the prophet is told to "describe the temple to the people of Israel, that they may be ashamed of their sins." The purpose of the elaborate description and temple measurement in Ezekiel is to indicate the glory and holiness of God in Israel's midst and convict them of their defilement of his sanctuary (43:12). Likewise, John's prophetic ministry calls for a clear separation between those who are holy and those who have defiled themselves with the idolatry of the beast.

John is to measure "the temple of God." There are two Greek words used in the NT for temple. One (*hieron*) is a broad term that refers to the whole structure of Herod's temple, including courts, colonnades, etc. (e.g., Matt 4:5; John 2:14). The other (*naos*) is narrower and refers to the sanctuary or inner house where only the priests were allowed (Matt 23:35; 27:51; and always in Rev). While the distinction between the two words is not always maintained (TDNT, 4: 884), yet in this context (11:1) it may be appropriate since the next verse mentions the outer precinct as a separate entity.

Does John mean the heavenly temple often mentioned in Revelation (cf. 11:19; 15:5, 8; 16:17), or does he refer to the Christian community as in 3:12: "Him who overcomes I will make a pillar in the temple of my God"? In the postapostolic Epistle of Barnabas (16:1ff.), the temple is the individual Christian or alternately the community of Christians as it is in Paul (1 Cor 3:16; 6:19; 2 Cor 6:16). Since John refers to the "outer court" in v.2, which is trampled by the nations, it is quite likely that he has in mind not the heavenly temple of God but an earthly one—either the (rebuilt?) temple in Jerusalem or, symbolically, the covenant people.

The word for temple (*naos*) always refers to the Jerusalem temple in the Gospels with the single exception of John's Gospel, where it refers to Jesus' own body (John 2:19–21; cf. Rev 21:22). Outside the Gospels it refers either to pagan shrines (Acts 17:24; 19:24) or, in Paul's letters, metaphorically to the physical bodies of Christians or to the church of God (1 Cor 3:16; 6:19; 2 Cor 6:16; Eph 2:21). In only one case is it debatable whether Paul means the literal Jerusalem temple or the church (2 Thess 2:4).

While to take the temple in this verse (11:1) as representing the church in the Great Tribulation is not without problems, this seems the best view. Other NT usage outside the Gospels, the figurative usage of temple in John 2:19–21, and his usage in Revelation all point to the image of the temple representing the messianic community of both Jews and Gentiles, comparable to his symbol of the woman in chapter 12 (so Alf, 4:657).

The "altar" would then refer to the huge stone altar of sacrifice in the court of the priests, and the expression "the worshipers" would most naturally indicate the priests and others in the three inner courts (the court of the priests, the court of Israel, the court of the women). These represent symbolically the true servants of God and the measuring symbolizes their recognition and acceptance by God in the same manner as the numbering in chapter 7. The writer of Hebrews likewise speaks of an "altar" that Christians eat from, but that Jewish priests who serve in the temple are not qualified to eat from (Heb 13:10). By this language he speaks of the once-for-all sacrifice of Christ on the cross utilizing the background of the temple images, as does John.

2 As the "outer court" in the Jerusalem temple was frequented by a mixed group including Gentiles and unbelievers, so in John's mind the earthly temple or community of God may involve a part where those who are impure or unfaithful will be (21:8; 22:15). The effect of not measuring this part of the temple is to exclude it and those in it from spiritual security and God's blessing, in contrast to the way the measuring secured these things for the true community. So in measuring the temple, Ezekiel is instructed to exclude from the sanctuary "the foreigners uncircumcised in heart and flesh" (Ezek 44:5–9)—viz., pagans who do not worship the true God and whose presence would desecrate the sanctuary. Previously, John has shown concern over those who were associated with the local churches but were not true worshipers of Christ (cf. 2:14–16, 20–25; 3:1–5, 16). When the great test comes, they will join the ranks of the beast and reveal their true colors.

On the other hand, while Swete (in loc.) suggests that the outer court is perhaps the rejected synagogue (cf. 2:9; 3:9), it may be better to understand the desecration of the outer court as a symbolic reference to the victory of the beast over the saints, which is described in v.7. Thus by using two slightly different images, the "temple-altar-worshipers" and the "outer court-Holy City," John is viewing the church under different aspects. Though the Gentiles (pagans) are permitted to touch the "outer court" and to trample on the "Holy City" for a limited time ("42 months"), they are not able to destroy the church because the "inner sanctuary" is measured or protected in keeping with Christ's earlier words: "And the gates of Hades will not overcome it" (Matt 16:18) (so Morris, *Revelation of St. John*, p. 146; Mounce, *Revelation*, p. 220).

Since John says the outer court will be "given to the Gentiles," it is important to establish the best translation of *ethnē* ("Gentiles"). *Ethnē* may have, in the NT, the more general sense of "nations," describing the various ethnic or national groups among mankind (e.g., Matt 24:9, 14; Luke 24:47; Rom 1:5; 15:11). In other contexts, it may be used as a narrower technical term to denote "Gentiles" in contrast to the Jewish people (e.g., Matt 4:15; 10:5; Luke 2:32; Acts 10:45; Rom 11:11). In many cases the broader sense may shade off into the narrower, producing ambiguity.

But there is another usage of *ethnē*. Just as the Jews referred to all other peoples outside the covenant as "Gentiles," so there gradually developed a similar Christian usage of the term that saw all peoples who were outside of Christ as *ethnē*, including also unbelieving Jews (1 Cor 5:1; 12:2; 1 Thess 4:5; 1 Peter 2:12; 3 John 7). Our word "heathen" may parallel this usage of the word (TDNT, 2: 370, n.19). When the sixteen cases of the plural form (*ethnē*) in Revelation are examined, not once is the sense "Gentiles" appropriate. Everywhere the *ethnē* are the peoples of the earth, either in rebellion against God (11:18; 14:8; 19:15; 20:3) or redeemed and under the rule of Christ (2:26; 21:24, 26; 22:2). There is no good reason why John does not intend the same sense in 11:2. Nevertheless, the versions reflect the uncertainty of the translators: "Gentiles" (KJV, Knox, NEB, NIV) or "nations" (RSV, NASB, Ph).

To sum up, John's words "given to the Gentiles" refer to the defiling agencies that will trample down the outer court of the church, leading either to defection from Christ or physical destruction, though all the while the inner sanctuary of the true believers will not be defiled by idolatry. This spiritual preservation of the true believers will be accomplished by John's prophetic ministry, which distinguishes true loyalty to Christ from the deception of the beast.

The nations will "trample on the holy city for 42 months." Opinion varies between the literal and the symbolic significance of the term "the holy city." The more literal viewpoint sees "the holy city" as the earthly city of Jerusalem. Support for this is found (1) in the OT's use (Neh 11:1; Isa 48:2; 52:1; Dan 9:24) and Matthew's use of "holy city" for Jerusalem (Matt 4:5; 27:53), (2) the proximity of the term "the holy city" to the temple reference (v.1), and (3) the mention in v.8 of the "great city" that is "where also their Lord was crucified."

Since Jerusalem was destroyed in A.D. 70, and since Revelation was presumably written about 95 (cf. Introduction), the more literalistic interpreters hold two views about the meaning of this reference to the city. Some believe it to refer to the rebuilt city and temple during the future Tribulation period (Walvoord, p. 177). Others see the city as merely a representative or symbolic reference to the Jewish people without any special implication of a literal city or temple (Beckwith, p. 588; Ladd, *Commentary on Revelation*, pp. 152–53; Rissi, *Time and History*, pp. 96f.). But if John does in fact differentiate here between believing Jews (inner court) and the nation as a whole (outer court), this would be the only place in the book where he does so. Furthermore, such a reference at this point in the context of chapters 10 and 11 would be abrupt and unconnected with the main themes in these chapters, the subject of which is the nature of the prophetic ministry and the great trial awaiting Christians.

Far more in keeping with the emphasis of the whole book and of these chapters in particular is the view that in the mind of John "the holy city," like the temple, refers to the church. The consistent usage of the expression "holy city" means the community of those faithful to Jesus Christ, composed of believing Jews and Gentiles (21:2, 10; 22:19; cf. 3:12; 20:9). It should also be noted that the name Jerusalem nowhere appears in chapter 11 but that there is a circumlocution for it in v.8, "where also their Lord was crucified," which is prefaced with the word "figuratively" (*pneumatikōs*, lit., "spiritually"). While the vision of the future Holy City (chs. 21–22) describes the condition of the city when she has completed her great ordeal and is finally delivered from the great deceiver, the present reference is to the people as they must first endure the trampling of the pagan nations for "42 months."

Does the trampling (*pateō*) indicate defilement and apostasy, or does it instead mean persecution? The word "trample" can metaphorically mean either of these (BAG, p. 640).

Two factors favor the latter sense. The time of the trampling is "42 months," which is the exact time John attributes to the reign of the beast (13:5–7). Furthermore, in

Daniel's prophecy the trampling of the sanctuary and host of God's people by Antiochus Epiphanes (Dan 8:10, 13; 2 Macc 8:2, *katapateō*, LXX) is clearly a persecution of the people of God. The apocryphal Psalms of Solomon relate that the trampling of Jerusalem by the pagans will be reversed by the Messiah (Pss Sol 17:24, 42–47).

But what of the term "42 months"? This exact expression occurs in the Bible only here and in 13:5, where it refers to the time of the authority of the beast. Mention is also made of a period of 1,260 days (i.e., 42 months of 30 days each) in 11:3 and 12:6. In 12:14 a similar length of time is referred to as "a time, times [i.e., two times] and half a time." All these expressions equal a three-and-one-half-year period.

In the various usages of the terms, "42 months" refers to the period of oppression of the Holy City and the time of the authority of the beast (11:2; 13:5). As for the "1,260 days," this is the period the two witnesses prophesy and the time the woman is protected from the dragon's reach (11:3; 12:6). "Time, times and half a time" seems to be used synonymously for the 1,260 days during which the woman will be protected in the desert (12:14). We cannot assume that because these periods are equal, they are identical. On the other hand, the three different expressions may well be literary variations for the same period. Daniel is generally taken to be the origin of the terms.

In Daniel 9:27 a week is spoken of ("seven," NIV), and the context makes it clear that this is a week of years, i.e., seven years (Glasson, p. 67). Further, the week is divided in half—i.e., three years and a half for each division. These half weeks of years are spoken of in Daniel 7:25 as "a time, times and half a time." Early Jewish and general patristic interpretation followed by the early Protestant commentators referred this to the period of the reign of the Antichrist (James A. Montgomery, *A Critical and Exegetical Commentary on the Book of Daniel*, ICC [Edinburgh: T. & T. Clark, 1964], p. 314).

In Daniel 12:7 the identical expression refers to the period "when the power of the holy people has been finally broken"; in 12:11 the equivalent period expressed in days (1,290) refers to the time of the "abomination" and defilement of the temple. Whether or not these references refer to the second-century B.C. activities of Antiochus Epiphanes must be left to the exegetes of Daniel; but it is known that the Jews and later the Christians believed that these events at least foreshadow, if not predict, the last years of world history under the Antichrist (Glasson, p. 68). Thus John would have a ready tool to use in this imagery for setting forth his revelation of the last days.

Glasson, following the early fathers Victorinus, Hippolytus, and Augustine, suggests that the first three and a half years is the period of the preaching of the two witnesses, while the second half of the week is the time of bitter trial when Antichrist reigns supreme (p. 70). Others believe the expressions are synchronous and thus refer to the identical period (Swete, p. 131). With some reservations, the view of Glasson may be followed. The 1,260-day period of protected prophesying by the two witnesses (11:3–6) synchronizes with the period of the woman in the desert (12:6, 14). When the death of the witnesses occurs (11:7), there follows the forty-two-month murderous reign of the beast (13:5, 7, 15), which synchronizes with the trampling down of the Holy City (11:2). This twofold division seems to be also supported by Jesus' Olivet Discourse, where he speaks of the "beginning of birth pains" (Matt 24:8) and then of the period of "great distress" shortly before his Parousia (Matt 24:21).

Finally, are the two periods of three and a half years symbolic or do they indicate calendar years? Not all will agree, but a symbolic sense that involves a real period but understands the numbers to describe the kind of period rather than its length is in keeping with John's use of numbers elsewhere (cf. 2:10; 4:4; 7:4). Hence, if we follow the twofold division of Daniel's seventieth week of seven years, the preaching of the two witnesses occupies the first half, while the second half is the time of bitter trial when the beast reigns supreme, and during which time the fearful events of chapters 13–19 take place. Since these time references are by no means clear, any explanation must be tentative.

3 Perhaps more diversity of interpretation surrounds these two personages than even the temple in the previous verses. They are called "two witnesses" (v.3), "two prophets" (v.10), and, more figuratively, "two olive trees and the two lampstands who stand before the Lord of the earth" (v.4). Identifications range all the way from two historic figures raised to life, to two groups, to two principles, such as the law and the prophets. Tertullian (d.220) identified the two with Enoch and Elijah.

On the other hand, Jewish tradition taught that Moses and Elijah would return, and this view is followed by a number of Christian interpreters. According to Jochanan ben Zakkai (first century A.D.), God said to Moses, "If I send the prophet Elijah, you must both come together" (Charles, *Commentary on Revelation*, 1: 281; also Seiss, J.B. Smith, Gundry; cf. Mark 9:11–13). Beckwith believes they are two prophets of the future who will perform the functions of Moses and Elijah (p. 595). Others understand the figures to represent the church (Primasius [d.552]). In the words of Swete, "The witness of the church, borne by her martyrs and confessors, her saints and doctors, and by the words and lives of all in whom Christ lives and speaks, is one continual prophecy" (p. 132; also Beasley-Murray). Ladd cannot make up his mind between the witnessing church to Israel and two historical eschatological prophets (*Commentary on Revelation*, p. 154). Bruce believes they are symbolic of the church in its royal and priestly functions ("Revelation," p. 649). Others identify them as representative of the martyrs (Morris, *Revelation of St. John*, p. 147; Caird, p. 134).

More recently Munck has identified them with the Christian prophets Peter and Paul (cited by Bruce, "Revelation," p. 649). Rissi sees them as representatives of the Jewish believers and Gentile believers in the church (Mathias Rissi, "The Kerygma of the Revelation to John," Int, 22 [January 1968]: 16). Minear understands the two to represent all the prophets (*I Saw a New Earth*, p. 99).

Since opinion varies so greatly at this point, it may be wise not to be dogmatic about any one view. Minear's arguments, however, seem more persuasive than the others. The two witnesses represent those in the church who are specially called, like John, to bear a prophetic witness to Christ during the whole age of the church. They also represent those prophets who will be martyred by the beast. Indications that they are representative of many individuals and not just two are that (1) they are never seen as individuals but do everything together—they prophesy together, suffer together, are killed together, are raised together, and ascend together—and all this is hardly possible for two individuals; (2) the beast makes war on them (v.7), which is strange if they are merely two individuals; (3) people throughout the whole world view their ignominious deaths (v.9)—something quite impossible if only two individuals are involved; (4) they are described as two "lamps" (v.4), a figure applied in chapters 1 and 2 to local churches comprised of many individuals. They are "clothed in sackcloth" because they are prophets (cf. Isa 20:2; Zech 13:4) who call for repentance and humility (Jer 6:26; 49:3; Matt 11:21); it was the most suitable garb for times of distress, grief, danger, crisis, and humility. That God himself will appoint, or "give power," to them would encourage the church to persevere even in the face of strong opposition.

4 The reference to the "two olive trees and the two lampstands" is an allusion to Joshua and Zerubbabel in Zechariah's vision, who were also said "to serve the Lord of all the earth" (Zech 4:1–6a, 10b–14). The whole import of Zechariah's vision was to strengthen the two leaders by reminding them of God's resources and to vindicate them in the eyes of the community as they pursued their God-given tasks. Thus John's message would be that the witnesses to Christ who cause the church to fulfill her mission to burn as bright lights to the world will not be quenched (cf. Rev 1:20; 2:5).

Why there should be two olive trees and two lampstands has been variously answered. Some suggest that "two" is the number of required legal witnesses (Num 35:30; Deut 19:15; cf. Matt 18:16; Luke 10:1–24); others suggest that "two" represents the priestly and kingly aspects of the church or the Jewish and Gentile components, etc. Perhaps the dualism was suggested to John by the two olive trees from Zechariah and the two great prophets of the OT who were connected with the coming of the Messiah in Jewish thought, i.e., Moses and Elijah (v.6); cf. Matt 17:3–4). What Joshua (the high priest) and Zerubbabel (the prince) were to the older community and temple, Jesus Christ is to the new community. He is both anointed Priest and King, and his church reflects this character especially in its Christian prophets (1:6; 5:10; 20:6).

5 Here the prophets' divine protection from their enemies is described in terms reminiscent of the former prophets' protection by God (2 Kings 1:10; Jer 5:14). Fire is understood symbolically as judgment from God; and since it proceeds from the witnesses' mouths, we understand that their message of judgment will eventually be fulfilled by God's power (Gen 19:23f.; 2 Sam 22:9; Ps 97:3). Their Lord gives them immunity from destruction until they complete their confirmation of God's saving deed in Christ. This assures the people of God that no matter how many of its chosen saints are oppressed and killed, God's witness to Christ will continue until his purposes are fulfilled.

6 The words "power to shut up the sky . . . and power to turn the waters into blood" clearly allude to the ministries of the prophets Elijah and Moses (1 Kings 17:1; Exod 7:17–21). There is, however, no need for the literal reappearing of these two if it is understood that the two witnesses come in the same spirit and function as their predecessors. Thus Luke interprets the significance of John the Baptist as a ministry in the "spirit and power of Elijah" (Luke 1:17). The author of Revelation is simply describing the vocation of certain Christian prophets, indicating that some follow in the same tradition as the former prophets of Israel. According to Luke 4:25 and James 5:17, Elijah's prophecy shut up the heaven for "three and a half years," a curious foreshadowing, perhaps, of the span of time that these prophets witness (i.e., 1,260 days [v.3]).

7 When they finish their witness, the witnesses are killed by the beast from the Abyss. This is the first reference to the "beast" in the book. The abruptness with which it is introduced seems not only to presuppose some knowledge of the beast but also to anticipate what is said of him in chapters 13 and 17. Only here and in 17:8 is the beast described as coming "up from the Abyss" (cf. 9:1), showing his demonic origin. He attacks the prophets (lit., "makes war with them," *polemon;* cf. 9:7; 12:7, 17; 13:7; 16:14; 19:19; 20:8). This possibly reflects Daniel 7:21: "As I watched, this horn was waging war [*polemon,* LXX] against the saints and defeating them." This attack is again described in 12:17 and 13:7: "Then the dragon was enraged at the woman and went off to make war against the rest of her offspring . . . [the beast] was given power to make war against the saints and to conquer them." This is the second and final phase of the dragon's persecution of the Christian prophets and saints.

8 Here we have the place of the attack on the witnesses and the place of their death: "The street of the great city, which is figuratively called Sodom and Egypt, where also their Lord was crucified." Verse 8 is both full of meaning and difficult to interpret. At first glance, it seems apparent that John is referring to the actual city of Jerusalem where Christ died. This allusion seems obvious. Yet John's terminology also implies more than this. The city is called the "great city," a designation that refers to Babylon throughout the rest of the book (16:19; 17:18; 18:10, 16, 18–19, 21). Moreover, John's use of the word "city," from the very first occurrence in 3:12, is symbolic. In fact, there are really only two cities in the book, the city of God and the city of Satan, which is later referred to as Babylon. A city may be a metaphor for the total life of a community of people (Heb 11:10; 12:22; 13:14).

Here the "great city" is clearly more than merely Jerusalem, for John says it is "figuratively called Sodom and Egypt." "Figuratively" comes from the Greek word *pneumatikōs*, which BAG (p. 685) says means "spiritually, in a spiritual manner, full of the divine Spirit." Elsewhere in the NT, the word characterizes that which pertains to the Spirit in contrast to the flesh (1 Cor 2:14–15; Eph 1:3; 5:19; Col 3:16; 1 Peter 2:5, etc.). RSV and NEB translate it "allegorically," which is questionable, since there is the Greek word *allēgoreō*, which means precisely that (cf. Gal 4:24); and nowhere else does *pneumatikōs* have this sense. NASB has "mystically." Closer may be Knox, who renders *pneumatikōs* "in the language of prophecy," or Minear's "prophetically" ("Ontology and Ecclesiology in the Apocalypse," NTS, 12 [1966], p. 94, n.1), or Phillips's "is called by those with spiritual understanding."

The spiritually discerning will catch the significance of the threefold designation of this city. It is called "Sodom," which connotes rebellion against God, the rejection of God's servants, moral degradation, and the awfulness of divine judgment (cf. Ezek 16:49). In Isaiah's day the rebellious rulers of Jerusalem were called the rulers of Sodom (Isa 1:10; cf. Ezek 16:46). The second designation is "Egypt." Egypt, however, is a country, not a city. It is virtually certain that by John's day, Egypt had become a symbolic name for antitheocratic world kingdoms that enslaved Israel (K. Jose b. Chalaphta, "All kingdoms are called by the name of Egypt because they enslave Israel" [SBK, 3:812]). The third designation is "the great city, . . . where also their Lord was crucified" (cf. Matt 23:28–31, 37–38; Luke 13:33ff.; 21:20–24).

If, as most commentators believe, John also has Rome in mind in mentioning the "great city," then there are at least five places all seen by John as one—Babylon, Sodom, Egypt, Jerusalem, and Rome. (This one city has become, in the eyes of the spiritually discerning, all places opposed to God and the witness of his servants— Sodom, Tyre, Egypt, Babylon, Nineveh, Rome, et al.) Wherever God is opposed and his servants harassed and killed, there *is* the "great city," the transhistorical city of Satan, the great mother of prostitutes (cf. 17:1ff.). What can happen to God's witnesses in any place is what has already happened to their Lord in Jerusalem. Bunyan's city, called "Vanity Fair," approaches this idea, though not precisely, since John uses actual historical places where this great transhistorical city found its manifestation. Mounce suggests that "the great city in which the martyred church lies dead is the world under the wicked and oppressive sway of Antichrist" (*Revelation*, p. 227). It is curious that in the Greek the singular noun *ptōma* ("body") is used for both witnesses in vv.8–9a, but the plural *ptōmata* ("bodies") is used in 9b. Their dead bodies lie in full public view "in the street."

9–10 People from every nation—Jew and Gentile—will "gloat over" their corpses and refuse them the dignity of burial. To have his dead body lie in view of all was the worst humiliation a person could suffer from his enemies (Ps 79:3–4; Tobit 1:18ff.). Further-more, the pagan world will celebrate the destruction of the witnesses and the victory over them by exchanging gifts, a common custom in the Near East (Neh 8:10, 12; Esth 9:19, 22). Thus the beast will silence the witness of the church to the glee of the beast-worshiping world. The time of their silence corresponds in days to the time of their witness in years. It denotes only a brief time of triumph for the beast.

11–12 The witnesses now experience a resurrection and an ascension to heaven following their three-and-one-half-day death. In regard to this puzzling passage, it is generally held that Ezekiel's vision of the restoration of the dry bones was in John's mind (Ezek 37:5, 10–12). Just as interpretations of Ezekiel's vision vary, so interpreta-tions of vv.11–12 of Revelation 11 also vary. Some hold that the dry bones vision refers to the spiritual quickening of the nation of Israel (KD, *Ezekiel*, 2:120). Others, following rabbinic interpretation and certain church fathers, understand the descrip-tions to refer to the physical resurrection of the dead. If the two witnesses represent the witness of the church, then physical resurrection and ascension could be in mind. (The summons "Come up here" followed by "they went up to heaven in a cloud" perhaps points to the Rapture [1 Thess 4:16–17].)

On the other hand, John may be using the figure of physical resurrection to represent the church's victory over the death blow of the beast. In Romans 11:15 Paul uses the figure of resurrection symbolically to depict a great spiritual revival among the Jews in a future day. Here in Revelation 11:12 the reference to the "cloud" may be significant. The "cloud" depicts the divine power, presence, and glory; and yet this is the only instance in the book where strictly human figures are associated with a cloud. This must be significant. The two witnesses share in Christ's resurrection. The cloud is a sign of heaven's acceptance of their earthly career. Even their enemies see them, as they will see Christ when he returns with the clouds (1:7). The events of Christ's return and the ascension of the witnesses seem to be simultaneous. Thus in the two witnesses John has symbolized the model of all true prophets, taking as a central clue the story of Jesus' appearance in Jerusalem and describing the common vocation of appearing in the Holy City (or temple) in such a way that reaction to their work would separate the worshipers of God from the unbelievers in language drawn from the stories of many prophets (Minear, *I Saw a New Earth*, p. 103).

13 The earthquake is God's further sign of the vindication of his servants (cf. 6:12). But unlike the earthquake under the sixth seal, this one produces what appears to be repentance: "The survivors . . . gave glory to the God of heaven." The opposite response in 16:9, "they refused to repent and glorify him," seems to confirm that 11:13 speaks of genuine repentance (cf. 14:7; 15:4). Although Ladd (*Commentary on Revela-tion*, p. 159) understands the entire chapter as a reference to the conversion of the Jews, since the death, resurrection, and ascension of the two witnesses is more worldwide in scope (vv.9–10), we may infer that the earthquake is also symbolic of a world-wide event. Verse 13 shows that even in the midst of judgment, God is active in the world to save those who repent. If there is such hope in the terrible time of final judgment, how much more now! God has not abandoned the human race, regardless of the recurring waves of unbelief. Neither should we!

14 All the events from 9:13 to 11:14 fall under the sixth trumpet and are called the second woe (see comments on 8:13 and 9:12). Since there are further judgments (woes) mentioned in this chapter, it is natural to see at the sounding of the seventh trumpet (vv. 15–19) the third woe taking place. Its nature is described in the bowl judgments (16:11ff.). Apparently the third woe will come without further delay. Indeed, the seventh trumpet (v. 15) brings us to the final scenes of God's unfolding mystery (10:7).

Notes

1 A. McNicol has recently argued that 11:1–14 represents a Christian response to the fall of Jerusalem. He sees the section as reflecting the post–A.D. 70 conflict between Christians and Jews. "Revelation 11:1–14 and the Structure of the Apocalypse" *Restor Quart* 22/4 (1979), 193–202.
3 David Hill argues that the two prophets represent the messianic remnant that survives the destruction of unbelieving Israel and that bears within its life the continuing testimony of the Law and the Prophets: "In its readiness to proclaim the truth of God in the face of Jewish unbelief, and even to die for that truth, the entire church is being symbolized." Hill also argues that John, the author of Revelation, while identifying himself with the prophets, sees himself as "unique in his community and as standing closer to the tradition of the Old Testament prophets than the function of the New" ("Prophecy and Prophets in the Revelation of St. John," NTS, 18 [1971–72], 401–18).

4. *Sounding of the seventh trumpet*

11:15–19

[15]The seventh angel sounded his trumpet, and there were loud voices in heaven, which said:

"The kingdom of the world has become the kingdom of
    our Lord and of his Christ,
  and he will reign for ever and ever."

[16]And the twenty-four elders, who were seated on their thrones before God, fell on their faces and worshiped God, [17]saying:

"We give thanks to you, Lord God Almighty,
  who is and who was,
because you have taken your great power
  and have begun to reign.
[18]The nations were angry;
  and your wrath has come.
The time has come for judging the dead,
  and for rewarding your servants the prophets
and your saints and those who reverence your name,
  both small and great—
and for destroying those who destroy the earth."

¹⁹Then God's temple in heaven was opened, and within his temple was seen the ark of his covenant. And there came flashes of lightning, rumblings, peals of thunder, an earthquake and a great hailstorm.

15 The seventh trumpet sounds, and in heaven loud voices proclaim the final triumph of God and Christ over the world. The theme is the kingdom of God and of Christ—a dual kingdom eternal in its duration. The kingdom is certainly a main theme of the entire Book of Revelation (1:6, 9; 5:10; 11:17; 12:10; 19:6; 20:4; 22:5). This kingdom involves the millennial kingdom and its blending into the eternal kingdom (chs. 20–22). The image suggests the transference of the world empire, once dominated by a usurping power, that has now at length passed into the hands of its true owner and king (Swete). The present rulers are Satan, the beast, and the false prophet. The announcement of the reign of the king occurs here, but the final breaking of the enemies' hold over the world does not occur till the return of Christ (19:11ff.).

Verses 15–18 are reminiscent of Psalm 2. The opening portion of this psalm describes the pagan nations and kings set in opposition to God and his Messiah (Anointed One). Then there follows the establishment of the Son in Zion as the Sovereign of the world and an appeal to the world rulers to put their trust in the Son before his wrath burns. John does not distinguish between the millennial kingdom of Christ and the eternal kingdom of the Father (but cf. 3:21) as Paul does (1 Cor 15:24–28). This should be viewed as a difference merely of detail and emphasis, not of basic theology. Furthermore, in John's view this world becomes the arena for the manifestation of God's kingdom. While at this point the emphasis is on the future visible establishment of God's kingdom, in John's mind that same kingdom is in some real sense now present; and he is participating in it (1:9).

16–17 As the other features in these verses are anticipatory, so the expression "have begun to reign" looks forward to the millennial reign depicted in chapter 20. Significantly, the title of God found earlier in the book, "who is, and who was, and who is to come" (1:8; 4:8), now is "who is and who was." He has now *come!* God has taken over the power of the world from Satan (Luke 4:6).

18 This passage contains a synopsis of the remaining chapters of Revelation. The nations opposed to God and incited by the fury of the dragon (12:12) have brought wrath on God's people (Ps 2:1–3). For this, God has brought his wrath upon the nations (14:7; 16:1ff.; 18:20; 19:19b; 20:11–15). The time (*kairos,* "season") has now come for three further events: the judgment of the dead (20:11–15); the final rewarding of the righteous (21:1–4; 22:3–5); and the final destruction of the destroyers of the earth (Babylon, the beast, the false prophet, and the dragon) (19:2, 11; 20:10).

In Revelation there are three groups of persons who receive rewards: (1) God's "servants the prophets" (cf. 18:20; 22:9); (2) the "saints" (perhaps the martyrs; cf. 5:8; 8:3–4; 13:7, 10; 16:6; 18:20, 24; or simply believers in every age, cf. 19:8; 20:9); and (3) "those who reverence [God's] name" (cf. 14:7; 15:4). In whatever way these groups are denoted, it is important to note that in Revelation the prophets are specially singled out (16:6; 18:20, 24; 22:6, 9).

19 In the heavenly temple John sees the ark of God's covenant. In the OT the ark of the covenant was the chest that God directed Moses to have made and placed within the holiest room of the tabernacle sanctuary (Exod 25:10–22). He was directed to put in the ark the two tables of the Decalogue—the documentary basis of God's redemptive covenant with Israel (Exod 34:28–29). It is presumed that the ark was destroyed when Nebuchadnezzar burned the temple in 586 B.C. There was no ark in the second temple (Jos. War V, 219 [v.5]).

A Jewish legend reported in 2 Maccabees 2:4–8 indicates that Jeremiah hid the ark in a cave on Mount Sinai until the final restoration of Israel. There is no reason, however, to believe that John is alluding in v.19 to this Jewish tradition, since he is clearly referring to a heavenly temple and ark, which is symbolic of the new covenant established by the death of Christ. As the way into the holiest was barred under the old covenant to all except the high priest, now full and immediate access for all, as well as a perfect redemption, has been secured by Christ's death (Heb 9:11–12; 10:19–22).

In v.19 the kingdom of God is seen retrospectively as having fully come. Yet its coming will be elaborated in chapters 20 to 22. Prospectively, this sight of the ark of the covenant also prepares us for the following chapters, which concern the faithfulness of God to his covenant people. As the ark of the covenant was the sign to Israel of God's loyal love throughout their wilderness journeys and battles, so this sign of the new covenant will assure the followers of Christ of his loyal love through their severe trial and the attack by the beast. "Flashes of lightning, rumblings, peals of thunder" call our attention to God's presence and vindication of his people (cf. comments on 6:12; 8:5).

Notes

15–19 Elisabeth S. Fiorenza has argued that the author of Revelation does not seek to comfort the persecuted Christian community with reference to past and future history (as in the Jewish apocalyptic literature) but with reference to the eschatological reality of God's kingdom. She sees this main theme briefly but precisely expressed in the hymn in 11:15–19 and presents an outline for structuring the whole book around this concept ("The Eschatology and Composition of the Apocalypse," CBQ, 30 [1968], 537–69).

C. The Seven Signs 12:1–14:20

In this section there is what might be called a Book of Signs. While no signs (*sēmeia;* cf. comments on 12:1) appear in chapters 1 to 11, at least seven signs are mentioned in chapters 12 to 19 (cf. the seven signs in John 1–11). Three are in heaven (12:1, 3; 15:1); four on earth (13:13–14; 16:14; 19:20). Only one is a sign of good (12:1); the others are omens of evil or judgment from God. These signs explain and amplify previous material (e.g., the beast in 11:7 is more fully described in ch. 13) and also advance the drama to its final acts. More specifically, chs. 12 to 14 contain seven further images though only two are directly identified as signs.

This intermediary section (chs. 12–14), preceding the final bowl judgments (15:1ff.), picks up and develops the theme of the persecution of God's people, which has already appeared (3:10; 6:9–11; 7:14; 11:7–10). Chapter 12 gives us a glimpse into the dynamics of the persecution of God's people under the symbolism of the dragon who wages war on the woman and her children (v.17). Chapter 13 continues the same theme by

114

telling of the persecution of the saints by the dragon-energized beasts. Finally, the section closes with (1) the scene of the redeemed 144,000 on Mount Zion who are triumphant over the beast (14:1–5) and (2) looks at the final hour of judgment on the beast worshipers (14:6–20).

1. The woman and the dragon

12:1–17

¹A great and wondrous sign appeared in heaven: a woman clothed with the sun, with the moon under her feet and a crown of twelve stars on her head. ²She was pregnant and cried out in pain as she was about to give birth. ³Then another sign appeared in heaven: an enormous red dragon with seven heads and ten horns and seven crowns on his heads. ⁴His tail swept a third of the stars out of the sky and flung them to the earth. The dragon stood in front of the woman who was about to give birth, so that he might devour her child the moment it was born. ⁵She gave birth to a son, a male child, who will rule all the nations with an iron scepter. And her child was snatched up to God and to his throne. ⁶The woman fled into the desert to a place prepared for her by God, where she might be taken care of for 1,260 days.

⁷And there was war in heaven. Michael and his angels fought against the dragon, and the dragon and his angels fought back. ⁸But he was not strong enough, and they lost their place in heaven. ⁹The great dragon was hurled down—that ancient serpent called the devil or Satan, who leads the whole world astray. He was hurled to the earth, and his angels with him.

¹⁰Then I heard a loud voice in heaven say:

"Now have come the salvation and the power and the
    kingdom of our God,
  and the authority of his Christ.
For the accuser of our brothers,
  who accuses them before our God day and night,
  has been hurled down.
¹¹They overcame him
  by the blood of the Lamb
  and by the word of their testimony;
they did not love their lives so much
  as to shrink from death.
¹²Therefore rejoice, you heavens
  and you who dwell in them!
But woe to the earth and the sea,
  because the devil has gone down to you!
He is filled with fury,
  because he knows that his time is short."

¹³When the dragon saw that he had been hurled to the earth, he pursued the woman who had given birth to the male child. ¹⁴The woman was given the two wings of a great eagle, so that she might fly to the place prepared for her in the desert, where she would be taken care of for a time, times and half a time, out of the serpent's reach. ¹⁵Then from his mouth the serpent spewed water like a river, to overtake the woman and sweep her away with the torrent. ¹⁶But the earth helped the woman by opening its mouth and swallowing the river that the dragon had spewed out of his mouth. ¹⁷Then the dragon was enraged at the woman and went off to make war against the rest of her offspring—those who obey God's commandments and hold to the testimony of Jesus.

In this chapter there are three main figures: the woman, the child, and the dragon. There are also three scenes: the birth of the child (vv. 1–6), the expulsion of the dragon (vv. 7–12), and the dragon's attack on the woman and her children (vv. 13–17).

1 John sees a dazzling sight—a pregnant woman, "clothed with the sun, with the moon under her feet," and wearing a victor's crown (*stephanos*, cf. 2:10; 3:11; 4:4, 10; 6:2; 9:7; 14:14) of twelve stars. John calls the sight a "great sign" (*mega sēmeion*). This shows that the woman is more than a mere woman. She signifies something. Generally John uses *sēmeion* ("sign") to refer to a miraculous sign that points to some deeper spiritual significance in connection with the event or object (John 2:11, 18, et al.; Rev 12:1, 3; 13:13–14; 15:1; 16:14; 19:20). In classical Greek, the word referred especially to the constellations as signs or omens (LSJ, p. 1593).

The basic plot of the story was familiar in the ancient world. A usurper doomed to be killed by a yet unborn prince plots to succeed to the throne by killing the royal seed at birth. The prince is miraculously snatched from his clutches and hidden away, until he is old enough to kill the usurper and claim his kingdom. In the Greek myth of the birth of Apollo, when the child's mother, the goddess Leto, reached the time of her delivery, she was pursued by the dragon Python who sought to kill both her and her unborn child. Only the tiny island of Delos welcomed the mother, where she gave birth to the god Apollo. Four days after his birth, Apollo found Python at Parnassus and killed him in his Delphic cave. In Egypt it is Set the red dragon who pursues Isis, the pregnant mother of Horus. When the child is grown, he too kills the dragon. These stories were living myths in the first century and were probably known to both John and his Asian readers.

While it is easy to point to parallels between these earlier myths and Revelation 12, the differences are striking enough to eliminate the possibility that John merely borrowed pagan myths. As Mounce points out, "Would a writer who elsewhere in the book displays such a definite antagonism toward paganism draw extensively at this point upon its mythology? As always, John is a creative apocalyptist who, although gathering his imagery from many sources, nevertheless constructs a scenario distinctly his own" (*Revelation,* p. 235). To this argument could be added also the evidence of the patristic testimony of the first eight centuries. Not a single voice was raised in favor of interpreting the woman as the embodiment of a mythological figure (Bernard J. LeFrois, *The Woman Clothed With the Sun* [Roma: Orbis Catholicus, 1954], p. 210). Did he, then, draw more directly on OT parallels? Some cite Genesis 37:9–11, where the heavenly bodies of sun, moon, and eleven stars are associated together in Joseph's vision. Joseph's father, Jacob, and his mother, Rachel (the sun and the moon), together with his eleven brothers (the stars), bow down before Joseph. Yet while the sun, moon, and twelve stars are parallel in both accounts, the other details are quite different. For example, the woman and the child who are central to John's account are totally absent from the Joseph dream. It thus seems highly unlikely that John intended his readers to interpret this chapter from the Genesis material.

Others see a more conscious parallelism between the story and the activities of the emperor Domitian around 83 A.D. After the death of his ten-year-old son, Domitian immediately proclaimed the boy a god and his mother, the mother of god. Coinage of this period shows the mother Domitia as the mother of the gods (Cerea, Demeter, Cybele) or enthroned on the divine throne or standing with the scepter and diadem of the queen of heaven with the inscription "Mother of the Divine Caesar." Another coin shows the mother with the child before her. In his left hand is the scepter of world dominions, and with his right hand he is blessing the world. Still another coin shows the dead child sitting on the globe of heaven, playing with seven stars, which represent the seven planets, symbolic of his heavenly dominion over the world. A recently discovered coin of the same period shows on the obverse, like the others, the head of Domitia; but instead of the child on the reverse, it has the moon and the other six planets, emblematic of the golden age. Stauffer interprets this coin's imagery as representing the imperial Zeus child, who has been exalted to be lord of the stars, who will usher in the age of universal salvation that is to come (Ethelbert Stauffer, *Christ and the Caesars* [London: SCM, 1965], pp. 151–52).

Whereas the coinage of Domitian glorifies the son of Domitia as the lord of heaven and savior of the world, Revelation 12 presents Jesus Christ, the Lord of heaven and earth, as he who will rule all nations with a rod of iron (v.5). Tenney says, "The parallel imagery seems almost too similar to be accidental" (Merrill F. Tenney, *New Testament Times* [Grand Rapids: Eerdmans, 1955], p. 337). From this viewpoint, what John does is to demythologize the contemporary Domitian myth by presenting Christ as the true and ascended Lord of heaven, the coming Ruler and Savior of the world.

Another approach to the source problem in this chapter is to compare the chapter with a passage in the DSS. The Hymn scroll contains this disputed passage:

> She who is big with the Man of distress is in her pains. For she shall give birth to a man-child in the billows of Death, and in the bonds of Sheol there shall spring from the crucible of the pregnant one a Marvellous Counsellor with his might; and he shall deliver every man from the billows because of Her who is big with him (1QH E.3:9–10).

In notes explaining the above translation, Dupont-Sommer indicates that not only is the man-child (also called Marvelous Counselor and firstborn) a reference to Messiah based on Isaiah 9:5–6 but that the "crucible" refers to the suffering of the Messiah. The woman symbolizes the "congregation of the just, the Church of the Saints, victim of the persecution of the wicked," and is also associated with the redeeming work of the Messiah. Dupont-Sommer also notices that in the verses of the hymn that immediately follow, there is a reference to another pregnant woman who represents the community of the wicked. She gives birth to the "Asp" or serpent (from Gen 3), which refers to Satan (*The Essene Writings from Qumran*, tr. G. Vermes [Cleveland: World, 1962], p. 208, nn. 1–5).

Other OT references to the birth of the Messiah through the messianic community (Isa 9:6–7; Mic 5:2) and to the travailing messianic community (Isa 26:17; 66:7) should also be noted. In the OT, the image of a woman is frequently associated with Israel, Zion, or Jerusalem (Isa 54:1–6; Jer 3:20; Ezek 16:8–14; Hos 2:19–20). If the main thrust of Dupont-Sommer's interpretation can be accepted (see Notes, v.1), this background seems to provide a much closer link to the intended significance of chapter 12 than the other proposed parallels. In any case, there seems to be in chapter 12 a blending of elements from OT concepts, Jewish materials, ancient mythical stories, and possibly the Domitian child myth. Regardless of the sources or allusions, John reinterprets the older stories and presents a distinctively Christian view of history in the imagery of the woman and her children.

Who then *is* the woman? While it is not impossible that she is an actual woman, such as Mary, the evidence clearly shows that she, like the woman in chapter 17, has symbolic significance. At the center of chapter 12 is the persecution of the woman by the dragon, who is definitely identified as Satan (v.9). This central theme, as well as the reference to the persecution of the "rest of her offspring" (v.17), renders it virtually certain that the woman could not refer to a single individual. Thus, even some recent Roman Catholic interpreters have departed from this view (Ford, p. 207; Heidt, p. 85; but for a strong case for Mary as the woman, see LeFrois, *Woman Clothed With the Sun*, esp. pp. 211–35).

Some identify the woman exclusively with the Jewish people, the nation of Israel (Walvoord, p. 188). This view seems to be supported by the reference to the woman giving birth to the Messiah or "male child" (v.5); the twelve stars would refer to the twelve tribes (Gen 37:9–11). The twelve signs of the zodiac were thought by the Jews to represent the twelve tribes; their tribal standards corresponded to the zodiacal names (*Berakoth* 32; cf. Ford, p. 343). (On the floor of the ancient sixth-century synagogue of Beth Alpha [near Gilboa in Israel] lies a mosaic with the crescent moon and the sun and the twelve signs of the zodiac with twenty-three stars scattered around a figure representing the sun god.) While these factors must be taken seriously, there are internal problems with this view. The dragon's persecution of the woman after the Messiah's birth could hardly refer to the devil's attack on the nation as a whole but could apply only to the believing part of the people. The whole intent of the passage is to explain the persecution of the believing community, not the persecution of the nation of Israel as a whole.

Since the context indicates that the woman under attack represents a continuous entity from the birth of Christ until at least John's day or later, her identity in the author's mind must be the believing covenant-messianic community. This group would include the early messianic community, which under John the Baptist's ministry was separated from the larger Jewish community to be the people prepared for the Lord (Mark 1:2–3). Later this group merged into the new community of Christ's disciples called the church, or less appropriately, the new Israel, composed of both Jews and Gentiles. John does not at this point seem to distinguish between the earlier almost totally Jewish community and the one present in his day. Their continuity in identity is so strong that whatever ethnic or other differences they have does not affect his single image representing one entity.

The woman's dazzling appearance like the sun relates her to the glory and brilliance of her Lord (Rev 1:16) as well as to her own light-bearing quality (1:20). With the moon under her feet signifying her permanence (Pss 72:5; 89:37; cf. Matt 16:18) and a crown of twelve stars on her head indicating her elect identity (cf. comments at 7:4ff.), she appears in her true heavenly and glorious character despite her seemingly fragile and uncertain earthly history (vv.13–16). A possible allusion to her priestly nature may be suggested by the cosmic imagery of stars, sun, and moon, figures that Josephus uses in describing the high priestly vestments (Antiq. III, 179–87 [vii. 7]; cf. Rev 1:6; 5:10; see Ford, p. 197). Peter likewise refers to the priestly function of the church (1 Peter 2:5, 9). The church viewed as a woman is found elsewhere in the NT as well as in early Christian literature (2 Cor 11:2; Eph 5:25–27, 32; 2 John 1, 5, with 3 John 9; *Hermas* 5.1.i–ii).

2 The woman is in the throes of childbirth. The emphasis is on her pain and suffering, both physical and spiritual. The meaning of her anguish is that the faithful messianic community has been suffering as a prelude to the coming of the Messiah himself and the new age (Isa 26:17; 66:7–8; Mic 4:10; 5:3). The "birth" (*tiktō*) itself does not necessarily refer to the actual physical birth of Christ but denotes the travail of the community from which the Messiah has arisen (see same word in Heb 6:7 and James 1:15).

3 The second "sign" now appears. It likewise is a heavenly sign and introduces us to the second character, the ultimate antagonist of the woman. The dragon is clearly identified with the "ancient serpent called the devil or Satan" (v.9; cf. 20:2–3). The description of him as an "enormous red dragon" symbolically suggests his fierce power and murderous nature. He is further described as having "seven heads and ten horns and seven crowns on his heads." Except for the exchange of the crowns from the heads to the horns, the same description is used for the beast from the sea in chapter 13 and the beast of chapter 17. There is no way of understanding how the horns fit on the heads. While some have tried to find specific meaning for each of the heads and horns, John probably intends to give no more than a symbolic sense of the whole impression rather than of its parts. It is a picture of the fullness of evil in all its hideous strength. (Compare here the OT references to Rahab and Leviathan: Ps 74:13–14; Isa 27:1; 51:9–10; Dan 7:7; 8:10.) There is more than a coincidental similarity in these descriptions and John's image. The diadem crowns on the heads may indicate fullness of royal power (13:1; 19:12).

4 So great is the dragon's power that his tail can even sweep away a large number of the stars and cast them down to the ground (for "a third," see comments on 8:7). This should probably be understood simply as a figure to represent the dragon's power and not as a reference to Satan's victory over some of the angels. In any event, the stars cast down would, after the analogy of Daniel 8:10, 24, refer to the saints of God who were trampled by Satan and not to fallen angels. Satan has placed himself before the woman, thus expecting certain victory over the messianic child. As Lilje (in loc.) notes, it is through this figure that the church shows her awareness that Satan is always threatening the purposes of God within history. Although the attack of Herod against the children of Bethlehem and many incidents during the life of Jesus—such as the attempt of the crowd at Nazareth to throw him over the cliff (Luke 4:28–39)—must also be included, the greatest attempt to devour the child must certainly be the Crucifixion.

5 This verse records the last element of the story. The messianic child comes, finishes his mission, is delivered from the dragon, and is enthroned in heaven. John again refers to the destiny of the child in once more alluding to Psalm 2:9: "Who will rule all the nations with an iron scepter" (Rev 2:27; 19:15). It is not clear whether John also intends a collective identity in the birth of the male child. Daniel 7:13–14, 27 seems to fuse the individual son of man with the people of God. Likewise in Revelation John seems to alternate between the rule of Christ (1:5; 11:15) and the rule of the saints (1:6; 2:26–27). It is, however, difficult to see how the child as well as the woman could be a group of believers. Nevertheless, many early interpreters such as Tyconius (d.390), Pseudo-Augustine (d.542), Primasius (d.552), Quodvultdeus (d.453), and others understood the male child to be simultaneously Christ and the members of Christ; and even a few (Methodius [d.312]; Venerable Bede [d.735]) saw the child as a reference only to the church (LeFrois, *Woman Clothed With the Sun*, pp. 58–61). Through Christ's resurrection and ascension, the dragon's attempt to destroy God's purposes through the Messiah has been decisively defeated.

6 What is this flight into the desert? Is it a symbolic or an actual historic event? Among those who take it literally, some have understood the reference as the escape of the early Jerusalem Christians to Pella (modern Tabaqat Fahil, about twenty miles south of the Sea of Galilee) in A.D. 66 to escape the Roman destruction of Jerusalem. Pella continued to be an important Christian center even after a large portion of the community returned to Jerusalem in 135. Others refer the event to the future, when a portion of the Jewish people will be preserved through the Tribulation period to await the return of Christ (Walvoord). Other approaches view the desert as a symbol for the hiddenness of the church in the world because of persecution (Swete) or as a symbol of its pure condition (Lilje).

Most commentators, however, understand the wilderness to mean the place of safety, discipline, and testing (Caird, Farrar, Ford). This view is preferable because of the highly symbolic nature of the whole chapter, the symbolic use of "desert" in 17:3 (q.v.), and the parallelism to the Exodus where the children of Israel fled from Pharaoh. All are agreed that the reference here to the flight of the woman is anticipatory of vv. 13ff. The intervening verses show why the dragon is persecuting the woman (vv. 7–12).

For a discussion of the 1,260 days, see comments at 11:2.

7 All agree that the section beginning with this verse, which describes the battle in heaven between Michael and the dragon (vv. 7–12), provides the explanation as to why the dragon has turned on the woman and caused her to flee into the desert for protection (vv. 6, 13ff.). The account is in two parts: (1) the battle in heaven between Michael and his angels and the dragon and his angels, which results in the ejection of Satan from heaven to the earth (vv. 7–9), and (2) the heavenly hymn of victory (vv. 10–12).

As elsewhere in the book, the narrative material can be interpreted only in the light of the hymns. This principle is especially important in vv. 7–9, where the victory takes place in heaven as the result of Michael's defeat of the dragon. Were this the only thing told us about the "war in heaven," it might be concluded that the dragon's defeat was unrelated to Jesus Christ. But the interpretative hymn (vv. 10–12) says that it was in fact the blood of Christ that dealt the actual death blow to the dragon and enabled the saints to triumph (v. 8; cf. 5:9). Does this not suggest that the redeeming work of Christ is here depicted by the cosmic battle of Michael and the dragon as it is elsewhere seen as a loosing from sin (1:5), as a washing of our garments (7:14), and as a purchasing to God (5:9)? The time of the dragon's defeat and ejection from heaven must therefore be connected with the incarnation, ministry, death, and resurrection of Jesus (v. 13: Luke 10:18; John 12:31). Christ has appeared in order that he may destroy the works of the devil (Matt 12:28–29; Acts 10:38; 2 Tim 1:10; 1 John 3:8).

Early Jewish belief held the view that Michael would cast Satan from heaven as the first of the last-time struggles to establish the kingdom of God on earth. John, in contrast, sees this event as already having taken place through Jesus Christ's appearance and work. Only the final, permanent blow of Satan's ejection from earth remains (Rev 20:10; cf. Charles, *Commentary on Revelation*, 1: 324). The fact that the battle first takes place in heaven between Michael, the guardian of God's people (Dan 10:13, 21; 12:1; Jude 9), and the dragon shows that evil is cosmic in dimension (not limited merely to this world) and also that events on earth are first decided in heaven. By way of contrast, in the DSS the decisive final battle takes place on earth, not in heaven (1QM 9.16; 17.6–7). The single intent of the passage is to assure those who meet satanic evil on earth that it is really a defeated power, however contrary it might seem to human experience (Ladd, *Commentary on Revelation*, p. 171).

8–9 The triumph of the archangel results in the ejection of the dragon and his angels from heaven to earth. Apparently, prior to this event Satan had access to the heavens and continually assailed the loyalty of the saints (Job 1:9–11; Zech 3:1), but now, together with his angels, he has been cast out (cf. Luke 10:18). Whatever appears to be the earthly situation for God's people now, the victory has already been won. When the battle grows fiercer and darker for the church, it is but the sign of the last futile attempt of the dragon to exercise his power before the kingdom of Christ comes (v. 12). The "ancient serpent" who tempted Eve with lies about God (Gen 3:1ff.) is in John's mind the same individual as the "devil" and "Satan." As Farrer says, "It is precisely when Satan has lost the battle for the souls of the saints in heaven that he begins the fruitless persecution of their bodies (Austin Farrer, *A Rebirth of Images: the Making of St. John's Apocalypse* [London: Darce, 1949], p. 142). Satan is also the one who "leads the whole world astray." His power lies in deception, and by his lies the whole world is deceived about God (2:20; 13:14; 18:23; 19:20; 20:3, 8, 10; 2 John 7; cf. Rom 1:25).

10 This anonymous hymn, which interprets the great battle of the preceding verses, has three stanzas: the first (v. 10) focuses on the victorious inauguration of God's kingdom and Christ's kingly authority; the second (v. 11) calls attention to the earthly victory of the saints as they confirm the victory of Christ by their own identification with Jesus in his witness and death; the third (v. 12) announces the martyrs' victory and the final woe to the earth because of the devil's ejection and impending demise.

In the first stanza (v. 10), the triumph of Christ is described as the arrival of three divine realities in history: God's "salvation" or victory (7:10; 19:1), God's "power," and God's "kingdom." This latter reality is further identified as Christ's assumption of his "authority." The historic event of Christ's life, death, and resurrection has challenged the dominion of Satan and provoked the crisis of history. At the time of Christ's death on earth, Satan was being defeated in heaven by Michael. As Caird has said, "Michael . . . is not the field officer who does the actual fighting, but the staff officer in the heavenly room, who is able to remove Satan's flag from the heavenly map because the real victory has been won on Calvary" (p. 154).

In times past, Satan's chief role as adversary was directed toward accusing God's people of disobedience to God. The justice of these accusations was recognized by God, and therefore Satan's presence in heaven was tolerated. But now the presence of the crucified Savior in God's presence provides the required satisfaction of God's justice with reference to our sins (1 John 2:1–2; 4:10). Therefore, Satan's accusations are no longer valid and he is cast out. What strong consolation this provides for God's faltering people!

11 This stanza is both a statement and an appeal. It announces that the followers of the Lamb also become victors over the dragon because they participate in the "blood of the Lamb," the weapon that defeated Satan, and because they have confirmed their loyalty to the Lamb by their witness even to death. The blood of the martyrs, rather than signaling the triumph of Satan, shows instead that they have gained the victory over the dragon by their acceptance of Jesus' Cross and their obedient suffering with him. This is one of John's chief themes (1:9; 6:9; 14:12; 20:4).

Verses 12 and 17 lead to the conclusion that only a portion of the martyrs are in view (cf. 6:11). Thus this hymn of victory also becomes an appeal to the rest of the saints to do likewise and confirm their testimony to Christ even if doing so means death. This seems to suggest that in some mysterious sense the sufferings of the people of God are linked to the sufferings of Jesus in his triumph over Satan and evil (John 12:31; Rom 16:20; Col 1:24). Since the martyrs have gotten the victory over the dragon because of the Cross of Jesus (i.e., they can no longer be accused of damning sin, since Jesus has paid sin's penalty [1:5b]), they are now free even to give up their lives in loyalty to their Redeemer (John 12:25; Rev 15:2).

12 Satan has failed. Therefore, the heavens and all who are in them should be glad. But Satan does not accept defeat without a bitter struggle. His final death throes are directed exclusively toward "the earth and the sea." Therefore their inhabitants will mourn, for the devil will now redouble his wrathful effort in one last futile attempt to make the most of an opportunity he knows will be brief (three and one-half years; cf. vv.6, 14).

13–14 The narrative is resumed after the flight of the woman into the wilderness (v.6). Why? Because she is under attack from the defeated but still vicious dragon (vv.7–12). No longer able to attack the male child who is in heaven or to accuse the saints because of the victory of Jesus on the Cross, and banned from heaven, the devil now pursues the woman, who flees into the desert. The word "pursue" was no doubt carefully chosen by John because it is also the NT word for "persecute" (*diōkō*, Matt 5:10 et al.). Since the woman has already given birth to the child, the time of the pursuit by the dragon follows the earthly career of Jesus.

The reference to eagle's wings once again introduces imagery borrowed from the Exodus account where Israel was pursued by the dragon in the person of Pharaoh: "You yourselves have seen what I did to Egypt, and how I carried you on eagles' wings and brought you to myself" (Exod 19:4). As God's people were delivered from the enemy by their journey into the Sinai desert, so God's present people will be preserved miraculously from destruction (cf. Deut 32:10–12; Isa 40:31).

15–16 The serpent spews a floodlike river of water out of his mouth to engulf and drown the woman. The water imagery seems clear enough. It symbolizes destruction by an enemy (Pss 32:6; 69:1–2; 124:2–5; Nah 1:8) or calamity (Ps 18:4). As the desert earth absorbs the torrent, so the covenant people will be helped by God and preserved from utter destruction (Isa 26:20; 42:15; 43:2; 50:2). The dragon-inspired Egyptians of old were swallowed by the earth: "You stretched out your right hand and the earth swallowed them" (Exod 15:12). In similar fashion, the messianic community will be delivered by God's power. Whatever specific events were happening to Christians in Asia in John's day would not exhaust the continuing significance of the passage.

17 This attack of Satan against "the rest" of the woman's offspring seems to involve the final attempt to destroy the messianic people of God. Having failed in previous attempts to eliminate them as a whole, the dragon now strikes at individuals who "obey God's commandments and hold to the testimony of Jesus." To "make war" (*poiēsai polemon*) is the identical expression used of the beast's attack on the two witnesses in 11:7 and on the saints in 13:7. Could this possibly correlate the three groups and indicate their common identity under different figures?

Those attacked are called "the rest of her [the woman's] offspring." Some identify this group as Gentile Christians in distinction from the Jewish mother church (Glasson). Others who identify the mother as the nation of Israel see the "rest" as the believing remnant in the Jewish nation who turn to Christ (Walvoord)—a view that depends on the prior identification of the woman with the whole nation of Israel. Others have suggested that the woman represents the believing community as a whole, the universal or ideal church composed of both Jews and Gentiles, whereas the "offspring" of the woman represent individuals of the community (Jews and Gentiles) who suffer persecution and martyrdom from the dragon in the pattern of Christ (Swete, Caird, Kiddle). The close identification of the seed of the woman as first of all Jesus and then also those who have become his brethren through faith agrees with other NT teaching (Matt 25:40; Heb 2:11–12). While Satan cannot prevail against the Christian community itself, he can wage war on certain of its members who are called on to witness to their Lord by obedience even unto death, i.e., "those who obey God's commandments and hold to the testimony of Jesus" (Matt 16:18; Rev 11:7; 13:7, 15). The church, then, is paradoxically both invulnerable (the woman) and vulnerable (her children) (cf. Luke 21:16–18).

Notes

1 On whether the Qumran Hymn (1QH, III) bears a direct relation to John's image of the woman as the Christian community, see pro Dupont-Sommer, *Writings from Qumran,* pp. 207–8, nn. 1–5; Ford, pp. 204–5; contra William LaSor, *The Dead Sea Scrolls and the New Testament* (Grand Rapids: Eerdmans, 1972), pp. 208–9.

6 The third person plural τρέφωσιν (*trephōsin*) may be a Semitism for the simple singular passive, meaning, "she might be taken care of." No plural antecedent fits, and the sense is passive. Such occurrences are found in the OT and possibly also in Rev 11:2, "they will trample," meaning, "the holy city shall be trampled." For this idiom, see Ronald J. Williams, *Hebrew Syntax: An Outline* (Toronto: University of Toronto, 1967), p. 32, par. 160.

7 The infinitive construction τοῦ πολεμῆσαι (*tou polemēsai;* NIV, "fought") has been discussed by Charles (*Commentary on Revelation,* 1:322) and G. Mussies (*The Morphology of Koine Greek as Used in the Apocalypse of St. John* [Leiden: E.J. Brill, 1971], p. 96), who both conclude that this is a pure Semitism and should be translated as "Michael and his angels had to fight with the Dragon." Almost all translations fail to catch this nuance, so illuminating to the context.

On the dragon myths of the ancient world, see Bruce Waltke's "The Creation Account in Genesis 1:1–3," BS, 132 (January-March 1975), pp. 32ff.

11 NIV does not translate the connective particle καί (*kai,* normally "and") that begins this verse in the Gr. text. The particle could be translated "for" and would, if so rendered, give an additional connection between the defeat of Satan and the death of the martyrs.

2. *The two beasts*

13:1–18

[1]And the dragon stood on the shore of the sea.

And I saw a beast coming out of the sea. He had ten horns and seven heads, with ten crowns on his horns, and on each head a blasphemous name. [2]The beast I saw resembled a leopard, but had feet like those of a bear and a mouth like that of a lion. The dragon gave the beast his power and his throne and great authority. [3]One of the heads of the beast seemed to have had a fatal wound, but the fatal wound had been healed. The whole world was astonished and followed the beast.

⁴Men worshiped the dragon because he had given authority to the beast, and they also worshiped the beast and asked, "Who is like the beast? Who can make war against him?"

⁵The beast was given a mouth to utter proud words and blasphemies and to exercise his authority for forty-two months. ⁶He opened his mouth to blaspheme God, and to slander his name and his dwelling place and those who live in heaven. ⁷He was given power to make war against the saints and to conquer them. And he was given authority over every tribe, people, language and nation. ⁸All inhabitants of the earth worship the beast—all whose names have not been written in the book of life belonging to the Lamb that was slain from the creation of the world.

⁹He who has an ear, let him hear.

¹⁰If anyone is to go into captivity,
   into captivity he will go.
If anyone is to be killed with the sword,
   with the sword he will be killed.

This calls for patient endurance and faithfulness on the part of the saints.

¹¹Then I saw another beast, coming out of the earth. He had two horns like a lamb, but he spoke like a dragon. ¹²He exercised all the authority of the first beast on his behalf, and made the earth and its inhabitants worship the first beast, whose fatal wound had been healed. ¹³And he performed great and miraculous signs, even causing fire to come down from heaven to earth in full view of men. ¹⁴Because of the signs he was given power to do on behalf of the first beast, he deceived the inhabitants of the earth. He ordered them to set up an image in honor of the beast who was wounded by the sword and yet lived. ¹⁵He was given power to give breath to the image of the first beast, so that it could speak and cause all who refused to worship the image to be killed. ¹⁶He also forced everyone, small and great, rich and poor, free and slave, to receive a mark on his right hand or on his forehead, ¹⁷so that no one could buy or sell unless he had the mark, which is the name of the beast or the number of his name.

¹⁸This calls for wisdom. If anyone has insight, let him calculate the number of the beast, for it is man's number. His number is 666.

This chapter forms part of the theme of the persecution of God's people John began to develop in chapter 12. Turning from the inner dynamics of the struggle, chapter 13 shifts to the actual earthly instruments of this assault—viz., the two dragon-energized beasts. In accord with the discussion in chapter 12, we may assume that the beast-related activities constitute the way the dragon carries out his final attempts to wage war on the seed of the woman (12:17). A contest is going on to seduce the whole world—even the followers of Jesus—to worship the beast. As Minear shows (*I Saw a New Earth,* p. 118), John seeks to emphasize three things about the first beast: he shows (1) the conspiracy of the dragon with the beast (vv. 2–4); (2) the universal success of this partnership in deceiving the whole world to worship them (vv. 3–4, 8); and (3) that the partnership will succeed in a temporary defeat of the saints of God, thus accomplishing the greatest blasphemy of God (vv. 6–7a).

Finally, not being able to seduce all the earth alone, the conspirators summon yet a third figure to their aids—the beast from the earth. He must remain loyal to his associates and at the same time be sufficiently similar to the Lamb to entice even the followers of Jesus. He must be able to perform miraculous signs (*sēmeia*) much as the two witnesses did (vv. 11ff.; cf. 13:13 with 11:5). As the battle progresses, the dragon's deception becomes more and more subtle. Thus the readers are called to discern the criteria that will enable them to separate the lamblike beast from the Lamb himself (13:11 with 14:1).

Two basic interpretative problems confront the reader. These have led students of the book to different understandings of this chapter: (1) The identification of the beast and his associate—are they personal or some other entity? (2) The time of the beast's rule—is it past, continuous, or still future? In seeking some satisfactory answers to these questions, it may be helpful to first set forth the facts about the beast. He (1) rises from the sea (v.1); (2) resembles the dragon (v.1); (3) has composite animal features (v.2); (4) is dragon empowered (v.2); (5) has one head wounded to death but healed (vv.3–4, 7b–8); (6) blasphemes God and God's people for forty-two months (vv.5–6); (7) makes war against the saints and kills them (vv.7a, 15); and (8) gives to those who follow him his "mark," which is either his name or his number, 666 (vv.16–18).

In addition, there are no fewer than a dozen further references in Revelation to the beast (11:7; 14:9, 11; 15:2; 16:2, 10, 13; 19:19–20; 20:4, 10), excluding the nine references to the scarlet-colored beast in chapter 17, which should probably be included. These further references contain no new information, but 11:7 indicates that the beast rises from the Abyss. Also, 19:19 refers to a coalition of the beast with the "kings of the earth," and 19:20 describes his final end in the lake of fire.

The history of the interpretation of chapter 13 is far too extensive for this commentary to cover. As early as the second century, two different understandings of the Antichrist appeared. Some early interpreters take the position that the Antichrist will be a person, a world deceiver who will reign for the last half of Daniel's seventieth week (Dan 7:25). The Epistle of Barnabas (A.D. 70–100?) warns believers to be alert to the imminent appearing of "the final stumbling-block," who is identified with the "little horn" of Daniel 7:24 (4.3–6, 9–10; ANF, 1:138–39). The Didache (early second century?) refers to a "world deceiver [who] will appear in the guise of God's Son. He will work 'signs and wonders' and the earth will fall into his hands and he will commit outrages such as have never occurred before" (16.4, in Cyril C. Richardson, ed., *Library of Christian Classics*, vol. 1, *Early Christian Fathers*, [Philadelphia: Westminster, 1953], p. 178). Justin Martyr (d. 165) likewise looked for the appearance in his lifetime of the Antichrist prophesied by Daniel, who would reign for three and one-half years according to Daniel 7:25 (*Dialogue* 32; ANF, 1:210).

Irenaeus (d. 202) gives the first extensive discussion of the Antichrist. He is to be an unrighteous king from the tribe of Dan, the little horn of Daniel 7:8, who will reign over the earth during the last three and one-half years of Daniel's seventieth "week" (Dan 9:27). Irenaeus identifies the Antichrist with the first beast of Revelation 13 and the "man of sin" ("lawlessness," NIV) of 2 Thessalonians 2:3–4, who will exalt himself in the Jerusalem temple (rebuilt) (*Contra Haereses* 5.25.1–5; 5.28.2; 5.30.2; ANF, 1:553, 556–59). This view, with modifications, is followed by Irenaeus's student Hippolytus (d. 235), also by Tertullian (d. 220) and Victorinus (d. 304), and in recent times by many commentators, including Barnhouse, Bruce, Gaebelein, Ladd, Morris, Mounce, Scofield, and Walvoord. In its favor is the more literal reading of 2 Thessalonians 2:1–10 and the natural understanding of the Antichrist as being the personal counterpart to the personal Christ.

On the other hand, from the earliest times some interpreters have understood the Antichrist as a present threat of heresy, depending more on the concept found in the Johannine Epistles (1 John 2:18, 22; 4:3; 2 John 7). Thus Polycarp (d. 155), said to be a disciple of the apostle John, understands the Antichrist to be revealed in the docetic heresies of his time (*Philippians* 7.1; ANF, 1:34). Likewise, Tertullian identifies the many false prophets of docetism with the Antichrist but sees these teachers as the forerunners of the future Antichrist, who as the Arch Deceiver will come "in all kinds of counterfeit miracles, signs and wonders" to mislead those who "have not believed the truth but have delighted in wickedness" (2 Thess 2:9–12) (*Against Marcion* 5.16; ANF, 3:463–64).

Luther, Calvin, and other Reformers adopting this general view identified the beast with the papacy of the Roman Catholic Church. Only one recent interpreter, Henry Alford, seems to follow the Reformers in their view. However, other modern commentators adopt the theological heresy interpretation of the Antichrist (Berkouwer, Minear, Newman). In its favor are the references to the Antichrist in the Johannine Epistles and the advantage of seeing the beast as a present threat to the church and not merely as an eschatological figure of the last time. This view also argues that the 2 Thessalonians 2 passage need not be understood as referring to a single future individual (see G.C. Berkouwer, *The Return of Christ* [Grand Rapids: Eerdmans, 1972], pp. 268–71). The issue is difficult to settle with any finality. However, I will develop chapter 13 more in accord with the theological heresy view, while recognizing at the same time that Tertullian's position as stated above is consistent with my position and that the personal future Antichrist view has strong support. (See also the comments at v.11.)

In modern interpretation, as Minear points out, there is almost complete agreement that the "wounded head" (v.3) refers to the Nero redivivus legend. It will be helpful to have Minear's summary of the legend before us:

> Let us look first, then, at the Neronic legend itself. Toward the end of his reign Nero's unpopularity among Roman citizens had assumed high proportions. In 67 and 68 open revolts had broken out against his authority in Gaul and Spain. At length he had been repudiated by the praetorian guard and by the Senate. Fleeing from the city, he had taken refuge in a friend's suburban villa, where he had received word that the Senate had proclaimed him a public enemy and had approved Galba as his successor. Having been warned that pursuing soldiers were approaching his hideout, he had cut his own throat with a sword (June 9, 68). After his death a rumor spread abroad that he had not actually died but had escaped to Parthia, whence he would soon return to regain his throne. This rumor circulated most quickly in the eastern provinces, and assumed strange forms. At one stage, popular expectation envisaged the return of Nero from Parthia, with a huge army subduing all opposition:
>
> > And to the west shall come the strife of gathering war and the exile from Rome, brandishing a mighty sword, crossing the Euphrates with many myriads.
>
> On the basis of this rumor, impostors arose in the east who assumed the name of Nero in the effort to exploit the legend. There are records of at least two such claimants. There seems to have been a later stage in the legend in which Nero's figure has become invested with supernatural status. Now his return from the abyss with hordes of demons is anticipated as an omen of the "last days." Among the oracles of the Sibyl we find an extensive reference to this expectation:
>
> > There shall be at the last time about the waning of the moon, a world-convulsing war, deceitful in guilefulness. And there shall come from the ends of the earth a matricide fleeing and devising sharp-edged plans. He shall ruin all the earth, and gain all power, and surpass all men in cunning. That for which he perished he shall seize at once. And he shall destroy many men and great tyrants, and shall burn all men as none other ever did (vv.361ff.) (*I Saw a New Earth*, pp. 248–49.).

This Neronic interpretation presupposes an identification in John's mind between the sea beast and the Roman Empire, a view espoused in our day by both preterist and not a few preterist-futurist interpreters of Revelation (most recently by Mounce, *Revelation*, pp. 250–51). This in turn usually assumes that Revelation 17 identifies the seven heads of the beast as the successive emperors of the Roman Empire. Yet a question concerning the reliability of this whole Neronic approach must be raised. Minear argues convincingly that the Nero redivivus view will fit neither the facts of history nor the text of Revelation 13 and 17 (*I Saw a New Earth*, pp. 228–60). (See comments at 17:8–9.)

Newman also impressively calls the Nero myth into question. He argues that Irenaeus, the best source for the Domitian dating of the book, never refers either to a Domitian persecution as the background for John's thought or to any Nero-myth interpretation, even though he is attempting to refute the identification of the number 666 with any Roman emperor. Newman concludes that Revelation could just as well be viewed as a theological polemic against some form of Gnosticism than, as popularly held, a political polemic. Newman also challenges the widely held assumption that all apocalyptic literature—and especially the Book of Revelation—must be understood as arising out of some contemporary political crisis for the saints. Little evidence can be cited for more than a selective and local persecution of Christians under Domitian's rule (E.T. Merrill, *Essays in Early Christian History* [London: Macmillan & Co., 1924], pp. 157–73; F.F. Bruce, *New Testament History* [New York: Doubleday, 1972], pp. 412–14; Barclay Newman, "The Fallacy of the Domitian Hypothesis," NTS, 10 [1963], 139–49; G. Edmundson, *The Church in Rome in the First Century* [London: Longmans, Green, 1913]).

Likewise rejecting the beast-equals-Rome hypothesis is Foerster, who points out that rabbinic exegesis up to the first century A.D. identified the fourth beast of Daniel 7 as Edom-equals-Rome. Since the beast of Revelation 13 is a composite that unites all the features of the four beasts of Daniel 7, it therefore cannot be identified with Rome (TDNT, 3:134–35, esp. n.11). An attempt will be made in this exposition to demonstrate that the Rome hypothesis is untenable. This leaves the question open as to whether John sees the Antichrist (or beast) as a person or some more encompassing entity.

1a NIV and most other modern translations include v. 1a as the concluding verse of chapter 12 because a variant Greek reading changes the KJV text "I stood" to "he stood" (i.e., the dragon). The latter reading is favored by a majority of textual scholars, though the KJV text may be the original (see Notes). If "he stood" is the correct reading, the sense would be that the dragon, who has now turned his rage on the children of the woman (12:17), stands on the seashore to summon his next instrument, the beast from the sea. But if the text reads "I stood," the sense is that John receives a new vision (cf. 10:1) as he gazes out over the sea in the same manner as Daniel (7:2).

1b–2 The beast (*thērion*, "wild beast") has already been described in 11:7 as rising from the "Abyss" (cf. 17:8). Thus the sea may symbolize the Abyss, the source of demonic powers that are opposed to God (cf. 9:1; 20:1–3), rather than "the agitated surface of unregenerate humanity (cf. Isa 57:20), and especially of the seething caldron of national and social life" (Swete, p. 158). This view agrees with the OT images of the sea as the origin of the satanic sea monsters—the dragon (Tannin), Leviathan

("Coiled One"), and Rahab ("Rager") (Job 26:12–13; Pss 74:13–14; 87:4; 89:10; Isa 27:1; 51:9; cf. also Ezek 32:6–8). The ancient Hebrews demythologized the sea-monster myths to depict the victory of the Lord of Israel over the demonic forces of evil that in various manifestations had sought to destroy the people of God. Thus John later foresees the final day of Christ's victory when there will "no longer [be] any sea" or source of demonic opposition to God and his people (21:1).

John describes the beast in words similar to those he used in 12:3 of the dragon: "He had ten horns and seven heads, with ten crowns on his horns." There is a slight difference here in the matter of the crowns, which may represent some change in the dragon's authority. As previously indicated (cf. comments on 12:3), any attempt to identify the heads or horns as separate kings, kingdoms, etc., should be resisted.

The image of the seven-headed monster is well attested in ancient Sumerian, Babylonian, and Egyptian texts. A cylinder seal coming from Tel Asmar (ancient Eshnunna, some fifty miles northeast of modern Baghdad), dating back to about 2500 B.C., shows two divine figures killing a seven-headed monster with flames arising from its back. Four of its heads are drooping as if already dead. A spear is in the hand of a figure who is striking the fourth head (see Alexander Heidel, *The Babylonian Genesis* [Chicago: University of Chicago, 1942], pp. 107–14, and figs. 15, 16; E.A. Wallis Budge, *The Gods of the Egyptians* [New York: Dover Publications, 1969], 1:278–79).

Courtesy of the Oriental Institute, University of Chicago

THE CHAOS MONSTER

Cylinder seal from Tell Asmar (in ancient Mesopotamia) dated c. 2500 B.C., showing two gods spearing a four-legged, seven-headed hydra, four of whose heads hang dead and three still live and show projected forked tongues; six tongues of flame arise from the monster's back; two worshipers and a star in the field are also seen. See Revelation 12:3-4; 13:1, 3, 14; 17:3, 8-11.

It may be argued that John's beast from the sea is to be connected with Leviathan in the OT. See Psalm 74:14, where the "heads" of the monster are specifically mentioned: "It was you who crushed the heads of Leviathan." The seven heads and ten horns, regardless of the imagery used in Daniel or elsewhere, are not to be separately identified. It is true that Leviathan, Rahab, and the dragon (serpent) in the cited OT texts have a reference to political powers, such as Egypt and Assyria, that were threatening Israel. In the minds of the OT writers, however, the national entities were inseparably identified with the archetypal reality of the satanic, idolatrous systems represented by the seven-headed monster (Leviathan, Rahab, and the dragon) so that the beast represented, not the political power, but the system of evil that found expression in the political entity (Budge, *Gods of the Egyptians*, 1:278). The reason this point is so important is that it helps us see that the beast itself is not to be identified in its description with any one historical form of its expression or with any one institutional aspect of its manifestation. In other words, the beast may appear now as Sodom, Egypt, Rome, or even Jerusalem and may manifest itself as a political power, an economic power, a religious power, or a heresy (1 John 2:18, 22; 4:3).

In John's mind, the chief enemy is diabolical deception; his description therefore has theological overtones, not political ones. This interpretation does not exclude the possibility that there will be a final climactic appearance of the beast in history in a person; in a political, religious, or economic system; or in a final totalitarian culture combining all these. The point is that the beast cannot be limited to either the past or the future.

John further states that this beast had "on each head a blasphemous name." This prominent feature is repeated in 17:3 (cf. 13:5–6). Arrogance and blasphemy also characterize the "little horn" of Daniel's fourth beast (7:8, 11, 20, 25) and the willful king of Daniel 11:36. John alludes to the vision of Daniel but completely transforms it.

In keeping with the Rome hypothesis, many have tried to identify the blasphemous names with the titles of the emperor: "Augustus" ("reverend," "to be worshiped"); *divus* ("deified"); "Savior"; *dominus* ("Lord"). But was this in John's mind? In 2:9 he refers to the blasphemy "of those who say they are Jews and are not," a reference that seems to refer to the fact that some Jews at Smyrna had spoken against the lawful messianic claims of Jesus. They may also have charged the Christians with disloyalty to the empire and thus sided with the pagan officials in persecuting them. Could these Jews be part also of the blasphemous names? In 13:6 the blasphemies are directed against God and are further defined: "to blaspheme God, by blaspheming his name, his temple, those who dwell in heaven" (my translation). Thus the beast challenges the sovereignty and majesty of God by denying the first commandment: "You shall have no other gods before me" (Exod 20:3). Therefore, whatever person or system—whether political, social, economic, or religious—cooperates with Satan by exalting itself against God's sovereignty and by setting itself up to destroy the followers of Jesus, or entices them to become followers of Satan through deception, idolatry, blasphemy, and spiritual adultery, embodies the beast of Revelation 13.

The description John gives of the beast from the sea does not describe a mere human political entity such as Rome. Rather, it describes in archetypal language the hideous, Satan-backed system of deception and idolatry that may at any time express itself in human systems of various kinds, such as Rome. Yet at the same time John also seems to be saying that this blasphemous, blaspheming, and blasphemy-producing reality will have a final, intense, and, for the saints, utterly devastating manifestation.

3 The beast has a fatal wound, but the wound is healed. This results in great, world-wide influence, acceptance, and worship for both the beast and the dragon. Verse 3 is important and requires careful exegesis because of the widespread Nero redivivus viewpoint that is read into the wounded head (see introduction to this chapter). There are a number of features of John's description that are inconsistent with both the Nero redivivus and the Roman Empire interpretations. I am indebted for the following arguments to Newman ("Domitian Hypothesis," pp. 133–39) and to Minear (*I Saw a New Earth,* ch. 5).

1. It should be observed that the wounded "head" of v.3 is elsewhere in the chapter a wound of the whole beast (vv.12, 14). A wound inflicted in a former and rejected emperor is not a wound inflicted on the whole empire. If the reference is to Nero, it is difficult to see how his self-inflicted wound could have wounded the whole empire or how the legendary healing of his throat enhanced the authority of the beast or the dragon's war against the saints.

2. The "wound" unto death or fatal wound, must be carefully examined. In the Greek, the word for "wound" is *plēgē,* which everywhere in Revelation means "plague," in fact, a divinely inflicted judgment (9:18, 20; 11:6; 15:1ff.; 16:9, 21; 18:4, 8; 21:9; 22:18). Elsewhere in the NT the word is used of "beatings" or official "floggings" (Luke 10:30; 12:48; Acts 16:23, 33; 2 Cor 6:5; 11:23). In 13:14 we find that the beast has the plague of the "sword" (*machaira*), which supposedly refers to Nero's dagger. Elsewhere in Revelation the "sword" (*machaira,* or *rhomphaia*) (1) symbolically refers to the divine judgment of the Messiah (1:16; 2:12, 16; 19:15, 21); (2) is the sword of the rider on the red horse and equals divine judgment (6:4, 8); and (3) is a sword used as a weapon against the saints of God (13:10). We are, then, nearer to John's mind if we see the sword, not as referring to an emperor's death, but as the symbol of God's wrath that in some event had struck a death blow to the authority of the beast (and the dragon), yet which had been deceptively covered up or restored (for a probable antecedent, see Isa 27:1).

3. The correct identification, therefore, of the beast's enemy will enable us to understand what event John had in mind in the death blow. Everywhere in the book the only sufficient conqueror of the beast and the dragon is the slain Lamb, together with his faithful saints (12:11; 19:19–21). Furthermore, it is the event of the life and especially the crucifixion, resurrection, and exaltation of Jesus that dealt this death blow to the dragon and the beast (1:5; 5:9; 12:11). This same thought is paralleled by other NT teaching (Luke 10:17–24; 11:14–22; John 12:31–33; Col 2:15). Irenaeus suggests that the wound, so central to the Apocalypse, must be understood as an appeal to Genesis 3:13ff. (*Contra Haereses* 5.25–34).

Yet the same paradox found in chapter 12 also appears here in chapter 13. While the dragon (ch. 12) is, on the one hand, defeated and cast out of heaven, on the other hand, he still has time and ability to wage a relentless war against the people of God. Likewise, the beast (ch. 13) has been dealt a fatal blow by the cross of Christ and yet still has time and ability to wage war against the saints. He appears to be alive and in full command of the scene; his blasphemies increase. What the sea beast cannot accomplish, he commissions the earth beast to do (vv.11ff.). All three—the dragon, the sea beast, and the earth beast—though distinguishable, are nevertheless in collusion to effect the same end: the deception that led the world to worship the dragon and the sea beast and the destruction of all who oppose them.

It is this description that leads to the fourth reason why identifying the beast exclusively with any one historical personage or empire is probably incorrect. In John's description of the beast, there are numerous parallels with Jesus that should alert the reader to the fact that John is seeking to establish, not a historical identification, but a theological characterization (though in this there is no implication against the historicity of Jesus): Both wielded swords; both had followers on whose foreheads were inscribed their names (13:16–14:1); both had horns (5:6; 13:1); both were slain, the same Greek word being used to describe their deaths (*sphazo*, vv. 3, 8); both had arisen to new life and authority; and both were given (by different authorities) power over every nation, tribe, people, and tongue as well as over the kings of the earth (1:5; 7:9; with 13:7; 17:12). The beast described here is the great theological counterpart to all that Christ represents and not the Roman Empire or any of its emperors. So it is easy to understand why many in the history of the church have identified the beast with a future, personal Antichrist.

It is curious that in her commentary on Revelation, Ford refers to Minear's "most challenging argument against this [Nero] theory" (p. 220) without offering any refutation. She then proceeds, contrary to Minear's whole thesis, to try her own hand at another *historical* identification that is even less convincing than the long succession of previous ones (see comments on v. 11).

While the references in the Johannine literature may be taken as supporting the view that the Antichrist is manifested in multiple persons and was a reality present in John's day (1 John 2:18, 22; 4:3; 2 John 7), Paul's description in such personal terms of the coming "man of lawlessness" (2 Thess 2:3–4, 8–9) has led the majority of ancient and modern interpreters to adopt the viewpoint that it is a personal Antichrist. Bavinck believes that the solution to the conflict between Paul and John lies in seeing John as describing the forerunners (anti-Christian powers in history) while Paul talks about the day when these powers will be embodied in one king(dom) of the world, the epitome of apostasy (cited by Berkouwer, *Return of Christ*, p. 265). John, however, says that in the false teachers "the antichrist" was actually present (2 John 7). Berkouwer shows that it is not necessary to understand Paul's apocalyptic language as describing a personal Antichrist (ibid., p. 270).

But the question must remain open as to whether John in the Apocalypse points to a *single* archenemy of the church—whether past or future—or to a transhistorical reality with many human manifestations in history. Thus the imagery would function similarly with regard to the image of the woman of chapter 12 or the harlot of chapter 17. If such is the case, this does not mean that John would have denied the earthly historical manifestations of this satanic reality; but it would prevent us from limiting the imagery merely to the Roman Empire or to any other single future political entity.

4 The goal of the dragon and the beast in their conspiracy is to promote the idolatrous worship of themselves. This perversion is further enhanced by the earth beast (vv. 12, 15). The means of deception varies because not all mankind is deceived in the same way. People follow and worship the beast because he is apparently invincible: "Who can make war against him?" His only real enemy seems to be the saints of Jesus, whom he effectively destroys (2:10, 13; 12:11; 13:15). But little does he realize that in the death of the saints the triumph of God appears. As they die, they do so in identification with the slain Lamb who through the Cross has decisively conquered the dragon by inflicting on him a truly fatal wound. "Who is like the beast?" echoes in parody similar references to God himself (Exod 15:11; Mic 7:18).

5–6 (See comments on v. 1.) The period of the beast's authority is given as "forty-two months," the same period already referred to in 11:2–3; 12:6, 13 (see comments at 11:2).

7 Here, to "make war," as elsewhere in the Apocalypse, does not mean to wage a military campaign but refers to hostility to and destruction of the people of God in whatever manner and through whatever means the beast may choose (study carefully 2:16; 11:7; 12:7, 17; 16:14; 17:14; 19:11, 19; 20:8; 2 Cor 10:4). "To conquer" them refers not to the subversion of their faith but to the destruction of their physical lives (cf. Matt 10:28). As in T.S. Eliot's *Murder in the Cathedral*, (New York: Harcourt, Brace & Co., 1935), their apparent defeat by the beast and his victory turns out in reality to be the victory of the saints and the defeat of the beast (15:2). Messiahlike universal dominion was given the beast by the dragon (Luke 4:4–7; 1 John 5:19).

8 John further identifies the worshipers of the beast as "all whose names have not been written in the book of life belonging to the Lamb" (for a discussion of the meaning of the "book of life," see comments at 3:5; also 17:8; 20:12, 15; 21:27). This contrast further emphasizes the theological nature of the description of the beast. The beast from the earth represents the idolatrous system of worship instigated by the dragon to deceive mankind into breaking the first commandment.

It has been debated whether the words "from the creation of the world" (also 17:8) belong grammatically with "have not been written" or with "that was slain." In other words, is it the Lamb who was slain from the creation of the world, or is it the names that were not recorded in the book of life from the creation of the world? In Greek, either interpretation is grammatically acceptable. But the reference in 17:8 implies that the word order in the Greek (not the grammar) favors the latter view and suggests that John is deliberately providing a complementary thought to 17:8. In the former instance, the emphasis would rest on the decree in eternity to elect the Son as the redeeming agent for mankind's salvation (13:8; 1 Peter 1:20); in the latter, stress lies on God's eternal foreknowledge of a company of people who would participate in the elect Son's redeeming work (17:8). In any event, the words "from the creation of the world" cannot be pressed to prove eternal individual election to salvation or damnation since 3:5 implies that failure of appropriate human response may remove one's name from the book of life. Therefore, we must allow John's understanding of predestination to qualify both earlier rabbinic and Qumran as well as later Christian views. This verse strikes a sharp note of distinction between the followers of the beast and those of the slain Lamb. It also calls for faithful commitment and clear discernment of error on the part of the Lamb's people.

9–10 These verses are both important and difficult. This is the only occurrence in Revelation of the words "he who has an ear, let him hear" apart from their use in each of the messages to the seven churches (chs. 2–3). Here they call special attention to the need for obedience to the exhortation in v. 10b. Kiddle feels that v. 10 is the focal point of the whole chapter, as it calls on the Christian to display faith and patience in the face of the divinely permitted predominance of evil (p. 248). Most agree that the language of v. 10 alludes to Jeremiah 15:2 and 43:11 (LXX 50:11), where the prophet describes the certainty of divine judgment that will come upon the rebels in Israel—they will suffer captivity, famine, disease, and death from the sword. Yet it is difficult to see how Jeremiah's words are appropriate here in this context of an exhortation for believers to be faithful. John's meaning must be different—viz., that as the rebels in Jeremiah's day would certainly encounter the divine judgment, so the faithful to Christ are assured that their captivity and martyrdom are in God's will. (For the textual problem in v.10, see Notes.)

No completely satisfying resolution of the problems in v.10 is available. Since the difficult part (10a) is both preceded by (v.9) and followed by (v.10b) appeals to obedience and loyalty, it seems best to stay with the sense of obedient faithfulness and follow the textual readings that support it. Charles puts it this way: "The day of persecution is at hand: the Christians must suffer captivity, exile or death: in calmly facing and undergoing this final tribulation they are to manifest their endurance and faithfulness" (*Commentary on Revelation*, 1: 355). Paul's statement is similar: "Without being frightened in any way by those who oppose you. This is a sign to them that they will be destroyed, but that you will be saved—and that by God" (Phil 1:28). While the DSS reveal that the Essenes held to an active, violent participation in the final eschatological battle for the elect, and while the then current Zealot holy-war doctrine advocated violent revolution, John seems to call believers here to passive resistance against their enemies. Yet this resistance, which may result in captivity and even martyrdom, seems to contribute to the eventual defeat of evil (cf. Adela Yarbo Collins, "The Political Perspective of the Revelation to John," JBL, 96–2 [1977], 241–56).

11 John sees another (*allo*, "one of a similar kind") beast rising from the earth. This second beast completes the triumvirate of evil—the dragon, the sea beast, and the land beast. The land beast is subservient to the beast from the sea and seems utterly dedicated to promoting not himself but the wounded beast from the sea. Elsewhere the land beast is called the "false prophet" (16:13; 19:20; 20:10). As with the first beast, identification is a problem. That this beast comes from the land rather than the sea may simply indicate his diversity from the first, while other references stress their collusion.

A survey of the history of interpretation reveals in general, as with the first beast, two main lines: the beast either represents a power or a movement, or describes a human being allied with the Antichrist at the close of the age (cf. Berkouwer, *Return of Christ*, pp. 260f.). Early Christian interpreters, such as Irenaeus (second century), who identify the first beast not with Rome but with a personal Antichrist, find in the second beast the "armour-bearer" of the first, who employs the demonic forces to work magic and deceive the inhabitants of the earth (*Contra Haereses* 5.28.2). Hippolytus (third century) identified the second beast as "the kingdom of the Antichrist" (*Christ and Anti-Christ*, ANF, 5:214, par. 48). Victorinus (late third century) speaks of this beast as the false prophet who will work magic before the Antichrist. Victorinus then blurs the identification of the second beast with the first in further remarks (*Apocalypse* 13.11–13). Andreas (sixth century) reports that in his day "some say this [second] beast is the Antichrist, but it seems to others that he is Satan, and his two horns are the Antichrist and the false prophet" (Swete, p. 166).

Calvin and Luther, as well as other Reformers, drawing on earlier traditions, were led to identify this beast with the papacy or specific popes. Berkouwer notes that while the Reformers may have been mistaken as to their actual identifications, they were right in seeing the beast as a present threat and not some entity awaiting a yet future manifestation (*Return of Christ*, pp. 262–63). Most modern commentators, following the Nero redivivus view of the first beast, identify this beast as the priesthood of the imperial cultus (Charles, *Commentary on Revelation* 1:357). Alford and others would extend the symbolism to all ages and see in the second beast "the sacerdotal persecuting power, pagan or Christian," and would call special attention to the Roman papacy, though by no means limiting it to this priesthood (Alf, 4: 679). While recognizing that no view is without problems, the following discussion takes the position that the land beast is John's way of describing the false prophets of the Olivet Discourse (Matt 24:24; Mark 13:22). This identification is consistent with the previously stated view of the sea beast as describing not just a specific political reality but the world-wide anti-God system of Satan and its manifestation in periodic, historical human antichrists. The land beast is the antithesis to the true prophets of Christ symbolized by the two witnesses in chapter 11 (cf. Berkouwer, *Return of Christ*, ch. 9, for a full and helpful discussion of the whole Antichrist issue). If the thought of a nonpersonal antichrist and false prophet seems to contradict the verse that describes them as being cast alive into the lake of fire (19:20), consider that "death" and "Hades" (nonpersons) are also thrown into the lake of fire (20:14).

The reference to the "two horns like a lamb" can be understood as highlighting the beast's imitative role with respect to the true Lamb in the rest of the book (e.g., 5:6ff.; 13:8; 14:1). Could the two horns be in contrast to the two witnesses in chapter 11? Since one of the primary characteristics of this second beast is his deceptive activities (v.14; 19:20), his appearance as a lamb would contribute to the confusion over the beast's true identity. If the land beast represents satanic false teaching and false prophets, their evil is intensified because of its deceptive similarity to the truth. Even though the beast is like the Lamb, in reality he is evil because "he [speaks] like a dragon," i.e., he teaches heresy. Jesus gave such a twofold description of false prophets in the Sermon on the Mount: "Watch out for false prophets. They come to you in sheep's clothing, but inwardly they are ferocious wolves" (Matt 7:15). On the other hand, the lamblikeness may simply be a reference to the beast's gentle outward manner in contrast to his true identity as a fierce dragon.

12 The activity of the land beast is repeatedly described as that of promoting the first beast's worship (v.14). Could this be the kind of activity referred to in the reference to the false prophets in Pergamum and Thyatira seducing the servants of God to idolatry (2:14–15, 20, 24)? NIV misses a nuance by rendering the Greek *enōpion* ("in behalf of ") as if the second beast exercised all the authority of the first beast merely as the latter's representative. The preposition *enōpion* occurs no fewer than thirty-four times in Revelation and in every instance means "in the presence of " or "before." The same word is used of the two witnesses in 11:4: "These are the two olive trees and the two lampstands that stand before [*enōpion*] the Lord of the earth." Kiddle points out how this word in such a context indicates "prophetic readiness to do the bidding of God, and with the authority inalienable from divine communion" (p. 255). As the antitheses of the two witnesses, the false prophets derive their authority and ministry from the first beast.

13 One of the strategies the land beast uses to deceive people into following the first beast is the performance of "miraculous signs" (*sēmeion;* see discussion at 12:1). The ability of the Satan-inspired prophets to perform deceiving miracles is attested elsewhere in Revelation and in other parts of the Bible (16:14; 19:20; Deut 13:1–5; Matt 7:22; 24:24; Mark 13:22; 2 Thess 2:9). Distinguishing between the true and false prophets has always been difficult but not impossible. The followers of Jesus must be constantly alert to discern the spirits (1 John 4:1–3).

The reference to "fire . . . from heaven" deserves brief comment. It could refer to the fire that the prophet Elijah called down from heaven (1 Kings 18:38) or to the fire coming out of the mouths of the two witnesses (Rev 11:5). Either reference is preferable to the attempt to see here some indication of the imperial cult priests of Rome. John may intend a deliberate contrast between the true witnesses' use of fire and its use by the false prophets (11:5; cf. Luke 9:54).

A quite elaborate theory was worked out by E. Watson and B. Hamilton that connects the fire of God with the true word of God and the Holy Spirit's witness (such as at Pentecost [Acts 2:3]). The false fire would then be a reference to pseudo-charismatic gifts that create a counterfeit church community whose allegiance is to the Antichrist (cited by Minear, *I Saw a New Earth*, pp. 124–27). (In regard to "the fire . . . from heaven," remember the priests Nadab and Abihu, who offered "unauthorized fire" before the Lord, apparently by their own self-will, and received God's judgment in the form of "fire" that "consumed them" [Lev 10:1–2].) In any case, the reference to fire from heaven indicates that no mighty deed is too hard for these false prophets, because they derive their power from the Antichrist and the dragon. Christ's true servants are not to be deceived by even spectacular miracles the false prophets may perform. Such miracles in themselves are no evidence of the Holy Spirit.

14a Here more must be involved than the deceptions of the imperial priesthood. The quality of the miracles deceives those who follow the beast—viz., "the inhabitants of the earth." "Deceive" (*planaō*) is John's term for the activity of false teachers who lead people to worship gods other than the true and living God (2:20; 12:9; 18:23; 19:20; 20:3, 8, 10; cf. 1 John 2:26; 3:7; 4:6; also Matt 24:11, 24).

14b–15 The second beast orders the setting up of an "image" (*eikōn*) of the first beast. Elsewhere, the worship of the first beast, his "image," and his "mark" are inseparable (14:9, 11; 15:2; 16:2; 19:20; 20:4). The *eikōn* of something is not a mere copy but partakes in its reality and in fact constitutes its reality (TDNT, 2: 389). Most interpreters, following the Roman-emperor exegesis, readily identify the image with the statue of Caesar and refer the "breath" and speaking of the image to the magic and ventriloquism of the imperial priests. But as has been argued earlier (see comments on vv. 1, 11), serious questions can be raised against such an exegesis of John's language, which is much more theologically descriptive than the Roman hypothesis allows. This is not to deny that the imperial worship could be included as one form of the beast worship. But the reality described is much larger and far more transhistorical than the mere worship of a bust of Caesar. John, however, would not deny that these realities have their historical manifestations, for in every age the beast kills those who will not worship his image. In terms reminiscent of the great golden image Nebuchadnezzar made and commanded every person to worship on the threat of death (Dan 3:1–11), John describes the world-wide system of idolatry represented by the first beast and the false prophet(s) who promotes it. John describes this reality as a blasphemous and idolatrous system that produces a breach of the first two commandments (Exod 20:3–5).

In speaking about giving "breath" (*pneuma*) to the image, John implies the activity of the false prophets in reviving idolatrous worship, giving it the appearance of vitality, reality, and power. Curiously, the two witnesses were also said to receive "breath" (*pneuma*) (11:11). The idolatrous satanic system has the power of death over those who worship the true God and the Lamb. The same "image" tried to kill Daniel and his friends, killed many of the prophets of God, crucified the Lord Jesus, put to death Stephen (Acts 7:60), James the apostle (Acts 12:1–2), and Antipas (Rev 2:13). Thus he demonstrated to his followers the apparent healing of his wounded head. To limit the image to the bust of Caesar or to some future statue or ventriloquistic device constricts John's deeper meaning and eliminates the present significance of his language.

The contemporary phenomenon of the Korean religious leader Sun Myung Moon and his official interpreter and prophetess, Young Oon Kim, embody what seems to be a clear example of John's teaching about antichrists and false prophets (cf. Young Oon Kim, *Divine Principle and Its Application* [Washington, D.C.: The Holy Spirit Association for the Unification of World Christianity, 1969]). Moon is being heralded as the "Lord of the Second Advent" by Kim and others. His whole stance clearly embodies heresy and blasphemy and many are being deceived into following him and his teaching (cf. Harry J. Jaeger, Jr., "By the Light of a Masterly Moon," CT [19 December 1975], 13–16). Moon's idolatrous image receives continual breath by worship from his followers.

16 The immediate effect of the worship of the beast involves receiving a mark on the right hand or forehead. By comparing the other passages where the beast, image, mark, and name of the beast are mentioned, it seems clear that the "mark" (*charagma*) is an equivalent expression to the "name of the beast" (13:17; 14:11; also 14:9; 15:2; 16:2; 19:20; 20:4), which is also the "number of his name" (13:17; 15:2).

In Greek *charagma* may refer to a work of art such as a carved image of a god (Acts 17:29), to any written inscription or document, to the "bite" of a snake, to a red "seal" (an impress) of the emperor and other official attestors of documents, or to a "brand" on camels indicating ownership (TDNT, 9: 416; MM, p. 683; Deiss BS, pp. 240–47). No evidence, however, can be cited from the ancient world where a *charagma* is placed on a *person*, let alone on the "right hand" or on the "forehead," though a seal (*sphragis*) was customarily put on slaves and soldiers. This lack of concrete evidence has led Swete, who is committed to the Roman-emperor view, to reject any connection between the *charagma* and a literal mark of the emperor. He argues that as the servants of God receive on their foreheads the impress of the divine seal (7:3; 14:1), so the servants of the beast are marked with the stamp of the beast (p. 170). In other words, the *charagma* is not a literal impress seal, certificate, or similar mark of identification, but it is John's way of symbolically describing authentic ownership and loyalty. Those who worship the beast have his *charagma* or brand of ownership on them, as the followers of Jesus have the brand of God's possession on them. The fact that the Babylonian Talmud prohibits the Jew from wearing the tephillim (prayer scroll) on the forehead or on the hand may lie in the background as to why John uses these two places to describe the idolatrous mark (*Megillah* 24b).

17 Those having the *charagma* ("mark") can "buy or sell," those without it cannot. This statement apparently refers to some sort of socio-economic sanctions that would, of course, affect the social and economic condition of Christians in the world. Earlier, John alluded to certain such conditions. Smyrna was a greatly persecuted church and was "poor" (2:9); Philadelphia was of "little strength" (3:8); those faithful to Christ in the Great Tribulation are seen in heaven as never again hungering (7:16), while the great harlot grows rich and wallows in luxury (18:3). Other NT writers also apparently refer to socio-economic sanctions practiced against Christians (Rom 15:26; Heb 10:34). Such a sanction was more social than political, imposed not by the government but by the communities. When governmental Rome took official notice of an illegal religion, it was always by criminal charges in the courts, not by economic sanctions (Caird, p. 173).

18 In v.17, John indicates that the *charagma* ("mark") is the name of the beast or the number of his name. He now reveals the number of the beast: "His number is 666." The list of conjectures concerning the meaning of the number (or its alternates—see Notes) is almost as long as the list of commentators on the book. Taking their cue from the words "let him calculate the number of the beast," most of these interpreters have tried to play the ancient Hebrew game of gematria or, as it is called by the Greeks, *isopsēphia*. Ancient languages, including Hebrew and Greek, use standard letters from their alphabets as numerical signs. For example, α (alpha) in Greek can represent the number one, β (bēta) the number two, $\iota\beta$ (iōta bēta) twelve, etc. A series of letters could form a word and at the same time indicate a number. Gematria took many forms and consisted in trying to guess the word from the number or trying to connect one word with another that had the same numerical value. On the walls of Pompeii, there are some graffiti, dated no later than A.D. 79, that illuminate the practice. One reads: "Amerimnus thought upon his lady Harmonia for good. The number of her honorable name is 45 ($\mu\varepsilon$ [mu epsilon])." The key to the puzzle seems to be in the word "Harmonia," which was probably not the girl's actual name but refers to the nine Muses (the goddesses of song and poetry); and 45 is the sum of all the digits from 1 to 9 (E.M. Blaiklock, *The Archaeology of the New Testament* [Grand Rapids: Zondervan, 1970], p. 131). Another runs: "I love her whose number is 545 ($\phi\mu\varepsilon$ [phi mu epsilon])" (Deiss LAE, p. 277). In these cases, the number conceals a name, and the mystery is perhaps known for certain only by the two lovers themselves.

Similarly, the Jews (esp. Hasidim) used Hebrew alphabetical numbers to indicate concealed names and mysterious connections with other words of the same numerical value. For example, the Hebrew word *nāḥāš* ("serpent") has the same numerical value as the Hebrew word *māšîaḥ* ("Messiah") (358). From this it was argued that one of the names of the Messiah was "serpent." Some suggest that this may relate to Moses' lifting up the "serpent" in the wilderness (cf. Num 21; John 3:14). (For these and many other examples, see William Barclay, "Great Themes of the New Testament. Part V. Revelation xiii (continued)," ExpT, 70, [1959], 292–96.)

Thus it is not difficult to understand why most commentators have understood John's words "Let him calculate the number. . . . His number is 666" to be an invitation to the reader to play gematria and discover the identity of the beast. This interpretation is not new. Irenaeus (second century) mentions that many names of contemporary persons and entities were being offered in his day as solutions to this number mystery. Yet he cautioned against the practice and believed that the name of the Antichrist was deliberately concealed because he did not exist in John's day. The name would be secret till the time of his future appearance in the world. Irenaeus expressly refutes the attempt of many to identify the name with any of the Roman emperors. He feels, however, that the gematria approach is John's intended meaning but warns the church against endless speculations (*Contra Haereses* 29.30).

Irenaeus's fear was not misplaced. Endless speculation is just what has happened in the history of the interpretation of v. 18, as Barclay has well documented it ("Great Themes," pp. 295–96). Barclay himself (following Charles, perhaps) is quite certain that the only possible solution is to use Hebrew letters, and so he comes up with "Neron Caesar," which equals 666. This identification is linked with the view that the Antichrist would be Nero redivivus (see introduction to 13:1). Yet this use of Hebrew letters requires a spelling for "caesar" that is not normal for the word (*qsr*). However, in a publication of an Aramaic document from the Dead Sea cave at Murabbaat, dated to the second year of the emperor Nero, the name is spelled *nrwn qsr*, as required by the theory (BASOR, 170 [April 1963], 65).

More recently the whole line of Nero redivivus interpretation has been seriously challenged by Minear and others (*I Saw a New Earth*, ch. 5; cf. commentary at introduction to 13:1). In the first place, none of the key words of v. 18—name, number, man, 666—requires the effort to find an emperor (or future political dictator) with a name whose letters will add up to 666. The sheer disagreement and confusion created through the years by the gematria method should have long ago warned the church that it was on the wrong track. After surveying all the evidence, Rühle says, "It may be said that all the solutions proposed are unsatisfactory" (TDNT, 1: 464). If John was seeking to illumine believers so that they could penetrate the deception of the beast as well as to contrast the beast and his followers with the Lamb and his followers (14:1ff.), he has clearly failed—that is, if he intends for us to play the gematria game. How Nero could fit these requirements is, on closer examination, difficult to see. If some Christians of John's time did succumb to Caesar worship, it was due less to their being deceived than to their fear of death. Moreover, several exegetical factors argue strongly for another sense of John's words.

In the first place, nowhere does John use gematria as a method. Everywhere, however, he gives symbolic significance to numbers (e.g., seven churches, seals, trumpets, and bowls; twenty-four elders; 144,000 sealed; 144 cubits for the New Jerusalem, etc.). Furthermore, in 15:2 the victors have triumphed over three enemies: the beast, his image, and *the number of his name*, which suggests a symbolic significance connected with idolatry and blasphemy rather than victory over a mere puzzle solution of correctly identifying someone's name.

John seeks to give "wisdom" (*sophia*) and "insight" (*nous*) to believers as to the true identity of their enemy. Curiously, while Mounce favors the gematria explanation, citing that it is a commonly used device in apocalyptic literature and tended to protect the user against sedition (both assertions made without citing any evidence), he ends his discussion by conceding in the light of the confusion that "it seems best to conclude that John intended only his intimate associates to be able to decipher the number" (*Revelation*, pp. 264–65). A similar use of *nous* and *sophia* occurs in 17:9, where John calls attention to the identity of the beast ridden by the harlot. What John seems to be asking for in both cases is divine discernment and not mathematical ingenuity! Believers need to penetrate the deception of the beast. John's reference to his number will help them to recognize his true character and identity.

The statement "it is man's number" (*arithmos . . . anthrōpou*) further identifies the kind of number the beast represents. Does John mean that the beast is a man, that he has a human name? In 21:17 John uses similar words for the angel: "by man's measurement, which the angel was using." The statement is difficult. How can the measure be both "man's" and at the same time of an "angel"? Kiddle seems to sense the peculiarity of the statement in 21:17 and suggests that John is attempting to call attention to some inner meaning in the number of the size of the height of the wall in respect to the size of the city. The meaning perhaps is a mild polemic against first-century tendencies to venerate angels unduly by stating that both men and angels can understand and enter the future city (see comments at 21:15–21). In any case, the statement "it is man's number" alerts the reader to some hidden meaning in 666. From this it may be concluded that the number of the beast is linked to humanity. Why would it be necessary for John to emphasize this relationship unless he assumed that his readers might have understood the beast to be other worldly without any connection to humanity. Might it be, then, that the statement signifies that the satanic beast, which is the great enemy of the church, manifests itself in human form? Thus as the similar phrase in 21:17 linked the angelic and the human, so here it joins the satanic with the human.

Finally, how are we to understand 666? The best way is to follow Minear (*I Saw a New Earth*, ch. 5) and Newman ("Domitian Hypothesis," pp. 133ff.) and return to one of the most ancient interpretations, that of Irenaeus. Irenaeus proposed (while still holding to a personal Antichrist) that the number indicates that the beast is the sum of "all apostate power," a concentrate of six thousand years of unrighteousness, wickedness, deception, and false prophecy. He states that "the digit six, being adhered to throughout, indicates the recapitulations of that prophecy, taken in its full extent, which occurred at the beginning, during the intermediate periods, and which shall take place at the end." Irenaeus also held that the wound of the beast has reference to Genesis 3:13ff. The Messiah has freed men from this wound by wounding Satan and by giving them the power to inflict wounds on the beast by overcoming his blasphemy (*Contra Haereses* 5.29.30).

The significance of the name of the beast is abundantly clear in Revelation (12:3; 13:1–6; 14:11; 17:3ff.). Wherever there is blasphemy, there the beast's name is found. The number 666 is the heaping up of the number 6. Minear adds, "Because of its contrast with 7 we may be content with an interpretation which sees in 666 an allusion to incompleteness, to the demonic parody in the perfection of 7, to the deceptiveness of the almost-perfect, to the idolatrous blasphemy exemplified by false worshipers, or to the dramatic moment between the sixth and the seventh items in a vision cycle (cf. seals, trumpets, bowls, and kings 17:10)" (*I Saw a New Earth*, p. 258). This interpretation of 666 as a symbolic number referring to the unholy trinity of evil or to the human imperfect imitation of God rather than a cipher of a name is not restricted to Minear. It has been held by a long line of conservative commentators— A.C. Gaebelein (*The Revelation* [New York: Our Hope, 1915]), J.A. Seiss (*The Apocalypse* [Grand Rapids: Zondervan, 1957]), J.F. Walvoord, T.F. Torrance (*The Apocalypse Today* [Grand Rapids: Eerdmans, 1959]), L. Morris, J. Ellul (*The Apocalypse: The Book of Revelation* [New York: Seabury, 1977]), and others.

Notes

1 In many critical editions of the Gr. text, the sentence "And the dragon stood on the shore of the sea" is made v. 18 of ch. 12 rather than v.1 of ch. 13 following the reading ἐστάθη (*estathē*, "he stood") instead of ἐστάθην (*estathēn*, "I stood"). The third person reading is well supported and may be correct, though the first person yields good sense and the MS evidence is not such as to eliminate it from consideration. A single letter in the Gr. text makes the difference.

10 A major textual problem in the last half of this verse presents a difficulty to understanding its meaning. The problem involves whether the first reference to the verb ἀποκτείνω (*apokteinō*, "kill") should be read with the majority as ἀποκτενεῖ (*apoktenei*, "will kill," a future indicative) or with A as ἀποκτανθῆναι (*apoktanthēnai*, "be killed," an aorist passive infinitive). KJV, RSV, Phillips, NASB all follow the first reading and render it "If any one kills with the sword." Combining this with the last phrase, the latter part of the verse yields either a warning directed toward Christians for them not to turn to violence and killing to vindicate themselves or a promise of requital to believers that their persecutors will be judged by God.

If, on the other hand, we follow the reading of A (preferred by Bruce M. Metzger [*A Textual Commentary on the Greek New Testament* (New York: UBS, 1971), p. 750] and Charles [*Commentary on Revelation*], 1:355), the translation will be as in NIV (cf. NEB, TEV). This yields the sense that Christians who are destined by God for death must submit to his will and not resist the oppressor. It is an appeal to loyalty. In adopting this reading and sense, Charles points out that the construction in A is the same idiomatic Heb. as that in 12:7 (where see note) and yields this sense: "If anyone must be killed with the sword, with the sword he must be killed." Metzger argues that the majority-text reading reflects an altered text influenced by the retribution idea found in Matt 26:52: "For all who draw the sword will die by the sword." No entirely satisfactory solution is available.

11 A curious interpretation of the first and second beasts is offered by Ford (pp. 227–30). She holds that the first beast is the emperor Vespasian and peculiarly identifies the second beast tentatively with Flavius Josephus, the renegade Jew and historian. While Ford's attempt is not without interesting parallels, it founders chiefly on the fact that she should be the first to suggest it. On such a premise, how could we explain the fact that Josephus's writings were not preserved by Jews but by Christians if he were, in fact, recognized as one of their great enemies?

16 The apocalyptic Pss Sol refers to the "mark of God" on the righteous and the "mark of destruction" on the wicked (15.8).

17 When John says "the name of the beast or the number of his name," the "or" (ἤ [*ē*]) may signify mere interchangeability so that the name and/or the mark are equivalent (BAG, p. 342).

18 Instead of 666, which is strongly supported, one good MS and a few lesser witnesses have 616, which is explained as either a scribal slip or a deliberate alteration to give the numbers necessary for the Gr. "Caesar god" (Deiss LAE, p. 278, n.3), or "Gaios Caesar" (Caligula) (Barclay, "Great Themes," p. 296), or the Latin form of Nero Caesar (Metzger, *A Textual Commentary*, p. 752). Irenaeus strongly deplored this 616 reading as heretical and deceptive (*Contra Haereses* 5.30).

A few MSS read 646 or 747 according to Hoskier (H.C. Hoskier, *Concerning the Text of the Apocalypse*, 2 vols. [London: Bernard Quaritch, 1929], 2:364).

---

3. *The Lamb and the 144,000*

14:1–5

> [1]Then I looked, and there before me was the Lamb, standing on Mount Zion, and with him 144,000 who had his name and his Father's name written on their foreheads. [2]And I heard a sound from heaven like the roar of rushing waters and like a loud peal of thunder. The sound I heard was like that of harpists playing their harps. [3]And they sang a new song before the throne and before the four living creatures and the elders. No one could learn the song except the 144,000 who had been redeemed from the earth. [4]These are those who did not defile themselves with women, for they kept themselves pure. They follow the Lamb wherever he goes. They were purchased from among men and offered as firstfruits to God and the Lamb. [5]No lie was found in their mouths; they are blameless.

The two previous chapters have prepared Christians for the reality that as the end draws near they will be harassed and sacrificed like sheep. This section shows that their sacrifice is not meaningless. A glance back at chapter 7 reminds us that there the 144,000 were merely sealed; here, however, they are seen as already delivered. When the floods have passed, Mount Zion appears high above the waters; the Lamb is on the throne of glory, surrounded by the triumphant songs of his own; the gracious presence of God fills the universe (Lilje).

Chapter 14 briefly answers two pressing questions: What becomes of those who refuse to receive the mark of the beast and are killed (vv. 1–5)? What happens to the beast and his servants (vv. 6–20)?

1 The Lamb standing on Mount Zion is contrasted to the dragon standing on the shifting sands of the seashore (13:1). Although the rapid movement mood of the previous chapters gives way to one of victorious rest (1–5, 13), activity continues because the battle between the dragon and the woman (cf. 12:11) is still going on. Immediately the question arises whether the 144,000 here are the same as those in chapter 7. The only reason for viewing the 144,000 in chapter 7 differently is that here they are described as "firstfruits" and "pure" who "did not defile themselves with women" (v.4). The two-group viewpoint has been defended especially by some Roman Catholic exegetes but has been effectively refuted by other Roman Catholic exegetes (see comments at v.4 and Heidt, pp. 94–95; Ford, p. 234).

The problem of the location of this group of 144,000 is more complex. Mount Zion may refer to the hilly area in southeast Jerusalem, the temple mount, the whole city of Jerusalem, or, as in postexilic days, the whole land of Judah and the whole Israelite nation (ZPEB, 5:1063–65). In the prophetic tradition, Zion came to symbolize the place where the Messiah would gather to himself a great company of the redeemed (Ps 48:1ff.; Isa 24:23; Joel 2:32; Obad 17, 21; Mic 4:1, 7; Zech 14:10). Likewise, in late Jewish apocalyptic literature there is a similar idea: "But he shall stand upon the summit of Mount Zion. . . . And whereas thou didst see that he summoned and gathered to himself another multitude which was peaceable, these are the ten tribes" (4 Ezra 13:35, 39–40; also 4 Ezra 2:42 is similar). Zion may here symbolize the strength and security that belong to the people of God (Swete).

In the seven NT references to Zion, five occur in OT quotations. Of the other two, one is here in Revelation and the remaining reference (Heb 12:22–23) implies a connection between Mount Zion and the church: "But you have come to Mount Zion, to the heavenly Jerusalem, the city of the living God . . . to the church of the firstborn." Some, connecting the reference in Hebrews to the one here in Revelation 14:1, have argued for the heavenly location of the 144,000 (Kiddle). Beckwith's view, by contrast, is significant: "The 'mount Zion, the city of the living God, the heavenly Jerusalem' in Heb 12:22, the 'Jerusalem that is above' in Gal 4:26, denote the perfect archetype or pattern of the earthly, which in Hebrew thought now exists in heaven, and in the end is to descend in full realization: they are not designations of heaven, the place of God and his hosts" (p. 647). For Beckwith and others, Mount Zion refers to the earthly seat of the messianic or millennial kingdom (also Beasley-Murray, Charles, Walvoord). Whether this Mount Zion has any connection (as to locality) with ancient and historical Zion, John does not say. At any rate, that the 144,000 are singing "before the throne" (v.3) is not an objection to seeing them as the earthly Zion; it is not the redeemed who are singing but the angelic harpists (Alf, 4:684).

The 144,000 have on their foreheads the names of the Father and the Lamb, showing that they belong to God, not the beast. In 7:3ff., the elect group has the seal of God on their foreheads, linking them to this group in chapter 14, while the further description that "they follow the Lamb" (v.4) may show their connection with the second group in 7:9ff. (see esp. 7:17: "lead them"). One of the most beautiful and assuring promises in the whole book is that God's servants will have his name on their foreheads (cf. 3:12; 22:4).

Chapter 14 advances the drama a step further than chapter 7. While the members of the multitude are the same, the circumstances in which they are seen have altered (Charles). In chapter 7 the whole company of God's people are sealed (7:1–8), readied for the satanic onslaught, and then a company (a martyred portion?) are seen in heaven serving before the throne of God (7:9ff.); whereas in chapter 14, the whole body of the redeemed is seen (resurrected?) with the Lamb in the earthly eschatological kingdom. The repetition of the reference to the 144,000 may also be a liturgical phenomenon, a chief characteristic of the book—either the repetition of the introit or of antiphons.

The background of the scene (vv.1–5) may reflect John's reinterpretation of Psalm 2, which he had alluded to elsewhere and which describes the battle between the rebellious nations and God, with God suppressing the revolt by enthroning his Son on Mount Zion (Caird). John, however, does not see the warrior-king the writer of Psalm 2 hoped for, but he sees the Lamb and those who repeated his victory over the enemy by their submission (his name on their forehead). Psalm 76 may also be part of the background, where Zion is the symbol of the defeat of God's enemies and the salvation of his people.

2 The "sound" John hears is probably a "voice" (*phōnē*) as in 1:15. It is important to recognize that this voice is not that of the redeemed; it is a loud angelic chorus (cf. 5:11), sounding like "the roar of rushing waters," like "a loud peal of thunder," and like "harpists playing their harps" (1:15; 5:8; 6:1; 19:1, 6; cf. comments on 5:8 and note on 5:9–10). Charles indicates that grammatically the sentence is Hebraistic. Again the scene is liturgical, emphasizing the connection between the earthly victory and the heavenly throne.

3 This "new song" should be related to the "new song" in 5:9, also sung by the angelic choirs (q.v.). It is the song of redemption and vindication. What was seen in chapter 5 as secured for the redeemed by Christ's death (i.e., that "they will reign on the earth" [v.10]) has now been realized on Mount Zion. In the one further reference to a song (*ōdē*) in Revelation, the redeemed "victors" now sing "the song [*ōdē*] of Moses . . . and the song of the Lamb" (15:3), which may also relate to the new song of chapters 5 and 14 (see comments at 15:3). This heavenly example of worship may help us understand and appreciate Paul's references to songs inspired by the Spirit (*ōdais pneumatikais*) and sung in the first-century congregations (Eph 5:19; Col 3:16). Also instructive are the OT references to a "new song" (Pss 33:3; 40:3; 96:1; 144:9; 149:1; Isa 42:10). A "new song," in consequence of some mighty deed of God, comes from a fresh impulse of gratitude and joy in the heart (KD, *Psalms*, 1:402). The angels sing a new song because now the victors themselves have become victorious. We are reminded again of the Passover motif (Exod 15:1ff.).

While the angels sing, only the 144,000 can "learn" the new song, for they alone of earth's inhabitants have experienced God's mighty deed of victory over the beast through their ordeal of suffering and death. Possibly, the word "learn" (*manthanō*) in this context may mean to "hear deeply" (TDNT, 4:407). In the Gospel of John, the word is used in the sense of a deep listening to divine revelation that results in learning: "Everyone who listens to the Father and learns from him comes to me" (John 6:45).

The 144,000 who were "redeemed" or "purchased" (agorazō) from "the earth" or "from among men" (v.4) must be the same as those "purchased" (agorazō) from all the earth's peoples in 5:9 and those sealed in 7:4–8, who have washed their garments in the blood of the Lamb (7:14ff.).

4 John's most difficult statement about this group is that they did "not defile themselves with women." Does he mean that this group consists only of men who had never married? Or should it be understood as referring to spiritual apostasy or cult prostitution? It is unlikely that "defiled" (molynō) refers merely to sexual intercourse since nowhere in Scripture does intercourse within marriage constitute sinful defilement (cf. Heb 13:4). On the other hand, the word "defiled" is found in the Letter of Aristeas (15.2) in connection with the promiscuous intercourse practiced by the Gentiles that defiled them but from which the Jews have been separated by the commandments of God (R.H. Charles, *The Apocrypha and Pseudepigrapha of the Old Testament*, 2 vols. [New York: Oxford, 1913], 2:109). Therefore, the words can refer only to adultery or fornication; and this fact, in turn, establishes "pure" as the meaning of parthenoi ("virgins") in this context (NIV is paraphrastic here, but accurately so). In fact, parthenos can be used of formerly married persons in this figurative way and is so used of widows by Ignatius (*Smyrna* 13). The same masculine plural word (parthenous) is used in the LXX of Lamentations 2:10, which Ford suggests may be in parallel with "the elders of the daughter of Zion" (p. 242).

Kiddle thinks the reference is to actual celibacy, which alone could fit a man to be a sacrificial lamb for God (p. 268; also Glasson, p. 85). Caird connects the purity reference with holy-war regulations for soldiers who were ceremonially unclean because of sexual reasons (Deut 23:9–10; 1 Sam 21:5; 2 Sam 11:11). Each of these views founders because of the assumption that "uncleanness" (akathartos) is the equivalent of "defile" (molyno). Such an assumption not only fails on linguistic grounds but involves us in a scriptural contradiction, i.e., that the marriage bed is defiling and sinful. It is better, then, to relate the reference to purity to the defilement of idolatry. In fact, John seems to use molyno this way elsewhere of cult prostitution (3:4; cf. 2:14, 20, 22).

The group as a whole has remained faithful to Christ; "they follow the Lamb wherever he goes" in obedient discipleship. They are purchased by Christ's blood and offered to God as a holy and pure sacrifice of firstfruits. Surely this symbolically implies that the bride of Christ must be pure from idolatry. Paul, likewise, uses this figure: "I promised you to one husband, to Christ, so that I might present you as a pure virgin to him" (2 Cor 11:2–3).

Those spoken of in v.3 are "firstfruits" (aparchē) (v.4) presented to God. The word can have two meanings. It may designate the initial ingathering of the farmer, after which others come. So it may mean a pledge or downpayment with more to follow. Though it is difficult to find this sense of the word in the OT, it seems to be its meaning in several NT references (Rom 8:23; 11:16?; cf. 1 Cor 15:20; 16:15). On the other hand, in the usual OT sense and alternate NT usage, aparchē means simply an offering to God in the sense of being separated to him and sanctified (wholly consecrated), where no later addition is made, because the firstfruits constitutes the whole (Num 5:9 [NIV, "sacred contributions"]; Deut 18:4; 26:2; Jer 2:3; James 1:18). That this is John's intended sense is evident from the expression "offered as firstfruits to God."

5 The "lie" that would bring "blame" refers to the blasphemy of the beast worshipers who deny the Father and the Son and ascribe vitality to the beast by believing his heresies and worshiping his image (21:27; 22:15; cf. John 8:44–45; Rom 1:25; 2 Thess 2:9–11; 1 John 2:4, 21–22, 27).

Notes

4 The extensive discussion of this passage in Beckwith's commentary is especially helpful (pp. 646ff.).

4. The harvest of the earth

14:6–20

> [6]Then I saw another angel flying in midair, and he had the eternal gospel to proclaim to those who live on the earth—to every nation, tribe, language and people. [7]He said in a loud voice, "Fear God and give him glory, because the hour of his judgment has come. Worship him who made the heavens, the earth, the sea and the springs of water."
> [8]A second angel followed and said, "Fallen! Fallen is Babylon the Great, which made all the nations drink the maddening wine of her adulteries."
> [9]A third angel followed them and said in a loud voice: "If anyone worships the beast and his image and receives his mark on the forehead or on the hand, [10]he, too, will drink of the wine of God's fury, which has been poured full strength into the cup of his wrath. He will be tormented with burning sulfur in the presence of the holy angels and of the Lamb. [11]And the smoke of their torment rises for ever and ever. There is no rest day or night for those who worship the beast and his image, or for anyone who receives the mark of his name." [12]This calls for patient endurance on the part of the saints who obey God's commandments and remain faithful to Jesus.
> [13]Then I heard a voice from heaven say, "Write: Blessed are the dead who die in the Lord from now on."
> "Yes," says the Spirit, "they will rest from their labor, for their deeds will follow them."
> [14]I looked, and there before me was a white cloud, and seated on the cloud was one "like a son of man" with a crown of gold on his head and a sharp sickle in his hand. [15]Then another angel came out of the temple and called in a loud voice to him who was sitting on the cloud, "Take your sickle and reap, because the time to reap has come, for the harvest of the earth is ripe." [16]So he that was seated on the cloud swung his sickle over the earth, and the earth was harvested.
> [17]Another angel came out of the temple in heaven, and he too had a sharp sickle. [18]Still another angel, who had charge of the fire, came from the altar and called in a loud voice to him who had the sharp sickle, "Take your sharp sickle and gather the clusters of grapes from the earth's vine, because its grapes are ripe." [19]The angel swung his sickle on the earth, gathered its grapes and threw them into the great winepress of God's wrath. [20]They were trampled in the winepress outside the city, and blood flowed out of the press, rising as high as the horses' bridles for a distance of 1,600 stadia.

This section forms a transition from the scene of the saints' final triumph (14:1–5) to the seven bowls (16:1ff.), which depict the final judgments on the enemies of the Lamb. As such, it forms a consoling counterpart to the first vision as it assures the 144,000 that God will judge the beast, his followers, and his world-wide system— Babylon.

6–7 The first angel announces that there is still hope, for even at this crucial moment in history God is seeking to reclaim the beast followers by issuing a message appealing to the people of the world to "fear God . . . and worship him." That this appeal is called a "gospel" (*euangelion*) has raised a question. How can it be good news? Yet is not the intent of the gospel message that men should fear God and worship him? Is it not the "eternal" gospel because it announces eternal life (John 3:16)? Could this be John's way of showing the final fulfillment of Mark 13:10? Let us not fail to see how in the NT the announcement of divine judgment is never separated from the proclamation of God's mercy.

The reference to the coming of the hour of judgment (v.7) supports the view that there is chronological progression in Revelation and that not everything described by John is simultaneous (see comments at 15:1). This is the first reference in the book to the "judgment [*krisis*] of God" (16:7; 18:10; 19:2), though the "wrath" (*thymos* or *orgē*) of God, which appears to be a synonymous term (v.19), has been mentioned earlier (6:16–17; 11:18; 14:8, 10; 15:1; cf. 16:1, 19; 18:3; 19:15).

8 In anticipation of a more extended description in chapters 17 and 18, the Fall of Babylon, the great anti-God system of idolatry, is announced. The actual fall does not occur until the final bowl judgment (16:19). There may be in 11:8 a previous allusion to Babylon as the "great city" (cf. 17:18).

9–12 The explicit reference to the certain judgment of the beast worshipers ties this section to chapter 13. Through an OT figure of eschatological judgment, unmixed wine (not diluted with water) in the cup of God's wrath (Ps 75:8; Jer 25:15) and "burning sulfur" (Isa 30:33; 34:8–10; cf. Gen 19:24; Rev 19:20; 20:10; 21:8), John describes God's judgment inflicted on those who refused his truth and worshiped a lie (Rom 1:18, 25). For those who drink Babylon's cup (v.8), the Lord will give his own cup of wrath.

The reference to "torment" (*basanizō;* cf. 9:5; 11:10; 12:2; 20:10) has troubled some commentators since the torment takes place "in the presence . . . of the Lamb" (so Ford, p. 237). Thus Glasson calls the passage "sub-Christian" (p. 86), while Caird only concedes a momentary final "extinction," the force mitigated by the further statement that "the smoke of their torment rises for ever and ever" (v.11), which is more appropriate to cities than individuals. While the view that some recalcitrant individuals will suffer eternal deprivation seems repugnant to Christian sensitivity, it is clear that it is not only John's understanding but that of Jesus and other NT writers as well (Matt 25:46; Rom 2:3–9; 2 Thess 1:6–9).

John's imagery conveys a sense of finality and sober reality. It is not clear whether the imagery points only to permanency and irreversibility of God's punitive justice or whether it also includes the consciousness of eternal deprivation (cf. Rev 20:10; John 5:28–29). Berkouwer wisely says that preaching about hell should never be used as a terror tactic by the church but should always be presented in such a way as to show that God's mercy is the final goal (G.C. Berkouwer, *The Return of Christ* [Grand

Rapids: Eerdmans, 1972], pp. 417–23). C.S. Lewis acknowledges that hell is a detestable doctrine that he would willingly remove from Christianity if it were in his power. But, as he goes on to point out, the question is not whether it is detestable but whether it is true. We must recognize that the reality of hell has the full support of Scripture and of our Lord's own teaching. Indeed, it has always been held by Christians and has the support of reason (*The Problem of Pain* [New York: Macmillan, 1954], ch. 8).

The worshipers of the beast will be unable to rest day and night. Notice the contrast with the saints who will "rest" from their labor (v.13). While the beast worshipers have their time of rest, and while the saints are persecuted and martyred, in the final time of judgment God will reverse their roles (7:15ff.; cf. 2 Thess 1:6–7).

The great test for Christians is whether through patient endurance they will remain loyal to Jesus and not fall prey to the deception of the beasts (see comments at 13:10). They do this by their serious attention to God's Word and their faithfulness to Christ Jesus (1:3; 2:26; 3:8, 10; 22:7, 9; cf. Phil 1:28–30).

13 A fourth voice comes from heaven (an angel's or Christ's?), pronounces a beatitude, and evokes the Spirit's response. This is the second beatitude in Revelation (cf. comments at 1:3). Its general import is clear. But how are the words "from now on" to be understood? Do they mean that from the time of the vision's fulfillment onward (i.e., the judgment of idolaters and the 144,000 with the Lord on Mount Zion), the dead will be blessed in a more complete manner (Alford)? Or do they refer to the time of John's writing onward? If the latter, why from *that* time? While either interpretation is grammatically possible, the preceding verse, which implies an exhortation to Christians in John's day, favors the latter view (Beckwith). John expects the imminent intensification of persecution associated with the beast, and the beatitude indicates that those who remain loyal to Jesus when this occurs will be blessed indeed.

Apart from 22:17, this is the only place in Revelation where the Spirit speaks directly (cf. Acts 13:2; Heb 3:7; 10:15). The beatitude is no doubt intended to emphasize the reality of the martyrs' future. Their blessedness consists in "rest" from the onslaught of the dragon and his beasts and the assurance that their toil (*kopos*, cf. 2:2) for Christ's name will not be in vain but will be remembered by the Lord himself after their death (Heb 6:10; cf. 1 Tim 5:24–25).

14–16 After a brief pause to encourage the faithfulness of the saints, John returns to the theme of divine judgment on the world. He does this by first describing the judgment in terms of a harvest (14:14–20) and then by the seven bowl plagues (chs. 15–16). John sees a white cloud and seated on it one resembling a human being ("a son of man"). He has a crown of gold and a sharp sickle, the main instrument of harvest. John clearly wishes to highlight this exalted human figure and his role in the eschatological judgment. The question of the identity of the "son of man" is not unlike the problem of the identity of the rider of the white horse (6:1). The same words *homoion huion anthrōpou* ("like a son of man") are used of Jesus in 1:13, in both places without the definite article. Some have noted the close association of the one "seated on the cloud" with the words "another angel" in v.15 and the similar implications in v.17, that another angel "too" had a sharp sickle, implying that the former figure with the sickle was likewise an angel. Further, if the figure on the cloud is Jesus, how can we account for an angel giving a command to him to reap the earth (v.15).

Though there are difficulties, Charles is no doubt right when he says, "There can be no question as to the identity of the divine figure seated on the cloud. He is described as 'One like a Son of Man.'" Charles shows how Daniel 7 comes to be associated with the person of the Messiah under the title "a son of man" (*Commentary on Revelation*, 2:19). Indeed, it is quite appropriate for John to use the term Son of Man, since in the Gospels that term is most frequently associated with the Messiah's suffering and the glory of the Second Advent as well as with his right to judge the world (Matt 26:64; John 5:27). Both themes are present in the context of Revelation. The imagery of Daniel 7, frequently used in the Apocalypse, links the suffering people of God ("the saints") to the Son of Man who sits in judgment over the kingdoms of the world (cf. Richard N. Longenecker, *The Christology of Early Jewish Christianity* [London: SCM, 1970], pp. 82–93; R.T. France, *Jesus and the Old Testament* [Downers Grove, Ill.: InterVarsity, 1971], pp. 202–5). It should, of course, be remembered that this is a highly symbolic description of the final judgment.

The harvest is an OT figure used for divine judgment (Hos 6:11; Joel 3:13), especially on Babylon (Jer 51:33). Jesus also likens the final judgment to the harvest of the earth (Matt 13:30, 39). He may use the instrumentality of angels or men, but it is his prerogative to put in the sickle. While this reaping may be the gathering of his elect from the earth (so Caird citing Matt 9:37–38; John 4:35–38, et al.), the context favors taking the harvest to be a reference not to salvation but to judgment.

17–20 "Another" angel here has no more necessary connection with the Son of Man than the "another" angel in v.15; it may simply mean another of the same kind of angel mentioned in the succession of personages in the book (cf. 14:6, where no other angel is involved except the one mentioned). This angel (v.17) will gather the vintage of the earth. He is associated with the angel from the altar who has authority over its fire. Though opinion about the identification of the altar is divided, it is the incense altar; and the fire is symbolic of God's vindication of his martyred people (cf. 8:3–5 and comments at 6:9–11).

The divine eschatological judgment is presented in a threefold imagery: the unmixed wine in the cup (v.10), the grain harvest (vv.14–16), and the vintage harvest (vv.17–20). These are best understood as three metaphors describing different views of the same reality, i.e., the divine judgment. Again the OT provides the background for this imagery of divine judgment (Isa 63:1–6; Lam 1:15; Joel 3:13; cf. Rev 19:13, 15). Caird certainly strains the text when he argues that the vintage overflowing with blood does not refer to the enemies of Christ but, connecting the "earth's vine" (v.18) with the new Israel, argues that the vintage must refer to the death of the martyrs of Jesus (p. 192). The reference to the "great winepress of God's wrath" in v.19 should clarify the imagery and leave no doubt that it denotes God's judgment on the rebellious world and not the wrath of the beast on the followers of the Lamb.

The final verse (v.20) is gruesome: blood flows up to the horses' bridles for a distance of about two hundred miles (sixteen hundred stadia). Again the source of the imagery is Isaiah 63:1–6, heightened by John's hyperbole. A similar apocalyptic image for the final judgment on idolators occurs in the pre-Christian Book of Enoch, where the righteous will slay the wicked: "And the horse shall walk up to the breast in the blood of sinners, and the chariot shall be submerged to its height" (1 Enoch 100.1.3, cited in R.H. Charles, *The Apocrypha and Pseudepigrapha of the Old Testament*, 2 vols. [New York: Oxford, 1913], 2:271). Here in Revelation the judgment is not the task of human vengeance but belongs exclusively to the Son of Man and his angelic reapers (cf. Rom 12:19–21). The symbolism is that of a head-on battle, a great defeat of the enemy, a sea of spilled blood. To go beyond this and attempt to find a symbolic meaning of the sixteen hundred stadia or to link the scene to some geographic location (cf. 16:4–6) is pure speculation.

The term "outside the city" requires explanation. It may refer merely to ancient warfare when a besieging army was slaughtered at the city walls, and the blood flowed outside the city. Some think John may have had an actual city in mind and have suggested Jerusalem because of the OT predictions of a final battle to be fought near the city (Dan 11:45; Joel 3:12; Zech 14:4; but cf. Rev 16:16—"Armageddon" is not near Jerusalem; so Beckwith, Ford, Mounce, Swete, etc.). On the other hand, John's symbolic use of "city" in every other reference favors taking the word symbolically in this verse. In Revelation there are only two cities (the "cities" of the seven churches in Rev 2–3 are not called cities), the city of God, which is the camp of the saints, and the city of Satan, Babylon, which is made up of the followers of the beast (Beasley-Murray, Kiddle). There is no way to be really sure of the identity of the city, nor is its identity important. It is sufficient to take it as the same city that was persecuted by the pagans (11:2) and is seen in 20:9, i.e., the community of the saints (Charles).

Notes

14 A few of the many who identify the figure on the cloud as Christ are Beckwith, Bruce, Caird, Charles, Ford, France, Ladd, Lilje, Morris, Mounce, Walvoord, and I.H. Marshall ("Martyrdom and the Parousia in the Revelation of John," *Studia Evangelica*, 4 [1968], 337). Others identify the figure with an angel (Glasson, Kiddle, Beasley-Murray).

18 The "sickle" is a δρέπανον (*drepanon*), which is a "reaping hook" used both for reaping grain and for pruning the vine and cutting off clusters at vintage (Beckwith, p. 664).

20 Some commentators have seen in the number sixteen hundred stadia the approximate length of Palestine from Dan to Beersheba (Ladd, *Commentary on Revelation*, p. 202). Taking four as a universal number and the multiplier forty times four, Victorinus suggested that the number was symbolic, i.e., "throughout all the four parts of the world" (ANF, 7:357).

D. *The Seven Bowls* (15:1–19:10)

It is difficult to know where the divisions should fall in these further visions. Since the last series of sevens in Revelation includes the fall of Babylon under the seventh bowl (16:19), it has seemed appropriate to include the extensive description of the city's fall under the bowl-series division.

Chapter 15, a sort of celestial interlude before the final judgment, is preparatory to the execution of the bowl series described in chapter 16, while chapters 17 and 18 elaborate the fall of Babylon. What has already been anticipated under the three figures of the divine eschatological judgment—the cup of wine (14:10), the harvest of the earth (14:14–16), and the vintage (14:17–20)—is now further described under the symbolism of the seven bowls. In typical Hebrew fashion, each cycle repeats in new ways the former events and also adds fresh details not in the former series.

It is clear that in these final judgments only the unbelieving world is involved; therefore, they are punitive plagues (16:2). Yet even in these last plagues, God is concerned with effecting repentance, though none abandon their idolatry (16:9, 11). But are the faithful still on earth? Verse 2 of chapter 15 locates the whole company of conquerors not on earth but before the throne. So intense are these final judgments that Victorinus argues: "For the wrath of God always strikes the obstinate people with seven plagues, that is, perfectly, as it is said in Leviticus; and these shall be in the last time, when the church shall have gone out of the midst" (ANF, 7:357). It is difficult to support or refute such a view. Farrer also argues that the saints are now gone (Austin Farrer, *A Rebirth of Images: the Making of St. John's Apocalypse* [London: Darce, 1949], p. 155).

My position is that the inclusive series of bowl judgments constitute the "third woe" announced in 11:14 as "coming soon" (so Alford, Beckwith, Ladd, etc.—see comments at 11:14). Since the first two woes occur under the fifth and sixth trumpets, it is reasonable to see the third woe, which involved seven plagues, as unfolding during the sounding of the seventh trumpet, when the mystery of God will be finished (10:7). The actual woe events were delayed till John could give important background material concerning not only the inhabitants of the earth but also the church herself, her glory and shame, her faithfulness and apostasy (12:1–14:20). These last plagues take place "immediately after the distress of those days" referred to by Jesus in the Olivet Discourse and may well be the fulfillment of his apocalyptic words: "The sun will be darkened, and the moon will not give its light; the stars will fall from the sky, and the heavenly bodies will be shaken" (Matt 24:29). Significantly, the next event that follows this judgment, the coming of the Son of Man in the clouds, is the same event John describes following the bowl judgments (19:11).

1. *Preparatory: The seven angels with the seven last plagues*

15:1–8

[1]I saw in heaven another great and marvelous sign: seven angels with the seven last plagues—last, because with them God's wrath is completed. [2]And I saw what looked like a sea of glass mixed with fire and, standing beside the sea, those who had been victorious over the beast and his image and over the number of his name. They held harps given them by God [3]and sang the song of Moses the servant of God and the song of the Lamb:

"Great and marvelous are your deeds,
  Lord God Almighty.
Just and true are your ways,
  King of the ages.
[4]Who will not fear you, O Lord,
  and bring glory to your name?
For you alone are holy.
All nations will come
  and worship before you,
  for your righteous acts have been revealed."

[5]After this I looked and in heaven the temple, that is, the tabernacle of Testimony, was opened. [6]Out of the temple came the seven angels with the seven plagues. They were dressed in clean, shining linen and wore golden sashes around their chests. [7]Then one of the four living creatures gave to the seven angels seven golden bowls filled with the wrath of God, who lives for ever and ever. [8]And the temple was filled with smoke from the glory of God and from his power, and no one could enter the temple until the seven plagues of the seven angels were completed.

Chapter 15 is tied closely to chapter 16. Both deal with the seven last plagues of God's wrath. One is preparatory and interpretative, the other descriptive. Chapter

15 is largely oriented to the OT account of the Exodus event and is strongly suggestive of the liturgical tradition of the ancient synagogue. The chapter has two main visions: the first portrays the victors who have emerged triumphant from the great ordeal (vv.2–4); the second relates the appearance from the heavenly temple of seven angels clothed in white and gold who hold the seven bowls of the last plagues (vv.5–8).

1 This verse forms a superscription to chapters 15 and 16. The final manifestation of the wrath of God takes the form of seven angels of judgment and is called a "sign" (*sēmeion*). This is the third explicitly identified heavenly "sign" (cf. the woman and dragon at 12:1, 3). The qualifying adjective "marvelous" (*thaumaston*, cf. v.3) apparently is added because John understood the seven angels to represent the completion of God's wrath, viz., the last plagues. They are awesome as well as final in character. The word *teleō* means to "finish," "to bring to an end," "to accomplish," "to perform" (BAG, p. 818; cf. Rev 10:7; 11:7; 15:8; 17:17; 20:3, 5, 7). While these plagues may be the finale to the whole historical panorama of God's judgments, it would be exegetically preferrable to find a connection of them with events related in Revelation itself. As has already been argued, the first reference to the eschatological judgments is found in 6:17: "For the great day of their wrath has come, and who can stand?" After the interlude of the sealing of the saints from spiritual harm (ch. 7), the seven trumpets are sounded (8:1ff.). The sixth one involves three plagues that kill a third of mankind (9:18). The third woe (11:14) includes the bowl judgments that are called the "last" plagues. From this we may conclude that the trumpets begin the eschatological wrath of God that is finished in the seven bowls.

2 As in 14:1ff., John again focuses his attention on a scene that contrasts sharply with the coming judgment, an indication of his pastoral concern. He sees before the throne the likeness of a sea of glass shot through with fire (cf. 4:6). It is a scene of worship, and its imagery is suitable for depicting the majesty and brilliance of God, which the sea of glass is reflecting in a virtual symphony of color. No further symbolic significance than this needs to be sought here. Firmly planted on (*epi* can also mean "beside," NIV) the sea are those who were "victorious over the beast." They are the same ones who are seen throughout Revelation as having won out over the idolatrous beasts through their faithful testimony to Christ, even to the extent of martyrdom (e.g., 2:7, 11, 26; 12:11; 21:7; cf. 3:21; 5:5). They are the 144,000, the elect of God (7:4; 14:1), the completed company of martyrs (6:11). Note the absence of "received his mark" since mention is made of the equivalent expression "the number of his name" (see comments at 13:17). Suddenly in this dazzling scene the sound of harps and singing is heard.

3–4 The song sung by the redeemed is the "song of Moses, the servant of God and the song of the Lamb"—a single song as vv.3–4 show. The Song of Moses is in Exodus 15:1–18. It celebrates the victory of the Lord in the defeat of the Egyptians at the Red Sea. In the ancient synagogue it was sung in the afternoon service each Sabbath to celebrate God's sovereign rule over the universe, of which the redemption from Egypt reminds the Jew (Joseph Hertz, *The Authorized Daily Prayer Book*, rev. ed. [New York: Block, 1948], p. 100). Such is the emphasis in the liturgical collection of psalms and prophets John quotes from (e.g., "King of the ages"). As the deliverance from Egypt, with its divine plagues of judgment on Israel's enemies, became for the Jew a signpost of God's just rule over the world, so God's eschatological judgment and the deliverance of the followers of the Lamb bring forth from the victors over the beast exuberant songs of praise to God for his righteous acts in history.

Each line in vv.3–4 picks up phrases from the Psalms and Prophets. Compare the following OT words with vv.3–4: "Then Moses and the Israelites sang this song" (Exod 15:1); "your works are wonderful" (Ps 139:14); "LORD God Almighty" (Amos 4:13); "all his ways are just. A faithful God . . . upright and just is he" (Deut 32:4); "who shall not revere you, O King of the nations" (Jer 10:7); "they will bring glory to your name" (Ps 86:9), etc. John may or may not have heard the victors over the beast singing these actual words. But it was revealed to him that they were praising God for his mighty deliverance and judgment on their enemies. His rendering of the song may be drawn from the liturgy of the synagogue and no doubt from the early Christian church. In fact, it is precisely in connection with the ancient Easter liturgy that the church's dependence on the synagogue Passover liturgy is most easily recognizable (Massey H. Shepherd, Jr., *The Paschal Liturgy and the Apocalypse* [Richmond: John Knox, 1960], p. 96). The Exodus background is quite obvious throughout both chapters 15 and 16 (cf. 8:7ff. and see comments at 1:10). On the possible theme of resurrection in the hymn, see Notes.

5–8 A second and still more impressive scene follows. The door to the temple in heaven is again opened (cf. 11:19), and the seven angels dressed in white and gold come out of the temple. In a dignified manner, one of the living creatures gives a bowl to each of the seven messengers. The bowls (*phialē*) are the vessels used in the temple ministry especially for offerings and incense (5:8). *Phialē* translates the Hebrew *mizrāq* (a bowl for throwing liquids) in most instances in the LXX. This might have been a large banquet bowl for wine (Amos 6:6), but more often it was a ritual bowl used for collecting the blood of the sacrifices (Exod 27:3). Golden bowls seem to be always associated with the temple (e.g., 1 Kings 7:50; 2 Kings 12:13; 25:15). *Phialē* in the Greco-Roman world was a broad, flat bowl or saucer used ritually for drinking or for pouring libations (LSJ, p. 1930).

The "smoke" that filled the temple refers to the shekinah cloud first associated with the tabernacle and then with the temple. It symbolizes God's special presence and that he is the source of the judgments (Exod 40:34ff.; 1 Kings 8:10–11; Ezek 11:23; 44:4). His awesome presence in the temple until the plagues are finished (16:17) prohibits even angels from entering it (cf. Isa 6:4; Hab 2:20).

Notes

3 K. Boronicz argues that according to Jewish tradition the doctrine of resurrection is implicitly contained in the Law and is exemplified by the Canticle of Moses (Exod 15:1–18). Revelation 15:3–4 has a prophetic and messianic sense and points to resurrection. In their prophetic symbolism, the Song of Moses and the Song of the Lamb are identical ("*Canticum Moysi et agni*"—Apoc. 15:3, Ruch Biblit, 17 [1964], 81–87). Could this also be the reason why all the early church liturgies included the Song of Moses somewhere in the Easter commemoration and some also included it on other Sundays (Eric Werner, *The Sacred Bridge: Liturgical Parallels in Synagogue and Early Church* [New York: Schocken Books, 1970], p. 142)?

In the ancient synagogue, the Haftorah (prophetic reading) accompanying the Seder on Exodus 15:1ff. was Isaiah 26:1: "In that day this song will be sung in the land of Judah: We have a strong city; God makes salvation its walls and ramparts"; and Isaiah 65:24: "Before they call I will answer; while they are still speaking I will hear." Both prophetic portions are part of the texts called "Consolation of Israel" and emphasize the strengthening of the faith of Israel (Jacob Mann, *The Bible as Read and Preached in the Old Synagogue*, 2 vols. [New York: Ktav, 1971], 1: 431–32). The Song of Moses was apparently not so frequently used in the synagogue but principally in the temple services (Werner, *Sacred Bridge*, p. 141).

6 There is good MS evidence for reading that angels were dressed in λίθον (*lithon*, "stone") instead of λίνον (*linon*, "linen"). But the sense of "stone" is strained and thus both Metzger (Bruce M. Metzger, *A Textual Commentary on the Greek New Testament* [New York: UBS, 1971], p. 756) and Swete argue for *linon* as the preferred reading.

---

2. Pouring out of the seven bowls

16:1–21

[1]Then I heard a loud voice from the temple saying to the seven angels, "Go, pour out the seven bowls of God's wrath on the earth."

[2]The first angel went and poured out his bowl on the land, and ugly and painful sores broke out on the people who had the mark of the beast and worshiped his image.

[3]The second angel poured out his bowl on the sea, and it turned into blood like that of a dead man, and every living thing in the sea died.

[4]The third angel poured out his bowl on the rivers and springs of water, and they became blood. [5]Then I heard the angel in charge of the waters say:

"You are just in these judgments,
   you who are and who were, the Holy One,
   because you have so judged;
[6]for they have shed the blood of your saints and prophets,
   and you have given them blood to drink
     as they deserve."

[7]And I heard the altar respond:

"Yes, Lord God Almighty,
   true and just are your judgments."

[8]The fourth angel poured out his bowl on the sun, and the sun was given power to scorch people with fire. [9]They were seared by the intense heat and they cursed the name of God, who had control over these plagues, but they refused to repent and glorify him.

[10]The fifth angel poured out his bowl on the throne of the beast, and his kingdom was plunged into darkness. Men gnawed their tongues in agony [11]and cursed the God of heaven because of their pains and their sores, but they refused to repent of what they had done.

[12]The sixth angel poured out his bowl on the great river Euphrates, and its water was dried up to prepare the way for the kings from the East. [13]Then I saw three evil spirits that looked like frogs; they came out of the mouth of the dragon, out of the mouth of the beast and out of the mouth of the false prophet. [14]They are spirits of demons performing miraculous signs, and they go out to the kings of the whole world, to gather them for the battle on the great day of God Almighty.

[15]"Behold, I come like a thief! Blessed is he who stays awake and keeps his clothes with him, so that he may not go naked and be shamefully exposed."

[16]Then they gathered the kings together to the place that in Hebrew is called Armageddon.

[17]The seventh angel poured out his bowl into the air, and out of the temple came a loud voice from the throne, saying, "It is done!" [18]Then there came flashes of lightning, rumblings, peals of thunder and a severe earthquake. No earthquake like it has ever occurred since man has been on earth, so tremendous was the quake.

¹⁹The great city split into three parts, and the cities of the nations collapsed. God remembered Babylon the Great and gave her the cup filled with the wine of the fury of his wrath. ²⁰Every island fled away and the mountains could not be found. ²¹From the sky huge hailstones of about a hundred pounds each fell upon men. And they cursed God on account of the plague of hail, because the plague was so terrible.

1 This chapter describes the "third woe" (see comments at introduction to ch. 15) in the form of the outpouring of seven bowl judgments. They occur in rapid succession with only a brief pause for a dialogue between the third angel and the altar, accentuating the justice of God's punishments (vv.5–7). This rapid succession is probably due to John's desire to give a telescopic view of the first six bowls and then hasten on to the seventh, where the far more interesting judgment on Babylon occurs, of which the author will give a detailed account. Again, seven symbolizes fullness, this time fullness of judgment (cf. Lev 26:21). The striking parallelism between the order of these plagues and those of the trumpets (8:2–9:21), though clearly not identical in every detail, has led many to conclude that the two series are the same. The similarity, however, may be merely literary.

Each plague in both series (the trumpets and the bowls) is reminiscent of the plagues on Egypt before the Exodus. The first four in both series cover the traditional divisions of nature: earth, sea, rivers, sky. But in each of the bowls, unlike the trumpets, the plague on nature is related to the suffering of mankind. Furthermore, each bowl plague seems to be total in its effect ("every living thing . . . died" [v.3]), whereas under the trumpets only a part is affected ("a third of the living creatures . . . died" [8:9]). Therefore, it seems better to understand the trumpets and bowls as separate judgments; yet both are described in language drawn from the pattern of God's judgment on Egypt under Moses (see comments at 8:7ff.). The final three plagues are social and spiritual in their effect and shift from nature to humanity.

The question arises whether these descriptions should be taken more or less literally. The answer is probably less literally. But the important point is that they depict God's sure and righteous judgment that will one day be literally and actually done in this world.

2 *The first bowl* has no strict counterpart in the trumpets but recalls the sixth plague of boils under Moses (Exod 9:10–11). As the antagonists of Moses were affected by the boils, so the enemies of Christ who worship the beast will be struck by this plague. Perhaps "painful" sore might be translated "malignant" sore (Swete).

3 *The second bowl* turns the sea into polluted blood (see comments at 8:8). Genesis 1:21 is reversed; all marine life dies (cf. Exod 7:17–21).

4 *The third bowl* affects the fresh waters of the earth, which are essential to human life. They too become polluted as blood (cf. Exod 7:17–21).

5–7 Here the reference to blood calls forth the dialogue between the angel and the altar concerning the logic of the plagues. The blood that sinners drink, which is poured out on them, is just requital for their shedding of the blood of the saints (15:1–4) and prophets (11:3–13; cf. 17:6; 18:20). With blood, God vindicates the blood of the martyrs of Jesus. God's wrath is exercised in recognition of their love. People must choose whether to drink the blood of saints or to wear robes dipped in the blood of the Lamb (Minear, *I Saw a New Earth,* in loc).

8–9 *The fourth bowl* increases the intensity of the sun's heat; it is the exact opposite of the fourth trumpet, which produced a plague of darkness (cf. 8:12). The earth dwellers, instead of repenting of their deeds and acknowledging the Creator, the only act that could even now turn away God's wrath, curse (*blasphēmeō,* "slander," "blaspheme") God for sending them agonizing pain (vv. 11, 21). Yet their problem goes beyond the awful physical pain and is moral and spiritual (cf. Isa 52:5; Rom 1:25; 2:24).

10–11 *The fifth bowl* plunges the kingdom of the beast into darkness. This is not a reference to the fall of the Roman Empire or Caesar worship, though John's words would include this level of meaning. In 2:13, John used the word "throne" (*thronos*) to designate the stronghold of Satan at Pergamum. Thus "the throne of the beast" symbolizes the seat of the world-wide dominion of the great satanic system of idolatry (the Abyss? cf. 20:1). This system is plunged into spiritual darkness or disruption, bringing chaos on all who sought life and meaning in it. Charles seeks to connect this darkness to the darkness and pain caused by the demon-locusts of the fifth trumpet (9:1ff.). But in the trumpet plague the locust-demons are the direct cause of the pain, while the darkness is incidental. This bowl plague, however, though similar to the fifth trumpet, strikes at the very seat of satanic authority over the world; and the darkness is probably moral and spiritual rather than physical (cf. 21:25; 22:5; John 8:12; 12:35–36, 46; 1 John 1:5–7; 2:8–10; Wisd Sol 17:21). Again the terrible refrain is repeated: "But they refused to repent of what they had done."

12–16 *The sixth bowl* is specifically aimed at drying up the Euphrates River and so will allow the demonically inspired kings from the East to gather at Armageddon where God himself will enter into battle with them. The reference to the Euphrates in the sixth trumpet is a striking parallel to the sixth bowl plague (9:14). Thus many identify the two series as different aspects of the same plagues. But while the sixth trumpet releases demonic hordes to inflict death on the earth dwellers, the sixth bowl effects the assembling of the rulers (kings) from the East to meet the Lord God Almighty in battle.

The Euphrates was not only the location of Babylon, the great anti-God throne, but the place from which the evil hordes would invade Israel (see comments at 9:14). Thus, by mentioning the Euphrates by name, John is suggesting that the unseen rulers of this world are being prepared to enter into a final and fatal battle with the Sovereign of the universe. It is a warfare that can be conceived only in terms that describe realities of a primordial and eschatological order, an order that is more descriptive of contemporary actualities than political history (Minear). Thus John does not, in my opinion, describe the invasion of the Parthian hordes advancing on Rome or any future political invasion of Israel (contra Mounce, *Revelation,* p. 12). How could such political groups be involved in the battle of the great day of God Almighty? Instead, in terms reminiscent of the ancient battles of Israel, John describes the eschatological defeat of the forces of evil, the kings from the East.

Further confirmation that these Eastern kings represent the combined forces of evil in the world is John's reference to the three froglike evil (*akatharta,* "unclean") spirits that proceed out of the mouths of the dragon, the beast, and the false prophet. Frogs were considered unclean (*akatharta*) animals by the Jews (Lev 11:10, 41). The background for this figure is not clear but probably relates more to pagan metaphors for evil than to any specific OT references. To the Persian, the frog was the double of Ahriman, god of evil and agent of plagues (Moffatt, EGT, 5:447).

To the Egyptian, the frog was not loathsome, as some suggest, but the symbol of the goddess Heqt, a goddess of resurrection and fertility. But to a Jewish mind, such gods were demons (*daimoniōn*, v.14), Satan's emissaries, and inseparable from idolatry (9:20; 18:2; 1 Cor 10:20–21). These demons produce miraculous signs like the false prophet (13:13–14), and this connects their activity to the deception of the earth's kings. Since these demons come from the "mouths" of the figures, lying and deceptive words are implied (cf. the sword from Christ's mouth that is equal to his word of truth). These kings are summoned to the battle of the great day of God Almighty. It is not necessary to limit John's language to the imperial emperor cult or to the Nero redivivus myth (see introduction to ch. 13). Under the sixth bowl, the kings are only gathered. Not until the seventh bowl do the confrontation and defeat actually occur (19:19–21).

Somewhat abruptly, but not inappropriately so, a warning is issued. Those who worship and serve the Lamb must be constantly vigilant lest their loyalty to him be diverted through the satanic deception (cf. Matt 24:43ff.; 1 Thess 5:2, 4). The Parousia (coming) of Christ is here connected with the judgment of Armageddon and the fall of Babylon. After John has described the latter in more detail (chs. 17–18), he describes the vision of the return of Jesus (19:11–16). In v.15 the third of the seven beatitudes is pronounced (cf. 1:3; 14:13; 19:9; 20:6; 22:7, 14).

Similar to the exhortation given to those in the churches at Sardis (3:2–4) and Laodicea (3:18), the warning about Jesus' coming "like a thief" implies a need for alertness to the deception of idolatry and disloyalty to Jesus. Like a guard who watches by night, the true Christian will remain steadfast and prepared. It is not necessary to relate this warning only to the end time as in the context, since the appeal for the steadfast loyalty of Christians is relevant at any time. Such appeals, however, are associated in the Gospels with the return of Christ (Mark 13:32–37). There is no evidence that John is here reinterpreting the second coming of Christ, seeing that event in the crises of history as Caird suggests (p. 208). Since John's description does not refer to the Roman Empire but to the eschatological judgment, there is no need to resort to any reinterpretation hypothesis.

Many modern interpreters identify Armageddon with the Galilean fortified city of Megiddo and believe that a literal military battle will be fought in the latter days in that vicinity (cf. New Scofield Reference Bible, notes at Judg 5:19 and Rev 16:16; H. Lindsay; Seiss; J.B. Smith; Walvoord). While this sense is not impossible, it is better to take the name as being symbolic. In Hebrew *har* means hill or mountain, while *m^egiddôn* (Gr., *magedōn*) could mean Megiddo, a Canaanite stronghold in the Jezreel Plain later captured by the Israelites (Josh 12:21; Judg 5:19). Megiddo, however, is a tell (artificial mound—only seventy feet high in John's day according to Mounce, *Revelation*, p. 301) and not a hill or mountain and is never so designated, though the fact that over two hundred battles have been fought in this vicinity makes the site an appropriate symbol for the eschatological battle (Swete). Neither can it mean Mount Carmel near Megiddo (Lohmeyer), for such a designation is never used and would be totally obscure to the residents of Asia to whom John writes and who probably were for the most part ignorant of Hebrew. Therefore it is better to understand the term symbolically in the same manner as "in Hebrew" in 9:11 alerts us to the symbolic significance of the name of the angel of the Abyss.

Several other possibilities for the meaning of *har m^egiddôn* have been suggested. Rissi derives the word from *har mô'ēd* ("mount of the assembly") and connects this with Isaiah 14:12–15, where the king of Babylon, lifted up in pride, tries to ascend to the "mount of the assembly," i.e., the throne of God (Rissi, *Time and History* pp. 84–85). While the theory is interesting, it rests on a conjectural emendation of the Greek text without any MS evidence and has no direct support from the immediate context (vv. 12–16). Another suggestion derives from the Hebrew *har m^egiddô* the phrase "his fruitful mountain," i.e., Jerusalem, and connects the reference to the final battle to be fought near Jerusalem (Joel 3:2; Zech 14:2ff.; cited by Charles, *Commentary on Revelation*, 2:50). Caird (p. 207) mentions a view where *magedōn* (from *'Armagedōn*, "Armageddon") is related to the Hebrew *gādad*, which means "to cut," "attack," or "maraud"; as such with *har* ("mountain") it would mean "marauding mountain" and would be John's variation on Jeremiah's "destroying mountain" (Jer 51:25).

It is surprising that no one has suggested taking *magedōn* as deriving from the secondary sense of the Hebrew *gādad* that means "to gather in troops or bands" (BDB, p. 151). The simple way in Hebrew to make a noun from a verb is to prefix a *ma* to the verbal form. Thus we have *magēd*, "a place of gathering in troops," and the suffix *ô*, meaning "his," yielding "his place of gathering in troops." This is almost equivalent to the expressions in vv. 14, 16—"to gather them [the kings] for the battle on the great day of God Almighty"—and would allude to the prophetic expectation of the gathering of the nations for judgment (Joel 3:2, 12). In any case, the name is symbolic and probably does not refer to any geographical location we can now identify, whether in Palestine or elsewhere; but it describes the eschatological confrontation where God will meet the forces of evil in their final defeat. As Mounce states:

> Har-Magedon is symbolic of the final overthrow of all the forces of evil by the might and power of God. The great conflict between God and Satan, Christ and Antichrist, good and evil, which lies behind the perplexing course of history will in the end issue in a final struggle in which God will emerge victorious and take with him all who placed their faith in him. This is Har-Magedon (*Revelation*, p. 302).

Nevertheless, it refers to a real point in history and to real persons who will encounter God's just sentence.

17–21 The seventh bowl is poured out into the air. Nothing further is said about the "air"; rather, John is concerned with the loud voice that cries out, "It is done" (*gegonen*), or, "It has come to pass." With this seventh bowl, the eschatological wrath of God is completed (cf. 6:17; 21:6; John 19:30). Flashes of lightning, peals of thunder, and a severe earthquake occur (cf. 4:5; 8:5; 11:19). These eschatological signs symbolize the destruction of the anti-God forces throughout the world (cf. Heb 12:27). So great is the earthquake of God's judgment that it reaches the strongholds of organized evil represented by the cities of the pagans (*ethnē*, "nations"). Even the great city Babylon, which seduced all the earth's kings and inhabitants (17:2), now comes under final sentence (see comments on 11:8).

The judgment of Babylon will occupy John's attention in chapters 17 and 18. While the catastrophe continues to be described in geophysical terms (islands and mountains disappearing, huge hailstones accompanying a gigantic storm), there is a question whether John intends the destruction to be merely natural or even politico-historical entities or exclusively of the unseen powers of evil. Like the Egyptian plague of hail that further hardened Pharaoh's heart, this plague of hail falls on the unrepentant to no avail; they curse God for sending his judgment on them (cf. Exod 9:24). By such language John describes the rising pitch of God's wrath on the rebellious powers of the earth. His words should not be politicized as if he spoke merely of Rome or of some impending historical crisis for the church. He is speaking of the great realities of the end, when God has put down all his enemies.

3. *The harlot and the beast*

17:1–18

> ¹One of the seven angels who had the seven bowls came and said to me, "Come, I will show you the punishment of the great prostitute, who sits on many waters. ²With her the kings of the earth committed adultery and the inhabitants of the earth were intoxicated with the wine of her adulteries."
>
> ³Then the angel carried me away in the Spirit into a desert. There I saw a woman sitting on a scarlet beast that was covered with blasphemous names and had seven heads and ten horns. ⁴The woman was dressed in purple and scarlet, and was glittering with gold, precious stones and pearls. She held a golden cup in her hand, filled with abominable things and the filth of her adulteries. ⁵This title was written on her forehead:
>
> MYSTERY
> BABYLON THE GREAT
> THE MOTHER OF PROSTITUTES
> AND OF THE ABOMINATIONS OF THE EARTH.

⁶I saw that the woman was drunk with the blood of the saints, the blood of those who bore testimony to Jesus.

When I saw her, I was greatly astonished. ⁷Then the angel said to me: "Why are you astonished? I will explain to you the mystery of the woman and of the beast she rides, which has the seven heads and ten horns. ⁸The beast, which you saw, once was, now is not, and will come up out of the Abyss and go to his destruction. The inhabitants of the earth whose names have not been written in the book of life from the creation of the world will be astonished when they see the beast, because he once was, now is not, and yet will come.

⁹"This calls for a mind with wisdom. The seven heads are seven hills on which the woman sits. They are also seven kings. ¹⁰Five have fallen, one is, the other has not yet come; but when he does come, he must remain for a little while. ¹¹The beast who once was, and now is not, is an eighth king. He belongs to the seven and is going to his destruction.

¹²"The ten horns you saw are ten kings who have not yet received a kingdom, but who for one hour will receive authority as kings along with the beast. ¹³They have one purpose and will give their power and authority to the beast. ¹⁴They will make war against the Lamb, but the Lamb will overcome them because he is Lord of lords and King of kings—and with him will be his called, chosen and faithful followers."

¹⁵Then the angel said to me, "The waters you saw, where the prostitute sits, are peoples, multitudes, nations and languages. ¹⁶The beast and the ten horns you saw will hate the prostitute. They will bring her to ruin and leave her naked; they will eat her flesh and burn her with fire. ¹⁷For God has put it into their hearts to accomplish his purpose by agreeing to give the beast their power to rule, until God's words are fulfilled. ¹⁸The woman you saw is the great city that rules over the kings of the earth."

In an important sense, the interpretation of this chapter controls the interpretation of the whole Book of Revelation. For a majority of exegetes, Babylon represents the city of Rome. The beast stands for the Roman Empire as a whole, with its subject provinces and peoples. The seven hills (v.9) are the seven selected dynasties of Roman emperors from Augustus to Domitian. The ten kings are heads of lesser and restless states, eager to escape their enslavement to the colonizing power. John's prediction of the fall of Babylon is his announcement of the impending dissolution of the Roman Empire in all its aspects. For such a view there is considerable evidence. Babylon was a term used by both Jews and Christians for Rome (2 Baruch 11:1; Sib Oracles 5.143, 158; 1 Peter 5:13; Hippolytus *Christ and Antichrist* 36; TDNT, 1:516). Rome was a great city (v.18), a city set on seven hills (v.9), and by the time of Domitian (A.D. 85) it was notorious for persecuting and killing the saints (v.6). Thus the argument goes. Many scholars of unquestioned competence have been fully convinced of the certainty of these equations.

Yet there is evidence that casts doubt on this exegesis and impels us to look for a more adequate—if also a more subtle—understanding of John's intention. It is simply not sufficient to identify Rome and Babylon. For that matter, Babylon cannot be confined to any one historical manifestation, past or future. Babylon has multiple equivalents (cf. 11:8). The details of John's description do not neatly fit any past city, whether literal Babylon, Sodom, Egypt, Rome, or even Jerusalem. Babylon is found wherever there is satanic deception. It is defined more by dominant idolatries than geographic or temporal boundaries. The ancient Babylon is better understood here as the archetypal head of all entrenched worldly resistance to God. Babylon is a transhistorical reality including idolatrous kingdoms as diverse as Sodom, Gomorrah, Egypt, Babylon, Tyre, Nineveh, and Rome. Babylon is an eschatological symbol of satanic deception and power; it is a divine mystery that can never be wholly reducible to empirical earthly institutions. It may be said that Babylon represents the total culture of the world apart from God, while the divine system is depicted by the New Jerusalem. Rome is simply one manifestation of the total system.

Chapters 17 and 18 form one continuous unit dealing with the judgment on Babylon. The woman is identified as the great city (17:18) whose fall is described in chapter 18. From internal evidence, the identity of Babylon the woman (ch. 17) with Babylon the great city (ch. 18) is so unmistakable that it would be inappropriate to make them different entities. Neither should chapter 17 be viewed as an interpolation, as some have suggested (Mathias Rissi, "The Kerygma of the Revelation to John," Int, 22 [January 1968], 4), simply on the grounds that it seems to be politically specific in the manner of ordinary Jewish apocalyptics (see Introduction: General Nature and Historical Background). While the Roman Empire theory leads more readily to this conclusion, if we reject it, the contents of chapters 17 and 18 are wholly compatible with John's emphasis elsewhere. These two chapters form an extended appendix to the seventh bowl, where the judgment on Babylon was mentioned (16:19). They also expand the earlier references to this city (11:8; 14:8) and look forward by way of contrast to the eternal Holy City (chs. 21–22).

Chapter 17 may be divided as follows: the vision of the great harlot (vv.1–6) and the interpretation of the vision (vv.7–18). In suspenseful literary fashion, John first describes the nature of the harlot and the beast she rides (ch. 17); then he describes her momentous fall in terms drawn from the OT descriptions of the fall of great cities (ch. 18).

1 "One of the seven angels" connects this vision with the preceding bowl judgments, showing that it is a further expansion or appendix of the final bowl action and not an additional event.

John sees a great prostitute (*pornē*) established on many waters. The verse forms a superscription for the chapter. The relationship between prostitution (*porneia*) and idolatry has already been discussed (see comments at 2:14, 20). The prevalence of cult prostitution throughout the ancient world makes this figure appropriate for idolatrous worship. The expressions "abominable things" (17:4) and "magic spell" (18:23) confirm this connection. In the OT, the same figure of a harlot city is used of Nineveh (Nah 3:4), of Tyre (Isa 23:16–17), and frequently of idolatrous Jerusalem (Ezek 16:15ff.). The best background for understanding the language of the chapter is not the history of the Roman Empire or pagan god parallels but the descriptions of Jerusalem the harlot in Ezekiel 16 and 23 and Babylon the harlot in Jeremiah 51. A quick reading of these chapters will confirm the many parallels to John's language.

But the great prostitute (*pornē*), Babylon, that Revelation describes is not any mere historical city with its inhabitants, whether in John's past, present, or future. Rather, this city is the mother of all these historical prostitutes, the archetypal source of every idolatrous manifestation in time and space. Therefore, it is as much a mistake to identify Babylon with Rome (though many scholars do, most recently Mounce, *Revelation*, p. 310) as it is with Jerusalem (so Ford, p. 285). Babylon could equally well be seen in any of these classic manifestations from the past or in modern times—viz., Nazi Germany, Idi Ammin's Ugandan regime, Soviet Russia, Mao's China, British colonialism, or even in aspects of American life (so William Stringfellow, *An Ethic for Christians and Other Aliens in a Strange Land* [Waco: Word, 1973]).

Amazingly, all the harlot-city societies mentioned in Scripture have certain common characteristics that are also reflected in John's description of the great Babylon, in which he merges the descriptions of ancient Babylon and Jerusalem into one great composite. Royal dignity and splendor combined with prosperity, overabundance, and luxury (Jer 51:13; Ezek 16:13, 49; Nah 2:9; cf. Rev 18:3, 7, 16–17); self-trust or boastfulness (Isa 14:12–14; Jer 50:31; Ezek 16:15, 50, 56; 27:3; 28:5; cf. Rev 18:7); power and violence, especially against God's people (Jer 51:35, 49; Ezek 23:37; Nah 3:1–3; cf. Rev 18:10, 24); oppression and injustice (Isa 14:4; Ezek 16:49; 28:18; cf. Rev 18:5, 20); and idolatry (Jer 51:47; Ezek 16:17, 36; 23:7, 30, 49; Nah 1:14; cf. Rev 17:4–5; 18:3; 19:2) are all here. Wherever and whenever these characteristics have been manifested historically, *there* is the appearance of Babylon.

The great prostitute "sits on many waters." This goes back to Jeremiah's oracle against historical Babylon, situated along the waterways of the Euphrates, with many canals around the city, greatly multiplying its wealth by trade (Jer 51:13). While the description alludes to ancient Babylon, it also has a deeper significance, explained in v. 15 as "peoples, multitudes, nations and languages"—figurative for the vast influence of the prostitute on the peoples of the world.

2 Earth's kings and inhabitants committed fornication with the prostitute. This language goes back to references to the harlot cities of the past (e.g., Jer 51:7) and means that the peoples of the world have become drunk with abundance, power, pride, violence, and especially false worship. The expression "kings of the earth" may be in poetic synonymous parallelism (i.e., an equivalent term) with "inhabitants of the earth." If this were so, the exegesis of the former term would be enriched. The evidence for this is not, however, conclusive (cf. 14:8; 17:4–5; 18:3, 9). "The kings of the earth" may describe simply the rulers in contrast to the hoi polloi.

3 John is carried in the Spirit (see comments at 1:10 and cf. 4:2; 21:10) into a "desert." Again the allusion is to ancient Babylon (Isa 14:23; 21:1; cf. Rev 18:2; see comments at 12:6). Caird (p. 213), following more the imagery of 12:6, thinks that John was taken to the desert to be free from the charms and attractions of the whore so that he could understand her exact nature. Yet it is in the desert that he sees the prostitute seated on "a scarlet beast"—scarlet, presumably, because the color symbolizes the beast's blasphemy in contrast to the white-horse rider and those dressed in white, who are faithful and true (19:8, 11, 14). Since this beast is a seven-headed monster, there is no cogent reason against identifying it with the first beast in chapter 13, which is also inseparable from the seven-headed dragon of chapter 12.

4 Dressed in queenly attire (Ezek 16:13; cf. Rev 18:7), the woman rides the beast, swinging in her hand a golden cup full of her idolatrous abominations and wickedness. Note the contrast—beauty and gross wickedness. Her costly and attractive attire suggests the prostitute's outward beauty and attraction (Jer 4:30). The golden cup filled with wine alludes to Jeremiah's description of Babylon's world-wide influence in idolatry (Jer 51:7). Her cup is filled with "abominable things" (*bdelygmatōn*). The *bdelygmatōn* are most frequently associated with idolatry, which was abhorrent to the Jew and likewise to the Christian (21:27). It is the same word Jesus used in referring to Daniel's "abomination that causes desolation" standing in the temple (Mark 13:14; cf. Dan 9:27; 11:31; 12:11). Babylon is the archetype of all idolatrous obscenities in the earth (v.5). "Filth" (*akatharta*, "uncleannesses") is a word frequently associated in the NT with evil (unclean) spirits (e.g., Matt 10:1; 12:43) and also with idolatry (2 Cor 6:17) and perhaps cult prostitution (Eph 5:5).

5 The woman has a title written on her forehead, showing that in spite of all her royal glamour she is nothing but a prostitute. From the writings of Seneca and Juvenal, we know that it was the custom for Roman prostitutes to wear their names in the fillet that encircled their brows (Swete, p. 214). The OT also refers to the peculiar brow of the prostitute (Jer 3:3, "a harlot's brow," NEB).

The first word in the woman's title is "MYSTERY" (*mystērion*, cf. 1:20; 10:7; 17:7). But does the word belong to the name "MYSTERY BABYLON" itself, or is it a prefix before the actual name—viz., "She has a name written on her forehead, which is a mystery, 'Babylon . . .'?" Scholars disagree, but the latter explanation fits better with John's use of *mystērion* as a word denoting a divine mystery or allegory that is now revealed. Furthermore, his use of *pneumatikōs* ("figuratively") before the words "Sodom and Egypt" in 11:8 (q.v.), by which the reader is alerted to a special symbolic significance in what follows, likewise supports this.

No doubt, as Lilje suggests, the specific part of the title that is a divine mystery is that this prostitute is the *mother* of all earth's idolatrous prostitutes (p. 223). She is the fountainhead, the reservoir, the womb that bears all the individual cases of historical resistance to God's will on earth; she is the unholy antithesis to the woman who weds the Lamb (19:7–8) and to the New Jerusalem (21:2–3). Therefore, she cannot be merely ancient Babylon, Rome, or Jerusalem, because these are only her children—*she* is the mother of them all. While at its beginning Babel was associated with resisting and defying God (Gen 11:1–11), it is probably the epoch of the Babylonian captivity of Israel that indelibly etched the proud, idolatrous, and repressive nature of Babylon on the memories of God's people and thus provided for succeeding generations the symbolic image that could be applied to the further manifestations of the mother prostitute.

6 This mother prostitute is also the source of the shed blood of the followers of Jesus, the martyrs referred to throughout the book (6:9; 7:9ff.; 13:8; 18:24). The same mother harlot who had killed the saints of old throughout salvation history is now also responsible for the deaths of the Christians (cf. 2:13). Though there is no direct reference here to Rome or Jerusalem, early Christian readers would understand that whenever they were threatened with death by any temporal power—whether political, religious, or both—they were in reality facing the blood-thirsty mother prostitute God was about to judge and destroy once for all. To be drunk with blood was a familiar figure in the ancient world for the lust for violence (Charles, *Commentary on Revelation*, 2:66; cf. Isa 34:7; 49:26).

7 Verses 7–18 contain an extended interpretation of the vision that parallels the method used in apocalyptic sections in OT prophecy (cf. Zech 1:8ff., etc.; Rev 7:9ff). First the beast is described and identified (vv.7–8), then the seven heads (vv.9–11), the ten horns (vv.12–14), the waters (v.15), and finally the woman (v.18). John's astonishment over the arresting figure of the woman on the beast is quickly subdued by the interpreting angel's announcement that John will be shown the explanation of the divine mystery of the symbolic imagery of woman and beast.

8 Much difficulty in interpreting this section has resulted from incorrectly applying John's words either to the Roman emperor succession (the seven heads), to the Nero redivivus myth ("once was, now is not, and will come up out of the Abyss" [see comments at introduction to ch. 13]), or to a succession of world empires. None of these views is satisfactory for reasons that will be stated below. John's description is theological, not political. He describes a reality behind earth's sovereigns, not the successive manifestations in history. When this is seen to be the case, it is unnecessary to revert to source theories (contra Beasley-Murray, "The Revelation," p. 1300), to interpolation theories (Charles, *Commentary on Revelation*, 2:67; Eller, pp. 165–67), or to other theories in an attempt to relate John's descriptive language to past events.

The beast is the monster from the Abyss, i.e., the satanic incarnation of idolatrous power, described in 13:1ff. (q.v.), mentioned earlier in 11:7, and whose destruction is seen in 19:19–20. John is told that the beast "once was, now is not, and will come up out of the Abyss." This seems clearly to be a paraphrase of the idea in chapter 13 of the sword-wounded beast who was healed (13:3, 14); the language is similar, the astonishment of the world's inhabitants identical, and the threefold emphasis on this spectacular feature is repeated in both contexts (13:3, 12, 14; 17:8 bis, 11).

The play here on the tenses "was, . . . is not, . . . will come" refers to a three-stage history of the beast that requires a mind with wisdom to understand its mystery. Isaiah refers to the chaos monster as "Rahab the Do-Nothing," i.e., the monster thought to energize Egypt is in reality inactive, rendered impotent by the hand of the Lord (Isa 30:7). That John's beast "is not" refers to his defeat by the Lamb on Calvary. To those who worship only the Father and the Son, all other gods are nothing or nonexistent (1 Cor 8:4–6). Satan once had unchallenged power over the earth ("was," cf. Luke 4:6; Heb 2:14–15). Now he is a defeated sovereign ("is not," cf. John 12:31–32); yet he is given a "little time" to oppose God and his people (12:12c; 13:5; 20:3b) before his final sentencing to "destruction" (*apōleia*, v.11; cf. Matt 7:13; John 17:12; Rom 9:22; 2 Thess 2:3). It is this apparent revival of Satan's power and authority over the world after his mortal wound (Gen 3:15) that causes the deceived of earth to follow him.

Note the subtle change in perspective from the way the first reference to the beast is stated (v.8a) to that of the second (v.8b). Whereas the first instance refers to his satanic origin ("out of the Abyss") and his final destruction, a divine revelation to believers, the second simply states how that he was, is not, and yet comes, an unbeliever's view. This twofold viewpoint is paralleled in vv.9–11 where one of the kings "is" (v.10) and an eighth king "is" (v.11); yet the beast "is not" (v.11). There seems to be an intentional double-talk whereby the author seeks to identify theologically the nature of the power that supports the profligate woman.

John's use of the present tense for the beast's coming up out of the Abyss (*anabainein*, cf. 11:7) may suggest a continuing aspect of his character, similar to the use of the present tense to describe the New Jerusalem descending from heaven (*katabainousa;* cf. 3:12; 21:2, 10). That the beast goes into perdition (present tense) may likewise indicate one of his continuing characteristics. There is also a possible parallelism in the expression "once was, now is not, and yet will come" with the divine attributes described in the phrase "who is, and who was, and who is to come" (1:8). On the meaning of the book of life, see comments at 3:5 (cf. 13:8).

9 This and the following verses form the key of the Roman emperor view of the Apocalypse. The woman not only sits on many waters (vv.1, 15), and on the beast (v.3), but she also sits on seven hills. As previously stated, most scholars have no doubt that the seven hills refer to the seven hills of Rome and the seven kings to seven successive emperors of that nation. Mounce states, "There is little doubt that a first-century reader would understand this reference in any way other than as a reference to Rome, the city built upon seven hills" (*Revelation,* pp. 313–14).

Yet there is very good reason to doubt that this interpretation, and its varieties, is the meaning John intended. The following dissenting view is drawn largely from Minear (*I Saw a New Earth,* pp. 237ff.). In the first place, the seven hills belong to the monster, not the woman. It is the woman (i.e., the city [v.18]) who sits upon (i.e., has mastery over) the seven heads (or seven hills) of the monster. If the woman is the city of Rome, it is obvious that she did not exercise mastery over seven successive Roman emperors that are also seven traditional hills of Rome. This introduces an unwarranted twisting of the symbolism to fit a preconceived interpretation. Also, how could the seven hills of Rome have any real importance to the diabolical nature of the beast or the woman? Nor does it help to make the prostitute the Roman Empire and the hills the city of Rome (so Kiddle) since the woman is explicitly identified in v.18 not as the empire but as the city. In fact, nowhere in the NT is Rome described as the enemy of the church.

If it is argued that what is really important in the mention of the seven hills is the identification with Rome, how then does this require any special divine wisdom ("This calls for a mind with wisdom" [v.9])? As Caird (in loc.) remarks, any Roman soldier who knew Greek could figure out that the seven hills referred to Rome. But whenever divine wisdom is called for, the description requires theological and symbolical discernment, not mere geographical or numerical insight (cf. comments at 13:18). Those who follow Charles and argue for a fusing of sources or images to explain the dual reference to the hills and kings simply evade the implications of the incongruity they have created.

In the seven other instances of the word *orē* in Revelation, it is always rendered "mountain," except here in 17:9, where it is translated "hills" (see Notes). Is this a case where previous exegesis has influenced even the best translations (KJV has "mountains")? On the other hand, mountains allegorically refer to world powers in the Prophets (Isa 2:2; Jer 51:25; Dan 2:35; Zech 4:7). It seems better, then, to interpret the seven mountains as a reference to the seven heads or kings, which describe not the city but the beast. The expression "they are also seven kings" seems to require strict identification of the seven mountains with seven kings rather than with a geographic location.

John's use of numbers elsewhere in the book likewise argues against the Roman Empire identification. He has already shown a strong disposition for their symbolic significance—e.g., seven churches, seals, trumpets, bowls, and thunders; twenty-four elders; 144,000 sealed, etc. By his use of seven, he indicates completeness or wholeness. The seven heads of the beast symbolize fullness of blasphemy and evil. It is much like our English idiom "the seven seas," i.e., all the seas of the world. Caird recognizes the patent absurdity of trying to take the symbolic number seven and make it refer to exactly seven Roman emperors. Yet he goes on to explain the seven kings as a reference to an indefinite number of emperors, including Nero redivivus (pp. 218–19). While Caird's view is much more in keeping with John's symbolism, it still labors under the unacceptable assumption that John is identifying the beast with Rome.

10 If the seven heads symbolically represent the complete or full source of evil power and blasphemy, why, then, does John talk about five fallen heads or kings, one existing head or king, and one yet to come? Does this not most readily fit the view of dynastic successions to the imperial throne? To be sure, there have been many attempts to fit the date of Revelation (the then contemporary king would be he who "is") into the emperor lists of the first century (for detailed discussions, see Caird, pp. 217–18; Ford, pp. 289–91). But immediately there are admitted problems. Where do we begin—with Julius Caesar or Caesar Augustus? Are we to count all the emperors or just those who fostered emperor worship? Are we to exclude Galba, Otho, and Vitellius who had short, rival reigns? If so, how can they be excluded on a completely arbitrary basis? A careful examination of the historic materials yields no satisfactory solution. If Revelation were written under Nero, there would be too few emperors; if under Domitian, too many. The original readers would have had no more information on these emperor successions than we do, and possibly even less. How many Americans can immediately name the last seven presidents? Furthermore, how could the eighth emperor who is identified as the beast also be one of the seven (v. 11)?

Recognizing these problems, others have sought different solutions to John's five-one-one succession of kings. Since the word "king" may also represent kingdoms, Seiss (followed recently by Ladd and Walvoord) has suggested an interpretation that takes the five-one-one to refer to successive world kingdoms that have oppressed the people of God: Egypt, Assyria, Babylon, Persia, Greece (five fallen), Rome (one is), and a future world kingdom (p. 393). While this solves some of the emperor succession problems and fits nicely, it too must admit arbitrary omissions, such as the devastating persecution of the people of God under the Seleucids of Syria, especially Antiochus IV, Epiphanes. This view also suffers in not respecting the symbolic significance of John's use of seven throughout the book. Also, how can these kings (kingdoms) survive the destruction of the harlot and be pictured as mourning over her demise (18:9)? And what logical sense can be made of the fact that the seventh king (kingdom), usually identified with Antichrist, is separate from the eighth king (kingdom), which is clearly identified with the beast (vv.10b–11)?

A convincing interpretation of the seven kings must do justice to three considerations: (1) Since the heads belong to the beast, the interpretation must relate their significance to this beast, not to Babylon. (2) Since the primary imagery of kingship in Revelation is a feature of the power conflict between the Lamb and the beast and between those who share the rule of these two enemies (cf. 17:14; 19:19), the kind of sovereignty expressed in 17:10 must be the true antithesis to the kind of sovereignty exercised by Christ and his followers. (3) Since the kings are closely related to the seven mountains and to the prostitute, the nature of the relationship between these must be clarified by the interpretation (Minear, *I Saw a New Earth*, p. 240).

If we can see that the seven heads do not represent a quantitative measure but show qualitatively the fullness of evil power residing in the beast, then the falling of five heads conveys the message of a significant victory over the beast. The image of a sovereignty falling is better related to God's judgment on a power than to a succession of kings (-doms) (cf. Jer 50:32; 51:8, 49; Rev 14:8; 18:2).

The imagery of the seven heads presented in 12:3 and 13:1 must be restudied. The ancient seal showing the seven-headed chaos monster being slain (see comments at 13:1b) well illustrates John's imagery here. In that ancient scene, the seven-headed monster is being slain by a progressive killing of its seven heads. Four of the heads are dead, killed apparently by the spear of a divine figure who is attacking the monster. His defeat seems imminent. Yet the chaos monster is still active because three heads still live. Similarly, John's message is that five of the monster's seven heads are already defeated by the power of the Lamb's death and by the identification in that death of the martyrs of Jesus (12:11). One head is now active, thus showing the reality of the beast's contemporary agents who afflict the saints; and one head remains, indicating that the battle will soon be over but not with the defeat of the contemporary evil agents. This last manifestation of the beast's blasphemous power will be short—"he must remain for a little while." This statement seems to go with the function of the ten horns (kings) who for "one hour" (v.12) will rule with the beast. The seventh king (head) represents the final short display of satanic evil before the divine blow falls on the beast (cf. 12:12c; 20:3c).

11 This verse presents all interpreters with a real difficulty. One of the common interpretations refers the language to the Nero redivivus myth (see comments at introduction to ch. 13)—viz., a revived Nero will be the reincarnation of the evil genius of the whole Roman Empire (Beasley-Murray, "The Revelation," p. 1300). Furthermore, among futurist interpreters there is no agreement as to whether the seventh or the eighth king is the Antichrist. It must be admitted that any king(-dom)-succession hypothesis founders on v.11. On the other hand, if John has in mind qualitative identification and not quantitative, a theological rather than historical or political sense, the passage may yield further insight into the mystery of the beast.

First, we note the strange (to us) manner in which the sequence of seven kings gives way to the eighth, which is really the whole beast. This pattern of seven-to-eight-equals-one was familiar to the early church. It is a concept those raised in the great liturgical traditions can grasp. The eighth day was the day of the resurrection of Christ, Sunday. It was also the beginning of a new week. The seventh day, the Jewish Sabbath, is held over, to be replaced by the first of a new series, namely Sunday. Austin Farrer has noted how even the whole theme of the Apocalypse is integrally related to this idea. "Sunday is the day of Resurrection. The 'week' with which the Apocalypse deals extends from the Resurrection of Christ to the General Resurrection, when death has been destroyed." He further states the relation between the seventh and eighth:

> God rests from his completed work, but in so resting he initiates a new act which is the eighth-and-first day. We may compare the Gospel once more. On the sixth day Christ conquered, and achieved his rest from the labours of his flesh. But the sabbath-day which follows is in itself nothing, it has no content: it is simply the restful sepulchre out of which, with the eighth and first day, the resurrection springs. (A Rebirth of Images; the Making of St. John's Apocalypse [London: Darce, 1949], pp. 70–71).

Each of the series of sevens in the book, except for the seven churches, follows a pattern of the seventh in the series becoming the first of a new series; thus seven to eight equals one. The eighth was the day of the Messiah, the day of the new age and the sign of the victory over the forces of evil (Alexander Schememann, *Introduction to Liturgical Theology* [London: Faith, 1966], pp. 60–64). Shepherd also calls attention to this phenomenon in Revelation (Massey H. Shepherd, Jr., *The Paschal Liturgy and the Apocalypse* [Richmond: John Knox, 1960], pp. 20–21, 80). But does this provide a key to interpret the symbolism of the chaos monster?

Of the three stages of the beast—was, is not, will come—only the last is related to his coming "up out of the Abyss" (v.8). These words appear to be the equivalent of the beast's healed wound (plague) mentioned in 13:3, 14. While, on the one hand, Christ has killed the monster by his death (Gen 3:15; Rev 12:7–9) and for believers he "is not" (has no power), yet, on the other hand, the beast still has life ("one is" [v.10]) and will attempt one final battle against the Lamb and his followers ("the other has not yet come; . . . he must remain for a little while"). In order to recruit as many as possible for his side of the war, the beast will imitate the resurrection of Christ (he "is an eighth king" [v.11]) and will give the appearance that he is alive and in control of the world (cf. Luke 4:5–7). But John quickly adds, for the pastoral comfort of God's people, that the beast belongs to the seven, i.e., qualitatively not numerically (as if he were a former king revived); he is in reality (to the eyes of the saints) not a new beginning of life but a part of the seven-headed monster that has been slain by Christ and, therefore, he goes "to his destruction." While this imagery may seem to us to be unnecessarily obscure, it reveals the true mystery of the beast in a fashion that exposes the dynamics of satanic deception so that every Christian may be forearmed.

12–14 Here John seems to allude to Daniel 7:7, 24. The ten horns are usually understood as either native rulers of Roman provinces, serving under the emperors or native rulers of satellite states, or governors of Palestine. Others see in them a ten-nation confederacy of the future revived Roman Empire (e.g., Walvoord, pp. 254–55). There are good reasons for abandoning these explanations. In the first place, the number ten should—like most of John's numbers—be understood symbolically. Ten symbolizes a repeated number of times or an indefinite number. It is perhaps another number like seven, indicating fullness (Neh 4:12; Dan 1:12; Rev 2:10). Thus the number should not be understood as referring specifically to ten kings (kingdoms) but as indicating the multiplicity of sovereignties in confederacy that enhance the power of the beast.

Second, since these kings enter into a power conflict with the Lamb and his followers (v.14), the kind of sovereignty they exercise must be the true antithesis of the kind of sovereignty the Lamb and his followers exercise. These rulers as well as the beast with which they will be allied can be no other than the principalities and powers, the rulers of the darkness of this world, the spiritual forces of evil in the heavenly realms that Paul describes as the true enemies of Jesus' followers (Eph 6:12). To be sure, they use earthly instruments, but their reality is far greater than any specific historical equivalents (see note on v.14). These "kings" embody the fullness of Satan's attack against the Lamb in the great eschatological showdown. They are the "kings from the east" (16:12–14, 16), and they are also the "kings of the earth" who ally themselves with the beast in the final confrontation with the Lamb (19:19–21).

Finally, there is a link between v.12 and v.11. The ten kings are said to receive authority for "one hour" along with the beast. This corresponds to the "little while" of the seventh king. From the viewpoint of the saints, who will be greatly persecuted, this promise of brevity brings comfort. These kings have "one purpose" (gnōmē); they agree to oppose the Lamb. But the Lamb will overcome them because he is Lord of lords and King of kings (cf. Deut 10:17; Dan 2:47; Rev 19:16). He conquers by his death, and those who are with him also aid in the defeat of the beast by their loyalty to the Lamb even to death (cf. 5:5, 9; 12:11)—a sobering thought.

15 On first reading, this verse appears to be out of place. However, closer examination shows that v.16 also refers to the prostitute and the horns. Verse 15 teaches that the influence of the idolatrous satanic system of Babylon is universal (cf. vv.1–2) and embraces all peoples, from the humblest to the kings of the earth.

16–17 On these verses the Roman hypothesis (empire and city) breaks down. For in that view the emperors (the beast and its heads) will turn against the city or empire and destroy her. Swete (p. 222) tries to locate this event in Rome's history and to argue that there is some supporting evidence for it. But the attempt is not convincing. Rather, the attack on the prostitute indicates that in the final judgment the kingdom of Satan, by divine purpose, will be divided against itself. The references to the prostitute being hated by her former lovers, stripped naked, and burned with fire are reminiscent of the OT prophets' descriptions of the divine judgment falling on the harlot cities of Jerusalem and Tyre (e.g., Ezek 16:39–40; 23:25–27; 28:18). The description of the punishment of convicted prostitutes who are priests' daughters (cf. Lev 21:9; the burning with fire is explained by Ford as "a pouring of molten lead down their throats" [p. 55]) is combined with the picture of judgment against rebellious cities (18:8). Caird aptly captures the meaning of John's imagery in v.16: "The ravaging of the whore by the monster and its horns is John's most vivid symbol for the self-destroying power of evil" (p. 221).

In the declaration "God has put it into their hearts to accomplish his purpose" (v. 17), there is another indication of God's use of the forces of evil as instruments of his own purposes of judgment (Jer 25:9–14; cf. Luke 20:18). Nothing will distract them from their united effort to destroy the prostitute till God's purposes given through the prophets are fulfilled (cf. 10:7; 11:18).

18 The "woman" and "the great city" are one. Yet this city is not just a historical one; it is the *great* city, the *mother* city, the archetype of every evil system opposed to God in history (see comments at introduction to ch. 17). Her kingdom holds sway over the powers of the earth. John's concept of the city in Revelation entails much more than a specific historical city even in its political and sociological aspects. The cities in Revelation are communities; they are twofold: the city of God, the New Jerusalem (3:12; 21:2, 10; 22:2ff.), and the city of Satan, Babylon the Great (11:8; 14:8; 16:19; 18:4, 20, etc.). The meaning cannot be confined to Sodom or Egypt or Jerusalem or Rome or any future city. Instead, John describes the real trans-historical system of satanic evil that infuses them all.

Notes

1 For Minear's general view, cf. *I Saw a New Earth*, pp. 228–46; idem, "Babylon in the New Testament," IDB, 1:338. While Ford presents five good reasons why Babylon cannot be the city of Rome, she falls into a similar error by identifying the city as Jerusalem (p. 216). But Jerusalem, like Rome, is only one of the multiple manifestations of Babylon in history. Josephus refers to Cleopatra in language very similar to that of the Apocalypse, but as a historical type Jezebel would probably come closer to John's imagery (cf. comments at 2:20; Jos. Antiq. XV, 97 [iv.2]).

Πόρνη (*pornē*, "prostitute") may be either male or female, married or unmarried. The word is generally used of unmarried sexual relations (μοιχεία [*moicheia*] is used for extramarital relations, i.e., adultery and cult prostitution), but it can denote sexual perversions in general, whether among married or unmarried (TDNT, 6:579ff.).

8 Ladd, following Zahn, interprets the play on tenses in a more literal manner, understanding the reference to the beast as the beast that "was" as pointing to the Syrian king Antiochus Epiphanes IV, the great persecutor of the people of God in the days of the Maccabees (c. 167 B.C.) (*Commentary on Revelation*, pp. 230–31). There is some support for this view in Dan 8:9, 21. But the beast that "was" could just as well have been the emperor Vespasian, who ordered Jerusalem destroyed in A.D. 70 by Titus. Or it could also refer to Nero, who undertook an attack on Christians in the city of Rome a short time earlier.

9 Translations that render ὄρη (*ore*) as "hills" include RSV, NEB, TEV, Ph, Knox, NIV; those translating the word as "mountains" include KJV, ASV, NASB. Places in Revelation where ὄρος (*oros*) or *ore* occurs and is translated "mountain(s)" in most all versions are 6:14–16; 8:8; 14:1; 16:20; 21:10. The early Christian work the Shepherd of Hermas (c. 90–140/150) refers to a vision of "twelve mountains" that are interpreted symbolically as the twelve tribes of Israel (*Similitudes* 9.17). The coinage of Vespasian depicts the goddess of the city, Roma, enthroned on the seven hills, with the Tiber and the she-wolf (Ethelbert Stauffer, *Christ and the Caesars* (tr. K. & R. Gregor Smith [London: SCM, 1955], p. 154). One could, however, count at least eight hills in Rome: the Capitol, the Palatine, the Aventine, the Caelian, the Oppian, the Esquiline, the Viminal, and the Quirinal. The Vatican would make a ninth (ZPEB, 5:162).

10 Caird refers to the symbolic significance of the seven heads as indicating not seven specific emperors but a whole line of emperors (pp. 218–19). Why the emperors should then be limited to Rome, Caird does not tell us. He also refers to the well-known Eagle Vision of 4 Ezra 11–12 as support for the emperor succession interpretation of Rev 17:10. However appropriate this interpretation is to Jewish apocalyptic writing, it remains to be demonstrated that John had such an intent in mind. The Jewish visions are more allegorical (language with a specific historical counterpart in mind) than Rev, while Rev is symbolical (language of universal reality having many historical counterparts).

11 In the early church there was an interpretation that took the seven mountains as referring to the seven millennia of world history, a theme current in that period. Thus after asserting that the Sabbath is a type of the millennial reign of Christ, Hippolytus says, "Since, then, in six days God made all things, it follows that six thousand years must be fulfilled. And

they are not yet fulfilled, as John says: five are fallen, one is, the other is not yet come (Rev 17:10). Moreover, in speaking of the other he specifies the seventh, in which there shall be rest" (*Commentary on Daniel* 4.23; see note on 20:1).

14 For an enlightening and thorough discussion of the relationship between the angel powers who rule and their earthly agents, see Oscar Cullmann, *The State in the New Testament,* "Excursus: on the most recent discussion of the ἐξουσίαις in Romans 13:1" (New York: Scribner's, 1956), pp. 95–114.

---

4. *The fall of Babylon the Great*

18:1–24

[1]After this I saw another angel coming down from heaven. He had great authority, and the earth was illuminated by his splendor. [2]With a mighty voice he shouted:

"Fallen! Fallen is Babylon the Great!
  She has become a home for demons
and a haunt for every evil spirit,
  a haunt for every unclean and detestable bird.
[3]For all the nations have drunk
  the maddening wine of her adulteries.
The kings of the earth committed adultery with her,
  and the merchants of the earth grew rich from her
    excessive luxuries."

[4]Then I heard another voice from heaven say:

"Come out of her, my people,
  so that you will not share in her sins,
  so that you will not receive any of her plagues;
[5]for her sins are piled up to heaven,
  and God has remembered her crimes.
[6]Give back to her as she has given;
  pay her back double for what she has done.
  Mix her a double portion from her own cup.
[7]Give her as much torture and grief
  as the glory and luxury she gave herself.
In her heart she boasts,
  'I sit as queen; I am not a widow,
  and I will never mourn.'
[8]Therefore in one day her plagues will overtake her:
  death, mourning and famine.
She will be consumed by fire,
  for mighty is the Lord God who judges her.

[9]"When the kings of the earth who committed adultery with her and shared her luxury see the smoke of her burning, they will weep and mourn over her. [10]Terrified at her torment, they will stand far off and cry:

" 'Woe! Woe, O great city,
  O Babylon, city of power!
In one hour your doom has come!'

[11]"The merchants of the earth will weep and mourn over her because no one buys their cargoes any more— [12]cargoes of gold, silver, precious stones and pearls; fine linen, purple, silk and scarlet cloth; every sort of citron wood, and articles of every kind made of ivory, costly wood, bronze, iron and marble; [13]cargoes of cinnamon and spice, of incense, myrrh and frankincense, of wine and olive oil, of fine flour and wheat; cattle and sheep; horses and carriages; and bodies and souls of men.

¹⁴"They will say, 'The fruit you longed for is gone from you. All your riches and splendor have vanished, never to be recovered.' ¹⁵The merchants who sold these things and gained their wealth from her will stand far off, terrified at her torment. They will weep and mourn ¹⁶and cry out:

" 'Woe! Woe, O great city,
    dressed in fine linen, purple and scarlet,
    and glittering with gold, precious stones and pearls!
¹⁷In one hour such great wealth has been brought to ruin!'

"Every sea captain, and all who travel by ship, the sailors, and all who earn their living from the sea, will stand far off. ¹⁸When they see the smoke of her burning, they will exclaim, 'Was there ever a city like this great city?' ¹⁹They will throw dust on their heads, and with weeping and mourning cry out:

" 'Woe! Woe, O great city,
    where all who had ships on the sea
    became rich through her wealth!
In one hour she has been brought to ruin!
²⁰Rejoice over her, O heaven!
    Rejoice, saints and apostles and prophets!
God has judged her for the way she treated you.' "

²¹Then a mighty angel picked up a boulder the size of a large millstone and threw it into the sea, and said:

"With such violence
    the great city of Babylon will be thrown down,
    never to be found again.
²²The music of harpists and musicians, flute players
        and trumpeters,
    will never be heard in you again.
No workman of any trade
    will ever be found in you again.
The sound of a millstone
    will never be heard in you again.
²³The light of a lamp
    will never shine in you again.
The voice of bridegroom and bride
    will never be heard in you again.
Your merchants were the world's great men.
    By your magic spell all the nations were led astray.
²⁴In her was found the blood of prophets and of the saints,
    and of all who have been killed on the earth."

Chapter 18 contains the description of the previously announced "judgment" (*krima;* NIV, "punishment") of the prostitute (17:1). It is important not to separate this chapter from the portrayal of the prostitute in chapter 17, for there is no warrant for making the prostitute in chapter 17 different from the city in chapter 18 (cf. 17:18). Under the imagery of the destruction of the great commercial city, John describes the final overthrow of the great prostitute, Babylon. He is not writing a literal description, even in poetic or figurative language, of the fall of an earthly city, such as Rome or Jerusalem; but in portraying the destruction of a city, he describes God's judgment on the great satanic system of evil that has corrupted the earth's history. Drawing especially from the OT accounts of the destruction of the ancient harlot cities of Babylon (Isa 13:21; 47:7–9; Jer 50–51) and Tyre (Ezek 26–27), John composes a great threnody that might well be the basis of a mighty oratorio. Here in chapters 17–18

169

is some of the most beautifully cadenced language in the whole book. John combines the song of triumph and the wailing strains of lamentation into a noble funeral dirge (cf. 2 Sam 1:17-27; Isa 14:4-21; Lam, in its entirety).

First, there is a kind of prelude in which the whole judgment is proclaimed (vv.1-3). Then there comes a call for God's people to separate themselves from the city because the divine plagues are about to descend upon her in recompense for her crimes (vv.4-8). The main movement that expresses the laments for the city's fall is divided into three parts: (1) the lament of the kings of the earth (vv.9-10), then (2) the lament of the merchants who traded with her (vv.11-17), and (3) the lament of the sea captains who became rich from the cargoes they took to the city (vv.18-20). Lastly, the finale sounds the death knell of the life of the city because she deceived the nations and killed God's people (vv.21-24).

1-3 So magnificent is the event about to be enacted that a dazzling angel of glory bears the divine news. Some interpreters have associated this glory with the shekinah glory that, in Ezekiel's vision, departed from the temple because of the harlotry of the Israelites (Ezek 11:23) but later on returned to the restored temple (Ezek 43:2).

In words very similar to those of the prophets who encouraged the people of God as they faced ancient Babylon, the angel announces that Babylon the Great, Mother of all the earthly prostitute cities, has fallen (cf. Isa 21:9; Jer 51:8 with Rev 14:8; 18:2). Again, in words reminiscent of the judgment announced against ancient Babylon when the city would be inhabited only by detestable creatures and evil spirits (Isa 13:19-22; 34:11; Jer 50:39), John hears the same fate announced for this Mother of prostitutes (v.2). "Demons" (*daimoniōn*) are associated elsewhere with idolatry (see comments at 9:20 and 16:14). The "haunt" (*phylakē*) is a watchtower; the evil spirits, watching over fallen Babylon like night birds or harpies waiting for their prey, build their nests in the broken towers that rise from the ashes of the city (Swete). She who was a great city has become a wilderness.

The prostitute city will be judged because of her surfeit of fornication (v.3). Here the same thought of 17:2 is expanded as we hear echoes of the judgments on ancient Tyre and Babylon (Isa 23:17; Jer 51:7; Rev 14:8). One of the great sins of Babylon was her luxury (*strēnos;* cf. at 18:7, 9). Because wealth may lead to pride, the prophets and John view surfeit as a manifestation of Babylon (Rev 18:7; cf. Ezek 28:4-5, 16-18). The close proximity of fornication with luxury may suggest that there is a fornication with Babylon that not only involves idolatry (cult prostitution) but that may be pride in excessive wealth.

4-8 "Come out of her, my people" forms the burden of Jeremiah's refrain concerning Babylon (Jer 50:8; 51:6-9; cf. Isa 48:20; 52:11; 2 Cor 6:17). Even in its OT setting, this was no mere warning to leave the actual city of Babylon, much less here in Revelation. John is burdened to exhort the churches to shun the charms and ensnarements of the queen prostitute (v.7) as her qualities are manifest in the world they live in. Wherever there are idolatry, prostitution, self-glorification, self-sufficiency, pride, complacency, reliance on luxury and wealth, avoidance of suffering, violence against life (v.24), there is Babylon. Christians are to separate themselves ideologically and, if necessary, physically from all the forms of Babylon. Already John has warned the churches of her deceit and snares (chs. 2-3). If they refuse to separate themselves, they will "share in her sins" and also in the divine judgments (NIV, "plagues"). It is not necessary to see this as one last call to repentance addressed to the beast worshipers (Caird). Rather, like the warnings in the letters to the churches (chs. 2–3), it is addressed to professing Christians who were being seduced by Satan through the wiles of the queen prostitute to abandon their loyalty to Jesus. If this occurred, Christ would be forced by their own decision to blot out their names from the book of life and include them in the plagues designed for Babylon when she is judged (cf. 3:5; so Farrer, *Revelation of St. John*, p. 155, n.2).

God will not forget her crimes (*adikēmata*), which are multiplied to the height of heaven (v.5; cf. Gen 18:20–21; Jer 51:9). Her punishment will fit her crimes (v.6; cf. Ps 137:8; Jer 50:15, 29, Matt 7:2). This OT principle of lex talionis is never enjoined on God's people in the NT but, as here, is reserved for God alone (Matt 5:38–42; Rom 12:17–21). "Mix her a double portion from her own cup" (cf. Exod 22:4, 7, 9; Isa 40:2) reflects both the ideas of the severity of God's judgment on those who persistently refuse to repent as well as the truth that God's wrath is related to the outworking of sin (cf. Rom 1:24–32). Verse 7 illustrates the latter point.

Babylon's threefold web of sin is described as satiety ("luxury"), pride ("boasts, . . . sit as a queen"), and avoidance of suffering ("I will never mourn"). The three may be interrelated. Luxury leads to boastful self-sufficiency (Ezek 28:5), while the desire to avoid suffering may lead to the dishonest pursuit of luxury (Ezek 28:18). "I sit as a queen" echoes Isaiah's description of judgment on Babylon (Isa 47:7ff.) and Ezekiel's description of Tyre (Ezek 27:3). As she avoided grief through her satiety, her punishment therefore is grief (*penthos*, "mourning," "sorrow," "misfortune"). Suddenly, "in one day," she will experience what she has avoided by her luxury: "death, mourning and famine." Like ancient Babylon, this queen of prostitutes will become unloved and barren (Isa 47:9). In spite of her many charms (v.23c), she will be powerless to avert her destruction (v.8). The words "consumed by fire" (cf. 17:16) may refer to the destruction of a city (cf. vv.9, 18) or to the OT punishment for prostitution if the woman is a priest's daughter (Lev 21:9). As strong as "Babylon the Great" is, the Lord God is stronger and will judge her.

9–19 Even quick reading of Ezekiel 27 shows that here in these verses John had in the back of his mind Ezekiel's lamentation over the Fall of ancient Tyre. Those who entered into fornication with the great mother prostitute wail over her destruction. In terms drawn from the fall of harlot cities in the past, John describes the end of the great reality of evil, Babylon the Great. While allusions to Rome may seem to appear, it is only because Rome, like Tyre, Babylon, or Jerusalem, is herself a prostitute city; and the characteristics of all these cities are found in the queen mother of prostitutes.

First, the kings of the earth cry out their dirge (vv. 9–10). There is a connection between their adultery with Babylon and their sharing of her luxury, as if sharing her luxury was part of their adultery (cf. Ezek 26:16; 27:30–35). So great is the heat and smoke of her burning that they must stand "far off" (v.10). Though ultimately the kings are all the heavenly powers that rule in the affairs of earthly kings and kingdoms (see comments at 17:10, 14; cf. 1 Cor 2:6, 8), in this extended poetic allegory they are the merchant princes who bewail the collapse of the last great city of man under Satan's rule. The lament "Woe, Woe" (cf. 8:13; 9:12; 11:14; 12:12) is repeated three times in this part of the threnody over Babylon and reflects pain at the suddenness of her downfall ("in one hour," cf. vv.8, 17) and the emptiness of their own existences apart from her.

The merchants wail (vv. 11–17). They have most to lose because Babylon the Great was built on luxury. The lists that follow are inventories of exotic items reminiscent of the great Oriental *suks* (marketplaces). Swete has an excellent discussion of the more important items (pp. 230–31). In v.13 "bodies and souls of men" require special mention. "Bodies" (*sōmata*) is a Greek idiom for slaves (cf. LXX of Gen 36:6), while "souls of men" (*psychas*) means essentially the same as bodies (slaves). Thus the whole expression means "slaves, that is, human beings."

The refrain (v.16) also shows the blending of the prostitute image of chapter 17 (dressed in fine linen, etc.; cf. 17:4) and the city image of chapter 18 ("O great city"). The wares are less suitable for Rome than for Asia Minor (Lilje, p. 236).

Finally, in vv.17–19 the sea captains and sailors add their lament because they too suffer irreparable loss because of the city's burning (cf. Ezek 27:28). This language is more appropriate to Tyre as a great port city than Rome, which was inland and had the not-too-distant Ostia as its port. But in any case, it is not John's intent to describe any one city but the great harlot city, the archetype of the earth's evil cities.

20 The threefold lament is balanced by a song of heavenly jubilation. Babylon has also persecuted the church of Jesus (saints, apostles, prophets). Except for the mention of false apostles earlier in the book (2:2), this is the only reference to apostles in Revelation (cf. 21:14). If it is correct to see in v.20 a reference to their being killed (cf. v.24), perhaps John had in mind Herod's martyring of James (Acts 12:1–2) or Rome's killing of Peter and Paul. The picture of Babylon cannot, however, be confined to the political activity of Rome. Therefore, John attributes the deaths of the martyrs to Babylon the Great. It is she who has killed Jesus (11:7–8) and Stephen by the hands of unbelieving Jews (Acts 7:57–60) and the martyr Antipas by the hands of pagan cultists (2:13; cf. Matt 23:34–37).

21–24 The final lament over the fall of Babylon, spoken by an angel, is poignant and beautiful. A mighty angel picks up a huge stone like a giant millstone (four to five feet in diameter, one foot thick, and weighing thousands of pounds) and flings it into the sea. One quick gesture becomes a parable of the whole judgment on Babylon the Great! Suddenly she is gone forever (cf. Jer 51:64; Ezek 26:21). The melancholy recollection of the pulsing life that once filled this great city with the joy of life sounds through these verses "like footsteps dying away in the distance in a desolate city which lies in ruins" (Lilje).

All nations were deceived (*planō*, "led astray") by her "magic spell" (*pharmakeia*, "sorcery"). John has previously used *pharmakeia* in conjunction with "murders," "fornicators," and "thefts" (see comments at 9:21). An element of drugging is involved that results in fatal poisoning (MM, p. 664). With her deceit, Babylon charmed the nations. Compare the similar charge against the harlot city Nineveh for her lies to other nations (Nah 3:4).

In the final verse (24), the great sin of Babylon is cited. She has martyred the prophets and followers of Jesus. John has already mentioned this blood-guiltiness (17:6; cf. 19:2). Elsewhere the death of martyrs is attributed to "the inhabitants of the earth" (6:10), the "beast that comes up from the Abyss" (11:7, 13:7), and the "beast, coming out of the earth" (13:15). In the OT, the city of Jerusalem (Ezek 24:6, 9; cf. Matt 23:37) and Babylon (Jer 51:35) are called cities of bloodshed. In v.24 "the blood . . . of all who have been killed on the earth" refers to all those who in history have been martyred because of their loyalty to the true God. John's word for kill (*sphazō*) is consistently used for martyrs (5:6, 9, 12; 6:4, 9; 13:8). In John's mind, Babylon the Great (v.2) is much more comprehensive than ancient Babylon, Nineveh, Jerusalem, or Rome. She encompasses all the persecution against the servants of God until the words of God are fulfilled (cf. 17:17).

5. Thanksgiving for the destruction of Babylon

19:1–5

[1]After this I heard what sounded like the roar of a great multitude in heaven shouting:

> "Hallelujah!
> Salvation and glory and power belong to our God,
> [2]for true and just are his judgments.
> He has condemned the great prostitute
>   who corrupted the earth by her adulteries.
> He has avenged on her the blood of his servants."

[3]And again they shouted:

> "Hallelujah!
> The smoke from her goes up for ever and ever."

[4]The twenty-four elders and the four living creatures fell down and worshiped God, who was seated on the throne. And they cried:

> "Amen, Hallelujah!"

[5]Then a voice came from the throne, saying:

> "Praise our God,
>   all you his servants,
> you who fear him,
>   both small and great!"

In stark contrast to the laments of Babylon's consorts, the heavenly choirs burst forth in a great liturgy of celebration to God. In these verses (1–5), we hear four shouts of praise for the Fall of Babylon. First, there is the sound of a great multitude praising God for his condemnation of the prostitute (19:1–2). Then they shout out in celebration of the city's eternal destruction (v.3). Following this, we hear in antiphonal response the voices of the twenty-four elders and the four living creatures (v.4). Finally, a voice from the throne calls on all the servants of God to praise him (v.5).

1–2 The word "Hallelujah" (*hallēlouia*) transliterates the Greek, which in turn transliterates the Hebrew *hal^elû yāh*, which means "Praise the Lord!" (In v.5, "Praise our God" [*Aineite tō theō hēmōn*] is equivalent to "Hallelujah.") The Hebrew transliteration occurs only in this chapter in the NT (vv.1, 3, 4, 6), but in the LXX it is a frequent title for certain of the psalms (Pss 111:1; 112:1; 113:1, et al.). This phenomenon clearly illustrates the connection of the early church's liturgical worship with the synagogue and temple worship of the first century. These praise psalms formed an important part of the Jewish festival celebrations.

> Hallel is the Jewish song of jubilation that has accompanied our wanderings of thousands of years, keeping awake within us the consciousness of our world-historical mission, strengthening us in times of sorrow and suffering, and filling our mouths with song of rejoicing in days of deliverance and triumph. To this day, it revives on each Festival season the memory of Divine Redemption, and our

confidence in future greatness (S.R. Hirsch, quoted in Joseph Hertz, *The Authorized Daily Prayer Book,* rev. ed. [New York: Block, 1948], p. 756).

The Hallel is the name especially applied to Psalms 113–118. These psalms are also called "The Hallel of Egypt" because of the references in them to the Exodus. They thus have a special role in the Feast of Passover (M *Pesahim* 10:5–7). The Midrashic sources also unanimously associate the Hallel with the destruction of the wicked, exactly as this passage in Revelation does (Eric Werner, *The Sacred Bridge: Liturgical Parallels in Synagogue and Early Church* [New York: Schocken Books, 1970], pp. 151, 158, 302–3).

The Hallel was most certainly what Jesus and the disciples sang after the Passover-Eucharist celebration, before going out to the Mount of Olives the night before his death (Matt 26:30). This close connection between the Hallel, Passover, and the death of Jesus no doubt explains why all the early church liturgies incorporated the Hallel into the propers for Easter and Easter Week (Massey H. Shepherd, Jr., *The Paschal Liturgy and the Apocalypse* [Richmond: John Knox, 1960], p. 96). This Easter liturgy is the Christian experience of the gospel of redemption from sin, Satan, and death in the victorious triumph of Christ, our Passover. The Paschal liturgy concludes with the celebration of the Eucharistic banquet of Christ, as he holds intimate communion with his church, giving it light and life. Shepherd links the great banquet of vv.7–9 to the Eucharist celebration in the early church. The psalms in the great Hallel (Pss 113:1; 115:13) are unmistakably cited in 19:5. One can hardly read this Hallel section of Revelation without thinking of the "Hallelujah Chorus" in Handel's *Messiah*.

The theme of "salvation" (*sōtēria*) has already been sounded in Revelation in connection with victory or divine justice (7:10; 12:10). God has indeed vindicated the injustice visited on his servants by meting out true justice on the great prostitute, Babylon. She deserves the sentence because she corrupted the earth (cf. 11:18; Jer 51:25) and killed the saints of God (cf. 18:24).

3 The second Hallel supplements the first one. Babylon's permanent end is celebrated in words reminiscent of ancient Babylon's judgment (Isa 34:10).

4 In response to the heavenly Hallels, the twenty-four elders cry out, "Amen, Hallelujah" (cf. comments at 1:7 on Amen, at 4:4 on the elders).

5 This final praise is spoken by a single voice from the throne (cf. 16:17). The voice is probably neither that of God nor that of Christ because of the words "*our* Lord God Almighty reigns" (v.6). Here is a clear reference to the great Hallel Psalms 113 and 115. "Praise our God, all you his servants" reflects Psalm 113:1, while "you who fear him, both small and great" reflects Psalm 115:13 (cf. Ps 135:1, 20). All socio-economic distinctions are transcended in the united worship of the church ("both small and great") (cf. 11:18; 13:16; 19:18; 20:12).

6. *Thanksgiving for the marriage of the Lamb*

19:6–10

⁶Then I heard what sounded like a great multitude, like the roar of rushing waters and like loud peals of thunder, shouting:

"Hallelujah!
  For our Lord God Almighty reigns.

⁷Let us rejoice and be glad
    and give him glory!
For the wedding of the Lamb has come,
    and his bride has made herself ready.
⁸Fine linen, bright and clean,
    was given her to wear."

(Fine linen stands for the righteous acts of the saints.)

⁹Then the angel said to me, "Write: 'Blessed are those who are invited to the wedding supper of the Lamb!' " And he added, "These are the true words of God."

¹⁰At this I fell at his feet to worship him. But he said to me, "Do not do it! I am a fellow servant with you and with your brothers who hold to the testimony of Jesus. Worship God! For the testimony of Jesus is the spirit of prophecy."

6–8 Finally, the cycle of praise is completed with the reverberating sounds of another great multitude. If the multitude in v.1 was angelic, then this one would most certainly be the great redeemed throngs (cf. 7:9). They utter the final Hallel in words reminiscent of the great kingship psalms (93:1; 97:1; 99:1). The first of these psalms is used in the synagogue Sabbath morning and evening services and also in the Armenian church liturgy for Easter Sunday (Werner, *Sacred Bridge,* p. 153). It is also the prelude to Psalms 95–99, which are messianic, and has as its theme the eternal sovereignty of God who will conquer all his enemies (Hertz, *Daily Prayer Book,* p. 362). The Greek verb *ebasileusen* ("reigns"), an ingressive aorist, may better be rendered "has begun to reign."

There is also rejoicing because the "wedding of the Lamb has come, and his bride has made herself ready" (v.7). It is John's way to give us a glimpse of the next great vision at the close of the former one (cf. 21:2, 9). Contrast the prostitute and her lovers in the preceding chapters with the Lamb and his chaste bride ("fine linen, bright and clean").

The bride is the heavenly city, the New Jerusalem (21:2, 9), which is the symbol of the church, the bride of Christ, the community of those redeemed by Christ's blood. The wedding imagery, including the wedding supper, was for the Jews a familiar image of the kingdom of God. Jesus used wedding and banquet imagery in his parables of the kingdom (Matt 22:2ff.; 25:1–13; Luke 14:15–24). The OT used the figure for the bride of Israel (Ezek 16:1ff.; Hos 2:19), and NT writers have applied it to the church (2 Cor 11:2; Eph 5:25ff.). Heaven's rejoicing has signaled the defeat of all the enemies of God. The time of betrothal has ended. Now it is the time for the church, prepared by loyalty and suffering, to enter into her full experience of salvation and glory with her beloved spouse, Christ. The fuller revelation of the realization of this union is described in chapters 21 and 22.

The church's garments are white linen—in marked contrast to the purple and scarlet clothing of the great mother of prostitutes (17:4; 18:16). Linen was an expensive cloth used to make the garments worn by priests and royalty. It has two qualities: brightness and cleanness (cf. 16:6). Bright (*lampros*) is the color of radiant whiteness that depicts glorification (TDNT, 4:27; cf. Matt 13:43). Clean (*katharos*) reflects purity, loyalty, and faithfulness, the character of the New Jerusalem (21:18, 21).

An explanatory interjection, probably added by John, states that "fine linen stands for the righteous acts of the saints." In 15:4, *dikaiōmata* ("righteous acts") describes the manifest deeds of God that relate to truth and justice. The *dikaiōmata* do not imply any kind of meritorious works that would bring salvation. Rather, there is a delicate balance between grace and obedient response to it. The bride is "given" the garments, but she "has made herself ready" for the wedding by faithfulness and loyalty to Christ (cf. 3:4–5, 18). In the parable of the man without a wedding garment, the garment he lacked was probably a clean one supplied by the host but either refused or soiled through carelessness by the rejected guest. The meaning of the clean garment is probably repentance and obedient response to Christ, both of which the Pharisees lacked (Matt 22:11f.; cf. J. Jeremias, *The Parables of Jesus*, rev. ed. [New York: Scribner's, 1963], pp. 188–89). Thus John contrasts the faithful disciples of Jesus, who have been true to God, with those who were seduced by the beast and the prostitute. The bride prepared herself, then, by her obedient discipleship (see comments at 12:11).

9–10 This beatitude is the fourth of seven (1:3; 14:13; 16:15; 20:6; 22:7, 14) in Revelation. In each beatitude there is a subtle contrast to those who are not loyal and faithful followers of the Lamb. The word translated "invited" is *keklēmenoi* ("called"), a form of the verb *kaleō* ("call"), which is used in the NT of the call to salvation (e.g., Matt 9:13; Rom 8:30; 9:24; 1 Cor 1:9; 2 Thess 2:14). However, the word may also mean "invited," with no connotation of election (cf. Matt 22:3, 8; Luke 14:16; John 2:2). The wedding supper began toward evening on the wedding day, lasted for many days, and was a time of great jubilation. Here in Revelation, the wedding is the beginning of the earthly kingdom of God, the bride is the church in all her purity, the invited guests are both the bride and people who have committed themselves to Jesus.

To assure John and his readers of the certainty of the end of the great prostitute and the announcement of the wedding supper of the Lamb, the angel adds, "These are the true words of God" (cf. 1:2; 17:17; 21:5). A similar sentence later seems to give the same assurance for the whole book (22:6).

John, who was himself a prophet and who had received such a clear revelation about idolatry, now falls prey to this temptation. After the final vision, he again slips into idolatry (22:8). Whether John included these references to his own failure because he knew of the tendency toward angel worship in the churches of Asia is not clear. Be that as it may, we need to recognize how easy it is to fall into idolatry. Whenever a Christian gives anyone or anything other than God control of his life, he has broken the first commandment. The "testimony of Jesus" is Jesus' own testimony that he bore in his life and teaching and especially in his death (cf. comments at 1:2, 9; and also the same expression in 6:9; 12:11; 14:12; 20:4). Those who hold to or proclaim this testimony are Christian prophets. Thus "the testimony of Jesus is the spirit of prophecy." The words spoken by the Christian prophets come from the Spirit of God, who is the Spirit of the risen Jesus; they are the very words of God.

Notes

10 See commentary at 1:2 for arguments supporting the identification of Ἰησοῦ (*Iēsou*, "Jesus") in this verse as a subjective genitive and rendering it as "Jesus' witness" (so Caird; Minear, et al.).

IV. Vision of the Return of Christ and the Consummation of This Age (19:11–20:15)

A. The Rider on the White Horse and the Destruction of the Beast

19:11–21

[11]I saw heaven standing open and there before me was a white horse, whose rider is called Faithful and True. With justice he judges and makes war. [12]His eyes are like blazing fire, and on his head are many crowns. He has a name written on him that no one but he himself knows. [13]He is dressed in a robe dipped in blood, and his name is the Word of God. [14]The armies of heaven were following him, riding on white horses and dressed in fine linen, white and clean. [15]Out of his mouth comes a sharp sword with which to strike down the nations. "He will rule them with an iron scepter." He treads the winepress of the fury of the wrath of God Almighty. [16]On his robe and on his thigh he has this name written:

KING OF KINGS AND LORD OF LORDS.

[17]And I saw an angel standing in the sun, who cried in a loud voice to all the birds flying in midair, "Come, gather together for the great supper of God, [18]so that you may eat the flesh of kings, generals, and mighty men, of horses and their riders, and the flesh of all people, free and slave, small and great."
[19]Then I saw the beast and the kings of the earth and their armies gathered together to make war against the rider on the horse and his army. [20]But the beast was captured, and with him the false prophet who had performed the miraculous signs on his behalf. With these signs he had deluded those who had received the mark of the beast and worshiped his image. The two of them were thrown alive into the fiery lake of burning sulfur. [21]The rest of them were killed with the sword that came out of the mouth of the rider on the horse, and all the birds gorged themselves on their flesh.

This new vision is introduced by the words "I saw heaven standing open." Earlier John had seen a door standing open in heaven (4:1), the temple in heaven standing open (11:19), and now, in preparation for a great revelation of God's sovereignty, he sees heaven itself flung wide open to his gaze (cf. Ezek 1:1). In one sense, this vision (vv.11–21), which depicts the return of Christ and the final overthrow of the beast, may be viewed as the climax of the previous section (vv.1–10) or as the first of a final series of seven last things—viz., the return of Christ; the defeat of Satan; the binding of Satan; the Millennium; the final end of Satan; the last judgment; and the new heaven, the new earth, and the New Jerusalem.

Early as well as modern interpretation has for the most part seen in 19:11–16 a description of the second coming of Christ—an event to which the NT bears a frequent and unified witness. As for the features of this event, they are variously understood by interpreters.

11 The great vision that begins here reminds us of the first vision of the book (1:12ff.), though its function is entirely different from that of the earlier vision. The whole scene looks alternately to the OT and to the previous references in Revelation to Christ, especially the seven letters (chs. 2–3). So strong are the parallels with chapters 1–3 that Rissi believes that the first section (vv.11–13) of this vision deals with the judgment on the church and the second section (vv.14–16) with the world (Mathias Rissi, *The Future of the World; an Exegetical Study of Revelation 19:11–22:15* [Naperville, Ill.: A.R. Allenson, 1972], p. 19). A white horse with a rider has appeared at 6:1 (cf. discussion in loc.). Both white horses represent conquest or victory, but with that the similarity changes to total contrast: The rider here in chapter 19 is "faithful and true" (cf. 1:5; 3:7, 14) in contrast to the forces of Antichrist with their empty promises and lies. Christ will keep his word to the churches. In contrast to those who pervert justice and wage unjust war, John says of Christ, "With justice [righteousness] he judges and makes war," an allusion to the messianic character described in Isaiah 11:3ff. In only one other place (2:16) is Christ described as making war (*polemeō*), and there the reference is to his judgment of the church. Furthermore, the questions in 13:4, "Who is like the beast? Who can make war against him?" anticipate the answer that Christ alone can do this, while in 17:14 the beast and the ten kings wage war against the Lamb.

Though John uses OT language descriptive of a warrior-Messiah, he does not depict Christ as a great *military* warrior battling against earth's sovereigns. John reinterprets this OT imagery while at the same time inseparably linking Christ to its fulfillment. The close proximity in v. 11 of justice and war shows us that the kind of warfare Christ engages in is more the execution of justice than a military conflict. He who is the faithful and true witness will judge the rebellious nations.

12 The reference to the blazing eyes definitely connects this vision with that of chapter 1 (cf. 1:14; 2:18). On his head are not just seven crowns (12:3), or ten (13:1) but many crowns of royalty (*diadēmata*). Perhaps they signify that the royal power to rule the world has now passed to Christ by virtue of the victory of his followers (11:15). All the diadems of their newly won empire meet on his brow (Caird).

So great is Christ's power that his name is known only by himself. Knowledge of the name is in antiquity associated with the power of the god. When a name becomes known, then the power is shared with those to whom the disclosure is made (cf. comments at 2:17). But since two names of Christ are revealed in this vision, "the Word of God" (v. 13) and "KING OF KINGS AND LORD OF LORDS" (v. 16), it may be concluded that the exclusive power of Christ over all creation is now to be shared with his faithful followers (3:21; 5:10; 22:5). On the other hand, the secret name may be one that will not be revealed till Christ's return.

13 The imagery in this verse has traditionally been related to Isaiah 63:1–6, a passage understood messianically by the Jews and one that John has used in portraying God's wrath in 14:9–11, 17–19. Isaiah pictures a mighty warrior-Messiah who slaughters his enemies. Their life-blood splashes on his clothing as he tramples them down in his anger, as the juice of the grapes splashes on the winetreader in the winepress. But is Christ's blood-dipped robe (v. 13) red from his enemies' blood or from his own blood? There are good reasons for accepting the latter (contra Mounce, *Revelation*, p. 345). If the blood is his enemies', how is it that Christ comes from heaven with his robe already dipped in blood before any battle is mentioned? Furthermore, the blood that is always mentioned in connection with Christ in the Apocalypse is his own life-blood (1:5; 5:6, 9; 7:14; 12:11). Caird, however, has no difficulty identifying the blood as that of the saints, which Christ turns into victory over his enemies. But Caird has understood the vintage passage (14:7–20) as a reference to the death of the saints (pp. 242–43).

Admittedly, there is a close connection between the discolored clothing of Christ, the Word of God (to whom the saints bear witness and give their lives), and "the armies of heaven"—i.e., the saints (v.14). Moreover, the word "dipped" (*bebamme-non*, from *baptō*) does not fit the imagery of Isaiah 63:2; but it does fit that used in Revelation of believers' garments being washed thoroughly in Christ's blood (7:14; 22:14). The interpretation of the blood as Christ's own is an early one (so Hippolytus, Origen, Andreas; cf. Swete, p. 249). Finally, the sword with which Christ strikes down the nations comes from his mouth and is not in his hand (v.15); and this too is incompatible with battle imagery. In any case, there is sufficient warrant not to press the allusion to Isaiah 63:1–6 too literally.

Applying the expression "the Word of God" (*ho logos tou theou*) to Jesus in a personal sense is peculiar to the Johannine writings (John 1:1, 14; cf. 1 John 1:1). In Revelation "the Word of God" refers to the revelation of God's purpose (1:2; 17:17; 19:9). It is also the message and lifestyle for which the saints suffer oppression and even death (1:9; 6:9; 20:4). The adjectives "true and faithful," which are applied to Christ, are likewise identified with the Word of God (19:9; 21:5; 22:6; cf. 1:5; 3:14; 19:11). Thus Jesus in his earthly life had borne reliable and consistent witness in all his words and actions to the purposes of God and had been completely obedient in doing this. In him the will of God finds full expression. The Word of God and the person of Christ are one.

14 This verse seems somewhat parenthetical because it does not refer directly to Christ's person or his actions. The armies of heaven mounted on white horses are understood by most to be angelic hosts since passages in the OT and NT, though infrequent, speak of the armies or soldiers of heaven as angels (Pss 103:21; 148:2; Luke 2:13; Acts 7:42). Moreover, elsewhere in the NT the coming of Christ is associated with angels (e.g., Matt 13:41; 16:27; 24:30–31). Yet this may not be John's meaning. These soldiers, like their leader, are riding white horses of victory—something hardly true of angels. Their clothing of bright and clean linen is identical to the bride's attire (cf. v.8). Thus it is probably the victors who accompany Christ, either all of them (resurrected and raptured [1 Thess 4:16–17]) or the company of the martyrs. Revelation 17:14 confirms this: "They [the beast and the ten kings] will make war against the Lamb, but the Lamb will overcome them because he is Lord of lords and King of kings—*and with him will be his called, chosen and faithful followers*" (italics added; cf. 15:1–2).

15 There are three OT allusions to the warrior-Messiah in this verse: he strikes down the nations (Isa 11:3ff.); he rules them with an iron rod (Ps 2:9); he tramples out the winepress of God's wrath (Isa 63:1–6). (For the last metaphor, see comments on v.13.) In the first OT allusion, there are significant changes in the imagery. In Revelation the Lamb-Messiah does not wield a sword in his hand, but his sword comes from his mouth (cf. comments at 1:16 and 2:16). This has no exact OT parallel and cannot be accidental, since John emphasizes it so much in Revelation (1:16; 2:12, 16; 19:15, 21). Christ conquers by the power of his word. Yet it is not necessary to see the reference to the sword coming from Christ's mouth as pointing to the expansion of Christianity and the conquest of the nations by their conversion to Christ (so Swete). The scene here is the eschatological return of Christ and his judgment of the nations, not the whole intervening age. Besides, Christ's words are also the instruments of his judgment as well as his salvation (Matt 12:37; John 12:48). On "the rod of iron" and the relationship between "rule" and "shepherd," see comments at 2:27. For the winepress figure, see 14:17ff.

179

16 This third name of Christ, which all can read, is displayed on that most exposed part of his cloak, the part that covers the thigh, where it cannot escape notice (Swete). The name has already appeared attached to the Lamb (17:14). He is the absolute Lord and King, full of the divine power and authority.

17–18 This section finally brings us to the second last thing (cf. comments at introduction to 19:11–21): the anticipated great confrontation between the beast and his soldiers and the Lamb (vv.17–21; cf. 16:12–16; 17:14). First, there is the summons to the vultures to come to God's great supper and gorge themselves on the slain corpses of the battlefield—a horrible picture of human carnage. The language is borrowed from Ezekiel 39:17ff., which describes the eschatological overthrow of Gog. It may be unnecessary to press the literalness of the description. This battlefield language is designed to indicate that a great victory is about to occur.

19–21 The contrast between the assembling of the beast's might with his kings and their soldiers and the ease by which he is overthrown and captured highlight the beast's powerlessness before his mighty conqueror. The "kings of the earth" refer to the ten horns (kings) of the beast, which is another way of describing the beast's power (see comments at 17:12–14). Both the beast and the false prophet (13:1ff.) are simply seized and thrown into the lake of fire (v.20). Their followers fall before the sword (word) of Christ (v.21). No battle is actually fought. Only the arrangement of the foes and the defeat of the beast is described. Is this accidental? Is John indicating that the battle has already been fought and this is simply the final realization of that previous victory? In chapter 5 the Lamb had overcome (won the victory) by his death (5:5, 9). Further, we are told that there was a battle in heaven, and Satan was cast out and defeated by the blood of the Lamb and the word of his followers' testimony (12:7–9, 11).

There seems to be only one actual battle described in Revelation. Thus these further scenes may be understood as more judicial in character than as literal battlefield descriptions. Because of John's christological reinterpretation, no great eschatological military battle, such as that envisaged in the Qumran War Scroll, will actually be fought. The decisive battle has already been won at the Cross. These armies and the beast are the destroyers of the earth (11:18), who ultimately are the satanic principalities of the world who ally themselves with the human puppets for their idolatrous ends. These have been positionally defeated at the Cross (Col 2:15), but they will finally be stripped of all power at Christ's return. Certainly John would not have denied that Satan and his evil powers are active in the world and that they use historical persons such as a Nero or a Hitler and oppose and harass Christians today.

Although Satan has been dealt a death blow at the Cross (cf. John 12:31; 16:11), he nevertheless continues to promulgate great evil and deception during this present age (cf. Eph 2:2; 1 Thess 3:5; 1 Peter 5:8–9; Rev 2:10). Yet he is a deposed ruler who is now under the sovereign authority of Christ but who for a "little time" is allowed to continue his evil until God's purposes are finished. In this scene of the overthrow of the beast and his kings and their armies, John is showing us the ultimate and swift downfall of these evil powers by the King of kings and Lord of lords. They have met their Master in this final and utterly real confrontation. (On the "lake of fire," see comments at 20:14.)

Notes

13 For references to the messianic interpretation of Isa 63:1ff. by the rabbis, see LTJM, 2:730; Swete, pp. 248–49.

The Targum on Gen 49:10ff. has a reference to the warring Messiah whose clothes are discolored with the blood of his enemies (M. McNamara, *Targum and Testament: Aramaic Paraphrases of the Hebrew Bible; A Light on the New Testament* [Grand Rapids: Eerdmans, 1962], p. 141). While this seems to add further evidence to support the view that the blood is from the enemies of Christ, it must still be asked whether John has reinterpreted the figure.

14 For angels accompanying the Messiah in his return, cf. MA Isa 4.14–17. This is probably a Christian document of the first century A.D.

15 While there are no other references in our literature to a sword from the Messiah's mouth, there are references to the destruction of the godless by the mouth of the Messiah, no doubt deriving from Isa 11:4: "He will strike the earth with the rod of his mouth; with the breath of his lips he will slay the wicked." Thus 4 Ezra 13:6, 19 and Pss of Sol 17:10, 45, 49 mention the Messiah in terms such as "He shall destroy the godless nations with the word of his mouth."

19–21 An eschatological military battle is described in both Jewish apocalyptic and Qumran literature (cf. 1 Enoch 90:13–19; 4 Ezra 13:1–13; As Moses 10; Pss Sol 17:23–51; 1QM; 1QH 6.25f.). In these references the war is still to be fought in the future; it involves actual earthly rulers of the godless; and, according to Qumran documents, it will require the military assistance of the godly to effect the defeat of the ungodly. However, this does not seem to be John's view, since Christ alone executes the wrath; and the decisive victory has already been won before the actual eschatological end. Christ *will* really defeat evil once and for all, but not in the literal military sense envisaged by the Jewish apocalyptists.

B. *Binding of Satan and the Millennium*

20:1–6

> [1]And I saw an angel coming down out of heaven, having the key to the Abyss and holding in his hand a great chain. [2]He seized the dragon, that ancient serpent, who is the devil, or Satan, and bound him for a thousand years. [3]He threw him into the Abyss, and locked and sealed it over him, to keep him from deceiving the nations any more until the thousand years were ended. After that, he must be set free for a short time.
>
> [4]I saw thrones on which were seated those who had been given authority to judge. And I saw the souls of those who had been beheaded because of their testimony for Jesus and because of the word of God. They had not worshiped the beast or his image and had not received his mark on their foreheads or their hands. They came to life and reigned with Christ a thousand years. [5](The rest of the dead did not come to life until the thousand years were ended.) This is the first resurrection. [6]Blessed and holy are those who have part in the first resurrection. The second death has no power over them, but they will be priests of God and of Christ and will reign with him for a thousand years.

Charles has described this passage as a constant source of insurmountable difficulty for the exegete. Berkouwer has called the Millennium one of the most controversial and intriguing questions of eschatology. He feels that one's view of Revelation 20 is internally connected with the rest of one's eschatology (G.C. Berkouwer, *The Return of Christ* [Grand Rapids: Eerdmans, 1972], p. 291). While the OT and later Jewish literature point forward to a time when the kingdom of God will be manifest in the world, nowhere in Jewish literature is the time of the reign of the Messiah stated to be a thousand years.

The exegesis of the passage leads me to a premillennial interpretation. It should be recognized, however, that there are problems with this view of Revelation 20:1–6, just as there are problems with other views of this difficult portion of the book, and that responsible Christian scholars vary in its interpretation according to their convictions and presuppositions.

For the moment the question of the duration of the reign of Christ (which is equal to the duration of the binding of Satan) may be delayed. The main problem concerns whether the reference to a Millennium indicates an earthly historical reign of peace that will manifest itself at the close of this present age or whether the whole passage is symbolic of some present experience of Christians or some future nonhistorical reality.

In the first place, we may note that the ancient church down to the time of Augustine (354–430) (though not without minor exceptions) unquestionably held to the teaching of an earthly, historical reign of peace that was to follow the defeat of Antichrist and the physical resurrection of the saints but precede both the judgment and the new creation (Jean Daniélou, *The Theology of Jewish Christianity* [Philadelphia: Westminster, 1964]; see note on v. 1). To be sure, in the ancient church there were various positions as to the material nature of the Millennium (see comments at v. 4), but the true conception of the thousand years was a balance between the worldly aspects of the kingdom and its spiritual aspects as a reign with Christ.

It is well known that the break with this earlier position came with the views of the late fourth-century interpreter Tyconius, an African Donatist, who, partly dependent on the Alexandrian allegorizing of Origen, developed a view of the Millennium based on a recapitulation method of interpretation. In applying this principle, Tyconius viewed Revelation as containing a number of different visions that repeated basic themes throughout the book. Though Tyconius's original work is not available, his exegesis of the Apocalypse can be largely reconstructed through his prime benefactor, Augustine, as well as Tyconius's many Roman Catholic followers. When he came to chapter 20, he interpreted the thousand years in nonliteral terms and understood the period as referring to the church age, the time between the first and second advents of Christ. Tyconius interpreted the first resurrection as the resurrection of the soul from spiritual death to the new life, while the second resurrection was the resurrection of the body at the end of history. The binding of Satan had already taken place in that the devil cannot seduce the church during the present age. Moreover, the reign of the saints and their "thrones of judgment" had already begun in the church and its rulers. Augustine, following Tyconius, "cast the die against the expectation of a millennial kingdom for centuries to come" (H. Berkhof, *Christ the Meaning of History* [Grand Rapids: Baker, 1979], p. 161). The recapitulation method adopted by Augustine continued through the centuries and is not without its modern exponents in both the Protestant and Roman Catholic branches of the church. This is the first main option in modern nonmillennial (or amillennial) interpretations of Revelation 20.

Augustine's approach, however, was not to remain unchallenged. Joachim of Floris (c. 1135–1202) saw in the Apocalypse a prophecy of the events of Western history from the time of Christ till the end. He thought the Millennium was still future in his time but soon to begin. The Franciscans, who followed Joachim, identified Babylon with ecclesiastical Rome and the Antichrist with the papacy. The Reformers followed suit. In modern times, Henry Alford (1810–71) adopted this view.

During Reformation times, still another type of interpretation developed, expounded by a Jesuit scholar named Ribeira (1537–91). He held that almost all the events described in the Apocalypse are future and apply to the end times rather than to the history of the world or contemporary Rome and the papacy. He still, however, held to Augustine's view of the Millennium as the period between the first and second advents of Christ. But at one important point he changed Augustine's view. Instead of the Millennium taking place on earth between the advents, Ribeira saw it as taking place in heaven. It is a reward for faithfulness. When the saints at any time in history are martyred, they do not perish but live and reign with Christ in heaven in the intermediate state before the final resurrection. This is the second main option today for nonmillennialists. John's basic message in Revelation 20 is, according to this viewpoint, pastoral. If Christians face the prospect of suffering death for Jesus, they should be encouraged because if they are killed, they will go to reign with him in heaven. This seems to be the drift of Berkouwer's conclusions (*The Return of Christ*, pp. 314ff.) and earlier those of B.B. Warfield ("The Millennium and the Apocalypse," PTR, 2 [1904], 599–617).

The Augustinian view of Revelation 20 and its variant espoused by Joachim cannot be harmonized with a serious exegesis of Revelation 20 on two important counts. In the first place, it founders on the statements concerning the binding of Satan (vv. 1–3); and, second, it must handle in an absurd fashion the statements about the coming to life of the martyrs, which cannot be exegetically understood as anything other than physical resurrection without seriously tampering with the sense of the words (cf. discussion on vv. 1–4). While it is popular among certain nonmillennialists to view 20:1–6 as a symbolic description of the reward to be granted the martyrs on their entrance into heaven (so Beckwith, Berkouwer, Boer, Schnackenburg), this variation of the Augustinian exegesis, while removing the criticism that the passage refers to the present rule of Christ in the church age, fails to deal seriously with the binding of Satan and other details of the text.

There is yet another view that, though not free of problems, does more justice to the Book of Revelation as a whole and to the exegesis of chapter 20 in particular. This view rejects both the Augustinian interpretation that the Millennium is the rule of Christ during this dispensation and the variant of Joachim that locates the resurrection and the reign of the martyrs in heaven for an interim period before their bodily resurrection and the return of Christ. It likewise rejects the variation of Augustine's view known as postmillennialism or evolutionary chiliasm, which teaches that the forces of Antichrist will gradually be put down and the gospel will permeate and transform the world into an interim of the reign of peace before the return of Christ (see note on v. 1 for representatives of this view). Berkouwer justly criticizes this postmillennial view as exegetically and theologically weak. He then goes on to espouse a totally mystical viewpoint of Revelation 20 that fails to grapple exegetically with the text. For him the millennial language is purely a figure of speech to depict the reality of the hidden triumph of Christ (*Return of Christ*, pp. 208–9). Such a view, however, fails to account for how the reality of the divine kingdom of God has actually invaded history in Jesus Christ.

If eschatological realities are simply mystical, figurative, and pastoral in intent and never impinge on the empirical world, then the Christ event as an eschatological event must likewise be abandoned. Instead, the view espoused in this commentary argues that the Millennium is in history and on the earth as an eschatological reality. Much in the same manner as the kingdom of God was eschatologically present in the life and ministry of Jesus—present, yet still future—so the Millennium is at once the final historical event of this age and the beginning of the eschatological kingdom of Christ in eternity. Oscar Cullmann, one of the principal advocates of this view, states:

> The millennium is future and is, so to speak, the very last part of Christ's lordship, which at the same time extends into the new aeon. Consequently, the thousand-year kingdom should be identified neither with the whole chronological extent of Christ's lordship nor with the present Church. That lordship is the larger concept; it has already begun and continues in the aeon for an undefined length of time. The thousand-year reign, on the other hand, belongs temporally to the final act of Christ's lordship, the act which begins with his return and thus already invades the new aeon (*The Christology of the New Testament* [Philadelphia: Westminster, 1959], p. 226).

This view is called the "end-historical" view. It follows the same chronological sequence as the early church's position, i.e., Parousia—defeat of Antichrist—binding of Satan—resurrection—Millennium—release of Satan—final judgment—new heavens and earth. It differs slightly from earlier chiliasm in viewing the Millennium as an end-historical event that at the same time is the beginning of the eternal reign of Christ and the saints.

The problem as to the limits of the description of the Millennium in Revelation 20–22 is a more difficult question. A group of expositors of varying theological thought (Beasley-Murray, R.H. Charles, Ford, A.C. Gaebelein, Kelly, Zahn) believe that 21:9–22:5, 14–15 belong with 20:1–10 as a further description of the millennial reign, whereas 21:1–5 refers to the eternal state, which follows the final judgment of the dead. This approach is an attempt to harmonize a more literal understanding of certain statements in 21:9ff. with the assumed conditions during the eternal state. For example, according to Beasley-Murray ("The Revelation," p. 1305) the references to nations and kings seem to describe an earthly kingdom better than they describe the eternal condition (21:24, 26); references to leaves "healing" the nations (22:2) seems to describe an imperfect condition better than they describe the perfected eternal state; and, finally, the blessing pronounced on those who come and eat the tree of life while a curse rests on all those outside the city (22:14–15) seems to relate better to the thousand years than to the eternal state when the wicked are in the lake of fire.

Admittedly, this is a possible solution that has the advantage of giving more descriptive content to the millennial reign. This approach, however, suffers from two serious criticisms. First, though it rightly assigns 21:1–5 to the postmillennial New Jerusalem in the context of the new heaven and earth, it arbitrarily assigns 21:9ff. to the millennial New Jerusalem without the slightest hint from the text that this is a recapitulation of 20:1–10. Thus, there is an eternal state New Jerusalem followed immediately by a millennial New Jerusalem, both bearing the same title. This is hardly plausible. Second, this view strongly argues for historical progression in 19:11–21:5; Parousia—defeat of Antichrist—binding of Satan—first resurrection—Millennium—release of Satan—last judgment—new heavens and earth—and then argues for recapitulation in 21:9ff.

It seems best, therefore, despite some problems, to regard the sequence begun at 19:11 as running chronologically through 22:6, thus placing all the material in 21:1ff. after the Millennium. At this point, a suggestion might be offered for further study.

If the Millennium is a true eschatological, historical event like the person, ministry, and resurrection of Jesus, may not 21:1ff. be viewed as the full manifestation of the kingdom of God, a partial manifestation of which will be realized in the thousand-year reign of Christ and the saints, during which Christ will defeat all his enemies, including death (1 Cor 15:23–28)? Some of the same conditions described in 21:1ff. would then, at least in part, characterize the Millennium.

Finally, why the Millennium? There are at least four answers to this question:

1. During the Millennium, Christ will openly manifest his kingdom in world history; the Millennium will provide an actual demonstration of the truthfulness of the divine witness borne by Christ and his followers during their life on earth. It will be a time of the fulfillment of all God's covenant promises to his people.

2. The Millennium will reveal that man's rebellion against God lies deep in man's own heart, not in the devil's deception. Even when Satan is bound and righteousness prevails in the world, some people will still rebel against God. The final release of Satan will openly draw out this hidden evil.

3. The release of Satan after the Millennium shows the invulnerability of the city of God and the extent of the authority of Christ, since the devil is immediately defeated and cast into the lake of fire forever.

4. The Millennium will serve as a long period required to do the general "house-cleaning" needed after the preceding ages of sin, during which sin was prevalent.

1–3 These verses are integrally related to 19:20–21. After the destruction of the beast and his followers and of the false prophet, Satan (the dragon, the ancient serpent) is dealt with. He is thrown into the Abyss to be imprisoned there for a thousand years, which is the third last thing (see comments at introduction to 19:11–21). The Abyss is the demonic abode (see comments at 9:1; cf. 11:7). The angel's mission is to restrain Satan from deceiving the nations—thus the key, the chain, and the violent casting into the Abyss. That this whole action is not a recapitulation of earlier descriptions of Satan is evident from a number of points. In 12:9 (q.v. for the same titles), Satan is "hurled" out of heaven "to the earth," where he goes forth with great fury to work his deception and persecute God's people (13:14; 18:23c). But in 20:1–3, the situation is completely different. Here Satan is cast *out of the earth* into a place where he is kept from "deceiving the nations." The former period of Satan's restriction to earth is described as a "short time" (12:9, 12), while the time here (20:1–3) of his binding is a thousand years. In the earlier references to Satan, he is very active on the earth (2:10, 13; 12:17; 16:13, cf. 1 Peter 5:8); here he is tightly sealed in "prison" (*phylaka*, v.7). The binding of Satan removes his deceptive activity among "the nations" (*ta ethnē*), a term never used to describe the redeemed community (until ch. 21, after Satan's permanent end).

From at least the time of Victorinus (d.c.303), some have interpreted the binding of Satan as the work of Christ in the lives of believers. Thus Satan is "bound" for believers since he no longer deceives them, but he is still "loose" for unbelievers who are deceived (Victorinus *Commentary on the Apocalypse* 20; also Minear, *I Saw a New Earth*, p. 162). This explanation, however, does not take seriously the language of the Abyss and the prison in which Satan is confined, nor does it account for the releasing of Satan after the thousand years. The binding of spirits or angels is mentioned in Isaiah 24:21–23; Jude 6 (cf. Tobit 8:3; 1 Enoch 10:4, 11–12; 88:1–3; Jub 23:29; T Levi 18:12). In all these references there is no question of the spirits being bound in some respects and not in others; it signifies a complete removal as to a prison, usually in the depths of the underworld (Beasley-Murray, "The Revelation," p. 1305).

185

Mounce's observation is well taken: "The elaborate measures taken to insure his custody are most easily understood as implying the complete cessation of his influence on earth (rather than a curbing of his activities)" (*Revelation*, p. 353).

In only one NT reference is there a question as to the limited binding of Satan. In Mark 3:27 Jesus refers in his parable to the strong man first being bound before his goods can be plundered. The reference is to Satan's being bound by Christ and, according to J. Jeremias, specifically relates to the temptation of Jesus (*The Parables of Jesus*, rev. ed. [New York: Scribner's, 1963], pp. 122–23), or, according to others, to Jesus' exorcisms mentioned in the immediate context. In any case, the binding of Satan by the ministry of Jesus did not totally immobilize the devil but struck him a vital blow. But does the reference in Mark provide a true analogy for the binding of Satan in 20:1–3, as Augustine claimed? A careful examination of Mark 3:27 and Revelation 20:1–3 leads to the conclusion that the two passages are not teaching the same truth. There is a sense in which, according to the Gospel account, Satan is in the process of being bound by the activity of Christ and the kingdom of God; but this is clearly an event different from the total consigning of Satan to the Abyss as taught in Revelation 20:1–3.

Finally, it may be noted that the thousand-year binding of Satan is concurrent with and inseparable from the thousand-year reign of the resurrected martyrs. For a thousand years on this earth, within history, the activity of Satan leading mankind into false worship and active rebellion against God and his people will be totally curbed under the authority of Christ in his kingdom. If that reign is yet future, the binding is future. If the binding refers to an earthly situation—which it clearly does—the thousand-year reign most naturally refers to an earthly situation.

4–6 The fourth last thing (see comments at introduction to 19:11–21) is the thousand-year reign of Christ on the earth. John gives us no picture of life in the Millennium in these verses; they contain only a statement about who will participate in it. He sees thrones, and judges sitting on them. The scene is usually connected with Daniel's vision of the Son of Man (Dan 7:9, 22, 27). In Daniel, justice was done for the saints by the Ancient of Days and they began their kingdom reign. The thought may be similar here. If this is the case, those who sit on the thrones are the angelic court. However, those on the thrones may be the resurrected martyrs who exercise judgmental and ruling functions during the Millennium. This possible reinterpretation of Daniel seems preferable in the light of other NT teaching as well as of Revelation itself (cf. Luke 22:30; 1 Cor 6:2; Rev 2:26). They who were once judged by earth's courts to be worthy of death are now the judges of the earth under Christ.

A more difficult question concerns the identity of those who will rule with Christ. They are the "beheaded" (with an axe, *pelekizō*, elsewhere *sphazō*, "slaughter," cf. 6:9) martyrs who have previously occupied John's attention. The cause of their death is attributed to their faithful witness to Jesus and the word of God (on these terms, see comments at 1:9; cf. 6:9; 12:11). The reference to "souls" (*psychas*) immediately recalls 6:9, where the same expression is used of the slain witnesses under the altar. The word describes those who have lost their bodily life but are nevertheless still alive in God's sight. This term prepares us for their coming to (bodily) life again at the first resurrection. It is a mistake to take *psychas* to imply a later spiritual resurrection or rebirth of the soul as did Augustine and many since (contra Swete, et al.).

These martyrs are also those who did not worship the beast or his image or receive his mark on them (cf. 13:1ff.; 15:2); in a word, they are the followers of the Lamb.

At this point, NIV omits a very important term. Between the description of those beheaded and the description concerning the beast worship in v.4 are the two words *kai hoitines* ("and who"). This construction is capable of bearing two different meanings. It could simply introduce a further qualifying phrase to the identification of the martyrs (so NIV, TEV). But it may also be understood to introduce a second group. There are (1) those who were beheaded for their witness and (2) "also those who" did not worship the beast (so Rissi, Swete; see JB; BV—"and of these also"; NASB—"and those who"). This immediately alleviates a thorny problem, i.e., why only the martyrs should live and reign with Christ. Usually in Revelation the relative pronoun *hoitines* ("who") simply refers to the preceding group and adds some further detail (2:24; 9:4; 17:12); but in one other reference, which alone has the identical introductory terms (*kai hoitines*), the phrase so introduced singles out a special class or group from the more general group in the preceding statement (1:7). Thus the *kai hoitines* clause introduces a special class of the beheaded, i.e., those who were so beheaded because they did not worship the beast, etc. In any case, it seems that John has only the beheaded in mind (cf. 14:13).

But this presents a problem because John has elsewhere indicated that the kingdom reign will be shared by every believer who overcomes (2:26–28; 3:12, 21) and is purchased by Christ's blood (5:10). Also, in 1 Corinthians 6:2–3, Paul clearly speaks of all believers—not just martyrs—exercising judgment in the future. Revelation 5:10 indicates that the kingdom will be a "reign on the earth." Unless only those beheaded by the beast will reign in the Millennium, another explanation is demanded. The pastoral approach would explain John's reference to only the martyrs as a piece of special encouragement to them, while not implying that others would be left out (Beasley-Murray).

I feel somewhat more comfortable with the view expressed earlier (see comments at 6:9)—viz., that the martyrs represent the whole church that is faithful to Jesus whether or not they have actually been killed. They constitute a group that can in truth be described as those who "did not love their lives so much as to shrink from death" (12:11). As such, the term is a synonym for overcomers (chs. 2–3). Thus John could count himself in this group, though he may never have suffered death by the axe of the beast. In 2:11 those who during persecution are faithful to Christ even to the point of death are promised escape from the second death, which in 20:6 is promised to those who share in the first resurrection, i.e., the beheaded (v.4). In fact, a number also of the other promises to overcomers in the letters to the seven churches find their fulfillment in chapter 20 (compare 2:11 with 20:6; 2:26–27 with 20:4; 3:5 with 20:12, 15; 3:21 with 20:4).

The martyrs "came to life." The interpretation of these words is crucial to the whole passage. Since Augustine, the majority of interpreters have taken the words to refer to a spiritual resurrection, or new birth, or to the triumph of the church. Caird, for example, sees the parallel to Christ's resurrection (2:8) but seems to spiritualize Jesus' resurrection and concludes that resurrection for the martyrs "means that they have been let loose into the world" (p. 255). This substitutes some symbolic sense of physical resurrection for the historical event. Others, rightly chastened by a more serious exegesis of the text, hold that the language teaches bodily resurrection but that the whole section (20:1–10) is not to be taken as predicting events within history but is apocalyptic language, figurative of the consolation and reward promised the martyrs (Beckwith, p. 737). Berkouwer's position typifies the mystical and vague language used by nonmillennialists to explain what the passage means:

We may not tamper with the real, graphic nature of the vision of Revelation 20, nor may we spiritualize the first resurrection. But one question is still decisive: does this vision intend to sketch for us a particular phase of *history?* If one does interpret it this way, it seems to me that he must include the first (bodily) resurrection in his concept of a future millennium. . . . This vision is not a narrative account of a future earthly reign of peace at all, but is the apocalyptic unveiling of the reality of salvation in Christ as a backdrop to the reality of the suffering and martyrdom that still continue as long as the dominion of Christ remains hidden (italics his) (*Return of Christ,* p. 307).

While alleviating the criticism of a spiritual resurrection, Berkouwer fails to take with equal seriousness the language of the thousand-year reign, which is everywhere in the Apocalypse a reign on the *earth* within *history*.

The verb *ezēsan* ("came to life," from *zaō*) is used in v.4 of the martyrs and also in v.5 of the "rest of the dead" who did not come to life till the thousand years were completed. When the context is that of bodily death, *ezēsan* is used in the NT to connote physical resurrection (John 11:25; Acts 1:3; 9:41), though the normal word is *egeirō* ("raise up"). More importantly, Revelation clearly uses *zaō* ("live") for the resurrection of Christ (1:18; 2:8) and also curiously for the sea beast (13:14). John 5:25 is sometimes cited as an evidence that *zaō* refers to spiritual life, not physical resurrection. But a careful reading of the context clearly shows that while John 5:25 does indeed use *zaō* in the sense of spiritual life (as do other NT passages), John 5:29 is definitely referring to physical resurrection and uses the phrase "rise to live" (*anastasin zōēs*, from *zaō*). John plainly says in Revelation 20:5 that "this is the first resurrection" (*anastasis prōtē*). The word *anastasis*, which occurs over forty times in the NT, is used almost exclusively of physical resurrection (Luke 2:34 is the only exception). There is no indication that John has departed from this usage in these verses.

Why does John call this the "first" resurrection? The term *prōtē* clearly implies the first in a series of two or more. John does not directly refer to a second resurrection; a second resurrection is, however, correctly inferred both from the use of *prōtē* and also from the expression "the rest of the dead did not come to life until the thousand years were ended" (v.5). Irenaeus (fl. c.175–c.195) clearly connects John's first resurrection with the "resurrection of the just" (Luke 14:14; Irenaeus *Contra Haereses* 39.3–10). Likewise Justin Martyr held to a physical resurrection before the Millennium (*Dialogue with Trypho* 80) and a general physical resurrection after the thousand years (ibid., 81), though he does not explain whether believers will also participate in the latter. From at least the time of Augustine, the first resurrection was understood as a regeneration of the soul and the second resurrection as the general physical, bodily resurrection of just and unjust (*City of God* 20.9–10). It must, however, be insisted that it is quite weak exegesis to make the first resurrection spiritual and the second one physical, unless the text itself clearly indicates this change, which it does not.

Another response would be to understand "the rest of the dead" who lived not until the close of the thousand years to be all the faithful except the martyrs, plus the entire body of unbelievers (so Mounce, *Revelation,* p. 360). This view, in our opinion, runs aground on the fact that John clearly seems to tie exclusion from the second death with those who are part of the first resurrection, thus strongly implying that those who participate in the second resurrection are destined for the second death.

Therefore, following the lead of the earlier exegesis of Irenaeus, we may understand the first resurrection as being the raising to physical life of all the dead in Christ (cf. 1 Cor 15:12ff; 1 Thess 4:13ff.); this is the resurrection to life of John 5:29 (NIV, "rise to live"). For those who participate in this resurrection, "the second death [the lake of fire (20:14)] has no power over them" (v.6). Therefore, they are "blessed and holy" (the fifth beatitude in Rev; see comments on 1:3) and shall be priests of God and Christ for the thousand years. On the other hand, those over whom the second death will have power must be "the rest of the dead" (v.5), who will be participants in the second resurrection, the "rise to be condemned" of John 5:29 (cf. Acts 24:15).

In the only place other than Revelation 2:11 and 20:6 where the second death is mentioned, it refers to exclusion from physical resurrection (v.14). Likewise, in the Palestinian Targum on Deuteronomy 33:6, the OT *locus theologicus* in rabbinic Judaism for proving the resurrection from the dead, the Targum reads: "Let Reuben live in this world and not die in the second death in which death the wicked die in the world to come." In the Targum the second death means exclusion from the resurrection. Not to die the second death, then, means to rise again to eternal life (cf. M. McNamara, *Targum and Testament: Aramaic Paraphrases of the Hebrew Bible; A Light on the New Testament* [Grand Rapids: Eerdmans, 1962], p. 123).

What now may be said as to the length of the kingdom reign? Nowhere in other literature is the kingdom reign of the Messiah specified as 1,000 years (on 2 Enoch 33, see note on v.6), though estimates of 400, 40, 70, 365, or an indefinite period (*Sanhedrin* 99a) are found. Thus parallels to John's use of 1,000 years must be sought elsewhere. According to Daniélou, the most primitive traditions in Asia relate the 1,000 years to Adam's paradisiacal time span. According to the Book of Jubilees, Adam's sin caused him to die at 930 years of age (Gen 5:5), "seventy years before attaining a thousand years, for one thousand years are as one day [Ps 90:4] in heaven. . . . For this reason [because he ate from the tree of knowledge] he died before completing the years of this day" (Jub 4:29–30). Here the 1,000 years are based on an exegesis of Genesis 2:17 in terms of Psalm 90:4—Adam dies on the day on which he eats the forbidden fruit; but according to Psalm 90:4, a day means 1,000 years, and therefore Adam dies before completing 1,000 years. Daniélou believes this is the origin of John's use of the 1,000 years.

Later, the thousand years began to be associated with the Jewish cosmic-week framework in which the history of the world is viewed as lasting a week of millennia, or seven thousand years. The last day millennium is the Sabbath-rest millennium, followed by the eighth day of the age to come. This idea was then linked interpretatively but inappropriately to 2 Peter 3:8. While early Christian writings, such as the Epistle of Barnabas, reflect this reasoning, it was not, according to Daniélou, the most primitive tradition (*Theology of Jewish Christianity*, pp. 377–404).

Is the thousand years, then, symbolic of a perfect human lifespan or some ideal kingdom environment on the earth? In the first place, the number symbolisms of John in Revelation should not be used to argue against an earthly kingdom. It might be said that the number is symbolic of a perfect period of time of whatever length. The essence of premillennialism is in its insistence that the reign will be on earth, not in heaven, for a period of time before the final judgment and the new heavens and earth. For example, we may rightly understand the 1,260 days (forty-two months) of earlier chapters as a symbolic number, but it still refers to an actual historical period of whatever length during which the beast will destroy the saints. If we look at the time of suffering of the Smyrna Christians, it is "ten days" (2:10), a relatively short time in comparison to a thousand years of victorious reign with Christ. In any case, it is not of primary importance whether the years are actual 365-day years or symbolic of a shorter or longer period of bliss enjoyed by believers as they reign with Christ on earth (cf. 5:10 with 11:15; 22:5).

Notes

1 Some selected bibliographic references on the millennial question may be helpful: Premillennial—Alford, "Revelation," Alf (1884); Tenney, *Interpreting Revelation* (1957); Cullmann, *Christology of the New Testament* (1959); Rissi, *Time and History* (1966); idem, *The Future of the World, An Exegetical Study of Revelation* 19:11–22:15 (Naperville, Ill.: A.R. Allenson, 1972); Walvoord, *The Revelation of Jesus Christ* (1966); Beasley-Murray, "The Revelation," NBCrev. (1970); Ladd, *Commentary on Revelation* (1972); Amillennial—Augustine *The City of God* 20.6–15; Caird, *Revelation of St. John* (1966); Rudolf Schnackenburg, *Present and Future; Modern Aspects of New Testament Theology* (South Bend, Ind.: University of Notre Dame, 1966); G.C. Berkouwer, *The Return of Christ* (1972); Harry Boer, "What About the Millennium?" *The Reformed Journal*, 25 (January 1975), 26–30; idem, "The Reward of Martyrs," *The Reformed Journal*, 25 (February 1975), 7–9, 28; Postmillennial—Lorraine Boettner, *The Millennium* (Philadelphia: Presbyterian and Reformed, 1958); Rousas J. Rushdoony, *The Institutes of Biblical Law* (Nutley, N.J.: Craig, 1973); H. Berkhof, *Christ the Meaning of History* (1979). For background material, see G.R. Beasley-Murray and H. Hobbs, *Revelation: Three Viewpoints* (Nashville: Broadman, 1977); Robert G. Clouse, ed., *The Meaning of the Millennium: Four Views* (Downers Grove, Ill.: InterVarsity, 1977); and Millard J. Erickson, *Contemporary Options in Eschatology. A Study of the Millennium* (Grand Rapids: Baker, 1977). For a helpful historical survey of the origins of millennial thought, see Daniélou, *Theology of Jewish Christianity*.

4–6 Second Enoch 33:1ff. (of doubtful age) is sometimes cited as evidence that the Jews believed in a thousand-year Messianic Age. However, the Jewish cosmic-week explanation for the history of the world did not explicitly connect the Messiah's reign to the seventh-day millennium. Thus there arose a multitude of different year periods assigned to the Messianic Age that would precede the eternal period or age to come.

On the possibility that the first resurrection refers to the intermediate state, see Meredith Kline, "The First Resurrection," WTJ, 37 (1974–75), 366–75; J.R. Michaels, "The First Resurrection: A Response," WTJ, 39 (1976), 100–109; P.E. Hughes, "The First Resurrection: Another Interpretation," WTJ, 39 (1977), 315–18; See also J.S. Deere, "Premillennialism in Revelation 20:4–6," BS, 135 (1978), 58–73.

4 The plural ἐκάθισαν (*ekathisan*, lit., "they sat"; NIV, "were seated") may be another instance of the Semitic idiom where the plural is used for the passive idea (cf. note on 12:6). In this case, the NIV rendering is perfectly justified.

C. *The Release and End of Satan*

20:7–10

> [7]When the thousand years are over, Satan will be released from his prison [8]and will go out to deceive the nations in the four corners of the earth—Gog and Magog—to gather them for battle. In number they are like the sand on the seashore. [9]They marched across the breadth of the earth and surrounded the camp of God's people, the city he loves. But fire came down from heaven and devoured them.

¹⁰And the devil, who deceived them, was thrown into the lake of burning sulfur, where the beast and the false prophet had been thrown. They will be tormented day and night for ever and ever.

7–10 The fifth last thing (see comments at introduction to 19:11–21) is the defeat of Satan. In v.3 the release of Satan after the Millennium was anticipated: "He must [*dei*] be set free for a short time [*mikron chronon;* cf. 12:12, *oligon kairon*]." Why must (*dei*) he once again be released? The answer is so that he can "deceive the nations" throughout the world and lead them into conflict against "God's people." But why should God allow this? Certainly if man alone were prophetically writing the history of the world, he would not bring the archdeceiver back after the glorious reign of Christ 20:4–6. But God's thoughts and ways are not man's (Isa 55:8). Ezekiel's vision of Gog brought out of the land of Magog seems to be clearly in John's mind (Ezek 38–39). Ezekiel also saw an attack on God's people, who had been restored for some time ("after many days" [Ezek 38:8])—i.e., after the commencement of the kingdom age.

In Ezekiel 38–39, Gog refers to the prince of a host of pagan invaders from the North, especially the Scythian hordes from the distant land of Magog. In Revelation, however, the names are symbolic of the final enemies of Christ duped by Satan into attacking the community of the saints. The change in meaning has occurred historically through the frequent use in rabbinic circles of the expression "Gog and Magog" to symbolically refer to the nations spoken of in Psalm 2 who are in rebellion against God and his Messiah (cf. Caird, p. 256, for Talmud references).

If the beast and his armies are already destroyed (19:19ff.), who are these rebellious nations? It may be that the beast and his armies in the earlier context refer to the demonic powers and those in 20:7ff. to human nations in rebellion—not an unlikely solution (see comments at 19:19ff.)—or it may be that not all the people in the world will participate in the beast's armies and thus those mentioned here in v.8 refer to other people who during the millennial reign defected in their hearts from the Messiah. In any case, this section shows something of the deep, complex nature of evil. The source of rebellion against God does not lie in man's environment or fundamentally with the devil but springs up from deep within man's own heart. The return of Satan will demonstrate this in the most dramatic manner once for all. The temporal reign of Christ will not be fulfilled till this final challenge to his kingdom occurs and he demonstrates the power of his victory at the Cross and puts down all his enemies (1 Cor 15:25).

The gathered army, which is extensive and world-wide, advances and in siege fashion encircles the "camp [*parembolē*] of God's people, the city he loves." Most commentators take the expressions camp and city as different metaphors for God's people. The word *parembolē* in the NT refers to either a military camp or the camp of Israel (Acts 21:34, 37; 22:24; Heb 11:34; 13:11, 13). It is a word that reminds us of the pilgrim character of the people of God even at the end of the Millennium, as long as evil is active in God's creation.

The "city he loves" presents more difficulty. According to standard Jewish eschatology, this should refer to the restored and spiritually renewed city of Jerusalem in Palestine (Ps 78:6–8; 87:2; Beckwith, p. 746). A number of modern commentators of various theological opinions have taken this Jewish identification as a clue and have so understood the passage (H. Berkhof, *Christ the Meaning of History*, p. 153; Ladd,

Commentary on Revelation, p. 270; Charles, *Commentary on Revelation*, 2:145). On the other hand, John may have intended to refer merely to the community of the redeemed without any specific geographical location in mind. This would be in harmony with his previous references to the city elsewhere in the book (cf. comments at 3:12; 11:2, 8). There are only two cities or kingdoms in the Apocalyse—the city of Satan, where the beast and harlot are central, and the city of God, where God and the Lamb are central. The city, then, is the kingdom of God in its millennial manifestation; it is the same city that appears in its final, most glorious form in the last chapters (21–22). Wherever God dwells among his people, there the city of God is (21:2–3). Following this understanding of the beloved city in no way weakens the validity of an earthly reign of Christ and the saints.

The swiftness and finality of the divine judgment (v.9) emphasizes the reality of the victory of Christ at the Cross. The fire imagery may reflect Ezekiel's vision of the destruction of Gog (Ezek 38:22; 39:6). Note that unlike the Qumran and Jewish apocalyptic literature, it is God, not the saints, who destroys the enemy (cf. comments at 19:19). The devil is now dealt the long-awaited final and fatal blow (Gen 3:15; John 12:31). The "lake of fire" imagery is probably related to the teaching of Jesus about hell (*gehenna*, Matt 5:22; 7:19; 10:28; 13:49–50; Mark 9:48, et al.). The lake image may be related to certain Jewish descriptions of eternal judgment (cf. 2 Enoch 10:2: "a gloomy fire is always burning, and a fiery river goes forth"). The figure may intensify the idea of the permanency of the judgment (cf. comments at 14:11; also 19:20; 20:14–15; 21:8). That the beast and false prophet are already there does not argue for their individuality (contra Beasley-Murray, "The Revelation," p. 1308) since later in the chapter "death" and "Hades," nonpersonal entities that for the sake of the imagery are personified, are cast into the same lake of fire (20:14).

Notes

8 On "Gog," see TDNT, 1: 789–91; Ralph Alexander, "A Fresh Look at Ezekiel 38 and 39," ETS, 17, no. 3 (1974), 157–69. Alexander argues for multiple manifestations of Gog in history and the close parallelism between Ezek 38–39 and Rev 20:7–10.

The Palestinian Targum on Exod 40 refers to the Messiah of Ephraim "by whose hand the house of Israel is to vanquish Gog and his confederates at the end of days" (cited by Ford, p. 356).

D. *Great White Throne Judgment*

20:11–15

[11]Then I saw a great white throne and him who was seated on it. Earth and sky fled from his presence, and there was no place for them. [12]And I saw the dead, great and small, standing before the throne, and books were opened. Another book was opened, which is the book of life. The dead were judged according to what they had done as recorded in the books. [13]The sea gave up the dead that were in it, and death and Hades gave up the dead that were in them, and each person was judged according to what he had done. [14]Then death and Hades were thrown into the lake of fire. The lake of fire is the second death. [15]If anyone's name was not found written in the book of life, he was thrown into the lake of fire.

11–15 John describes in vivid pictures the sixth last thing (see comments in introduction to 19:11–21), the final judgment of mankind. Unlike many of the vivid, imaginative paintings based on this vision, here John describes a strange, unearthly scene. Heaven and earth flee from the unidentified figure who sits on the majestic white throne. The language of poetic imagery captures the fading character of everything of the world (1 John 2:17). Now the only reality is God seated on the throne of judgment, before whom all must appear (Heb 9:27). His verdict alone is holy and righteous (white symbolism). It is possible that in Revelation the earth and sky refer more to the religio-political order than to the cosmological one (Caird). Since 20:11–12 makes use of the theophany of Daniel 7:9–10, the one seated on the throne is presumably God himself; but since 22:1, 3 mention the throne of God *and of the Lamb,* it may well be that here Jesus shares in the judgment (John 5:27; R.T. France, *Jesus and the Old Testament* [Downers Grove, Ill.: InterVarsity, 1971], p. 203). God has kept the last judgment in his own hands. This vision declares that even though it may have seemed that earth's course of history ran contrary to his holy will, no single day or hour in the world's drama has ever detracted from the absolute sovereignty of God (Lilje).

But who are the dead (vv. 12–13)? Earlier in the chapter, John has mentioned the "rest of the dead" who are not resurrected till the thousand years are completed (v.5). As Mounce observes: "If the first resurrection is limited to actual martyrs, then the judgment of verses 11–15 involves both believer and impenitent. If the second resurrection is of the wicked only, then the judgment is of those who will in fact be consigned to the lake of fire" (*Revelation,* p. 365). While no resurrection is mentioned in vv. 11–15, the dead may well be those who did not participate in the first resurrection. Since the second death has no power over those who were raised in the first resurrection (v.6), it may be argued that only those who are the enemies of God—i.e., the wicked dead—stand before this throne (John 5:24). This is by no means a necessary inference, though it is the most satisfying exegesis.

A moment of tension arrives. The books are opened. It is sobering to ponder that in God's sight nothing is forgotten; all will give an account of their actions (v.13). Judgment always proceeds on the basis of works (Matt 25:41ff.; Rom 2:6; 2 Cor 5:10; Heb 4:12–13). The "books" are the records of human deeds (v.12). While in Jewish thought there are references to books of good and evil deeds being kept before God (4 Ezra 6:20; 1 Enoch 47:3), John is probably alluding to Daniel 7:10: "The court was seated, and the books were opened." We are not told whether these books contain both good and evil works or only the latter. John is more concerned about another book, the book of life, which alone seems to be decisive (vv. 12, 15; cf. at 3:5; also 13:8; 17:8; 21:27). How can these two pictures be harmonized? In reality there is no conflict. Works are unmistakable evidence of the loyalty of the heart; they express either belief or unbelief, faithfulness or unfaithfulness. The judgment will reveal through the records whether or not the loyalties were with God and the Lamb or with God's enemies. John's theology of faith and its inseparable relation to works is the same as Jesus' and Paul's (John 5:29; Rom 2:6ff.). This judgment is not a balancing of good works over bad works. Those who have their names in the Lamb's book of life will also have records of righteous deeds. The opposite will also be true. The imagery reflects the delicate balance between grace and obedience (cf. comments at 19:6–8).

Three broad places are mentioned as containing the dead: the sea, death, and Hades (v.13). The sea represents the place of unburied bodies while death and Hades represent the reality of dying and the condition entered on at death (cf. 1:18; 6:8).

The imagery suggests release of the bodies and persons from their places of confinement following death; i.e., it portrays resurrection. They rise to receive sentence (John 5:29b). Death and Hades are personified (cf. 6:8) and in a vivid image are cast into the lake of fire to be permanently destroyed (cf. 19:20; 20:10). This not only fulfills Paul's cry concerning the last enemy, death, which will be defeated by the victorious kingdom of Christ (1 Cor 15:16), but also signals the earth's new condition: "There will be no more death" (21:4).

The final scene in this dark and fearful passage is in v.15. From the English rendering it might be inferred that John is doubtful whether anyone will be thrown into the lake of fire. The Greek construction, however, is not so indefinite. John uses a first-class condition, which assumes the reality of the first clause and shows the consequences in the second clause. Thus we might paraphrase the verse: "If anyone's name was not found written in the book of life, and I assume there were such, he was thrown into the lake of fire." When taken seriously, this final note evaporates all theories of universalism or *apocatastasis* (cf. Berkouwer's excellent discussion in *Return of Christ*, pp. 387–423).

Notes

15 The "second death" terminology does not occur in rabbinic teaching in this period, but it is found in the Targum to the Prophets on Isa 65:6, where it is said that the bodies (resurrected) of the wicked are delivered to the second death. This supports the idea of a second resurrection of the unjust that precedes the casting into the second death (cf. Israel Abraham's *Studies in Pharasaism and the Gospels* 2d ser. [New York: Ktav, 1967], pp. 41–49).

V. Vision of the New Heaven and the New Earth and the New Jerusalem (21:1–22:5)

A. *The New Jerusalem*

21:1–27

¹Then I saw a new heaven and a new earth, for the first heaven and the first earth had passed away, and there was no longer any sea. ²I saw the Holy City, the new Jerusalem, coming down out of heaven from God, prepared as a bride beautifully dressed for her husband. ³And I heard a loud voice from the throne saying, "Now the dwelling of God is with men, and he will live with them. They will be his people, and God himself will be with them and be their God. ⁴He will wipe every tear from their eyes. There will be no more death or mourning or crying or pain, for the old order of things has passed away."

⁵He who was seated on the throne said, "I am making everything new!" Then he said, "Write this down, for these words are trustworthy and true."

⁶He said to me: "It is done. I am the Alpha and the Omega, the Beginning and the End. To him who is thirsty I will give to drink without cost from the spring of the water of life. ⁷He who overcomes will inherit all this, and I will be his God and he will be my son. ⁸But the cowardly, the unbelieving, the vile, the murderers, the sexually immoral, those who practice magic arts, the idolaters and all liars—their place will be in the fiery lake of burning sulfur. This is the second death."

⁹One of the seven angels who had the seven bowls full of the seven last plagues

came and said to me, "Come, I will show you the bride, the wife of the Lamb." [10]And he carried me away in the Spirit to a mountain great and high, and showed me the Holy City, Jerusalem, coming down out of heaven from God. [11]It shone with the glory of God, and its brilliance was like that of a very precious jewel, like a jasper, clear as crystal. [12]It had a great, high wall with twelve gates, and with twelve angels at the gates. On the gates were written the names of the twelve tribes of Israel. [13]There were three gates on the east, three on the north, three on the south and three on the west. [14]The wall of the city had twelve foundations, and on them were the names of the twelve apostles of the Lamb.

[15]The angel who talked with me had a measuring rod of gold to measure the city, its gates and its wall. [16]The city was laid out like a square, as long as it was wide. He measured the city with the rod and found it to be 12,000 stadia in length, and as wide and high as it is long. [17]He measured its wall and it was 144 cubits thick, by man's measurement, which the angel was using. [18]The wall was made of jasper, and the city of pure gold, as pure as glass. [19]The foundations of the city walls were decorated with every kind of precious stone. The first foundation was jasper; the second sapphire, the third chalcedony, the fourth emerald, [20]the fifth sardonyx, the sixth carnelian, the seventh chrysolite, the eighth beryl, the ninth topaz, the tenth chrysoprase, the eleventh jacinth, and the twelfth amethyst. [21]The twelve gates were twelve pearls, each gate made of a single pearl. The street of the city was of pure gold, like transparent glass.

[22]I did not see a temple in the city, because the Lord God Almighty and the Lamb are its temple. [23]The city does not need the sun or the moon to shine on it, for the glory of God gives it light, and the Lamb is its lamp. [24]The nations will walk by its light, and the kings of the earth will bring their splendor into it. [25]On no day will its gates ever be shut, for there will be no night there. [26]The glory and honor of the nations will be brought into it. [27]Nothing impure will ever enter it, nor will anyone who does what is shameful or deceitful, but only those whose names are written in the Lamb's book of life.

The seventh last thing (see comments in introduction to 19:11–21) is the vision of the new heavens, the new earth, and the New Jerusalem. Moffatt's striking remark, which captures something of the freshness of this moment in the book, is worth remembering at the outset of the exposition of this incredibly beautiful finale:

> From the smoke and pain and heat [of the preceding scenes] it is a relief to pass into the clear, clean atmosphere of the eternal morning where the breath of heaven is sweet and the vast city of God sparkles like a diamond in the radiance of his presence" (J.B. Moffatt, EGT, 5:477).

Countless productions of art and music have through the ages been inspired by this vision. Cathedral architecture has been influenced by its imagery. John discloses a theology in stone and gold as pure as glass and color. Archetypal images abound. The church is called the bride (21:2). God gives the thirsty "to drink without cost from the spring of the water of life" (21:6). Completeness is implied in the number twelve and its multiples (21:12–14, 16–17, 21) and fullness in the cubical dimension of the city (21:16). Colorful jewels abound as do references to light and the glory of God (21:11, 18–21, 23, 25; 22:5). There is the "river of the water of life" (22:1) and the "tree of life" (22:2). The "sea" is gone (21:1).

Allusions to the OT abound. Most of John's imagery in this chapter reflects Isaiah 60 and 65 and Ezekiel 40–48. John weaves the New Jerusalem vision of Isaiah together with the new temple vision of Ezekiel. The multiple OT promises converging in John's mind seem to indicate that he viewed the New Jerusalem as the fulfillment of all these strands of prophecy. There are also allusions to Genesis 1–3—viz., the absence of death and suffering, the dwelling of God with men as in Eden, the tree of life, the removal of the curse, etc. Creation is restored to its pristine character (cf. Claus Westermann, *Beginning and End in the Bible* [Philadelphia: Fortress, 1972]).

The connection of this vision with the promises to the overcomers in the letters to the seven churches (chs. 2–3) is significant. For example, to the overcomers at Ephesus was granted the right to the tree of life (2:7; cf. 22:2); to Thyatira, the right to rule the nations (2:26; cf. 22:5); to Philadelphia, the name of the city of my God, the New Jerusalem (3:12 and 21:2, 9ff.). In a sense, a strand from every major section of the Apocalypse appears in chapers 21–22. Moreover, almost every major theme and image found in these chapters can be duplicated from Jewish literature (Mathias Rissi, *The Future of the World; an Exegetical Study of Revelation 19:11–22:15* [Naperville, Ill.: A.R. Allenson, 1972], pp. 46–51). But there is in the totality of John's vision a dimension that is clearly lacking in the Jewish parallels. Furthermore, his theology of the Lamb's centrality in the city and the absence of a temple in the New Jerusalem is unique.

In other NT passages, the vision of the heavenly city is described as having the character of eschatological promise. The kingdom reality of the age to come has already appeared in history in the life of Jesus and also in the presence of the Holy Spirit in the church. But the reality is now present only in a promissory way, not in actual fulfillment. Therefore, while the Jerusalem that is from above has present implications for believers (Gal 4:25–31), they are nevertheless, like Abraham, "looking forward to the city with foundations" (Heb 11:10; 13:14). In this sense, the medieval synthesis that made the church on earth and the kingdom synonymous and built its cathedrals to depict that notion was misdirected. John's vision in chapters 21–22 is one of eschatological promise, future in its realization, totally dependent on God's power to create it, yet having present implications for the life of the church in this age.

Outlines of the chapters are necessarily arbitrary because of the familiar Semitic style of doubling back and elaborating on previous subjects. Perhaps 21:1–8 may be seen as a preface or introduction to the vision of the New Jerusalem (21:9–22:6), and this in turn may be seen as followed by the conclusion in 22:7–21.

1 The new heavens and earth were foreseen by Isaiah (65:17) as a part of his vision of the renewed Jerusalem. It is remarkable that John's picture of the final age to come focuses not on a platonic ideal heaven or distant paradise but on the reality of a new earth and heaven. God originally created the earth and heaven to be man's permanent home. But sin and death entered the world and transformed the earth into a place of rebellion and alienation; it became enemy-occupied territory. But God has been working in salvation history to effect a total reversal of this evil consequence and to liberate earth and heaven from bondage to sin and corruption (Rom 8:21). The first heaven and earth refers to the whole order of life in the world—an order tainted by sin, death, suffering, and idolatry (cf. v.4: "the old order of things—death, mourning, crying, pain—has passed away"). John's emphasis on heaven and earth is not primarily cosmological but moral and spiritual. So Peter also speaks of the new heaven and earth, "the home of righteousness" (2 Peter 3:13).

The Greek word for "new" (*kainē*) means new in quality, fresh, rather than recent or new in time (*neos*) (TDNT, 3: 447). That it is a *kainē* heaven and earth and not a second heaven and earth suggests something of an endless succession of new heavens and earth. It is the newness of the endless eschatological ages (2:17; 3:12; 5:9;

cf. Eph 2:7). What makes the new heaven and earth "new" is above all else the reality that now "the dwelling of God is with men, . . . They will be his people, and God himself will be with them and be their God" (v.3). The heaven and earth are new because of the presence of a new community of people who are loyal to God and the Lamb in contrast to the former earth in which a community of idolaters lived.

The sea—the source of the satanic beast (13:1) and the place of the dead (20:13)— will be gone. Again, the emphasis is not geographic but moral and spiritual. The sea serves as an archetype with connotations of evil (cf. comments at 13:1). Therefore, no trace of evil in any form will be present in the new creation.

2–4 The Holy City, the New Jerusalem, occupies John's vision for the remainder of the book. How different is this concept of heaven from that of Hinduism, for example? Here heaven is depicted as a city, with life, activity, interest, and people, as opposed to the Hindu ideal of heaven as a sea into which human life returns like a raindrop to the ocean. First, John sees the city "coming down out of heaven from God"—a phrase he uses three times (3:12; 21:2, 10) in an apparent spatial reference. But the city never seems to come down; it is always seen as a "descending-from-heaven kind of city" (Caird, p. 257). Therefore, the expression stresses the idea that the city is a gift of God, forever bearing the marks of his creation.

Second, John calls the city a "bride" (*nymphē*) (cf. 21:9; 22:17). Earlier he referred to the bride of the Lamb (19:7–8) by a different word (*gynē*), though the reality is the same. The multiple imagery is needed to portray the tremendous reality of the city. A bride-city captures something of God's personal relationship to his people (the bride) as well as something of their life in communion with him and one another (a city, with its social connotations). The purity and devotedness of the bride are reflected in her attire.

The subtitle of the Holy City, "the new Jerusalem," raises a question. The "old" Jerusalem was also called the "holy city" and a "bride" (Isa 52:1; 61:10). Since the Jerusalem from above is the "new" (*kainē*) Jerusalem, we may suppose that it is connected in some manner with the old one so that the new is the old one renewed. The old Jerusalem was marred by sin and disobedience. In it was the blood of prophets and apostles. Still worse, it became a manifestation of Babylon the Great when it crucified the Lord of glory (11:8). The old city always involved more than the mere inhabitants and their daily lives. Jerusalem represented the covenant community of God's people, the hope for the kingdom of God on earth. Thus the OT looked forward to a renewed Jerusalem, rebuilt and transformed into a glorious habitation of God and his people. But the prophets also saw something else. They saw a new heaven and new earth and a Jerusalem connected with this reality. Thus it is not altogether clear precisely what the relationship is between the old and the new, the earthly, restored Jerusalem of the prophets and the Jerusalem associated with the new heaven and earth, the Jerusalem called a heavenly Jerusalem in later Jewish thought (cf. Gal 4:25–31; Heb 11:10; 12:22; 13:14; Rissi, *The Future of the World*, p. 50).

The key to the puzzle must be understood with due respect for the old city. Any exegesis, therefore, that completely rejects any connection with the old city cannot take seriously the name "new" (*kainē*) Jerusalem, which presupposes the old. To speak of the heavenly Jerusalem does not deny an earthly city, as some suggest, but stresses its superiority to the older Jewish hope and affirms the eschatological nature of that hope (TDNT, 5:540–41)—a hope that could not be fulfilled by the earthly Jerusalem, a hope John now sees realized in the Holy City of the future. This city is the church in its future glorified existence. It is the final realization of the kingdom of God.

God's dwelling (*skēnē*) among his people (v.3) is a fulfillment of Leviticus 26:11-13, a promise given to the old Jerusalem but forfeited because of apostasy. As a backdrop for the scene, consider Genesis 3, when man lost his fellowship with God (cf. Exod 25:8; Ezek 37:26-27). Thus the Holy Jerusalem is not only mankind's eternal home but the city where God will place his own name forever. God's presence will blot out the things of the former creation. In a touching metaphor of motherly love, John says that God "will wipe away every tear from their eyes" (cf. 7:17; cf. Isa 25:8). These tears have come from sin's distortion of God's purposes for man. They are produced by death or mourning for the dead, by crying or pain. An enemy has done this to the old order. Now God has defeated the enemy and liberated his people and his creation.

5 Now, for the second time in the book, God himself is the speaker (cf. 1:8). From his throne comes the assurance that the one who created the first heaven and earth will indeed make all things new (*panta kaina*). This is a strong confirmation that God's power will be revealed and his redemptive purposes fulfilled. Since these words are in truth God's words (cf. 19:9; 22:6), it is of utmost importance that this vision of the new heaven and the New Jerusalem be proclaimed to the churches.

6-8 With the same word that declared the judgment of the world finished, God proclaims that he has completed his new creation: "It is done" (*gegonan;* cf. 16:17). The names of God, "the Alpha and the Omega, the Beginning and the End," emphasize his absolute control over the world as well as his creatorship of everything (cf. comments at 1:8 and see 22:13).

To those who thirst for him, God offers the water of life without cost (cf. 7:17; 22:1, 17; John 7:37-39; Rom 3:24). Here salvation is beautifully depicted by the image of drinking at the spring of life. Twice in these last two chapters of Revelation, God offers an invitation to those who sense their need and are drawn toward him. John knows that the visions of God's glory among his people, which he is proclaiming as the Word of God, will create a thirst to participate in the reality of this glory. Nothing is required except to come and drink.

Those who come and drink and remain loyal to Christ as overcomers (*nikaō*, see comments at 2:7, 11, et al.) will inherit all the new things of the city of God. They will be God's children, and he will be their Father. This is the essence of salvation— intimate, personal relationship with God himself, age upon age unending (cf. John 17:3). For John this is really what the heavenly city is all about.

Before John shows us the city, however, he must first confront us with a choice. This choice must be made because there are two cities: the city of God and the city of Babylon. Each has its inhabitants and its destiny. Those who drink from salvation's springs supplied by God himself are true followers of Christ. The "cowardly" (*deilos,* "fearful") are those who fear persecution arising from faith in Christ. Not having steadfast endurance, they are devoid of faith (Matt 8:26; Mark 4:40; cf. Matt 13:20-21). Thus they are linked by John to the "unbelieving" and "vile" (a participial form of the verb *bdelyssomai,* "detest," "abhor," which is used of idolatry [Rom 2:22]). They are called "murderers" because they are guilty of the death of the saints (17:6; 18:24). The "sexually immoral" (fornicators), practitioners of "magic arts, the idolaters and all liars" are those associated with idolatrous practices (cf. 9:21; 18:23; 21:27; 22:15; contrast 14:5). By their own choice, Babylon, not the New Jerusalem, is their eternal home (Caird). Thus this passage is not a picture of universal salvation in spite of man's recalcitrance, though it contains a universal invitation for all who thirst to drink the water of life.

In this section (21:9–22:5), the vision of the New Jerusalem introduced in vv. 1–8 is fully described. (For reasons why this section does not describe the millennial kingdom of ch. 20, see comments at introduction to ch. 20.) Verses 9–14 focus on the description of the gates and the walls of the city. This is followed by the action of the angel who measures the city and John's precise mention of the precious stones in the twelve foundations (vv. 15–21). Finally, he describes various aspects of the life of the city (21:22–22:5).

9–10 Here the parallelism with 17:1 is clearly deliberate. The bride, the wife of the Lamb, contrasts with the great prostitute. As the prostitute was found to be John's archetypal image for the great system of satanic evil, so the bride is the true counterpart. She is pure and faithful to God and the Lamb, whereas the prostitute is a mockery. To see the prostitute, John was taken to the desert; but now he is elevated by the Spirit to the highest pinnacle of the earth to witness the exalted New Jerusalem (cf. at 1:10; 4:2; 17:3). As his vision will be a reinterpretation of Ezekiel's temple prophecy (Ezek 40–48), like the former prophet, he is taken to a high mountain (Ezek 40:2). For the moment, the author drops the bridal metaphor and in magnificent imagery describes the church in glory as a city with a lofty wall, splendid gates, and jeweled foundations. There is no warrant for thinking of the city descending like a space platform to the mountain or hovering over the earth as some suggest (see comments on v.2).

11–14 In John's description of the city, precious stones, brilliant colors, and the effulgence of light abound. The problem of the literalness of the city has received much attention. If the city is the bride and the bride the glorified community of God's people in their eternal life, there is little question that John's descriptions are primarily symbolic of that glorified life. This in no way diminishes the reality behind the imagery. In the most suitable language available to John, much of it drawn from the OT, he shows us something of the reality of the eschatological kingdom of God in its glorified existence.

Its appearance is all glorious, "with the glory of God" (v. 11; cf. Ezek 43:4). The city has a "brilliance" (*phōstēr*, "light-bearer") given it by God's presence that appears as crystal-clear jasper (Isa 60:1–2, 19; Rev 21:23). Jasper (*iaspis*) is mentioned three times in chapter 21 (vv. 11, 18–19); earlier in Revelation it refers to the appearance of God (4:3). Jasper is an opaque quartz mineral and occurs in various colors, commonly red, brown, green, and yellow, rarely blue and black, and seldom white. BAG suggests it is an opal (p. 369); others believe it to be a diamond, which is, of course, not quartz but a crystalline carbon. Ginzburg says of it, "This stone changes color even as Benjamin's feelings towards his brothers changed" (cited by Ford, p. 335). Ford thinks the rare and valuable white color is referred to here. Actually, there is no basis for certainty about it.

The wall is very high, its height symbolizing the greatness of this city as well as its impregnability against those described in 21:8, 27. The twelve gates (vv. 12–13) are distributed three on each of the four walls (v.13). These may be like the triple gates that can now be seen in the excavated wall of the old Jerusalem. Later John describes the gates as single pearls (v.21). What impresses him at this point about the gates is their angel guards and the inscribed names of the twelve tribes of Israel. The presence of angels proclaims that this is God's city, while the twelve tribes emphasize the complete election of God (cf. comments at 7:4). Here there seems to be a deliberate allusion to Ezekiel's eschatological Jerusalem on whose gates the names of the twelve tribes appear (Ezek 48:30–34). Ezekiel 48:35 says, "The name of the city from that time on will be: THE LORD IS THERE" (cf. Rev 21:3; 22:3–4).

Like the gates, the twelve foundations of the wall have twelve names written on them—in this case the names of the twelve apostles of the Lamb. Foundations of ancient cities usually consisted of extensions of the rows of huge stones that made up the wall, down to the bedrock. Jerusalem's first-century walls and foundation stones have recently been excavated. Huge stones, some of which are about five feet wide, four feet high, and thirty feet long, weighing eighty to one hundred tons each and going down some fourteen to nineteen layers below the present ground level, have been found.

In vv.19–21, John turns to the precious stones that make up the foundations. Here, however, he stresses the names of the twelve apostles. Theologically, it is significant that he brings together the twelve tribes and the twelve apostles of the Lamb and yet differentiates them. This is not unlike what Matthew and Luke tell us that Jesus said (Matt 19:28; Luke 22:30). The earlier symbolic use of twelve (see comments at 7:4), representing in Revelation completeness, implies that it is unnecessary for us to know precisely which twelve will be there. Judas fell and was replaced by Matthias (Acts 1:21–26), but Paul also was a prominent apostle. Furthermore, the number "twelve" is sometimes used to refer to the elect *group* when all twelve are not in view (John 20:24 has ten; 1 Cor 15:5 has eleven; cf. Luke 9:12). The group of apostles represents the church, the elect community built on the foundation of the gospel of Jesus Christ, the slain Lamb. The dual election here depicted admittedly entails some difficulty in identifying the twelve tribes in 7:4ff. with the church as this writer and other commentators have done (see comments at 7:1ff.). Thus some commentators have insisted that the "twelve tribes" refers to an eschatological purpose for the elect Jewish people (Rissi, *The Future of the World,* p. 73; Walvoord, pp. 322–23). It is a puzzling problem.

15–21 The angel measures the city with a golden measuring rod. (The significance of measuring was discussed at 11:1.) The act of measuring signifies securing something for blessing, to preserve it from spiritual harm or defilement. Ezekiel's elaborate description of the future temple and its measuring was to show the glory and holiness of God in Israel's midst (Ezek 43:12). The measuring reveals the perfection, fulfillment, or completion of all God's purposes for his elect bride. Thus the city is revealed as a perfect cube of twelve thousand stadia (12x1000 [about 1,400 miles]). The wall is 144 cubits (about 200 ft.) thick (12x12). These dimensions should not be interpreted as providing architectural information about the city. Rather, we should think of them as theologically symbolic of the fulfillment of all God's promises. The New Jerusalem symbolizes the paradox of the completeness of infinity in God. The cube reminds us of the dimensions of the Most Holy Place in the tabernacle (10x10 cubits [15x15 ft.]) and in the temple (20x20 cubits [30x30 ft.]). John adds that the measurement was both human and angelic (divine): "by man's measurement, which the angel was using" (v.17). This statement is not unimportant. In some sense it shows that both the human and the divine will intersect in the Holy City. Others take v.17 to be John's way of making the reader realize the "disparity" between the city and the size of the wall, thus forcing us to seek a deeper meaning in the angel's measurements (Kiddle).

In vv.18–21, John describes in more detail the priceless materials of which the city, with its foundations and gates, is made (cf. Isa 54:11–15). The symbolism is not meant to give the impression of wealth and luxury but to point to the glory and holiness of God. The wall of jasper points to the glory of God (4:2–3; see comments at 21:11), while the fabric of the city is pure gold—as clear as glass (v.21). Such imagery portrays the purity of the bride and her splendor in mirroring the glory of God (cf. Eph 5:27).

The foundation stones are made of twelve precious stones. Here the imagery may reflect three possible sources: (1) the high priest's breastplate (Exod 28:17–20), (2) the jewels on the dress of the king of Tyre (Ezek 28:13), or (3) the signs of the zodiac. The second one, though referring to only nine stones, suggests the splendor of ancient royalty and might be appropriate as a symbol for the glorious kingdom reign in the Holy City. Yet regardless of how one feels about the way some have identified the king of Tyre (Ezek 28:11ff.) with Satan (cf. Feinberg, A.C. Gaebelein, New Scofield Reference Bible), there is something inappropriate about taking this pagan king as symbolic of the future kingdom. Swete and Ford prefer the first option—that of the high priest's breastplate. But while the twelve stones are perhaps the same, the order of their mention is different. This leaves the third option. According to Philo and Josephus, Israel associated these same stones with the signs of the zodiac, and their tribal standards each bore a sign of the zodiac (Caird, p. 276). If we begin with Judah, the tribe of Christ (7:5), the sign is Aries, the Ram, which has the amethyst as its stone. The last sign is Pisces, the fishes, which has jasper as its stone (Charles, *Commentary on Revelation*, 2:167). So the first zodiacal sign agrees with the twelfth foundation and the last zodiacal sign with the first foundation. In fact, the whole list agrees with John's, though in reverse order. This may be a significant device to show John's disapproval of pagan cults. But these matters are uncertain.

The gates are twelve great pearls. Though pearls are not mentioned in the OT, some rabbinic texts refer to gates for Jerusalem hewn out of jewels about forty-five feet square (*Sanhedrin* 100a). As for the one main street of the Holy City, it is like the fabric of the city itself, of pure gold, clear as glass (see comments at 21:18).

22–27 John turns from this beautiful description of the city to the life within it. In antiquity every notable city had at least one central temple. The New Jerusalem not only differs in this respect from ancient cities but also from all Jewish speculation about the age to come. Illuminated by the overflowing radiance of the presence of the glory of God, the Holy City no longer needs a temple (*naos*). Yet paradoxically it has a temple, for the Lord God Almighty and the Lamb are its temple (v.22). And in another sense, the whole city is a temple, since it is patterned after the Most Holy Place (v.16). Jewish expectation was centered on a rebuilt temple and the restoration of the ark of the covenant. In his glorious vision, John sees the fulfillment of these hopes in the total presence of God with his purified people, while the Lamb, the sign of the new covenant, is the fulfillment of the restoration of the ark of the covenant (see comments at 11:19; cf. John 4:21, 23). As long as there is uncleanness in the world, there is need for a temple where God's presence and truth are in contrast to the uncleanness. But in the new city no such symbol is needed any longer. In fulfillment of Isaiah 60:19–20, there will be no further need, as in ancient temples, for any natural or artificial lighting because the glory of God will dim the most powerful earthly light into paleness (cf. Zech 14:7). In the earthly tabernacle and temple, there was, to be sure, artificial lighting (the seven-branched lampstand in the OT tabernacle and the temple); yet the Most Holy Place had no such lighting because of the shekinah, the light of God's own presence.

Verses 24–26 present a remarkable picture of "the nations" and "the kings of the earth" entering the city and bringing their splendor (*doxa*, "glory," "honor," "magnificence") into it. John sees a vision of social life, bustling with activity. Elsewhere in Revelation, the nations (*ethnē*) are the pagan, rebellious peoples of the world who trample the Holy City (cf. comments at 11:2; 11:18) and who have become drunk with the wine of Babylon, the mother of prostitutes (18:3, 23), and who will also be destroyed by the second coming of Christ (19:15). The same description applies to the kings of the earth. But there is another use of these terms in Revelation. They stand for the peoples of earth who are the servants of Christ, the redeemed nations who follow the Lamb and have resisted the beast and Babylon (1:5; 15:3; 19:16; 2:26; 5:9; 7:9; 12:5). It is this latter group that John describes figuratively as having part in the activity in the Holy City, the kingdom of God. What this may involve regarding the relation of this life to the future kingdom is not stated.

Life in the age to come will certainly involve continuing activities and relationships that will contribute to the glory of the Holy City throughout eternity. Instead of the nations bringing their precious possessions to Babylon, the harlot city, the redeemed nations will bring these offerings to the throne of God (cf. Isa 60:3ff.). So certain is its perpetual light and security that the gates will never be shut for fear of evil by night (v.25; cf. Isa 60:11). This imagery should not, however, be allegorized as indicating some sort of perpetual invitation to salvation.

One thing is absolutely certain. Nothing impure (*koinos*, "common," "profane") will ever enter the city's gates (v.27). By *koinos* John means ceremonial impurity (cf. at 21:8; 22:15). No idolatrous person may enter. Only those can enter whose names are in "the Lamb's book of life" and who thus belong to him through redemption (cf. 3:5; 20:12, 15). This should not be taken as implying that in the New Jerusalem there will still be unsaved roaming around outside the city who may now and then enter it by repenting (contra Caird). Instead, the exhortation warns present readers that the only way to participate in the future city is to turn one's total loyalties to the Lamb now (cf. 21:7).

Notes

16, 21 Many see a possible allusion to ancient Babylon, which was described in antiquity in language similar to John's. According to Herodotus, Babylon was four-square, magnificent beyond all other cities. As in Revelation, he gives the dimensions of the city in stadia and those of the wall in royal cubits (Herodotus 1.178). Ancient Babylon also had a great street down its center. While these allusions are no more than hypothetical, the similarities are striking.

19–21 Glasson argues that the jewels fulfill the allusion to Isa 54:11–12, which in turn is based on the high priestly breastplate. The city itself is as sacred as the Most Holy Place, and all the inhabitants are named priests of the Lord (Isa 61:6; cf. Rev 1:6)(*The Revelation*, p. 118; see also idem, "The Jewels of Revelation 21:19–20," JTS, 26 (April 1975), 95–99).

B. *The River of Life and the Tree of Life*

22:1-5

> [1]Then the angel showed me the river of the water of life, as clear as crystal, flowing from the throne of God and of the Lamb [2]down the middle of the great street of the city. On each side of the river stood the tree of life, bearing twelve crops of fruit, yielding its fruit every month. And the leaves of the tree are for the healing of the nations. [3]No longer will there be any curse. The throne of God and of the Lamb will be in the city, and his servants will serve him. [4]They will see his face, and his name will be on their foreheads. [5]There will be no more night. They will not need the light of a lamp or the light of the sun, for the Lord God will give them light. And they will reign for ever and ever.

1–5 This section continues the description of the Holy City begun in 21:9, but now with the emphasis on its inner life. John returns to his archetypal images from Genesis (1–3) and Ezekiel (40ff.). The paradisiacal quality of the future age is briefly but beautifully described. Here Paradise is regained. As in the OT imagery of the age to come, metaphors of water and light abound (cf. Isa 12:3; Zech 14:7–8). The river of the water of life recalls Ezekiel 47:1ff. (cf. Joel 3:18) and the pastoral scene of Revelation 7:17 (q.v.). In both Testaments water is frequently associated with the salvation of God and the life-imparting and cleansing ministry of the Holy Spirit (Isa 44:3; cf. John 3:5; 4:13–14; 7:37–39; 13:10; 19:34; Titus 3:5). In the new city of God the pure water does not issue from the temple as in Ezekiel but comes from the throne of God, since this whole city is a Most Holy Place with God at its center. Life from God streams unceasingly through the new world.

The tree of life spreads all along the great street of the city (v.2). What was once forfeited by our forebears in Eden and denied to their succeeding posterity is now fully restored (cf. Gen 3:22–24). In Ezekiel's vision these are multiple trees on each side of the river that bear fruit monthly, whose leaves are for healing (Ezek 47:12). Therefore, the tree (*xylon*) John speaks of may be a collective word for Ezekiel's trees. So abundant is its vitality that it bears a crop of fruit each month! Its leaves produce healing for the nations. The imagery of abundant fruit and medicinal leaves should be understood as symbolic of the far-reaching effects of the death of Christ in the redeemed community, the Holy City. So powerful is the salvation of God that the effects of sin are completely overcome. The eternal life God gives the redeemed community will be perpetually available, will sustain, and will cure eternally every former sin.

Thus the curse pronounced in Eden will be removed (v.3; cf. Gen 3:17). This may mean, according to Swete, that no one who is cursed because of idolatry will be in the city (v.15). Instead of Babylon and its servants occupying the earth, the throne of God will be central and his servants will serve him (cf. 2:13). Wherever the throne is in sight, the priestly service of the saints will be perpetual (cf. 1:6). Here our true liturgy is fulfilled (cf. Rom 12:1). Observe John's emphasis on God and the Lamb (21:22–23; 22:1, 3). They share the same glory, the same throne, the same temple significance. The Christology of John's vision is everywhere evident even though stated in functional terms.

With no restriction such as those that pertain to Moses (Exod 33:20, 23) or the high priests (Heb 9:7), the redeemed community will be in Christ's presence, beholding perpetually his glory (cf. Ps 17:15; Matt 5:8; 1 Cor 13:12; 2 Cor 3:18; 1 John 3:2).

Eternal life is perfect communion, worship, the vision of God, light, and victory. Since God and the Lamb are always viewed together, there is no point in saying that the redeemed will see Jesus but not the Father. (Concerning the name on their foreheads, see comments at 14:1.)

A final burst of light engulfs the whole scene, and an announcement that the saints will reign for ever and ever fulfills the first promise of the book (1:6; cf. 5:10; 20:4–6; and see esp. 11:15). The logical sequence as well as the inner relationship of the words "his servants will serve" (v.3) and "they will reign" (v.5) have deep implications for the whole nature of God's kingdom in contrast to that of the satanic Babylon. Surely it is fitting for such a book of prophecy as Revelation to close around the throne, with God's servants both worshiping and ruling.

VI. Conclusion

22:6–21

⁶The angel said to me, "These words are trustworthy and true. The Lord, the God of the spirits of the prophets, sent his angel to show his servants the things that must soon take place."

⁷"Behold, I am coming soon! Blessed is he who keeps the words of the prophecy in this book."

⁸I, John, am the one who heard and saw these things. And when I had heard and seen them, I fell down to worship at the feet of the angel who had been showing them to me. ⁹But he said to me, "Do not do it! I am a fellow servant with you and with your brothers the prophets and of all who keep the words of this book. Worship God!"

¹⁰Then he told me, "Do not seal up the words of the prophecy of this book, because the time is near. ¹¹Let him who does wrong continue to do wrong; let him who is vile continue to be vile; let him who does right continue to do right; and let him who is holy continue to be holy."

¹²Behold, I am coming soon! My reward is with me, and I will give to everyone according to what he has done. ¹³I am the Alpha and the Omega, the First and the Last, the Beginning and the End.

¹⁴"Blessed are those who wash their robes, that they may have the right to the tree of life and may go through the gates into the city. ¹⁵Outside are the dogs, those who practice magic arts, the sexually immoral, the murderers, the idolaters and everyone who loves and practices falsehood.

¹⁶"I, Jesus, have sent my angel to give you this testimony for the churches. I am the Root and the Offspring of David, and the bright Morning Star."

¹⁷The Spirit and the bride say, "Come!" And let him who hears say, "Come!" Whoever is thirsty, let him come; and whoever wishes, let him take the free gift of the water of life.

¹⁸I warn everyone who hears the words of the prophecy of this book: If anyone adds anything to them, God will add to him the plagues described in this book. ¹⁹And if anyone takes words away from this book of prophecy, God will take away from him his share in the tree of life and in the holy city, which are described in this book.

²⁰He who testifies to these things says, "Yes, I am coming soon." Amen. Come, Lord Jesus.

²¹The grace of the Lord Jesus be with God's people. Amen.

6 With consummate art, the notes of the introit (1:1–8) are sounded again in the conclusion. So the book ends with the voices of the angel, Jesus, the Spirit, the bride, and, finally, John (v.20). The book is a seamless garment. There are three major emphases in the conclusion: confirmation of the genuineness of the prophecy (vv.6–7, 16, 18–19); the imminence of Jesus' coming (vv.7, 12, 20); the warning against idolatry and the invitation to enter the city (vv.11–12, 15, 17–19). A similar word of assurance (v.6), such as that in 19:9 and 21:5, provides the transition from the glorious vision of the Holy City to the final words of the book. An angel declares that it is "the Lord, the God of the spirits of the prophets," the one from whom the prophets like John receive their message, that assures the readers of the speedy fulfillment of all that has been revealed (cf. 1:1; 10:6–7). John has been the recipient of divine prophecy that will have its immediate consequences (cf. v.10).

7 This first declaration of the imminent coming of Jesus is Jesus' own response to the yearnings of the church (cf. comments at 1:7; 2:25; and esp. 3:11). It is the sixth beatitude in Revelation; and, like the first one (1:3), it is directed toward those who keep (obey) the words of the prophecy (cf. vv.18–19).

8–9 The "I, John" is reminiscent of 1:4, 9. His confession that he "heard and saw these things" and the repetition of the prohibition (19:10) against John's worshiping the angel serve a purpose. No believer, not even one of great spiritual stature as John, is beyond the subtle temptation to worship what is good itself in place of God who alone is to be worshiped.

10–11 These verses stand in contrast to the command given Daniel to seal up his book (8:26; 12:4, 9–10) and in contrast to Jewish apocalypses in general. John's message cannot be concealed because the contents of the vision are needed immediately by the churches. (On the sealing metaphor, see comments at 7:3.) Verse 11 appears at first reading to be fatalistic. Yet on further reflection, the exhortation stresses the imminency of the return of Jesus and the necessity for immediate choices. It echoes the aphorism As now, so always. Far from being an encouragement to remain apathetic, it is evangelistic in spirit. It may also allude to the great ordeal John viewed as imminent. For the unfaithful and wicked, this appeal would be a deep confirmation of their choice, whereas for the faithful, it would alert them to the necessity of guarding themselves against apostasy (cf. Jude 20–21). There is no reason to take this passage as teaching the irreversibility of human choices (contra Swete). Repentance is always a live option as long as a person is living. After death, however, there remains only judgment, not repentance (Heb 9:27).

12–13 This second of three announcements of the imminent return of Jesus in this chapter (cf. vv.7, 20) is associated with the truth of rewards and judgment based on deeds (cf. comments at 20:12; also 11:18). (On the terms Alpha and Omega, etc., see comments at 1:8, 17.)

14 The seventh and last beatitude in Revelation is evangelistic in emphasis (cf. 21:6; 22:11, 17). Strands of the earlier imagery are blended in it. In 7:14 the washing of the robes indicates willing identification with Jesus in his death. It also carries the thought of martyrdom during the great ordeal for the saints (cf. 6:11). Thus it symbolizes a salvation that involves obedience and discipleship, since it is integrally related to the salvation imagery of the tree of life (cf. comments at 22:2) and the gates of the city (cf. 21:25).

15 John has already made it clear that no idolaters can ever enter the city but only those whose names are in the Lamb's book of life (cf. comments at 21:8, 27). Such are "the dogs," i.e., those who practice magic arts, etc.—viz., those who rebel against the rule of God (cf. Deut 23:18, where a dog signifies a male prostitute; Matt 15:26, where "dogs" refers to Gentiles; Phil 3:2–3, where "dogs" refers to the Judaizers). There is no doubt that such people will not be admitted through the gates of the Holy City. They will be in the lake of fire (20:15). But the problem involves what appears to be their present exclusion from the city at the time of John's writing. Are they "outside" now? As has been previously argued in this commentary, the city is future and is not to be identified with the present historical church (see introduction to ch. 21 and comments at 21:2). Only in an eschatological sense can it be maintained that the new city exists in the present.

On the other hand, it is not necessary to place the time of v.15 in the present (contra Caird). There is no verb in the Greek text of the verse. Therefore the time of the action is determined by the context. Since the fulfillment of v.14 lies in the future, the time of v.15 is also most naturally future. The word "outside" is simply a figure that agrees with the whole imagery of the Holy City. It means exclusion. To be outside the city means to be in the lake of fire. Thus it is not necessary either to place the Holy City in the present or to place it in a millennial Jerusalem. The Holy City, as we have previously argued, is a symbol for the future realization of the corporate community of God's people (i.e., the eschatological kingdom of God), and as such it does not have a geographical location other than that it is on the new earth.

16 As in 1:8, 17–20, in this verse Christ addresses John and the churches directly. The "you" is plural in the Greek text. Here Christ's words authenticate the whole Book of Revelation ("this testimony") as being a message to the churches. Therefore, any method of interpreting Revelation that blunts the application of this message in its entirety to the present church must disregard these words of Christ. He is the Messiah of Israel, "the Root and the Offspring of David" (cf. Isa 11:1; see comments at Rev 5:5) and the fulfillment of the promise to the overcomers at Thyatira (see comments at 2:28).

17 The first two sentences in this verse are not an evangelistic appeal but express the yearning of the Holy Spirit and the "bride" (the whole church, cf. 21:9) for the return of Christ. In v.20 John gives us the Lord Jesus' answer: "Yes, I am coming soon." Those who hear (i.e., "him who hears")—viz., the members of the local congregations in John's time—join in the invitation for Christ to return. Then, any in the congregations who are not yet followers of Jesus are invited to come and take the water of life as a free gift (*dōrean*, "freely," cf. Rom 3:24; Rev 21:6). (On the water of life, cf. 21:6; 22:1; also, for the liturgical and eucharistic use of this verse, see comments at v.20.)

18–19 These verses should not be taken as a warning against adding anything to the Bible. Early interpreters understood them as a warning to false prophets not to alter the sense of John's prophecy—i.e., Revelation (so Irenaeus *Contra Haereses* 30.2). Kline has likened the force of these words to the curses pronounced for disobedience in the covenant law codes of the OT period (Meredith Kline, *Treaty of the Great King*

[Grand Rapids: Eerdmans, 1963], p. 44; cf. Deut 4:2; 12:32). Verses 18–19 are a strong warning against any who would tamper with the contents of "this book" (Rev), either textually or in its moral and theological teaching (cf. 1 Cor 16:22). So severe is the danger he is warning against that John says that those who teach contrary to the message of Revelation will not only forfeit any right to salvation in the Holy City but will have visited on them the divine judgments (plagues) inflicted on the beast worshipers.

20 This is the third affirmation (in ch. 22) of Jesus' imminent return and perhaps the response to the longing cry in v.17. John responds to the Lord Jesus' declaration by saying, "Amen. Come, Lord Jesus." These fervent words are part of the liturgy of the early church. They were a prayer used at the close of the meal in the eucharistic liturgy (*Didache* 10.6). Cullmann believes that these words are the earliest expression of the recognition that the Lord's Day (Sunday) is the day of the Resurrection. As Jesus appeared to his disciples alive on the first day of the week, so he was expected to be present in the Spirit at every first-day Eucharist celebration and to appear again at the end, which is often represented by the picture of a messianic meal (Oscar Cullmann, *Early Christian Worship*, [London: SCM, 1953], pp. 13–14). The expression "Come, Lord Jesus" (*erchou, kyrie Iēsou*) is equivalent to the Aramaic *mārānā' 'ᵘṭāh* (Gr. *marana tha*; cf. 1 Cor 16:22, "Come, O Lord," NIV). So in closing Revelation, John alludes to chapter 1, with its reference to the Lord's Day (1:10).

21 A conclusion such as this, while quite unsuitable for a Jewish apocalypse, is wholly appropriate for this prophetic message addressed to the ancient church and, indeed, to the whole body of Christ. The benediction is reminiscent of Paul's usual practice (cf. the final verses of Rom, 1 Thess, Col, et al.). Whether in this benediction we should accept the textual reading "with all" (Bruce M. Metzger, *A Textual Commentary on the Greek New Testament* [New York: UBS, 1971], p. 769) or "with all the saints" (Swete, various MSS) cannot be completely settled. We may, however, agree that nothing less than God's grace is required for us to be overcomers and triumphantly enter the Holy City of God, where we shall reign with him for ever and ever.

Notes

14 Here most of the better textual witnesses read πλύνοντες τὰς στολὰς αὐτῶν (*plynontes tas stolas autōn*, "wash their garments"). Following a number of later minuscule MSS, KJV follows the reading ποιοῦντες τὰς ἐντυλὰς αὐτοῦ (*poiountes tas entylas autou*, "those who do his commands"). The former reading is preferred.
19 While only one or two late Gr. MSS have βιβλίον τῆς ζωῆς (*biblion tēs zōēs*, "book of life") instead of ξύλον τῆς ζωῆς (*xylon tēs zōēs*, "tree of life"), KJV curiously follows this inferior reading, probably because of its presence in the Lat. Vul.